'With incisive sensitivity and elegance of expression, Donnel B. Stern brilliantly defines, integrates and deepens our understanding of a cohesive relationalist view of what it means to be a person, a person in essence ever a part of the fabric of human connectedness. His clinical illustrations are alive, his insightful consideration of the implications of those analytic experiences richly extending as well as integrating our theories. This valuable work is engaging to read as well as rich in its contributions.'

Warren Poland, *author of* Intimacy and Separateness in Psychoanalysis

'Donnel B. Stern is one of our most penetrating thinkers on the subject of field theory. He gently reminds us that emotional connections are operating in ways that are outside of our awareness. The moment-to-moment experience carries with it an opening into areas that have long been dormant. In this extraordinary contribution into the unseen and the unheard, Stern activates the inner world of the 'other' and the 'self'. It is a major contribution that is a must-read.'

Glen O. Gabbard, MD, *clinical professor psychiatry,*
Baylor College of Medicine

'With equal measures of brilliance, intellectual rigor, and generosity, this book reminds us why and how psychoanalysis is magical. In a series of expansive gestures, Donnel B. Stern stages encounters with ideas that, while seemingly familiar, reveal themselves to be fresh with possibility: otherness, in these pages, aligns with psychic freedom, and Stern persuasively shows that witnessing and recognition remain critical ingredients of the psychoanalytic endeavor. This book renews the promise of psychoanalysis, which is to ask more of us, always.'

Avgi Saketopoulou, *psychoanalyst in private*
practice, and faculty of New York University's
postdoctoral program in psychotherapy and psychoanalysis

On Coming into Possession of Oneself

This book is Donnel B. Stern's latest contribution to the kind of understanding of the psychotherapeutic and psychoanalytic process offered by field theory.

Stern anchors his understanding of therapeutic action in the freedom of both patient and analyst to create a meaningful experience with minimum inhibition. The field's capacity to generate meaning—and thus to make possible fully realized human living—grows from its freedom to respond spontaneously to the feelings, wants, and needs of its participants. To whatever extent this spontaneity is diminished, as it is in unconscious mutual enactment, we can be sure that some part of the field is frozen or otherwise rigidified. This position serves as the foundation of the psychoanalysis that Stern practices. The analyst aims to feel their way into compromises in the field, and then do whatever they can to grasp and dissolve them, knowing that they will have to be visited repeatedly, and dissolved again. These insights into interpersonal and relational field theory lead to descriptions of clinical interventions that are focused on the moment-to-moment emotional experience of both the patient and the analyst.

With valuable contributions to theory and emotionally immediate clinical vignettes, this book is essential for all psychoanalysts and psychoanalytic psychotherapists wishing to understand how the analyst's interventions grow from the analyst's emotional involvement in the clinical process.

Donnel B. Stern, training and supervising analyst, member of the faculty at the William Alanson White Institute, and adjunct clinical professor of psychology at New York University.

PSYCHOANALYSIS IN A NEW KEY BOOK SERIES

DONNEL STERN

Series Editor

When music is played in a new key, the melody does not change, but the notes that make up the composition do: change in the context of continuity, continuity that perseveres through change. Psychoanalysis in a New Key publishes books that share the aims psychoanalysts have always had, but that approach them differently. The books in the series are not expected to advance any particular theoretical agenda, although to this date most have been written by analysts from the Interpersonal and Relational orientations.

The most important contribution of a psychoanalytic book is the communication of something that nudges the reader's grasp of clinical theory and practice in an unexpected direction. Psychoanalysis in a New Key creates a deliberate focus on innovative and unsettling clinical thinking. Because that kind of thinking is encouraged by exploration of the sometimes surprising contributions to psychoanalysis of ideas and findings from other fields, Psychoanalysis in a New Key particularly encourages interdisciplinary studies. Books in the series have married psychoanalysis with dissociation, trauma theory, sociology, and criminology. The series is open to the consideration of studies examining the relationship between psychoanalysis and any other field—for instance, biology, literary and art criticism, philosophy, systems theory, anthropology, and political theory.

But innovation also takes place within the boundaries of psychoanalysis, and Psychoanalysis in a New Key therefore also presents work that reformulates thought and practice without leaving the precincts of the field. Books in the series focus, for example, on the significance of personal values in psychoanalytic practice, on the complex interrelationship between the analyst's clinical work and personal life, on the consequences for the clinical situation when patient and analyst are from different cultures, and on the need for psychoanalysts to accept the degree to which they knowingly satisfy their own wishes during treatment hours, often to the patient's detriment.

A full list of all titles in this series is available at:
https://www.routledge.com/Psychoanalysis-in-a-New-Key-Book-Series/book-series/LEAPNKBS

On Coming into Possession of Oneself

Transformations of the Interpersonal Field

Donnel B. Stern

Routledge
Taylor & Francis Group

LONDON AND NEW YORK

Designed cover image: stellalevi © Getty Images

First published 2025

by Routledge
4 Park Square, Milton Park, Abingdon, Oxon OX14 4RN

and by Routledge
605 Third Avenue, New York, NY 10158

Routledge is an imprint of the Taylor & Francis Group, an informa business

British Library Cataloguing-in-Publication Data
A catalogue record for this book is available from the British Library

ISBN: 9781032688916 (hbk)
ISBN: 9781032688879 (pbk)
ISBN: 9781032688893 (ebk)

DOI: 10.4324/9781032688893

Typeset in Times New Roman
by Deanta Global Publishing Services, Chennai, India

For my grandchildren: Everett, Ellis, Asher, and Nathan.

Contents

Acknowledgments

I thank my patients, especially those who have given their permission for me to write about our work together. I am lucky that I found my way into the field in which I have spent over 50 years. I also thank my private study groups, my supervisees, the candidates in my institute classes, and those who have offered comments when I have presented my work to audiences of students and fellow professionals. I thank my friends, whose interest and thoughtful reactions to what I have had to say over the years have been irreplaceable. All of these friends, students, and colleagues have contributed to whatever is of value in the chapters of this book.

I am grateful to my wife, Kathe Hift, PhD, most of all. She is a psychoanalyst herself, generous beyond any reasonable expectation, and the best clinician I know. She understands and accepts my devotion to my work, partly because she is devoted to her own.

I thank Phillip Blumberg, PhD, my close friend and erstwhile editor, who reads everything I write and tells me whatever he can about how to make it better. I take his advice, which makes it a good thing that he is always right.

I am grateful to Taylor and Francis, LLC, for permission to reprint as chapters in this book the following articles, which first appeared in T&F journals and books:

Chapter 2: Donnel B. Stern (2022) On coming into possession of oneself: Witnessing and the formulation of experience. *The Psychoanalytic Quarterly*, 91:4, 639–667, DOI: 10.1080/00332828.2022.2153528

Chapter 5: Donnel B. Stern (2022) Feels like me: Formulating the embodied mind, *Psychoanalytic Inquiry*, 42:4, 232–243, DOI: 10.1080/07351690.2022.2059275

Chapter 7: Donnel B. Stern (2019) How I work with unconscious process: A case example, *Contemporary Psychoanalysis*, 55:4, 336–348, DOI: 10.1080/00107530.2019.1676579

Chapter 9: Donnel B. Stern (2022) Dissociation and unformulated experience: A psychoanalytic model of mind (revised and updated). In: M. Dorahy & S. Gold (eds.), *Dissociation and the Dissociative Disorders, 2nd Edition*. London & New York: Routledge, pp. 341–352. DOI: 10.4324/9781003057314

Chapter 12: Donnel B. Stern (2016) Dissociative enactment and interpellation. In: J. Petrucelli & S. Schoen (eds.), *Unknowable, Unspeakable, Unsprung*. New York: Routledge, pp. 42–49.

Chapter 13: Donnel B. Stern (2022) From interpersonal field to mind in the work of Philip Bromberg, *Contemporary Psychoanalysis*, 58:2–3, 285–291, DOI: 10.1080/00107530.2022.2136532

Chapter 14: Donnel B. Stern (2020) Field theory and the dream sense: Continuing the comparison of interpersonal/relational theory and Bionian field theory. *Psychoanalytic Dialogues*, 30:538–553. DOI: https://doi.org/10.1080/10481885.2020.1797416

Chapter 15: Donnel B. Stern (2018) Otherness in psychoanalysis: On recognizing the critics of relational psychoanalysis. In: L. Aron, S. Grand, & J. Slochower, (eds.), *Decentering Relational Theory: A Comparative Critique*. London: Routledge, pp. 27–48.

Chapter 16: Donnel B. Stern (2014). A response to LaFarge. (Published here as "Can there be a psychoanalysis without unconscious phantasy? Unformulated experience and the multiple self.") *International Journal of Psychoanalysis*, 95: 1283–1297. DOI: 10.1111/1745-8315.12291

I am grateful to Sage Publications, Inc., for permission to reprint the following material, which appeared first in journals published by Sage.

Preface: Donnel B. Stern (2020). A magic world: Why I write. *Journal of the American Psychoanalytic Association*, 67: 1113–1115. DOI: 10.1177/0003065119897242

Chapter 3: Donnel B. Stern (2023). Distance and relation: Emerging from embeddedness in the other. *Journal of the American Psychoanalytic Association*, 71: 641–668. DOI: 10.1177/00030651231198493

Chapter 4: Donnel B. Stern (2023). Interpretation: Voice of the field. *Journal of the American Psychoanalytic Association*, 71: 1127–1148. DOI: 10.1177/00030651241232703

Chapter 6: Donnel B. Stern (2018). How does history become accessible? Reconstruction as an emergent product of the interpersonal field. *Journal of the American Psychoanalytic Association*, pp. 493–506. DOI: 10.1177/0003065118781493

Chapter 11: Donnel B. Stern (2020). Dissociative multiplicity and unformulated experience: Commentary on Diamond. *Journal of the American Psychoanalytic Association*, 68: 907–920. https://doi.org/10.1177/0003065120967741

I am grateful to John Wiley and Sons for permission to reprint the following article, which appeared in a journal published by Wiley:

Chapter 10: Donnel B. Stern (2017). Unformulated experience, dissociation, and *Nachträglichkeit. Journal of Analytical Psychology*, 62: 501–525. DOI: 10.1111/1468-5922.12334

Preface
A magic world
Why I write

This brief piece was invited by the book review editors of the Journal of the American Psychoanalytic Association, *who founded and continue to edit an innovative series called, "Why I Write." Each issue of* JAPA *contains one psychoanalytic writer's very brief response to the series title. "A magic world" serves as a preface in this book because it is my attempt to say why I have written anything at all, including the chapters that follow.*

I love psychoanalysis. But my devotion to our literature and my desire to contribute to it, as much as they shape me, are not, at bottom, why I write. But don't misunderstand: without the love of a subject matter, neither I nor anyone else would have any reason to write. To write, you must love to think about something. But I think I would write even if it weren't psychoanalysis I loved.

Many years ago, in the *New York Times Book Review*, the novelist Joyce Carol Oates (1982) wrote, "If I say that I write with the enormous hope of altering the world—and why write without that hope?—I should first say that I write to discover what it is I will have written" (p. 1). Writing is just this kind of emergent process for me. I can't make it happen, and I have the very clear sense that it would be a shame if I could. I have no choice but simply to observe the unfolding of my own thoughts and feelings on the page. I am an onlooker at processes that, paradoxically, could not be more my own.

When I write, I hope to get out of the way and let something grow and change and come into focus, only to verge back into the unformulated and then begin to emerge again. I want to go through this cycle of experience, which never grows old, again and again. It gives me a feeling like no other, a feeling of becoming, of participating in the life of something bigger than myself, of contact with mystery.

As writers, we hope to bring ourselves so thoroughly to bear on the problem at hand, with so little reservation, holding back so little, that something comes into being at least a little bit differently than it has ever done before. We aim to access something we have always lived with but sensed only hazily, or never perceived at all. Writers, when successful, are mid- wives of being. We go deep inside ourselves and find … the world!

This is what I know about why I write. Or rather, it's why I couldn't *not* write. Life is an ongoing project of reinvention: the slippage of signifiers lies at the heart of creation.

* * *

I had my first conscious sense of emergent experiencing in stories, probably the stories read to me by my mother. L. Frank Baum's Oz books were the most compelling of the books she read aloud, but I loved Kipling's *Jungle Book* stories almost as much. Once I began reading independently, I found magic in Defoe's *Robinson Crusoe*, Wyss's *The Swiss Family Robinson*, H. Rider Haggard, H. G. Wells, and Jules Verne.

Whenever I was in the middle of a book I loved, and I had to interrupt my reading, I left the book behind with the vague sense that the story went on by itself. Or if it didn't go on inside those covers, if it really did stop when I stopped reading it, it began again the moment I returned to it, as if it had just been waiting for me, ready to spring again to life.

I couldn't have said it then in so many words, but it was as if my books did not already exist; they grew as I read them. The story was a living thing. My bookshelves were a kennel or stable for stories, not just a storage space for books. The public library was an enchanted place. Just as the toys in the magic toyshop cavorted as the toymaker slept, so my books continued to unfold inside their covers while I was away from them. Always there was magic about words, magic that reading and writing still have for me. But now I see that it isn't only my books that grow; it's also me. The meanings I find in what I read, and the meanings I create when I write, change to reflect who I have become.

I grew up in a time when home movies were exotic. There was no such thing as video—you had to film in 8-millimeter. My parents made such home movies sometimes, and perhaps because they were rare and expensive, they seemed to me to be marvels. There I was in the past, telling a story by portraying it, no less surely bringing it to life than an actor in a movie. And just as I felt about reading my books, I had the vague sense that the movies went on after the filming ended. Whatever happened in the futures of the events captured on those films was forever lost to me. Who knew in what universe the events that took place after the camera stopped might have come to life?

In one scene that particularly fascinated me, filmed on a trip my family took when I was nine, in the nearly unpopulated territories north of Saskatchewan, I was out in the middle of nowhere, sprinting down a long lakeside dock and leaping off the end of it. For some reason the film ended with me in mid-air, before I hit the water.

Did I hit the water after the scene ended? Did I *ever* hit the water? Did I hit the water over and over again? Did I hit the water *forever*? We think stories belong to us; meanwhile, they're doing what they want. We are wisest when we stay out of their way.

None of this means, of course, that we should merely sit back and wait for the arrival of new meanings. By studying and living with conscious and committed purpose, by coming to know things in that conventional way, we prepare ourselves, and because we are prepared, when language does seize us we are sometimes able to give it the materials it needs to invent something new. Of course we also need rational, conscious purpose to revise and polish what arrives from the gods, but I have to say that even carrying out revisions of syntax and wording has the effect of immersing me in that special way that makes me lose myself in the task. I love revision as much as I love writing the first draft. All writing carries me away.

I'm usually best off, I think, both as a clinician and as a writer, if I stay close to what things are like, what they *feel* like, resisting the temptation to use my rational mind to translate into a different form whatever it is that comes to me unbidden. I generally prefer not to give way to the urge to "know what it means." Once we find our way to an episode of freedom from a state of internal constriction—something I think we are always struggling to do—understanding very often takes care of itself, like water rushing in to fill an empty space. Language is not ours to wield, but is instead an agent of revelation: we learn what we think. It usually seems to me to be better for the purposes of creation to give writing its head than to use rational thought to steer it in one way or another.

But even when language takes us and uses us for its own ends, perhaps the greatest depths and the most profound meanings are those that exist between the words, or apart from them. Not everything should be said. Lucky for writers, not everything can be.

24 East 82nd Street
New York, NY 10028
E-mail: donnelstern@gmail.com

Reference

Oates, J.C. (1982). Stories that define me. *New York Times Book Review*, July 11, pp. 1, 15–16.

Chapter 1

Introduction

Transformations of the interpersonal field

I have thought of my work as field theory since I began writing in the early 1980s, and so in one sense every chapter in this book, despite the fact that each has its own particular subject, is also part of my latest attempt to contribute to the development of North American, or interpersonal and relational, field theory. The field's capacity to generate meaning, and thus fully realized human living, grows from its freedom to respond spontaneously to the feelings, wants, and needs of its participants. To whatever extent this spontaneity is diminished, we can be sure that some part of the field is frozen, constricted, or otherwise rigidified. That position about field events serves as the foundation of the psychoanalysis I practice: my goal is to identify and feel my way into the rigidities in the fields created between my patients and me, and to do what I can to grasp and dissolve them, with the understanding that every one of those compromises of freedom will have to be visited repeatedly and dissolved over and over again. These patterns of relatedness, while they routinely shape the analytic relationship itself, simultaneously configure the discourse of the treatment—i.e., what it is "about": fantasy, history, dreams, and everyday life. Therapeutic action for this reason cannot be understood as the analyst's revelation of the truth about the patient's mind, because those revelations, growing from the analytic relatedness, tend to take on the same configurations as the subject matter being interpreted (Levenson, 1972, 1983; see Chapter 4).

And so none of us can will our capacity simply to address compromises of the field's freedom. The analyst's capacity to participate in this way is instead emergent, a spontaneous process that must come about in its own time. Psychoanalytic work requires that analyst and patient find their uncharted way to a transformation of the unwitting compromises of the field's freedom. We clinicians can immerse ourselves in the field, and we

DOI: 10.4324/9781032688893-1

do; and we can study our own experience, especially our affective participation, and we do that, too. We have every confidence that those activities are necessary, even if they are not sufficient. To do our work, we must wait until we are capable of something we cannot describe in advance. As poet Paul Valéry (1952) wrote, in a favorite passage of mine (also quoted in Chapter 2), "[W]e must simply wait until what we desire appears. *We have no means of getting exactly what we wish from ourselves*" (p. 102; italics in the original).

Therapeutic action in this frame of reference does not rely on the revelation of any particular content, but on the creation of a new freedom to create meaningful experience with as little inhibition or constriction as possible. The therapeutic action of psychoanalysis, we can say, is not anchored in knowing anything in particular or in revealing previously hidden psychic content, but in the freedom and expansion of being and becoming. In Ogden's (2019a, 2020) words, this is "ontological psychoanalysis." Of course, knowing and understanding—what Ogden calls "epistemological psychoanalysis"—retain significance in this perspective. But knowing and understanding take their meaning, in my view, from their contributions to the freedom to experience (Stern, 2015), the freedom to be and become. In what I understand to be interpersonal/relational field theory, the spontaneity of our moment-to-moment emotional experience is valued more than anything else. Whatever it would mean to get "exactly what we wish from ourselves," in other words, it is hard to imagine that it would be desirable for that state of affairs to actually come about. Would it really be a good thing for us to be able to get what we wish from ourselves? Leaving aside the near-certainty that (as psychoanalysis has always taught) we could hardly define any one thing we "really" desire, would we even really *want* to be able to control our thoughts and feelings? Would it not take the joy out of living to know what we were going to think next? We feel free, real, and alive not when we force our minds to do our bidding (that way lies stagnation, entropy, *Thanatos*), but when we are able to welcome whatever arrives in our minds unbidden. It has always struck me as ironic that that unbidden quality—that sense that a thought or a feeling comes from elsewhere, but is nevertheless thoroughly our own—is the source of our spontaneity and vitality (Stern, 1990, 2015). Psychoanalysis teaches us, I think, that while our acceptance of whatever we can tolerate of our own spontaneous thought and feeling does not necessarily lead to the most comfortable existence, it does seem undeniable that our openness to our own unbidden thought and feeling is what makes life deep and interesting.

Over the decades, my interests have spread over a broader and broader range in psychoanalysis. It has seemed to me, especially over the last two decades, that becoming a good citizen of our discipline requires the study of psychoanalytic views that differ from those most familiar to us. This is a difficult undertaking, because psychoanalysis is taught and learned in an apprenticeship system. Without being an apprentice in the system you are trying to learn, it is very hard to grasp and feel what it is to be a member of that other school of thought. But difficult as it may be, I believe it is necessary to the survival of our discipline. And it is certainly interesting.

And so another thing, besides field thinking, that characterizes almost all of the chapters of this book is a comparative attitude. When the point of any particular chapter is not comparative, there are at least attempts in the chapter to make links with other points of view. But while I do favor ecumenicism—a sympathy for the community of psychoanalytic theories—I do not consider my view integrative or eclectic. I believe it is important to mine my own perspective as deeply as I can. It's just that I find the work of writers who think differently than I do to be useful in the pursuit of this goal, and as much I may disagree with them in certain respects, I am curious enough about them to want to grasp what they say. I want to understand how a reasonable person could see things differently than I do.

But the impact of reading beyond one's own backyard goes beyond that. I hope I allow writers who think differently than I do to broaden and deepen my views. I do believe that theories other than our own have that kind of impact on all of us, and I think that that influence often goes far beyond what we consciously grasp. I believe that someone besides me might be able to see better than I do the ways in which my thinking has been shaped not only by my long immersion in American psychoanalysis, but also by my enthusiastic reading over the years of many other psychoanalytic writers.

Let me not risk sounding, though, as if my purpose in these chapters is primarily theoretical or academic. I certainly do take up certain issues, such as those around the problem of psychic representation, that deserve to be called at least partially academic. But the book is, like my previous ones, clinical at its heart. The question animating every chapter is, "How can I best be of use? How I can help most effectively?" And so let me turn to clinical thinking.

Emotional connection

Psychoanalysis can be understood as variations on the theme of how one person can be of a certain special use to another. All of those ways of being helpful have one thing in common: they rely on emotional connection between patient and analyst.

Now, emotional connection is a more complicated thing in psychoanalysis than it is in everyday life. When I use the term "emotional connection" in a psychoanalytic context, I mean the capacity of the analytic participants to belong to the interpersonal field between them with as little reservation as possible. An equivalent expression would be that connection is what happens when the field is free to be spontaneous, to create within its participants whatever feelings, perceptions, thoughts, and memories are potentially present. Experience, when it is free to go its own way, always grows from both the present and the past, my mind and your mind, consciousness and the unconscious. It is neither a copy of a pre-existing state nor a creation from whole cloth. Unfettered experience, that is, is a dynamic conceptualization, and so, like all such conceptualizations, it cannot be absolute. What I have elsewhere described as "relational freedom" (Stern, 2015)—the state of the analytic relationship that I have also called "partners in thought" (Stern, 2010)—is not simply present or absent. Even when the field is at its most spontaneous, its freedom is relative, set against the background of its breaks, rigidities, stereotypies, and compromises.

It may be important to add, although this point probably should be taken for granted in the thinking of any psychoanalyst, that "emotional connection" refers not only to the colloquial understanding of the term as warmth or love (although it certainly can refer to those feelings), but rather to the state of affairs that obtains when the affective nature of whatever is going on between analyst and patient is taken in, owned, and accepted by each of them, even when it is painful—even, that is, when the acceptance by the analytic couple of their own affective lives with one another is accompanied by anger, dismay, shame, guilt, disappointment, desperation, deadness, emptiness, sadness, or regret. And so while emotional connection certainly does include warmth, in its profound forms it is most fully defined by emotional honesty (Levenkron, 2006; Bromberg, 2006b; Stern, 2006). And honesty, in turn, requires one's recognition that one's experience was made by *oneself*, no matter how little conscious intention may have been involved. Both analyst and patient must not only know and feel, that is; each must also come to recognize that *it is they themselves doing the knowing and feeling*. This is what I have called in Chapter 2 "'going meta' on an affective level," and it is what I mean by the phrase that is the title of both the book as a whole and of Chapter 2: "Coming into possession of oneself."

Because it is rooted in honesty, relational freedom is often not easy and seldom simply comfortable, although it can be. The crucial thing about relational freedom is that both participants not only allow themselves to know what they are feeling toward one another, but also find their way to an *acceptance* of that involvement. The common word "accept" takes on a distinctive meaning in my recent thinking (Stern, 2019). I intend "acceptance" to refer to the sense that one's experience is one's own, that it "feels like me" (Stern, 2019; Chapter 5 of this book). "Feels like me" leads to that same experience or state of mind I have just referred to as the subject of Chapter 2: "coming into possession of oneself." I have presented this way of thinking in my last book, *The Infinity of the Unsaid: Unformulated Experience, Language, and the Nonverbal* (Stern, 2019). In the present book, I offer clinical discussions of the idea in Chapters 2, 3, 4, and 5.

The acceptance of one's impact on the other and the other's impact on oneself, of course, is always alloyed with other kinds of experience that reflect its absence—i.e., with the analytic couple's inevitable intolerance, in any particular moment, of *some* of the influences passing between them. That intolerance, after all, is what we understand as mutual dissociative enactment, which is simultaneously perhaps the most significant obstruction to relational freedom and the greatest opportunity for its expansion (Stern, 2010, 2015). And so we really ought not to define emotional connection as the analytic couple's *accomplishment* of all the influences passing between them, but as an imperfectly realized *commitment* to that goal. We must be prepared, in other words, and not infrequently, to honor emotional connection, acceptance, and relational freedom in the breech.

"Enactment," in my frame of reference (see Stern, 2004, 2010), also has a very particular meaning: rooted in dissociation, it is a compromise or violation of the spontaneity of analytic relatedness. Enactment is expressed in either one or both of the following states of the field: (1) one or both of the participants cannot experience fully the affective involvement of the moment; or (2) one or both of the participants, even if they can experience their affective involvement, cannot accept it—cannot feel it as their own.

In practice, these two phenomena, experiencing and acceptance, usually occur simultaneously, since not being able to accept the possibility of a state of being (affect, usually) or cognitive content (memory, fantasy, thought, etc.) prevents its transformation from potentiality to actuality, and thus prevents its experience. Sometimes experience does occur in a depersonalized, intellectualized, deadened, or schizoid way, with blunted affect or without affect altogether. The most frequent context in which this occurs is the representation and experience of trauma, or experience that is infected by its imbrication in a traumatic context. In such circumstances, the traumatic event is recalled and may even be possible to imagine in sensory terms, but there is little affective involvement in it. It is not one's own; one cannot come into possession of it.

I feel called upon to revise immediately one aspect of what I have just said. In presenting both the points described just above—experiencing and accepting—I suggested that the state I was describing could apply to "one or both" of the therapeutic participants. Really, though, this is too simple a description. It certainly does happen often enough that either the patient or the analyst *believes* that only they (that is, not the other, but only themselves) are fully experiencing or accepting the situation at hand. But since both analyst and patient are always playing a role in constructing, maintaining, and playing out the field, whenever one of them believes that they are experiencing or accepting something fully and that the other is not, the case can be made that that belief is itself the evidence of its own falsity. In a relationship like psychoanalysis, which exists in order to pursue a collaborative goal, if you believe that you hold the truth and the other does not, you are probably missing something—and that is true for both the patient and the analyst.[1] The analyst is responsible for dealing with this state of affairs in a productive, responsive, professional way. This is not always easy, of course, since the analyst is just as vulnerable as the patient to falling into the adversarial quality that enactments often have, ranging from vague irritation to outright alienation.

Enactment, then, cannot affect one participant without affecting the other; if one of the participants enacts, the other responds reciprocally, no matter how difficult it may be to see it. As Edgar Levenson (1972, 1983) was one of the first to see, the analyst is unconsciously "transformed" by participation in the field. Even earlier, Benjamin Wolstein (1959) described the unconscious reciprocity of the analytic relationship as "the transference-countertransference interlock."

To come full circle, let me say this: to enact is to be unable to connect to the other. Dissociative enactment and emotional connection, in other words, are opposed to one another; they are each (partly) defined by the absence of the alternative. We can say that our relatedness with someone else always ranges between connection and enactment. In the terms in which I first put the point in 1983, "curiosity" and "dissociation" are two ends of a continuum. Curiosity is an active attitude of openness (Stern, 1990) to whatever experience is possible to formulate, and this openness allows the spontaneous development of the field, emotional connection with the other, and the transformation of unformulated experience into meaning. Curiosity is stymied by dissociation, which I understand to be the rigid limitation of experience to only a portion of its possibilities. Transformation is prevented; meaning may be either limited or prevented altogether. Dissociation leads to enactment, the unconsciously mediated shutdown of the field's spontaneity, accomplished by the constriction of each participant's contributions to it. (My understanding of enactment is presented most thoroughly in Stern, 2010, especially Chapter 4.)

There is a parallel here between the pair "enactment and connection" and Klein's (1946) paranoid-schizoid and depressive positions. The parallel is even clearer if we consider Bion's (1963) revision of Klein, in which the paranoid-schizoid and depressive positions are no longer static developmental milestones but a shifting set of dynamic experiential alternatives that one moves back and forth between, just as the field moves back and forth between different degrees of relational freedom, and its participants move back and forth between enactment and connection or, in terms introduced in Chapter 3, between "embeddedness in the other" and "emergence" from that embeddedness. Even more closely related to "enactment-connection" is Winnicott's (1971a) pair, "object relating" and "object usage," which can be read as a revision of Klein's original formulation. We might also cite in this context Winnicott's (1971a) concepts of the "subjective object" (object made meaningful by projection, existing within the area of omnipotence) and the "objective object" (object understood to exist independently in the external world, outside the area of omnipotence).

In all these pairs, the first term (enactment; paranoid-schizoid position; object relating; subjective object) describes relatedness that is less responsive to the external world than the second term (emotional connection or relational freedom; depressive position; object usage; objective object). The first terms in these pairs are largely shaped by the stereotyped imagos of the internal world, while the second terms refer to a greater freedom to grasp and accept the external world as separate from oneself, as what Winnicott (1971a) describes as "true externality." The depressive position (Klein), object usage (Winnicott), and emotional connection all result in relatedness that is more open to the influence of the other, and to the creation of experience that is more closely tailored to that other—in other words, an openness to the possibility of the transformation of experience into novel and more subtly differentiated forms. This point is the substance of Chapter 3, in which the clinical roles of separateness and psychic fusion are taken up.

Traditionally, interpersonal relatedness has been understood to be the product or outcome of structural aspects of mind. Conduct, that is, has generally been understood to be the expression of pre-existing psychic representations. We see this view in psychoanalysis from the beginning. Once Freud had rejected his trauma theory and replaced it with his theory of drive (Freud, 1905), psychic life was understood to be largely the creation of the interior—the unconscious processes of mind. If psychic life was to be modified by psychoanalytic treatment, the intrapsychic world—the mind's collection of unconscious psychic representations, each one an amalgam of drive and defense—had to be revealed by interpretation and thereby changed. Today, the Kleinian school perhaps most fully perpetuates this view, holding that transference is understood to be the expression of unconscious phantasy (psychic representation), and that interpretation of unconscious phantasy is the only means of changing this unconsciously mediated relatedness.

Interpretation and the field

But consider the possibility that meaning grows from relatedness, not from psychic representation. Consider, that is, that change may be more basically the product of new configurations in, and transformations of, the interpersonal situation than it is of changes in endogenously determined psychic representation. Keep in mind that, for interpersonal and relational analysts, relatedness can be just as dominated by unconscious process, and therefore just as recalcitrant to change, as unconscious phantasy.

From this perspective it is not interpretation that makes the new form of relatedness come about; instead, the interpretation becomes possible because there has been a shift in the field (the melting of a frozen place), which makes available the new freedom to see things in the way reflected in the interpretation. Useful interpretations become the signs of changes that have already taken place, not their causes (Stern, 2009, 2010, 2023—see Chapters 3 and 4 of this book).

As I have taken pains to say elsewhere, though (Stern, 2013, 2015, 2023—see Chapters 3 and 4 of this book), this point should not be taken to suggest that I repudiate interpretation. Nothing of the kind. While I am indeed suggesting that interpretation is more often an effect of the field than a cause of it, I also affirm that interpretation plays a central role in clinical practice—just not the role we have usually attributed to it. Instead, when we make an interpretation of the analytic relatedness, it has the effect of memorializing in symbolic form events that have already happened procedurally in the analytic situation. I also believe that even interpretations that do not have anything expressly to do with events in the analytic relationship arise in the analyst's mind because of shifts in the field. A new bit of history, for example, becomes accessible because of a relaxation of the field that may have no obvious bearing on that history. For an example of the link between field shifts and the new accessibility of history, see Chapter 6; and for other illustrations of the way that field shifts provoke the accessibility of new psychic content, and the transformation of the old, see an article of mine from 2015, republished as Chapter 5 of my book *Relational Freedom: Emergent Properties of the Interpersonal Field* (Stern, 2015) and all the chapters in the first section of the present book—Chapters 2–8. See especially Chapter 4, "Interpretation: Voice of the Field," which is entirely devoted to describing the role of interpretation in the interpersonal field.

And yet it is also true, of course, that all interpretations, merely by taking place, change the analytic landscape, which immediately becomes different than it would otherwise have been. And so we must also acknowledge that, in this way, interpretations do indeed affect the constitution of the field, even if they are themselves made possible by events in that same field.

I return here to the point that the relational analyst believes that the course and success of treatment are reflected in episodes of emotional connection and its absence. The analyst is always attempting to find the way, first, to an awareness of the absence of connection—which I have equated with enactment in the previous pages. Discovering these absences of connection is a substantial and often subtle part of the work, because these enactments, despite their profound influence on the shape of the field, are often invisible for long periods to both patient and analyst. If things go well, over time enactments become more visible, making it possible not to abide by their strictures, thereby creating conditions allowing connection where it did not exist before. These new possibilities for emotional connection are then reflected in positive outcomes in the treatment and the patient's life—outcomes that, because their very possibility was previously obscured by (invisible) enactments, neither the patient nor the analyst would necessarily have known to expect. A more spontaneous field leads to new possibilities for the construction of creative, spontaneous living: broader and deeper perception, thought, memory, and feeling; and a life of relatedness and work that reflect them.

But the nature of the changes that follow the appearance of new possibilities for emotional connection is unpredictable. Analyst and patient do what is possible to melt frozen places in the field and loosen the constraints on the field's spontaneity—but neither participant knows in advance exactly what new possibilities for living will be revealed when the spontaneity of the field expands.

Changes in the interpersonal field in the here-and-now, therefore, are responsible for new thoughts, feelings, perceptions, memories, and so on, and therefore also responsible for the expansion of the self and the growth of mind—two phrases that seem synonymous to me. It is the idea that metamorphoses of the field lead to the growth of mind that led me to the subtitle of this book—*Transformations of the Interpersonal Field*—a phrase that also serves as the title of this introductory chapter.

"Generative" enactments

A number of recent writers have described moments in which the patient's emotional deadness or other lack of vitality seems to be transcended by the analyst's spontaneous, unconsciously mediated efforts to connect, and in which these "enlivening" (Director, 2009), "generative" (Atlas & Aron, 2017), "positive" (Lenoff, 2014), or "vitalizing" (Schwartz Cooney, 2018; Schwartz Cooney & Sopher, 2021) influences awaken a new affective immediacy or liveliness in the patient. The emphasis in these accounts is on "positive" unconscious enactments that these authors see as contributions to treatment. The position is that our understanding of enactment should not be restricted to unconsciously limiting and dissociative involvements with the patient—rigid, stereotyped, deadening, and so on. We should also, these writers say, consider that the analyst can be unconsciously involved in enactments that are positive or generative in nature.

There is an implicit conflict of these views with writers who have presented the analyst's dissociation-mediated participation in enactments as a problematic but essential kind of affective involvement (e.g., Bromberg, 1998, 2006a, 2011; Davies, 1997, 1999, 2004; Chefetz, 2015; Howell, 2020; Stern, 1997, 2010, 2015, 2019). From this perspective, the spontaneous appearance of the analyst's lively affect and spontaneity in a treatment that had been characterized by deadness is not necessarily best understood as the outcome of the analyst's generative enactment. Instead, it is usually best understood to signal the dissolution (at least temporarily) of a dissociative enactment that may not even have been visible or understandable until that moment.

Analysts do frequently contribute to the vitalization of patients, of course. That is not at issue. And some of those contributions are spontaneous participations. But it is not clear to me that the examples used in the "generative enactment" literature to make this point come about in the way their authors believe they do. In my experience, interactions that qualify as enactments range in affective tone from slightly uncomfortable to deadened, tense, or adversarial. When these enactments are successfully addressed (a falsely euphemistic phrase, perhaps, because it may obscure the pain such success requires both patient and analyst to bear), the mutative outcome is exactly what is described in the literature on generative enactments and vitalization: there is an effulgence of affect and liveliness, and often a sense of considerable relief. We might say, adapting Winnicott's (e.g., 1954) description of "management" (as opposed to traditional psychoanalysis), that the successful address of dissociative enactments between patient and analyst removes the obstacles to environmental provision, which then takes place spontaneously. But whereas the authors of the literature on "generative" enactments see this new affective opening in the analytic relationship as having been provided by the analyst's unconsciously mediated, facilitative, and affectively "positive" participation, I think that such "positive" episodes are actually more likely to be the evidence that a previously existing and frequently painful and emotionally difficult dissociative enactment has been resolved by a shift in the field. The new connectedness between analyst and patient did not provoke the shift, but is instead an important sign that the shift has taken place. I find the analyst's key unconscious participation less in the provision of something unconsciously generative than in their very "stuckness" in the problematic aspect of the interaction, and their willingness to "stay with" the suffering that must be borne in order to preserve the hope of emerging from it. This "stuckness" may very well be replaced by new, positive affect, or environmental provision, when the rigidity characteristic of problematic relatedness relaxes.

In my view, in other words, the pursuit of emotional connection is less likely to be accomplished by the analyst's unconsciously mediated emotional encouragement, via unconsciously mediated enactment of the positive, than by the analyst's successful (and usually painful) dealings with the enactment—that is, by the analyst finding the path to an "act of freedom" (Symington, 1983) or "surrender" (Ghent, 1990), after which provision may become possible. I believe that positive affect is seldom created as the solution to the problem of the patient's deadness—that is, "unconsciously on purpose." Positive affect doesn't just bubble up spontaneously in contexts in which it is notably absent—in clinical situations of deadness, for instance. Emotional connection is instead made possible by the dissolution of the conditions that prevented it. And that dissolution rests on the analyst's willingness to suffer whatever must be suffered in order that the analyst can eventually deal with the patient in a way that results in the patient feeling understood and witnessed.

It is certainly true, in other words, as Avner Bergstein (2019) writes, that, "In order for the patient to reclaim his aliveness and pull himself out of his frozen states, it is up to the analyst to recognize the patient's hidden aliveness and bring it to light" (p. 96). So far, so good: the analyst must catalyze the patient's hidden aliveness. But Bergstein also makes the point repeatedly—and I agree with him—that the analyst's capacity to reach the patient's aliveness is rooted in the (often longstanding) enactment that preceded the new vitality: "Only when [the patient] perceives the analyst's internal struggle to bear the unbearable does he know that he has touched the analyst deeply, and only then does he feel capable of encountering something unbearable and encapsulated within himself" (p. 66). Bergstein is presenting his understanding of Bion's clinical attitude in these passages, but in this case Bion's clinical attitude is my own.

I believe, in other words, that there is a dynamic problem involved in these situations, one in which the analyst is psychically embedded and from within which he or she must work themselves out (we could say that they must work themselves into the experience so deeply that they come out the other side). In so-called "generative" enactments, what reason is there for the analyst's participation to be unconscious? Where is the pain in the analyst that would motivate a lack of awareness? Is this vitalizing participation itself an enactment?

It seems to me that it is not. But there is indeed an enactment going on in these situations. The enactment is the unconsciously mediated emotional inhibition existing in both the patient and the analyst that *preceded* the generative contribution. The generative contribution therefore, in this view, is not itself the enactment, but the *resolution* of the enactment. This is, in fact, the way I understand most of the clinical examples given in the literature as illustrations of generative enactment.

I certainly don't want what I've just said to suggest that I take issue with the significance of interventions by the analyst that enliven (Alvarez, 2012; Director, 2009), vitalize (Schwartz Cooney, 2018; Schwartz Cooney & Sopher, 2021), or facilitate the feeling of being real (Ogden, 2014, 2019b; Winnicott, 1971a, b). This literature is highly important to today's clinical practice, and I am very glad we have it. I do not think, though, that all of the analyst's unexpected participations should necessarily be considered enactments, even if they are entirely unplanned. I repeat my point: when emotionally vitalizing events emerge spontaneously from the analyst's experience, they are liable to represent the breach of an enactment, but are not themselves enactments.

Is this just a matter of vocabulary? Could we resolve the issue by simply agreeing that all unplanned conduct is enactment?

If we do that, I am afraid the concept of enactment will become so broad that it will lose its meaning. More important, some of the dynamic clinical import of moments of so-called "positive" enactment might be lost. The greatest of those losses would be an inadvertent flattening, or trivialization, of the clinical process. I know, of course, that none of those who have championed positive enactments intends anything like that. But if we believe that the analyst can break into the vicious circle of psychic deadness by simply enacting vitality, without having to work through the pain and deadness on the way to this outcome, we risk minimizing the significance of the suffering that I believe the analyst must struggle to accept, live with, and eventually find some way to use in communicating with the patient in a way that awakens vitality.

The organization of the book

Following the Preface ("A Magic World: Why I Write") and this introductory chapter, the book is divided into three sections: "The Formulation of Experience in the Clinical Situation" (Chapters 2–8); "Dissociation" (Chapters 9–13); and "Comparative Studies" (Chapters 14–16). I have a few words to say about each section here in these general introductory remarks, but I save most of my comments for the brief introductions that precede each chapter. Most of these introductions explain the meetings and invitations that were the occasions for each chapter. I have found that understanding this kind of context enhances my understanding of what I read. It is my hope that these introductions will do the same for the reader of this book.

"The formulation of experience in the clinical situation" Chapters 2–8

These seven chapters, recent presentations of the themes I have described in this introduction, are examinations, from different perspectives, of the process of psychoanalytic treatment as the formulation of experience. What does it mean to formulate what had been unformulated? How should we understand the failure to formulate? How can we best describe the process by which formulation takes place? Chapters 2, 3, 4, and 5 are statements of my most recent thoughts on these large and substantial problems. Each is illustrated with clinical material. Chapter 6 presents clinical material illustrating the way that a relaxation of the field opens the way to new historical material in the patient's life, even when the material has no direct relation to the issue that relaxed in the field. Chapters 7 and 8 focus on a single case at two different points in time and, like Chapters 2–5, are intended to illustrate a way of going about clinical practice.

"Dissociation," Chapters 9–13

Dissociation has always been, for me (Stern, 1983), the unconsciously mediated defensive unwillingness to formulate experience. Dissociation results in unformulated experience that remains unarticulated/unrealized for dynamic, defensive reasons. Dissociation is not a binary, absolute, either/or process, but a matter of the degree to which a particular potential source of meaning (unformulated experience) is invested with affective and cognitive significance. How "fully imagined" is the formulation in question (Stern,

1997, Chapter 5)? The degree to which a particular meaning is dissociated or formulated is a function of the nature of the interpersonal field. The field, by shaping the processes of curiosity (Stern, 1997) and formulation, on the one hand, and dissociation, on the other, determines the experience that analyst and patient can have in one another's presence. Dissociation, in other words, is simultaneously a field process, one of the means by which the field is shaped, and one of the outcomes of the operations of these processes. In its definition as a field process, it differs from repression, an intrapsychic process. For these reasons, dissociation is, for most interpersonal/relational psychoanalysts, the primary unconscious defensive process, occupying for them a place analogous in important respects to that of repression in Freud's thought.

Chapter 9 is a summary presentation of this theory of dissociation. Chapter 10 delineates relationships between this conception of dissociation and Freud's *Nachträglichkeit* (perhaps best known in its French translation as *aprés coup*—but translated into English by Strachey as "deferred action" [Laplanche & Pontalis, 1973] and by Laplanche [1998] as "afterwardsness"), emphasizing the role of the interpersonal field. This chapter could just as well have appeared in the "Formulation of Experience" or "Comparative Studies" sections of the book, since it has a comparative focus throughout and is centrally concerned with the clinical process of formulation. Chapter 11 is also comparative, laying out the ways that the interpersonal/relational model of dissociation, or "defensive multiplicity," differs from other ways of understanding dissociation in a way that makes it impossible to integrate repression and dissociation in a single model. Chapter 12 is a brief, highly schematic comparison of the model of dissociative enactment with the thinking of Jacques Derrida on binary thinking and Louis Althusser's (1969) understanding of interpellation. The final chapter in this section, Chapter 13, is a brief presentation of some of the ideas about dissociation that I learned from and with my good friend, Philip Bromberg. Philip and I have each contributed in our different ways to the view that problems in living, as well as the practices of creation and repair of mind that compose psychotherapy and psychoanalysis, are processes of the interpersonal field.

"Comparative studies," Chapters 14–16

Comparative studies have become more and more appealing and intellectually necessary to me as it has become clear that our theoretical world is unalterably pluralistic. I, for one, have always been in favor of pluralism, since I understand psychoanalysis to be an interpretive, hermeneutic discipline, not a natural science. I have described it that way for three decades (see Stern, 1990, 1991, 1992, 1996, 1997, 2002, 2010, 2012, 2013). From that point of view, the judgments we make between theories are less about which one is the correct answer to a question than about the clinical, political, and moral consequences of answering whatever question is at hand (and often the consequences of choosing which questions to ask) in one way rather than another (Stern, 2012). Two of the chapters in this section are applications of this point of view: Chapter 14 continues the comparison of the field theory of interpersonal/relational psychoanalysis with Bionian field theory; Chapter 16 compares psychoanalytic theories with and without the concept of unconscious phantasy, discussing how it could be that a theoretical feature so central to traditional psychoanalysis could be eschewed by any theory that identifies itself as psychoanalytic. Chapter 15 is a discussion of the comparative stance that I believe is the most productive and respectful attitude to take toward psychoanalytic theories that differ with one's own.

Besides cosmetic changes here and there, I have not revised the chapters of this book, most of which have been published recently. They are presented here as they originally appeared.

Note

1 You are *probably* missing something—but there are exceptions. For example, in a racialized enactment between people who believe they are collaborators (a situation that certainly does come up—in life, but of course also in treatment), it would seldom, if ever, make sense to say that the person of color is "missing something" in the same way the white person is. In this case, we would say that, while reciprocal, unconscious affective involvement is almost certainly present, reciprocal responsibility is not.

References

Althusser, L. (1969). Ideology and state apparatus. In S. Zizek (Ed.), *Mapping Ideology* (pp. 100–140). New York: Verso, 2000.
Alvarez, A. (2012). *The Thinking Heart*. London and New York: Routledge.
Atlas, G. & Aron, L. (2017). *Dramatic Dialogue: Contemporary Clinical Practice*. New York & London: Routledge.
Bergstein, A. (2019). *Bion and Meltzer's Expeditions into Unmapped Mental Life*. London and New York: Routledge.
Bion, W. R. (1963). *Elements of Psychoanalysis*. London: Heinemann.

Bromberg, P. M. (1998). *Standing in the Spaces: Essays on Clinical Process, Trauma, and Dissociation. Hillsdale*, NJ: The Analytic Press.

Bromberg, P. M. (2006a). *Awakening the Dreamer: Clinical Journeys*. Hillsdale, NJ: The Analytic Press.

Bromberg, P. M. (2006b). "Ev'ry time we say goodbye, I die a little …": Commentary on Holly Levenkron's "Love (and hate) with the proper stranger." *Psychoanalytic Inquiry* 26: 182–201.

Bromberg, P. M. (2011). *The Shadow of the Tsunami: And the Growth of the Relational Mind*. New York and London: Routledge.

Chefetz, R. (2015). *Intensive Psychotherapy for Persistent Dissociative Processes: The Fear of Feeling Real*. New York: Norton.

Davies, J. M. (1997). Dissociation, therapeutic enactment, and transference–countertransference processes: A discussion of papers on childhood sexual abuse by S. Grand and J. Sarnat. *Gender and Psychoanalysis* 2: 241–257.

Davies, J. M. (1999). Getting cold feet defining "safe-enough" borders: Dissociation, multiplicity, and integration in the analyst's experience. *Psychoanalytic Quarterly* 78: 184–208.

Davies, J. M. (2004). Whose bad objects are we anyway? Repetition and our elusive love affair with evil. *Psychoanalytic Dialogues* 14: 711–732.

Director, L. (2009). The enlivening object. *Contemporary Psychoanalysis* 45: 120–141.

Freud, S. (1905). Three essays on the theory of sexuality. *The Standard Edition of the Complete Psychological Works of Sigmund Freud* 7: 123–246.

Ghent, E. (1990). Masochism, submission, surrender—Masochism as a perversion of surrender. *Contemporary Psychoanalysis* 26: 108–136.

Howell, E. F. (2020). *Trauma and Dissociation-Informed Psychotherapy: Relational Healing and the Therapeutic Connection*. London & New York: Routledge.

Klein, M. (1946). Notes on some schizoid mechanisms. In *Envy and Gratitude and Other Works 1946–1963*. Hogarth Press and the Institute of Psycho-Analysis, 1975, 1–24.

Laplanche, J. (1998). Notes on afterwardsness. In J. Fletcher & L. Thurston (Eds.), trans. P. Slotkin & L. Hill, *Essays on Otherness*. London/New York: Routledge, 1999.

Lenoff L. (2014). Positive enactment as a clinical resource. *Psychoanalytic Inquiry* 34: 421–429.

Levenkron, H. (2006). Love (and hate) with the proper stranger: Affective honesty and enactment. *Psychoanalytic Inquiry* 26: 157–181.

Levenson, E. A. (1972). The fallacy of understanding. In *The Fallacy of Understanding & The Ambiguity of Change*. New York and Hove: Routledge, 2005.

Levenson, E. A. (1983). The ambiguity of change. In *The Fallacy of Understanding & The Ambiguity of Change*. New York and Hove: Routledge, 2005.

Ogden, T. H. (2014). Fear of breakdown and the unlived life. *International Journal of Psychoanalysis* 95: 205–224.

Ogden, T. H. (2019a). Ontological psychoanalysis or "What do you want to be when you grow up?" *Psychoanalytic Quarterly* 88: 661–684.

Ogden, T. H. (2019b). The feeling of real: On Winnicott's "Communicating and not communicating leading to a study of certain opposites". *International Journal of Psychoanalysis* 99: 1288–1304.

Ogden, T. H. (2020). Toward a revised form of analytic thinking and practice: The evolution of analytic theory of mind. *The Psychoanalytic Quarterly* 89(2): 219–243.

Schwartz Cooney, A. (2018). Vitalizing enactment: A relational exploration. *Psychoanalytic Dialogues* 28: 340–354.

Schwartz Cooney, A. & Sopher, R. (Eds.). (2021). *Vitalization in Psychoanalysis: Perspectives on Being and Becoming*. London and New York: Routledge.

Stern, D. B. (1983). Unformulated experience: From familiar chaos to creative disorder. *Contemporary Psychoanalysis* 19: 71–99.

Stern, D. B. (1990). Courting surprise: Unbidden perceptions in clinical practice. *Contemporary Psychoanalysis* 26: 452–478.

Stern, D. B. (1991). A philosophy for the embedded analyst: Gadamer's hermeneutics and the social paradigm of psychoanalysis. *Contemporary Psychoanalysis* 27: 51–58.

Stern, D. B. (1992). Commentary on constructivism in clinical psychoanalysis. *Psychoanalytic Dialogues* 2: 331–363.

Stern, D. B. (1996). The social construction of therapeutic action. *Psychoanalytic Inquiry* 16: 265–293.

Stern, D. B. (1997). *Unformulated Experience: From Dissociation to Imagination in Psychoanalysis*. New York: Routledge.

Stern, D. B. (2004). The eye sees itself: Dissociation, enactment, and the achievement of conflict. *Contemporary Psychoanalysis* 40: 197–237.

Stern, D. B. (2006). "Affective honesty" as example and metaphor: Discussion of Holly Levenkron's "Love (and hate) with the proper stranger: Affective honesty and enactment". *Psychoanalytic Inquiry* 26: 254–262.

Stern, D. B. (1997). *Unformulated Experience: From Dissociation to Imagination in Psychoanalysis*. New York: Routledge.

Stern, D. B. (2004). The eye sees itself: Dissociation, enactment, and the achievement of conflict. *Contemporary Psychoanalysis* 40: 197–237.

Stern, D. B. (2006). "Affective honesty" as example and metaphor: Discussion of Holly Levenkron's "Love (and hate) with the proper stranger: Affective honesty and enactment". *Psychoanalytic Inquiry* 26: 254–262.

Stern, D. B. (2009). Partners in thought: A clinical process theory of narrative. *Psychoanalytic Quarterly* 78: 701–731.

Stern, D. B. (2010). *Partners in Thought: Working with Unformulated Experience, Dissociation, and Enactment*. New York and London: Routledge.

Stern, D. B. (2012). Witnessing across time: Accessing the present from the past and the past from the present. *Psychoanalytic Quarterly* 81: 53–81.

Stern, D. B. (2013). Relational freedom and therapeutic action. *Journal of the American Psychoanalytic Association* 61: 227–255.

Stern, D. B. (2015). *Relational Freedom: Emergent Properties of the Interpersonal Field*. New York: Routledge.

Stern, D. B. (2019). *The Infinity of the Unsaid: Unformulated Experience, Language, and the Nonverbal*. London and New York: Routledge.

Stern, D. B. (2022). On coming into possession of oneself: Witnessing and the formulation of experience. *Psychoanalytic Quarterly* 91(4): 639–667.

Stern, D. B. (2023a). Distance and relation: Emerging from embeddedness in the other. *Journal of the American Psychoanalytic Association* 71: 641–668.

Stern, D. B. (2023b). Interpretation: Voice of the field. *Journal of the American Psychoanalytic Association* 71: 1127–1148.

Symington, N. (1983). The analyst's act of freedom as agent of therapeutic change. *International Review of Psycho-Analysis* 10: 283–291.

Valéry, P. (1952). The course in poetics: First lesson. Trans. J. Mathews. In B. Ghiselin (Ed.), *The Creative Process* (pp. 92–106). Berkeley, CA: University of California Press.

Winnicott, D. W. (1954). Metapsychological and clinical aspects of regression within the psycho-analytical set-up. In *Through Paediatrics to Psycho-Analysis* (pp. 278–294). New York: Basic Books, 1975.

Winnicott, D. W. (1971a). *Playing and Reality*. London: Tavistock.

Winnicott, D. W. (1971b). Fear of breakdown. In C. Winnicott, R. Shepherd and M. Davis (Eds.), *Psychoanalytic Explorations* (pp. 87–95). Cambridge, MA: Harvard University Press, 1989.

Wolstein, B. (1959). *Countertransference*. New York: Grune & Stratton.

Part I

The formulation of experience in the clinical situation

Chapter 2

On coming into possession of oneself

Witnessing and the formulation of experience

Witnessing, in my understanding, is a form of relatedness crucial to the formulation of experience. It mediates formulation, whether the witnessed relatedness goes on between states of mind or being inside the mind, or between two people in the wider world. Since I began to think about it (Stern, 2009), witnessing has become a central focus of my interest in clinical events. The earliest version of this chapter was written for a 2021 conference on field theory jointly sponsored by the Italian Society of Interpersonal Psychoanalysis and the Harry Stack Sullivan Institute of Florence, Italy.

In the interpersonal/relational theory of dissociation and enactment, when a meaning that has been dissociated emerges in one's mind, the creation of the meaning takes place because one can tolerate or accept something *now* that one could not tolerate or accept *then*. In the terms I have used elsewhere, *not-me* becomes *me* (Stern, 2003, 2004, 2010, 2015). Subjectivity that had been unformulated, non-meaningful, dissociated, intolerable, and non-self becomes formulated, meaningful, tolerable, or acceptable, and part of the self. *Not-me* becomes *feels-like-me* (Stern, 2019). Constriction in the relevant part of the interpersonal field relaxes somewhat, and there is a new possibility for vitality and spontaneity in both experience and conduct.

I have long held that we are able to accept a meaning that has been dissociated only when the interpersonal field, within which the meaning gains relevance, comes to feel safe enough to allow it (Stern, 1997, 2010, 2015, 2019). A new feeling of safety is crucial to the breach of a dissociative enactment.

Of course, the change does not happen all at once. Over time, in successful instances, spontaneity becomes more frequent in the relevant part of the field, so that eventually, events that in the past had to be dissociated and

DOI: 10.4324/9781032688893-3

rigidly enacted can more and more often be thought, felt, and acted with relative freedom.

In this chapter, I use clinical theory and illustration to explore details of the metamorphosis from not-me to feels-like-me. How does this change take place? This question has drawn my interest for most of my life, although I have just recently begun to find the words for it that I use here. In a nutshell, what I want to say is that the movement from not-me experience to feels-like-me (Stern, 2019), with the accompanying possibilities for formulating new meaning that open up at such moments, seems to me to happen when we not only know or feel something, but also and simultaneously, when we sense ourselves in the midst of this process—that is, when we know and feel that it is *we who are doing the knowing and feeling*. When these two events co-occur—the knowing and feeling, and knowing and feeling that we are knowing and feeling—we come into possession of ourselves. We feel something on the order of, "It is *I* who feels that (or sees it, hears it, remembers it, etc.); this experience is *mine*." Instances of coming into possession of ourselves take place virtually and continuously, ranging from tiny flares of bodily sensations, perceptions, memories, or thoughts to vast landscapes of personal insight or scientific or artistic inspiration (e.g., Ghiselin, 1952; Stern, 1990).

The phenomenon I want to address is not limited to our sense of *owning* experience. Ownership is part of what I want to describe, but the center of my interest is the role in the formulation of experience of our recognition of our own participation in the creation of meaning. There is a subtle difference between this phenomenon and the sense of the ownership of experience. To *recognize* our participation in the creation of meaning is not synonymous with *being aware of* it. *Recognition* goes beyond mere awareness. In fact, it would often be misleading to use the word *aware* in this context, because in becoming aware, the object of our attention usually is an explicit meaning. By contrast, more often than not the kind of recognition of our participation in the construction of experience that I want to describe is implicit, unspoken, even unthought. We could call it a feeling-sense of our participation, something that lets us know we are involved, vital, vibrant, alive. Winnicott called it "the sense of being real" (1960, p. 146), and wrote that, "Our patients, more and more, turn out to be needing to feel real, and if they don't, then understanding is of extremely secondary importance" (quoted by Caldwell & Robinson, 2017, p. ixx).

Of course, as soon as I refer to vitality in psychoanalytic treatment, I bring to mind many writers besides Winnicott (1960, 1971). Here is just a selection: Alvarez (1992, 2012; see also Director, 2009); Balint (1968); Ferenczi (1988, Ferenczi & Rank, 1925); Fromm (1955, 1964/1991, 1970); Gerson (2009); Green (1986); Laub (2005); Lichtenberg et al. (2015); Loewald (1978); Mitchell (2000); Ogden (2019a, b); Schwartz Cooney & Sopher (2021); Tauber (1959); and D. N. Stern and the Boston Change Process Study Group (2010)—and each of those resonances is entirely appropriate. But I want to find my way to something a bit different than what these writers have told us.

What I am looking for is something like *going meta* on an affective level: I do not only know and feel; I also *know that* I know and feel. That is, instead of merely feeling our experience washing over us, instead of just registering its presence as if it comes from elsewhere, we have a sense of our participation in these events, and we accept this sense of our participation. We accept our involvement, we *feel* it even if it seldom occurs to us to think it in words—that is, even though we cannot say exactly what we are doing or how we are doing it. This sensing of our participation is certainly *related* to vitality, agency, and the ownership of experience, as the writers I have just cited and others have brought to our attention; but the sense of our participation in the creation of meaning is not *synonymous* with these other qualities of experience. No doubt, vitality, agency, and ownership could not exist without our sense of participation. But they should not be confused with it.

The literature of witnessing

The activity and process that I will describe as *witnessing* is central to what I want to say. I have been writing about the subject for some time. But before turning to my own work, let me present a very brief overview of the literature.

Like so many important parts of life, witnessing is easier to refer to than to define. The difficulty in offering a definition here (at the beginning) is compounded by the fact that this chapter is meant to contribute to an understanding of what we mean when we use the word. But with those provisos, I offer this simple, preliminary description: witnessing is a process of recognition of the other or of the other in oneself. But witnessing is not only recognition, it is also affirmation. It takes more to witness the other than to accept and understand the experience to be witnessed. Witnessing is more than empathy and more than recognition. Witnessing must be embedded in a relationship that gives the phenomenon its power to affirm. What I mean will become clear, I hope, as this chapter moves along.

In recent decades, witnessing has become an important part of contemporary theories of therapeutic action, particularly in the case of trauma. The literature on this subject can be divided into two large categories: (1) work in which witnessing is conceptualized exclusively, or at least primarily, as the most significant tool in the understanding and treatment of trauma with a capital "T" (Boulanger, 2005; Gautier & Scalmati, 2019; Gerson, 2009; Goodman & Meyers, 2012; Grand, 2015; Laub, 1991, 1992a, b, 1995, 1989, 2005; Laub & Auerhahn, 1989; Mucci, 2019; Richman, 2006, 2014); and (2) literature in which witnessing (in Eshel's [2019] work, "withnessing") is given—as in this chapter—an expanded role rooted in the treatment of traditionally defined trauma but not limited to it. In this body of work (Amir, 2012; D'Ercole, 2012; Feldman, 2015; Gentile, 2013; Gondar, 2017; Poland, 2000, 2011; Reis, 2009; Richman, 2009, 2013; Seiden, 1996; Sheppard, 2017; Ullman, 2006), witnessing applies also to *developmental* or *relational trauma* (Bromberg, 1998, 2006, 2011), which today, in the view of many contemporary clinicians, comprises the largest proportion of the problems patients bring to treatment.

I share with all these writers the perspective that witnessing is a central part of treatment. We all agree on the role of witnessing in creating the capacity to give symbolic form to unsymbolized psychic material, especially trauma, and thereby to experience it explicitly. But many writers in both groups would also agree that the meaning of witnessing is not exhausted by its role in symbolization. Witnessing is also the interpersonal or intersubjective medium within which the *wordless registration* (Reis, 2009) of the memory/experience of trauma comes about. Helen Bamber, for instance, founder of the Medical Foundation for Victims of Torture, writes about her experience, as a 20-year-old in 1945, with just-liberated victims of the concentration camp of Bergen-Belsen:

> People were in very difficult situations, sitting on the floor, they would hold on to you and dig their fingers into your flesh and they would rock and they would rock and they would rock and we would rock together. You saw people rocking, but the act of rocking together and receiving their pain without recoil was essential.
>
> (Quoted by Gerson, 2009, p. 1352)

Clinicians generally acknowledge that witnessing without symbolization is an important part of any analyst's clinical responsiveness. But in my experience, more often than not, the position is held implicitly. Reis (2009) is one of the few who has explicitly recognized the point:

> The goal of psychoanalytic witnessing, if there may be said to be a goal, is to allow and witness memory in its varied forms, without attempting to symbolize or make personally understandable the experience— to accept the experience of trauma, without therapeutic ambition. The analyst occupying the position of witness in a treatment understands that performative and enactive features of traumatic experience are not to be simply translated or transduced into *symbolic* form, and that a part of the integrity of the experience of trauma is itself its wordless registration.
>
> (p. 1359, italics in original)

One last point about the literature of witnessing. For many writers, witnessing is a process that takes place between two separate people. Others, however, also refer to witnessing of a sort that we could describe as internal or imaginary—between parts of oneself (e.g., Amir, 2012; Gerson, 2009; Laub, 1992a, b; Laub & Auerhahn, 1989; Reis, 2009; Richman, 2006, 2013, 2014; Sheppard, 2017). I have frequently taken a form of this latter position (Stern 2004; 2009a, b; 2012), and I now take it up once again.

Witnessing: Picking up the thread

In 2004, I (Stern, 2004) argued that as long as the self is understood to be unitary, the problem of the analyst's countertransference awareness, because it is the problem of the eye seeing itself, is insoluble. The analyst's own experience is both the object to be observed and the observer. It is not clear how we should understand seeing our own being. And yet, of course, we know perfectly well that we often do.

But if the self is multiple, made of self-states that shift in and out of awareness according to the demands of the interpersonal field (Bromberg, 1998, 2006, 2011; Stern, 2004, 2010, 2015), we can observe one part of ourselves by simultaneously occupying a second part of ourselves, a part from which we can see and feel the first part (Stern, 2004). In this way, the problem of the eye seeing itself is resolved.

A few years later (Stern, 2009a), relying on this analysis of the problem of self-observation, I began an exploration of the role of witnessing in life and treatment (see also Stern, 2009b, 2012, 2015). I suggested that, throughout life, we need one part of ourselves to serve as a witness for another part. That is how we know our experience and grasp who we are. The first witnesses in our lives, I wrote then, are not parts of ourselves, but our earliest caregivers. We grasp ourselves by seeing, imaginatively, through our caregivers' eyes, hearing through their ears.

Winnicott (1956) tells us that babies need to see themselves and their states reflected in their mothers' faces. If this does not happen, babies may not be able to go on to learn who they are by exploring their mothers' minds. Channeling Winnicott, Fonagy, Target, and their collaborators (Fonagy et al., 2002) tell us that their purpose is "to capture and specify the processes by which infants fathom the minds of others and eventually their own minds." In other words, "we fathom ourselves through others" (p. 2). From this perspective, mind is created by the interaction of the infant's inborn potentials—Winnicott's true self—with caregivers' provision of a sensitive mirroring response to what they believe they can understand about the infant's relatively undifferentiated somatosensory experience— its proto-intentions and affects. Sharing this view, Alvarez (1992) tells us the caregiver, arousing "novelty, surprise, enjoyment and delight" (p. 63) in her baby (1992, p. 63), "[claims] her baby as her own, claiming his attention, calling him into relation with her and, in a way, calling him into psychological being" (p. 68).

Implied, and sometimes explicit, in these views is a further point that I take to be crucial: by creating the earliest portraits of those they care for, early caregiver-witnesses help to lay down the rudiments of self in the minds of their young charges. The role of these *reflected appraisals* in the formation of one's sense of oneself was emphasized by the influential Chicago School of Sociology (Cooley, 1902; Mead, 1934), and through them, by Harry Stack Sullivan (1940). Loewald (1960) and Winnicott (1971) have been both lucid and poetic on these points. Let me offer a brief, illustrative passage from the work of each of them. First, Loewald:

> The child, by internalizing aspects of the parent, also internalizes the parent's image of the child—an image which is mediated to the child in the thousand different ways of being handled, bodily and emotionally.

Early identification as part of ego-development, built up through intro-jection of maternal aspects, includes introjection of the mother's image of the child. Part of what is introjected is the image of the child as seen, felt, smelled, heard, touched by the mother ... The bodily han-dling of and concern with the child, the manner in which the child is fed, touched, cleaned, the way it is looked at, talked to, called by name, recognized and re-recognized—all these and many other ways of com-municating with the child, and communicating to him his identity, sameness, unity, and individuality, shape and mould him so that he can begin to identify himself, to feel and recognize himself as one and as separate from others yet with others. The child begins to experience himself as a centered unit by being centered upon.

(p. 19)

And here is one of many poetic passages one might choose from Winnicott (1971) about the interpersonal sources of the self:

It is only ... in this unintegrated state of the personality, that that which we describe as creative can appear. This if reflected back, *but only if reflected back*, becomes part of the organized individual personality, and eventually this in summation makes the individual to be, to be found; and eventually enables himself or herself to postulate the exist-ence of the self.

(p. 64, italics in original)

Eventually, our initial witnesses from the outside world are internalized and elaborated so that imaginary witnesses internal to the personality are created—and these internal presences are loving ones to the extent that our earliest witnesses have been. Self-affirmative internal conversation then becomes feasible. One self-state witnesses another, and the result is the formulation of a new and wider experience of oneself— thoughts, yes, but feelings, memories, and perceptions no less than thoughts. The boundaries of the self expand. Not-self becomes self. For this to happen, there must be a vantage point in one's own mind, a second *location*, from which to turn back and *see* or *hear* or *feel* ourselves and to care about what we see, hear, and feel. We begin to see ourselves through the eyes of others, hear and value ourselves through their ears. As I wrote then:

Even in the absence of others, we learn about ourselves by imaginatively listening to our own thoughts through the ears of the other. At the beginning of life, we need a witness to become a self. Later, patients listen to themselves as they imagine their analysts hear them ... The resolution of enactments is crucial in psychoanalytic treatment, not only because it expands the boundaries of the self, but also because it reinstitutes and broadens the range within which patient and analyst can witness one another's experience.

(Stern, 2009, p. 701)

In making reference to loving internal presences and self-affirmative internal conversation, I have already implied that witnessing is something more than the mere registration by the child of its presence in the caregiver's mind. Reliable and effective caretaking, that is, is not sufficient to create all the effects that I am addressing under the rubric of witnessing. I intend to refer not only to the creation of mind, but also to the development of an acceptable, stable, and comfortably valued sense of self—a dependable and sometimes pleasurable feeling of being a particular person. Only to the extent that the child senses that the image of itself in the caregiver's mind is beloved does the relationship result in the seeding and tending of a fully realized and valued sense of self— realized, that is, not just in the child's cognitive recognition of itself as what Loewald referred to in the passage above as a "centered unit," or what Fonagy et al. (2002) describe as the process by which infants "fathom ... their own minds" (p. 2). The self is most fully realized, in other words, when it is rooted in the confidence that one has a home in the mind of the other, a home that the child senses the other not only provides, but *wants* to provide (Bach, 2006; Benjamin, 1995, 1998, 2017).

What is needed is not only recognition, but also affirmation— "someone who is trusted and justifies the trust and meets the dependence" (Winnicott, 1971, p. 60). Only under these conditions can the caregiver's image of the child serve a fully developed witnessing function. The more widespread this kind of atmosphere becomes in the personality of the child, and then of the adult the child will become, the wider and deeper the range of formulations of experience that can be allowed to reach fruition is, and therefore, the more often thought and feeling can be allowed free rein. While Winnicott never expressed himself in just these words, he could have; and he is surely their ultimate source.

Here, Loewald (1960, see also Chodorow, 2018) again deserves mention since he beautifully conveys the links between the parent-child relationship and certain aspects of the therapeutic action of psychoanalysis. I think also of the clinical perspective presented by Fonagy and Target, heavily influenced by Winnicott and represented in one instance by these words:

> The analyst needs to infer and create a coherent representation of the patient's true self, separate from but concurrent with any counter-transference enactment. The psychotherapist's mentalistic elaborative stance ultimately enables the patient to find himself in the therapist's mind and integrate this image.
>
> (Fonagy & Target, 2000, p. 870)

The development of stable self-regard in childhood and later, the curative qualities of the analytic relationship, require more than two people becoming significant enough to one another to develop transferences and countertransferences—more than becoming psychic objects in one another's worlds. What is required is even more than that the relationship takes place in such a way that the child's (and the analysand's) raw sensory and affective experience is transformed into thought. (I am thinking here of Bion [1962, 1963] and Green [2005].) The caregiver's reverie, in other words—and the analyst's, too—becomes witnessing in the fullest sense, inspiring the most nuanced, inclusive, and emotionally complex formulation of experience, only when it grows from love.

This needs to be clarified: what do I mean by "love"? Let me just say, for the moment, that I am referring to a non-instrumental, affirmative bond or connection conceptualized as part of the analytic interaction since at the least the time of Searles's (1959) "Oedipal Love in the Counter-Transference," Balint's (1952, 1968) work on primary love and the basic fault, and Loewald's (1960) classic statement of therapeutic action. It is a variety of what Schachtel (1959) called the *allocentric attitude*. When analysts love their patients, they do not express this love in so many words and certainly not in their conduct. They are not looking to their patients to satisfy their needs; they seek the best for them.

In a classic 1961 panel, "The Curative Factors in Psycho-analysis," held at the 22nd Edinburgh Congress of the International Psychoanalytic Association, Nacht (1962a) put it this way:

It seems obvious to me that only a timely and technically appropriate attitude of gratification can allow the patient to accept his need to love and be loved, and to express it without fear. But this attitude must, of course, be expressed neither in words nor in gestures, but *solely by an inner state of being.*

(p. 209, italics in original)

In his very brief invited contribution to the ensuing discussion, Nacht (1962b) said that his attempt to define what the analyst's inner attitude should be had apparently "caused some astonishment," no doubt a euphemism for an uproar of controversy. The analyst's love for the patient, Nacht said by way of further explanation,

has a great importance when he tries to come into contact with his patient's unconscious, and I should say that that inner attitude should be impregnated with love for his patient. Of course not the same kind of love he has, for instance, for his brother, his wife, or his close friend.

(p. 233)

When I refer to love, I intend a further meaning, too—perhaps one that, in Nacht's terms, would be akin to some of the forms of love that we feel with our intimates outside the consulting room. This point I can only state, not explain, until I can take up the subject separately and in more depth in another presentation. Frequently in my experience, the love I intend here is fair to describe as affection or tenderness, whether it is the love of the parent for the child or the analyst for the patient—or whether it is the echo, the internalization, of those loves that imbues the perception and acceptance of one part of the self by another.

Of course, none of what I am saying should be taken as a denial of the reality that, in every kind of relationship, love is often nested in pain, hate, and struggle so that it seldom happens easily and sometimes cannot happen at all.

The last several paragraphs could give some readers the impression that I am rediscovering Kohut (1971, 1977). It is true that I have learned much from him. But what I am describing as witnessing differs from the selfobject relationship in several respects: (1) In my frame of reference, the analyst, while usually having a special degree of affective significance in the patient's mind, remains a human being like any other. The witness has no special status corresponding to the role of the selfobject. (2) Witnessing is a relational phenomenon: in the process of analyst and patient becoming partners in thought (Stern, 2009a, 2010), *acceptance of being witnessed* is as crucial a contribution as witnessing itself. (3) Witnessing often or usually contains empathy but cannot be reduced to it. (4) Most important, and overlapping with the former points, the selfobject is a special kind of object used to regulate and stabilize the self, while the witness is not an object at all, but another subject who is recognized as such by the one who is witnessed.

Dissociation and the interruption of witnessing

There are circumstances in which the state of mind that needs to be witnessed is dissociated from the states that could serve as its witness. The pain has just been too great in the past, enforcing a dissociation, which becomes structural over time (Bromberg, 1998, 2006, 2011). Consider a patient I have written about before (Stern, 2009), a man whose father treated him contemptuously with sufficient frequency that the patient grew up to take his contemptibility for granted. When I met him, he was unable to treat his contemptibility as an attribution, either by his father or by himself; for him, it was such an unquestioned (and unformulated) reality that he never really even saw it very clearly. It was the air he breathed; it was, in a word, dissociated.

One expression of this state of affairs, or perhaps just another way of saying the same thing, was that this man could not occupy a place in his mind from which he could grasp that he felt contemptible. In other words, he was incapable of thinking about his contemptibility. If he could have known that his feeling of contemptibility was an attribution, an active perception of his own—that is, if he could have grasped that his shame (which he hardly even knew how to experience directly) was a ceaseless creation, a representation of his own mind, not simply an objectively existing characteristic—then he might have had a chance of mustering curiosity about it. He might even have become able to challenge it.

Because this man could not create a witness in his internal world, he needed one in the outer world, some person (a psychoanalyst, or someone able and willing to carry out the crucial parts of that role) who, while not sharing the patient's feeling about his contemptibility, could somehow let him know, "It is *you* who feels contemptible; it is *you* who creates this representation of your experience." But it is seldom that it would be useful for the analyst to say such words as these. The role of the witness is not necessarily taken on in verbal language at all.

Here is a thumbnail sketch of the work with a dissociative enactment that set this man and me on a productive path.

The patient was a few minutes late, and I took the opportunity to have a quick snack; but he arrived while I was still eating. It took me a minute or so to finish, and I felt slightly guilty about that when I met him in the waiting room, where (as a result of this guilt, I think) I greeted him in a subdued way that lacked my usual warmth—although I did not make this observation until later, looking back at it. The patient sensed my coolness and took it as evidence (again, noted only later) that I regarded his neediness with the same contempt he was sure his father had felt about it. (It turned out that he had always secretly worried that his neediness was betrayed by the pleasure he routinely took in my appearance and warm greeting in the waiting room.)

The episode provoked rage on the patient's part. He bitterly accused me of being an inadequate analyst and, in fact, a cruel human being who should have known better than to have entered a helping profession. We went through a painful session; but as it went on, I eventually was able to explain what had happened in a way that led him to see that, in that same moment in which he had been convinced that I was (internally) rolling my eyes at what I thought was his pathetic weakness and neediness, I had actually been flustered and defensive about his attack and had not actually been thinking what he had thought I was thinking at all. Thus was a witness born (that is, me: the patient could now look back at himself through my eyes and see that he was suffering because he believed I felt something I did not feel). This was not something that could have come about through interpretation—although there was eventually a great deal to say about it, and some of those things were interpretations in the traditional sense.

Until we loosened the hold of that rigid enactment, until we could both think, until he could mentalize his own experience (Fonagy et al., 2002), this man had only two choices, neither of which could he formulate. That is, while an outside observer might be able to formulate the possibility of the man's choices, the patient himself could no more grasp his choices in words than he could sense his own participation in creating the problematic perceptions of himself in the first place. His two choices were as follows:

he could take on contemptibility as an intrinsic aspect of himself, in which case he would have had to blame himself and feel self-hateful and ashamed; or he could do as he did and attribute his feeling of contemptibility to mistreatment by me. That course, while temporarily freeing him from shame and self-hatred, led to an interpersonal impasse that, in most contexts in life, would probably have been fatal to the future possibilities of this relationship. His choices, in other words, were restricted to self-blame and intolerable shame or blame of the other with accompanying rage.

The latter solution, blaming the other, constitutes dissociative enactment: the contemptibility is located in the other, and the other is then treated—as in defensively motivated projective identification—as if they embody the not-me part of the self. Enactment is the last resort for those who face the disastrous collapse of dissociation, a collapse that not only threatens to flood consciousness with intolerable not-me experience that fills one with shame or terror, but also makes one unrecognizable to oneself (Bromberg, 1998, 2006, 2011). In this dissociative enactment, it was as if the patient organized the analytic field around the feeling that, "I must not, cannot, will not be my father's contemptible little boy."

By the end of that session, I had begun to serve as the witness the patient had never had. He saw me seeing him at the very moment that he felt most certain that he had aroused contempt in me; but that is not what happened, and he could see it. He experienced it. He knew that I did not feel the way he had been sure I did. The two of us eventually became partners in thought. "In such cases," I wrote about circumstances like these—which are not uncommon, even if they are not always so dramatic—"we not only profit from seeing a psychoanalyst, we need one" (Stern, 2009, p. 725). In other words, because dissociation prevents imaginative witnessing and mentalization of one's own experience, and therefore makes impossible the internal conversation of an experiencing state and a witnessing state, a witness in the outside world is required if the possibility of holding such a conversation is to come about. The witness reveals to us what and who we are, and in the very act of being witnessed, if we can accept it, we are brought into possession of ourselves. We have the thought, the feeling, the perception, and we know we have created them.

The patient, slowly, over time, with repetitions and variations on the theme, grasped that he did not need to fight me in order to avoid contemptibility; instead, he saw that, as much as his suffering deserved to be recognized and as little as he may have been responsible for its origins, it was at this point *his* suffering—his creation or co-creation. In accepting it, he began to be able to use the experience in the creation of different forms of living. Not-me began to become me. As time passed, he could sometimes question his suffering and, in some moments, experience himself differently enough to be free of it.

Observing ego

The point that one part of the mind can observe another, as in the conception of the imaginary witness, is hardly new. You may already have been reminded of the observing ego, the perspective offered long ago by Sterba (1934), who took the position that therapeutic action is based on a dissociation in the ego that allows observation by the patient of their own mind. This work led directly to later thinking on the therapeutic or working alliance (e.g., Loewald, 1960; Friedman, 1969; Greenson, 1965; Zetzel, 1956). Sterba understood the observing part of the patient's ego to be based on an identification with the analyst's interpreting function.

> Through this interpretation there emerges in the mind of the patient, out of the chaos of behaviour impelled by instinct and behaviour designed to inhibit instinct, a *new point of view of intellectual contemplation*. In order that this new standpoint may be effectually reached there must be a certain amount of positive transference, on the basis of which a transitory strengthening of the ego takes place through identification with the analyst. This identification is induced by the analyst. From the outset the patient is called upon to "co-operate" with the analyst against something in himself.
>
> (Sterba, 1934, p. 120, italics in original)

Soon after Sterba first delivered his paper in the early 1930s, Freud wrote in the *New Introductory Lectures* (1933) that,

> The ego can take itself as object, can treat itself like other objects, can observe itself, criticize itself, and do Heaven knows what with itself. In this, one part of the ego is setting itself over against the rest. So the ego can be split.
>
> (1933, p. 57)

Friedman (1969) suggests that Freud actually began his consideration of something on the order of the therapeutic alliance much earlier, in "The Dynamics of Transference" (1912). In this view, the idea of the observing ego or working alliance is longstanding, then, and was arguably inspired by Freud himself. Friedman (1969) also writes, though, that the working alliance is not a theory of therapeutic action, as Sterba and others styled it. It is instead, Friedman says, a means to an end, part of the working through process. Friedman (1969) says he does not intend to

> deny the alliance an instrumental value in the process of analysis, a function which may be pictured as analogous to—and perhaps an aspect of—working through. But just as working through is capitalizing on an achieved success, so the classical therapeutic alliance should not claim to explain the achievement which it propagates.
>
> (p. 143)

Note that Sterba describes the alliance as "*a new point of view of intellectual contemplation*" (see the above passage quoted from Sterba). This statement is consistent with conceptualizing the therapeutic alliance as a cognitive accomplishment, one that allows patients to observe and think about themselves more or less dispassionately—but not necessarily as a theory of therapeutic action. This is the view taken by all of those later writers who discussed the observing ego or the therapeutic alliance, with the exception of Loewald (1960), for whom the identification of the patient with the analyst is part of a relationship that has more significant aspects than the instrumental.

Friedman's (1969) observation that the alliance should not be understood as a component of therapeutic action highlights what separates the observing ego and the therapeutic alliance from the phenomena I am addressing as the internal witness and coming into possession of oneself. I am emphasizing the creation of the patient's grasp of their own involvement in the act of their own knowing or feeling, and I believe this process plays an important role in the therapeutic process. The patient's grasp of their own involvement is not only a sign that the patient can now master unconscious process by symbolization in words, as it is in the therapeutic alliance. Rather, the patient's grasp of their own active participation in the creation of their sense of who and what they are is an end in itself. *Not-me* becomes *feels-like-me*. The creation of this grasp is one way to describe therapeutic action.

I also want to draw attention to the fact that in Sterba's (1934) thera-peutic alliance, "the patient is called upon to 'co-operate' with the analyst *against* something in himself" (p. 120, italics added). This point differenti-ates Sterba's idea from mine even further than I have already described, because the kind of observation of one state by another that I have called "imaginary witnessing"—and that is encouraged by analytic treatment as I envision it—is not at all a matter of splitting (i.e., Sterba's pitting of one part of the mind against another) but is instead, in an important sense, quite the opposite: it is the *new linkage* of parts of the mind that have been sequestered from one another by dissociation.

Being witnessed: Feeling known, recognized, or understood

A clinical illustration

In the last part of these remarks, I address how it happens that witnessing leads to *feels-like-me*, and especially, why witnessing should result in com-ing into possession of oneself. Why should witnessing make it possible for us to know and feel that we know and feel?

I take the position that being effectively witnessed (which is to say, *feel-ing* witnessed) leads to the experience of being understood, and that *that*—feeling known, recognized, or understood—offers us the path that leads to our capacity to grasp our own participation in the creation of our own thinking and feeling.

Here is a clinical moment that illustrates what I mean. Near the end of a session, Emma, a talented, very bright, and highly self-critical white busi-nesswoman in her late thirties, with whom I meet four times a week, accused herself of being skillful at "duping" or "manipulating" people: "I'm false and superficial," she said, "because I put on a front so that people will think I am 'normal' and that I suffer less than I really do. I give the impression of being put together when I feel a mess underneath."

Emma and I had explored over and over again her worry that she had somehow managed to pull the wool over my eyes so that I could not see what a "mess" she is and how skillfully she manipulates me. She knows that I do not agree with this assessment of her impact on me, but she sometimes worries that, because I am a "nice person" and don't want her to suffer, I convince myself that she is "better" than she is. In her mind, I succumb, in this way, to her machinations. I do not carry on a battle with her about this point, of course, but I do insist that the way she sees it is meaningful—a point with which she agrees.

Emma suspects that she is involved in this same "manipulative" way with anyone who has not concluded that she is emotionally incompetent—and people generally do not conclude that at all. I have the impression that Emma is usually taken by others to be a capable, warm, friendly, and generous presence. People generally like her. I do not have the impression that this presentation of herself is dishonest, with me or with others, despite the fact that I really am deeply impressed with how profound a mess she often feels she is. (I know this largely because, despite her fears of pulling the wool over my eyes, Emma frequently tells me about it.)

You can see that this is a complicated situation, because of course Emma often really is more a mess inside than she lets on, and so her presentation of herself is, just as she says, partially designed to avoid the revelation of what she wants to keep to herself. Contributing to the complication is that I believe that Emma presents herself as she does not only to distract others' attention from the mess she is inside, but also because she actually does feel and believe that capability, warmth, and generosity are important in life. Emma, however, can take little satisfaction in her presentation of an emotionally capable self, since she needs to maintain the conviction that she is merely fooling those who don't see through it. Why? Because she is afraid that, if she accepts that she is more or less "good," someone else will see how "bad" or "toxic" she is, and she will feel caught out, humiliated, and hurt much more deeply than if she accuses herself first. And so the reason she accuses herself with such ferocity of abusing other people is, paradoxically, that it makes her feel safer than she would be if she let down her guard and allowed herself to believe that she generally treats people with basic warmth and respect. Her defensively skewed interpretation of her self-presentation therefore simply reinforces her sense that she is indeed duping and manipulating people. We might say that Emma is quite literally afraid to believe in herself and to trust my belief in her. I will not go into the parts of her history that result in this sad outcome, but the history is well known to both Emma and me.

And so, when Emma accused herself of duping people on this particular occasion, you should understand my response to her from within the context I have just described. This was one of the first times I had described to Emma what I felt was the positive side of her self-presentation. This is what I said (reconstructed from my notes):

As usual, you put your observation of yourself in a more negative way than I would. I don't see a good reason to call it "duping" or false when you present yourself as better put-together than you feel inside. I would say, as a matter of fact, that your capacity to present yourself as better-put-together than you feel is a notable strength. It grows from real self-esteem: you want to present yourself in a way that makes you feel better about yourself than you would if you just gave in to how things feel sometimes. I see it as a strength especially because you actually know you're doing it—you know that you have all those bad feelings, and you are able to hide them anyway. It's a choice you're making. It's an expression of wanting a certain kind of life, and wanting to be a certain sort of person. And it's not "made up," either, if you mean to say that being "made up" makes it inauthentic. What you call "put-together ways of being" are just as much a genuine part of you as the sadness and despair that the "put-together" parts sometimes let you keep to yourself.

In saying this, I was trying to represent a part of Emma that I believe exists, and that I was acutely aware of at the moment that Emma spoke about "duping," but that Emma tends to dissociate—as she often dissociates the parts of her that might offer a sympathetic account of her experience or conduct.

Emma's self-blame is only half the story, though. She also wants very badly to feel better, and so she is committed to thinking about why she falls into blaming herself at every turn. It is true that Emma is more or less continuously (that is, usually but not always) prepared to quash whatever thought or feeling might result in her feeling good about herself—especially if this thought or feeling originates with her. If it comes from someone else, it might just stand. But if she initiates it, feeling good is dangerous. However, it is also true that Emma is often courageous in questioning these inclinations and self-doubts, thereby leaving herself dangerously unprotected from the humiliation that threatens her whenever she is foolish enough to hope not to be unhappy. The depth and high stakes of her struggle, and her willingness to risk real danger in the service of her treatment and her own future, lead me to look forward to her visits.

What I have just reported that I said to Emma is prosaic and commonsensical, or at least not particularly surprising, but that is not how Emma felt about it. She actually *was* surprised. She said wonderingly, "It never occurred to me to think of it *that* way. Hmm ... (long silence) I have to ponder all that." There was another long silence, and then, just before the session ended, she added, "It feels hugely unburdening or relaxing or expanding or something."

Some hours later, I received the following email message from Emma:

> I just wanted to say thank you. I've had a few glimmers of a new feeling—a feeling that I have my own existence, independent of and separate from anyone else. That somehow it is okay to be my own person, separately. To just be myself, not me whose existence is contingent on other people. I never felt exactly this way before.

This is an eloquent expression of an experience of coming into possession of oneself, and it illustrates that such an experience requires feeling understood by someone else, or some part of oneself—someone (or some part) who is able to take a sympathetic view of whatever it is that, up to that point, one has had to bar from the domain of the self, of what is recognized as "me." This understanding is what is provided by the witness: in offering a sympathetic view of an unacceptable part of oneself, a view one would not create by oneself, the witness reveals the path by which one can, oneself, create this same view. The witness and the one being witnessed become partners in thought. *Not-me* becomes *feels-like-me*. Prior to having the feeling of being understood, one may have been familiar enough with the not-me part to recognize it—that is, one could have the thought or feeling, but that thought or feeling merely washes over one, like an ocean wave. It is experienced passively, as if it were a feature of the world, not a creation of one's own mind. Prior to feeling witnessed, in other words, one may be able to know or feel, but one cannot go meta-affective; one cannot know or feel that one knows or feels.

Emma's palpable sense of conviction, both in the session and the email, told me that I was right when I described the self-respecting part of her that I stood up for in the session. She listened to me, absorbed what I said, and later on, made it her own. What began as an alien thought began to "feel like me." She did not stop at recognizing and opening up a new possibility; she also was able to sense that *she* was the one doing the opening.

You can tell in Emma's email to me that she is not thanking me for a new insight. She is thanking me because she is experiencing a new, unbidden feeling/thought that she recognizes as coming from herself. She is mentalizing (Fonagy et al., 2002); she has the feeling that her mind is her own.

And once you do that, once you are no longer limited to a passive-receptive attitude toward the thought or feeling in question, but are able to make it yourself and know that it is you who have done it, you don't go back. You can't go back, not really, because the world has changed in a small way, and it can never be quite what it was before.

Information alone can't do that, no matter how subtle and accurate it may be. Interpretation, as any number of psychoanalytic writers have told us over the past decades, is not adequately defined by its semantic content. I believe that Emma could experience being understood by my act of witnessing only because she believed that I meant what I said to her. It would not have happened just because what I said was accurate, no matter how well intentioned. In fact, if Emma sensed I was making a statement that was accurate and well intentioned but not genuinely felt on my part, that itself would have been a strong reason for her not to take it seriously. She is highly sensitive to that sort of distinction. Emma's conviction derived from mine, and my conviction was rooted in my belief in her suffering.

Like a good poem, Jeanine Vivona (2013) reminds us, an interpretation makes one feel understood at the same moment that one sees "something new about oneself that has been articulated by someone else from within that person's own experience." And then Vivona says—expressing what seems to me to be what is most significant about witnessing in the process of formulation in the analytic situation—that insight "is an experience of resonance with another person's vision of things" (p. 1129).

Working through, or something like it

But I am not describing a magic psychoanalytic bullet. Even when there is a dramatic moment of coming into possession of oneself, there remains working through to do. I am sure that Emma and I will go through some version of the brief sequence I just described many times, in different ways. Her suffering, including the suffering she brings on herself, has hardly ended. The part of Emma that hates herself will try repeatedly to hurt or destroy the part that feels better about herself, and the hateful part will not always lose. And I will be part of the struggle. Sometimes I will be idealized, as I have been often enough already, in a way that results in Emma herself being cast in the devalued role. It will then seem to Emma, as it frequently does, that she has disappointed me, or worse, that she has hurt me or that she is toxic to me; and she will suffer for believing she is having this impact on me. If we do well, one day Emma will be able to be disappointed in me or angry at me, without having to feel that either of us is monstrous—neither her for being angry nor me for letting her down. All of this, and no doubt a good deal more, awaits us. I am hopeful that we will get there, because Emma has now had a number of experiences of finding her way—her own way—to perceptions of herself as good, or at least good enough. One of these experiences is the one I have just told you about: Emma's different sense of what she is doing when she presents herself as more put-together than she is.

The therapeutic action of witnessing depends on *feeling* witnessed. It would not be right to substitute *be* for *feel* here. It would not be right, that is, to say that to be witnessed is to *be* known, recognized, and understood. To word it that way would sound a falsely objectivistic note, as if being the object of someone's intention to witness is enough. If witnessing is to help, it must be rooted in an unconscious field process between the patient and the analyst, a web of meaning that, to exist, must usually have grown to its current status over a significant period of time. Let me say this another way. If the analyst is able to *mean* what he or she perceives, senses, feels, and speaks about the patient, about the analyst herself, and/or about the analytic relatedness—and let me emphasize that the emergence of the analyst's understanding from what is personally meaningful to the analyst is indeed what is required—it is because the analytic participants have already constructed between them a complex, affectively resonant, and (at least relatively) emotionally safe interpersonal field. The witnessing must be an emergent product of a deep, powerful, unconscious, nonrational involvement with the patient that the analyst can feel or sense, at least partly, but usually cannot describe in explicit terms.

The kinds of enactments that rigidify the field do not disappear just because dissociation has been breached, an enactment has been ended, and the field has become more spontaneous. The themes persevere; what is resolved is only these particular expressions of the themes. Each successful resolution does indeed loosen the structural, dissociative grip of mind on the formulation of experience that is yet to be created; but these moments of successful clinical work hardly do away with the patterns they express.

There are any number of theoretical perspectives from which to grasp the very simple interchange I have presented from Emma's treatment. Many of these perspectives, like mine, emphasize relational factors, and most of them might very well tell us something interesting and/or useful. My ideas about formulation, in other words, are not uniquely suited to describe this clinical moment. The vignette is, I hope, useful as an illustration, but it is not intended as empirical evidence for my point of view. My aim in this presentation has been to describe the way that the process of formulation—the determination of the shape, pattern, and content of consciousness—is thoroughly rooted in and emerges from relational life.

Coda

I end by reporting what Emma said when I requested her permission to use in this article the material from our work.

Among Emma's first reactions to my request was that she would like to read what I wrote about her because it might be like reading over the notes she takes after our sessions, which she said she likes to do. (This was the first time I had understood this, although Emma had told me she takes notes.) Emma said that she reads over her notes because they remind her of what we talked about, which pleases her. But she also likes reading them, she said, because during our sessions she can be so deeply involved in what she is talking about (and sometimes so self-conscious) that she is unable to pay close attention to what she thinks is my experience of her—at least those parts of my experience of her that she can believe are not critical. (She does generally believe that I feel warmly toward her, but of course that conclusion sometimes comes under attack by the self-hateful parts of her.) Reading her notes after the sessions allows Emma the freedom from urgency that she needs in order to imagine more fully and freely the positive parts of what I might have been thinking and feeling. She likes to imagine these things, she said, because, as she reads, Emma knows and can feel that I feel differently about her than she feels about herself. In her words, the surprise she experiences with every reading "feels freeing" (her words). She can feel her way into my experience of her, which is usually more sympathetic to her than the portrayals of herself she creates alone.

We see ourselves through our analysts' eyes, hear ourselves through our analysts' ears.

References

Alvarez, A. (1992). *Live Company: Psychoanalytic Psychotherapy with Autistic, Borderline, Deprived and Abused Children*. London: Routledge.

Alvarez, A. (2012). *The Thinking Heart: Three Levels of Psychoanalytic Therapy with Disturbed Children*. London/New York: Routledge.

Amir, D. (2012). The inner witness. *The International Journal of Psychoanalysis* 93: 879–896.

Bach, S. (2006). *Getting from Here to There: Analytic Love, Analytic Process*. Hillsdale, NJ: Analytic Press.

Balint, M. (1952). *Primary Love and Psychoanalytic Technique*. London: The Hogarth Press.

Balint, M. (1968). *The Basic Fault: Therapeutic Aspects of Regression*. London: Tavistock.

Benjamin, J. (1995). *Like Subjects, Love Objects*. New Haven, CT: Yale University Press.

Benjamin, J. (1998). *The Shadow of the Other*. New York/London: Routledge.

Benjamin, J. (2017). *Beyond Doer and Done To: Recognition Theory, Intersubjectivity, and the Third*. New York/London: Routledge.

Bion, W. R. R. (1962). *Learning from Experience*. London: Heinemann.

Bion, W. R. R. (1963). *Elements of Psychoanalysis*. London: Heinemann.

Boston Change Process Study Group. (2010). *Change in Psychotherapy: A Unifying Paradigm*. New York: W. W. Norton & Co.

Boulanger, G. (2005). From voyeur to witness: Recapturing symbolic function after massive psychic trauma. *Psychoanalytic Psychology* 22: 21–31.

Bromberg, P. M. (1998). *Standing in the Spaces: Essays on Clinical Process, Trauma, and Dissociation*. Hillsdale, NJ: Analytic Press.

Bromberg, P. M. (2006). *Awakening the Dreamer: Clinical Journeys*. Hillsdale, NJ: Analytic Press.

Bromberg, P. M. (2011). *The Shadow of the Tsunami: And the Growth of the Relational Mind*. New York: Routledge.

Caldwell, L. & Robinson, H. T. (2017). General introduction to the *Collected Works*. In L. Caldwell H. T. Robinson (Eds.), *The Collected Works of D. W. Winnicott, Volume 1: 1911–1938* (pp. lvii–lxxxii). Oxford: Oxford University Press.

Chodorow, N. J. (2018). Love, respect, and being centered upon: Loewald's image of development in childhood and the consulting room. *The Psychoanalytic Study of the Child* 71: 224–233.

Cooley, C. H. (1902). *Human Nature and the Social Order*. New York: Charles Scribner's Son, revised edition 1922.

D'ercole, A. (2012). Nella mia famiglia: Race, gender and the intergenerational dilemmas of being a witness. *Contemporary Psychoanalysis* 48: 451–482.

Director, L. (2009). The enlivening object. *Contemporary Psychoanalysis* 45: 120–141.

Eshel, O. (2019). *The Emergence of Analytic Oneness: Into the Heart of Psychoanalysis*. London/New York: Routledge.

Feldman, M. J. (2015). Ghost stories: Transgenerational trauma and witnessing in analyst and analysand. *Psychoanalytic Dialogues* 25: 600–613.

Ferenczi, S. (1988). *The Clinical Diary of Sandor Ferenczi*, ed. J. Dupont, trans. M. Balint & M. Z. Jackson. Cambridge, MA: Harvard University Press.

Ferenczi, S. & Rank, O. (1925). *The Development of Psychoanalysis*. New York: Nervous and Mental Disease Publishing.

Fonagy, P., Gergely, G., Jurist, E. & Target, M. (2002). *Affect Regulation, Mentalization, and the Development of the Self*. New York: Other Press.

Fonagy, P. & Target, M. (2000). Playing with reality: III. The persistence of dual psychic reality in borderline patients. *The International Journal of Psychoanalysis* 81: 853–874.

Freud, S. (1912). The dynamics of transference. *S. E.* 12.

Freud, S. (1933). *New introductory lectures on psycho-analysis. S. E.* 22.

Friedman, L. (1969). The therapeutic alliance. *The International Journal of Psychoanalysis* 50: 139–153.

Fromm, E. (1955). Remarks on the problem of free association. In D. B. Stern, C. Mann, S. Kantor & G. Schlesinger (Eds.), *Pioneers of Interpersonal Psychoanalysis* (pp. 123–134). Hillsdale, NJ: Analytic Press, 1995.

Fromm, E. (1964/1991). The causes for the patient's change in analytic treatment. *Contemporary Psychoanalysis* 27: 608–622.

Fromm, E., Suzuki, D. T. & De Martino, R. (1970). *Zen Buddhism and Psychoanalysis*. New York: Harpers.

Gautier, A. & Scalmati, A. S. (2019). *Bearing Witness: Psychoanalytic Work with People Traumatised by Torture and State Violence*. London/New York: Routledge.

Gentile, K. (2013). Bearing the cultural in order to engage in a process of witnessing. *Psychoanalytic Psychology* 30: 456–470.

Gerson, S. (2009). When the third is dead: Memory, mourning, and witnessing in the aftermath of the holocaust. *The International Journal of Psychoanalysis* 90: 1341–1357.

Ghiselin, B. (1952). *The Creative Process*. Berkeley, CA: Univerisity California Press.

Gondar, J. (2017). Between psychoanalysis and testimonial space: The analyst as a witness. *American Journal of Psychoanalysis* 77: 52–63.

Goodman, N. R. & Meyers, M. B. (Eds.). (2012). *The Power of Witnessing: Reflections, Reverberations, and Traces of the Holocaust*. London/New York: Routledge.

Grand, S. (2015). Circles of witnessing: On hope and atrocity. *Contemporary Psychoanalysis* 51: 262–275.

Green, A. (1986). *On Private Madness*. London: Hogarth.

Green, A. (2005). *Key Ideas for a Contemporary Psychoanalysis: Misrecognition and Recognition of the Unconscious*. London/New York: Routledge.

Greenson, R. R. (1965). The working alliance and the transference neurosis. *Psychoanalytic Quarterly* 34: 155–179.

Kohut, H. (1971). *The Analysis of the Self*. Madison, CT: International Universities Press.

Kohut, H. (1977). *The Restoration of the Self*. Madison, CT: International Universities Press.

Laub, D. (1991). Truth and testimony: The process and the struggle. *American Imago* 48: 75–91.

Laub, D. (1992a). Bearing witness or the vicissitudes of witnessing. In S. Felman & D. Laub (Eds.), *Testimony: Crises of Witnessing in Literature, Psychoanalysis, and History* (pp. 57–74). New York/London: Routledge.

Laub, D. (1992b). An event without a witness: Truth, testimony, and survival. In S. Felman & D. Laub (Eds.), *Testimony: Crises of Witnessing in Literature, Psychoanalysis, and History* (pp. 75–92). New York/London: Routledge.

Laub, D. (1995). Truth and testimony. In C. Caruth (Ed.), *Trauma: Explorations in Memory* (pp. 61–75). Baltimore: Johns Hopkins University Press.

Laub, D. (2005). Traumatic shutdown of symbolization and narrative: A death instinct derivative? *Contemporary Psychoanalysis* 41: 307–326.

Laub, D. & Auerhahn, N. (1989). Failed empathy: A central theme in the survivor's Holocaust experience. *Psychoanalytic Psychology* 6: 377–400.

Lichtenberg, J. D., Lachmann, F. M. & Fosshage, J. L. (2015). *Enlivening the Self: The First Year, Clinical Enrichment, and the Wandering Mind*. London/New York: Routledge.

Loewald, H. W. (1960). On the therapeutic action of Psychoanalysis. *The International Journal of Psychoanalysis* 41: 16–33.

Loewald, H. W. (1978). Primary process, secondary process, and language. In *The Essential Loewald: Collected Papers and Monographs* (pp. 178–204). Hagerstown, MD: University Publishing Group, 2000.

Mead, G. H. (1934). *Mind, Self, and Society*. Chicago: University of Chicago Press.

Mitchell, S. A. (2000). *Relationality*. London/New York: Routledge.

Mucci, C. (2019). Traumatization through human agency: "Embodied witnessing" is essential in the treatment of survivors. *American Journal of Psychoanalysis* 79: 540–554.

Nacht, S. (1962a). The curative factors in psychoanalysis. *The International Journal of Psychoanalysis* 43: 206–211.

Nacht, S. (1962b). The curative factors in psychoanalysis—contributions to discussion. *The International Journal of Psychoanalysis* 43: 233.

Ogden, T. H. (2019a). Ontological psychoanalysis or "what do you want to be when you grow up?" *Psychoanalytic Quarterly* 88(4): 661–684.

Ogden, T. H. (2019b). The feeling of real: on Winnicott's "on communicating and not communicating leads to a study of certain opposites." *The International Journal of Psychoanalysis* 99: 1288–1304.

Poland, W. S. (2000). The analyst's witnessing and otherness. *Journal of the American Psychoanalytic Association* 48: 17–34.

Poland, W. S. (2011). Self-analysis and creativity: Views from inside and outside. *Psychoanalytic Quarterly* LXXX: 987–1003.

Reis, B. (2009). Performative and enactive features of psychoanalytic witnessing: The transference as the scene of address. *The International Journal of Psychoanalysis* 90: 1359–1372.

Richman, S. (2006). Finding one's voice: Transforming trauma into autobiographical narrative. *Contemporary Psychoanalysis* 42: 639–650.

Richman, S. (2009). Secrets and mystifications: Finding meaning through memoir. *Psychoanalytical Perspective* 6: 67–75.

Richman, S. (2013). Out of darkness: Reverberations of trauma and its creative transformations. *Psychoanalytical Dialogues* 23: 362–376.

Richman, S. (2014). *Mended by the Muse: Creative Transformations of Trauma*. London/New York: Routledge.

Roussillon, R. (2011). *Primitive Agony and Symbolization*. London: Karnac Books.

Schwartz Cooney, A. (2018). Vitalizing enactment: A relational exploration. *Psychoanalytical Dialogues* 28: 340–354.

Schachtel, E. (1959). *Metamorphosis: On the conflict of human development and the psychology of creativity*. New York: Basic Books.

Schwartz Cooney, A. & Sopher, R. (2021). *Vitalization in Psychoanalysis: Perspectives on Being and Becoming*. London/New York: Routledge.

Searles, H. F. (1959). Oedipal love in the countertransference. *The International Journal of Psychoanalysis* 40: 180–190.

Seiden, H. M. (1996). The healing presence: Part I: The witness as self-object function. *Psychoanalytic Review* 83: 685–693.

Sheppard, A. (2017). Countering being envied: The need for a witness. *Canadian Journal of Psychoanalysis* 25: 79–87.

Sterba, R. (1934). The fate of the ego in analytic therapy. *The International Journal of Psychoanalysis* 15: 117–126.

Stern, D. B. (1990). Courting surprise: Unbidden perceptions in clinical practice. *Contemporary Psychoanalysis* 26: 452–478.

Stern, D. B. (1997). *Unformulated Experience: From Dissociation to Imagination in Psychoanalysis*. New York: Routledge.

Stern, D. B. (2003). The fusion of horizons: Dissociation, enactment, and understanding. *Psychoanalytic Dialogues* 13: 843–873.

Stern, D. B. (2004). The eye sees itself: Dissociation, enactment, and the achievement of conflict. *Contemporary Psychoanalysis* 40: 197–237.

Stern, D. B. (2009a). Partners in thought: A clinical process theory of narrative. *Psychoanalytic Quarterly* 78: 701–731.

Stern, D. B. (2009b). Shall the twain meet? metaphor, dissociation, and cooccurrence. *Psychoanalytic Inquiry* 29: 79–90.

Stern, D. B. (2010). *Partners in Thought: Working with Unformulated Experience, Dissociation, and Enactment*. New York/London: Routledge.

Stern, D. B. (2012). Witnessing across time: Accessing the present from the past and the past from the present. *Psychoanalytic Quarterly* 81: 53–81.

Stern, D. B. (2015). *Relational Freedom: Emergent Properties of the Interpersonal Field*. London/New York: Routledge.

Stern, D. B. (2019). *The Infinity of the Unsaid: Unformulated Experience, Language, and the Nonverbal*. London/New York: Routledge.

Stern, D. N. (2010). *Forms of Vitality: Exploring Dynamic Experience in Psychology and the Arts*. New York: Oxford University Press.

Sullivan, H. S. (1940). *Conceptions of Modern Psychiatry*. New York: Norton, 1953.

Tauber, E. S. (1959). The sense of immediacy in Fromm's conceptions. In S. Arieti (Ed.), *The American Handbook of Psychiatry* (pp. 1811–1815). New York: Basic Books.

Ullman, C. (2006). Bearing witness: Across the barriers in society and in the clinic. *Psychoanalytic Dialogues* 16: 181–198.

Vivona, J. M. (2013). Psychoanalysis as poetry. *Journal of the American Psychoanalytic Association* 61: 1109–1137.

Winnicott, D. W. (1956). Mirror role of the mother and father in child development. In D. W. Winnicott (Ed.), *Playing and Reality* (pp. 111–118). London: Tavistock, 2005.

Winnicott, D. W. (1960). Ego distortion in terms of true and false self. In *The Maturational Processes and the Facilitating Environment* (pp. 140–152). London: Hogarth Press, 1965.

Winnicott, D. W. (1971). *Playing and Reality*. London: Tavistock.

Zetzel, E. R. (1956). Current concepts of transference. *The International Journal of Psychoanalysis* 37: 369–376.

Chapter 3

Distance and relation

Emerging from embeddedness in the other

This chapter harks back to the beginning of my life in psychoanalysis, almost 50 years ago, when I arrived in New York, entered psychoanalytic training at the William Alanson White Institute, and began to discover writers who opened a whole new part of life to me. Two of the many writers who inspired me then were Ernest Schachtel and Martin Buber, both of whose work spurred me to write this chapter.

Schachtel had been a faculty member at White, but had died a few years before I arrived, so I never met him, but he seemed to me to be the ideal of the kind of psychoanalyst I wanted to become. He thought deeply and passionately, and he paid no attention at all to disciplinary boundaries,citing not only psychoanalysts but also novelists, artists, philosophers,biologists, and academic psychologists. His work challenged psychoanalysts to explore the life of the mind.

The original version of this chapter was written as an invited contribution to the Jahrbuch der Psychoanalyse. *The editor-in-chief of the journal told me that, while some of their readers had read relational psychoanalysis, they did not understand how relational analysts worked. The invitation was to write a paper for a special issue of the* Jahrbuch *being planned on the subject of "distance" in psychoanalysis, with the hope that the contribution would help German-speaking analysts learn something about the clinical practice of relational analysts. After that initial publication, I revised the article substantially for publication in the* Journal of the American Psychoanalytic Association. *It is the latter version of the paper that appears here.*

DOI: 10.4324/9781032688893-4

Something like 40 years ago, my imagination was fired by an essay by Martin Buber (1950), and so when I was invited by the editor of a German-language psychoanalytic journal, the *Jahrbuch der Psychoanalyse*, to write about the subject of distance in psychoanalysis, I decided to borrow Buber's title, "Distance and Relation," even before I had imagined more than the merest outline of what I would say. Eventually, that title became an article, which appeared in the *Jahrbuch*.[1] The remarks you are reading now, while they follow the same general thrust as the original essay, have been heavily revised. It was the origin of this chapter in the invitation to address the subject of distance, though, that drew me back, after all these years, to the work of Buber.

In rereading Buber and understanding his thesis more fully, I saw that I had to complicate it. Buber was a philosopher, and so he did not think about distance in clinical terms. But just as it was natural for him, as a philosopher, to think in terms of what makes human beings what they are, it is natural to me, as a psychoanalyst, to think of how the being of humans develops and how it can go awry—and of course how it can be healed. In this chapter I use Buber's thinking on the matter of distance somewhat differently than he used it himself, and I link it with the work of the psychoanalyst Ernest Schachtel (1959). I take up the relation of the phenomenon of embeddedness in the other—that is, psychic merger or fusion—with the capacity to set the other at a psychic distance from oneself (Buber), allowing the transformation of merger into the kind of relatedness in which people experience themselves as separate. Separateness, or the emergence from embeddedness (Schachtel), in turn, makes possible the appreciation of otherness. I lean on the concept of witnessing (Stern 2009, 2012, 2022b, in press) to describe the movement from embeddedness in the other to the emergence from embeddedness and the appreciation of otherness.

This chapter is written from a personal perspective. New understanding valuable to all of us often emerges not only from careful, objective observation, but also from a personal encounter with the object of study. I certainly intend to take a respectful, scholarly attitude toward the work of those who have come before me, but in this chapter I am also charting the course I have taken, and continue to take, through clinical psychoanalysis. What I want to communicate is an orientation to practice.

Buber's "Distance and Relation"

Buber (1950) begins his essay by telling us that he will be discussing "the principle of human life," by which he means what makes human beings unique among the phenomena of the world. He tells us not to imagine this principle in developmental terms: it "cannot be thought of … as a beginning in time" (p. 206). For Buber, the principle of human life does not seed and grow. It is, rather, an ontological matter, a special way of being that we must simply accept is present in the world. This principle, in fact, in Buber's eyes, is what allows us to make our being distinctively human. "It is not sensible," he writes, "to try to discover when and how a certain species of life [i.e., humans], instead of being content like the rest with the perception of things and conditions, began to perceive its own perceiving as well" (p. 206).

That is, instead of imagining the developmental trajectory of an individual life, as psychoanalysts might do, Buber takes "the principle of human life" as the ground of what it is to be human. And the core of that principle is that humans do something more than all other animals do. Animals, of course, perceive what faces them, just as humans do. But humans go further: we perceive our own act of perception; we perceive ourselves perceiving. In my recent presentation of a similar theme (Stern 2022b), we "come into possession of ourselves."

To perceive ourselves in the act of perceiving requires that we be able to experience what we are perceiving—something other than ourselves—apart from ourselves, "at a distance." This use of the word "distance" is metaphorical, of course: it is the *experience* of distance, not a measurable span. We cannot relate to the other as truly "other," that is, until we can experience that other as separate, as having an existence of its own. That experience of separateness requires that we *set the other at a distance*. This setting at a distance is an act. We will see later in these remarks that it may not be an act we decide to commit in any conscious way; but it is an act, nevertheless. Buber makes the point in these words:

> In this way, we reach the insight that the principle of human life is not simple but twofold, being built up in a twofold movement that is as such, one movement as the presupposition of the other. I propose to call the first movement "the primal setting at a distance" [*Urdistanz*], and the second "entering into relation" [*In-Beziehungtreten*]. That the

first movement is the presupposition of the other is plain from the fact that one can enter into relation only with a being that has been set at a distance or, more precisely, has become an independent opposite. And it is only for man that an independent opposite exists.

[p. 207]

This statement comes near the beginning of Buber's essay. He goes on to expand the idea, but I will soon break off further exploration of his thought, since this deceptively simple introductory point is what excited me when I first read the essay 40 years ago, and what eventually inspired the title of this chapter. My thinking in this chapter is based on the contrast between, on the one hand, human relatedness to an other, a *true* other, someone (or some "other" part of ourselves)[2] we can experience as a separate center of subjectivity, and, on the other hand, relatedness in which the other's independent subjectivity is shrouded, so that we do not recognize the other as a *true* other. In this latter case we unwittingly fill in our grasp of the other's subjectivity with assumptions made on the basis of our own.

But whereas psychoanalysts believe that both attitudes toward otherness—its appreciation, on the one hand, and its invisibility or outright denigration, on the other—exist very much within the range of human experience, Buber, given his ontological aims, writes that it is essentially human to grasp otherness, and that it is only the rest of nature, or the "animal," that lives otherwise. This understanding should not be taken as disagreement with the psychoanalytic view. Because Buber's thought is ontology and not psychology, his understanding of the relation with otherness does not map exactly onto psychoanalytic accounts. We can consult Buber for inspiration, while understanding that the purposes of ontology and psychology differ.

Buber writes that "an animal in the realm of its perceptions is like a fruit in its skin," sealed off from its world, always and forever instrumental. But humans are like wanderers in a house that goes on and on, beyond their capacity ever to explore fully, and yet humans know that they exist in a house, because they can grasp "the whole of the building," even if they can never experience every one of its rooms. "Man is like this because he is the creature [*Wesen*] through whose being [*Sein*] 'what is' [*das Saiende*] becomes detached from him and recognized for itself" (p. 207).

We can adapt these thoughts to psychoanalytic thinking if we recognize that persons and parts of persons (see footnote 2) occupy not only states that are what Buber describes as "human" (i.e., states in which one's own subjectivity is experienced as separate and distinct from the other's), but also other states that are, in Buber's terms, "animal" (i.e., states in which one's own subjectivity is fused with, or undifferentiated from, the subjectivity of the other).

I do wish that Buber had used a word other than "animal" here, because in today's world this use of the word is harder to justify. I do not mean to use "animal" to signify a moral judgment about "higher" and "lower" forms of life (nor do I believe that Buber himself intended such a judgment, although I can imagine his being read that way). I do not mean that "human" is better than "animal," although it is certainly true, as I will explain in the text, that certain precious parts of life—say, the appreciation of otherness—require separateness that in Buber's terminology would have to be called "human." I, though, use "human" and "animal" only because Buber does, and I use these terms to designate the presence or absence of the perception of separateness from the other, on the one hand, and the other's separateness from oneself, on the other. In addition to the unacceptable moral implication, I take issue with Buber's use of the word "animal" for pragmatic, empirical reasons. Anyone who has experienced the intimate devotion of a dog to its closest human companion might question whether it is always the case that animals are incapable of appreciating otherness. I use these two terms, "human" and "animal," then, only as placeholders, and only because Buber does. We know what we do and do not mean by them.

Going forward, let us neglect Buber's ontological purpose, and read his thinking through a psychoanalytic mindset. When we do that, we are immediately struck with the implication, recognized by Buber himself, that if the precondition for entering into a relation with another being is to set that being at a distance, then "one can enter into relation only with a being that has been set at a distance" (p. 207). And just like that, we are in a familiar clinical context: we have arrived at the proposition that establishing relatedness between separate centers of subjectivity is impossible when we cannot gain sufficient distance.

Schachtel: Emergence from embeddedness

Looking back, I see that when I first read Buber's essay, some 40 years ago, I added to it, without realizing I was doing so, the sense that setting the other at a distance, the first of Buber's two steps in the principle of human life, is not a discrete event, happening all at once, but a gradual one, a progressive differentiation that takes place over time. I see, in other words, that all those years ago I thought of setting the other at a distance—the creation of separateness—as an *emergent process*. I still think of it that way (Stern 1997, 2010, 2015, 2019).

However much I prize the work of the many psychoanalytic writers who have taught us about separation, though[3]—and I do prize the work of these writers—it was not they who awakened my interest in the role of emergence in psychic differentiation and the creation of separateness. I made my acquaintance with this kind of thinking earlier than I read these writers. I found it in the work of Ernest Schachtel (1959). Schachtel is not widely read today, and was never read as widely as writers such as Mahler, Loewald, or Winnicott. That outcome is not attributable to the substance of his work, which remains extraordinary, but to the fact that he was not a member of his era's psychoanalytic mainstream. He was an interpersonal psychoanalyst.

It was often said, in his day, that Schachtel gave depth, a developmental thrust, and intellectual heft to Erich Fromm's work (e.g., 1941, 1947), which was less thoroughly theorized than Schachtel's. Schachtel and Fromm were close, like-minded colleagues, and Schachtel, like Fromm, described psychological development as a process of individuation: the emergent growth of the self from less differentiated precursor states. But whereas classical psychoanalytic writers of that era, until Mahler (Mahler, Pine, and Bergman 1975), usually understood development as the succession of libidinal stages, Fromm and Schachtel, both of them deeply influenced by existentialism (as was Buber, of course) and interpersonal psychoanalysis (Lionells et al. 1995; Stern 2017; Stern and Hirsch 2017a,b; Stern et al. 1995), understood development as the ongoing struggle to individuate the self, with an emphasis on authentic engagement with the other and the fullest appreciation of the possibilities of being.

For the self to be fully awake and alive required, for Schachtel, what he referred to as "emergence from embeddedness." He understood life as a continuous series of challenges, each one provoked as one becomes familiar and comfortable with the level of development that has preceded it. As familiarity and comfort with one's present stage of development expand, anxiety about the next developmental challenge arises and increases, until there comes a point at which one must either shrink from the next challenge or muster the courage to take it on and become more than one was. And then the whole process starts again. The dialectic of embeddedness and the emergence from it, in changing iterations, is part of every developmental period, structuring what life is and how it feels. As we shall see, it is also part of every psychoanalytic treatment.[4]

The first embeddedness, for Schachtel, is embeddedness in the womb, and the first emergence from embeddedness is birth. From then on, life is one challenge after another, each offering the alternatives of the preservation of comfort and familiarity or the new reality of anxiety, pain, and growth. For Schachtel, since he was a psychoanalyst, much of what is most important in the registration and negotiation of these challenges goes on without awareness.

I have learned from Schachtel, or at least from living with Schachtel's contribution, that emergence from embeddedness should not be understood as a goal, as if it were something to be accomplished conclusively and then left behind, a proud artifact of history. We are, instead, faced with embeddedness every day—all of us, certainly including analysts in our consulting rooms with our patients. We disembed ourselves and discover our own separate perspective—and then we must be ready to leave behind our pleasure in having grown, and do it again. Our attitude toward life, and toward our patients, must be reexamined endlessly, and we must accept that the accomplishment of separateness, the patient's and our own, is always temporary. Relatedness is flux. What is separateness today could become embeddedness tomorrow.

Schachtel created his own vocabulary for these events. He began as a student of the Rorschach, and he published what is arguably the finest phenomenological account of the test (Schachtel 1966), complete with its own original scoring system. Because of these origins, no doubt, Schachtel was deeply involved in issues of perception, the process by which raw sensory data are given meaning and registered by the mind. He referred to instrumental perception—that is, perception organized around what one needs from an object of perception—as *autocentric* perception. Perception without any instrumental purpose, on the other hand—perception wholly devoted to the object, in all its myriad manifestations—he described as *allocentric*. And then Schachtel took one more step. He referred to two basic *attitudes toward the other*: the *autocentric attitude*, from within which we deal with the other on the basis of our needs of them; and the *allocentric attitude*, from within which the other is appreciated for itself, without the defining intrusion of needs of our own. It always seemed to me, in reading Schachtel, that the allocentric attitude was a fine description of the appreciation of otherness, while the autocentric attitude referred to embeddedness, an attitude in which we are unable to see or grasp objects or people as separate from ourselves.

And so, when I read Buber's "Distance and Relation," I think that, without being fully aware of it, I mapped Buber's "principle of human life" onto Schachtel's "emergence from embeddedness" and the dialectic of autocentricity and allocentricity, creating an implicit model: human relationships between separate beings cannot be taken for granted; they must be created, and when they are, there comes into being a differentiation between self and other: "animal" becomes "human," and one emerges from embeddedness into the allocentric attitude. When differentiation does not occur, relatedness is maintained as it was, the world does not change, and one remains embedded in the other, mired in the autocentric attitude. And even when the challenge is met and differentiation does occur, it is only a matter of time before it must be faced again.[5]

For me, adding Buber to Schachtel leads to the recognition that embeddedness is not best understood as a mere capitulation (often unconscious) to comfort and familiarity, as Schachtel would have it, but is instead something like being "buried" in the other—as Becker (1964) would say—or at least being buried in one's unconsciously determined *imagination* of the other. Jack Foehl (2014) puts it this way:

> Unconscious process is understood as … the loss or the failure to develop the crucial gap that allows for shifts of figure and ground in the formation of meaning. The unconscious is not *in* the subject; it is in the field of experiencing between subject and object, between subject and world.
>
> [p. 300]

It follows that to disembed oneself is to set the other at a distance and open the possibility that an invisible, unconscious part of the relationship will become visible and thinkable. Adding Buber to Schachtel, then, makes embeddedness a fully relational idea.

A cautionary note: Merger and separation are not a binary

To say, though, as I do, that separateness is necessary to the appreciation of otherness is not to say that the creation of a sense of separateness, however crucial it is to certain parts of living, is the only way to create intimacy. It is not even to say that appreciation of the other as a fully separate being is the only valuable or desirable kind of relatedness. Union and separateness should not be mapped onto binaries such as mental illness and mental health, intimacy or its absence, or maturity and immaturity.

Winnicott's views on the subject help in thinking about this problem. Play or "creative experience," said Winnicott (1971), in which we spend "a great deal of our time … enjoying ourselves" (p. 106), and which, he suggests, is perhaps the part of living we could least do without, takes place in "potential space," a third realm between the mind and the external world and, most important for our purpose here, *between oneness and separateness*. Play is the activity within which all transitional phenomena occur, including successful psychoanalysis and psychotherapy. There can be no doubt that, to the extent that it involves others, play is an intimate kind of relatedness. But because the materials and media of play exist *between* merger and separateness, the kind of intimacy that comes about at these times cannot be defined in any simple or absolute way as the appreciation of otherness. When the patient plays, the analyst, in Winnicott's understanding, is actually part of the patient, and the patient, too, is part of the analyst. Absolute separation from others is therefore not a state to be desired. It would be a disaster, in fact, because it would preclude our capacity to find ourselves in the other and the other in ourselves (Winnicott 1971, pp. 119–137). It would preclude the spontaneous gesture (Winnicott 1960), because it would be impossible to imagine that the other would be there to receive it. Absolute separateness would force upon us a cold and stark perception of otherness, not an appreciation of it. Potential space, therefore, is not just a way station on the route from oneness to separateness; it is also very much a destination of its own, with its own significances, and conferring its own advantages.

I want this point to be present in the background of this chapter, while in the foreground, for the purposes of my argument, I feature the view that we cannot fully grasp otherness, and thus are incapable of the particular kind of intimacy and affirmation that appreciation of otherness allows, from within states of being that are merged with the other.

These views do not have to contradict each other. Consider here the thinking of Loewald (2000), for whom, like Winnicott, mind comes about in relationship with others. Mind grows via the development of psychic states, structures, and functions—see especially his view of language (Loewald 1978)—and then their progressive differentiation. But if these increasingly differentiated mental phenomena do not also eventually turn back and reconnect to their vital and affectively immediate precursor states—if the individual mind fails to preserve a connection to its own origins in life with others—then the mind may become "mature" in certain technical respects, but it may also become more shallow and emotionally arid than we would wish. Language and intellect become intellectualization; expressions of feeling become sentimentality; separation cools into schizoid distance. And so for Loewald, as for Winnicott, aliveness is not well served by separateness unless separateness does not simply transcend its beginnings, but is leavened by them.

Enactment and emergence from it

What remains for me to do in the narrative I am constructing is to describe the movement from merger or fusion to separateness, and then back again, a process that amounts to an ongoing to-and-fro. What is the nature of embeddedness in the other, or the autocentric? Why are we sometimes unable to appreciate otherness? And what can we say about how we disembed ourselves from that kind of relatedness and emerge into the appreciation of otherness, Buber's "human" or Schachtel's allocentric attitude?

Remember the two steps of Buber's "principle of human life": first, "the primal setting at a distance"; and second, "entering into relation" (p. 207). Most psychoanalytic theories, in their accounts of the creation of separateness, focus almost entirely on the second step, "entering into relation." They do not give the same consideration to the first step, "the primal setting at a distance," and yet the second step is not possible without prior accomplishment of the first. The first is a prerequisite.

Let me translate this point into more specifically clinical terms: most psychoanalytic theories focus almost entirely on the developmental contribution made by the parent's facilitative treatment of the infant or child, or the analyst's facilitative treatment of the patient, but they do not attend to the question of how the parent or the analyst reaches the position from which facilitative treatment, or "entering into relation," can be launched in the first place. Somebody has to initiate the process of entering into relation, and in the case of parents and analysts, that "somebody" is frequently under considerable emotional pressure from the other—in Winnicott's picture of development (1971, 2016), the ruthless "attack" on the mother by the baby; in psychoanalytic treatment, the analogous "attack" of the patient on the analyst. The ruthless "attack," writes Winnicott (2016), is always "*potentially* 'destructive' but whether it *is* destructive or not depends on what the object is like; does the object *survive*, that is, does it retain its character, or does it *react*?" (p. 37). If the object "reacts"—that is, if it fails to survive, an outcome that does not necessarily require some hurtful variety of rejection, or the disappearance of the object, but might be the result of something as mild as a less-than-dramatic intolerance or defensive response—the moment cannot provide the growth-promoting environmental provision it might otherwise have created.

This theme in the work of Winnicott, that most humane of psychoanalysts, serves as the foil for my own argument here. Most of our theories, like Winnicott's, are well constructed to account for straightforward, successful instances of survival. And, indeed, such instances are common. In those cases, the creation of the separateness that the mother/analyst needs in order to recognize the needs of the other goes unconsidered. It is taken for granted that the mother/analyst can depend on having access to the state of separateness, and so it is also taken for granted that the mother/analyst is in a position to accept and tolerate the "ruthless" challenge from the baby/ patient that is necessary for its survival.[6]

Winnicott, along with every other clinician who presumes that parents and psychotherapists are more or less endlessly capable of treating the other as a differentiated subjectivity, was well aware, of course, that sometimes the analyst, despite having the overarching intention to offer crucial environmental provision, cannot manage to actualize that intention. But like almost all of his colleagues, Winnicott did not address those moments of failure as unconscious mutual enactments. That is, he did not discuss them as meaningful, unconsciously mediated conduct that is mutually created and carried out by analyst and patient. He did not address them as clinical events on the analyst's part that needed to be addressed if the treatment was to move forward. Nor did he address them as expectable events—although, of course, no doubt, he was compassionate about them. These failures on the analyst's part, or the mother's, remained for him mistakes to be regretted and corrected. Winnicott looked past the meaningfulness and frequency of these instances because, in important respects, and like virtually all of his psychoanalytic colleagues at the time, he did not assign the analyst's very particular subjectivity a formative role in the patient's experience, or in the nature of the analytic relationship. This observation of Winnicott's thought has been made by many (see, e.g., Benjamin 1988, 1995, 2017; Slochower 2014; McKay 2019).

Let me play devil's advocate for a moment. What about Winnicott's point (1963) that if analysts offer reliability adequate to make the patient feel safe enough to regress to dependence, then the analysts' failures, even quite small ones, may actually become sources of therapeutic action, via the experience of the original trauma, now in the transference? Winnicott writes that "the patient now hates the analyst for the failure that originally came as an environmental factor, outside the infant's area of omnipotent control, but that is *now* staged in the transference" (Winnicott 1963, p. 258). Does this part of Winnicott's thinking not challenge the point that he neglects the analyst's very particular subjectivity? It does not, because Winnicott understands the mutative aspect of the analyst's failure of reliability, like the failure itself, only in terms of the patient's mind and its history, not as an intersubjectively meaningful event between two particular people.

And consider Winnicott's influential acceptance of some instances of hate in the countertransference (1947), a position that the devil's advocate might argue contradicts my point. Is Winnicott not writing about unconscious mutual enactment here? He is not. The hate Winnicott is writing about in this famous article is not the expression of the subjectivity the analyst brings to the setting from her own life, but hate that is (in Winnicott's words) "objective" and "justified" by the nature of the patient's presence or conduct. In such cases, says Winnicott, analysts must do what they always must do: they must "maintain objectivity in regard to all that the patient brings, and a special case of this is the analyst's need to be able to hate the patient objectively" (p. 195). The analyst's experience of this kind of hatred, then, is not a failure, not an episode of nonsurvival, and not an expression of the analyst's own, personal unconscious involvement with the patient. It is, in fact, quite the opposite of these phenomena: it is an expression of the analyst's reliability, a variety of environmental provision.

And so, with these examples in mind, we are led to ask about all those other instances in which mothers/analysts, because they are under emotional pressure that is not necessarily "objective" (mothers dealing with a crying baby who cannot nurse, a raging toddler, or a recalcitrant teenager; analysts dealing with anger, envy, disappointment, or provocation of some other kind in the transference), must start out in a position of fusion or merger that cannot be understood to be simply "justified," and that is often adopted defensively, an autocentric position in which the other is not grasped on the other's own terms but is understood instead as the occasion of difficulty and/or frustration for the analyst. Under these circumstances the mother/analyst must then either work toward a stance of separateness, or fail to take on that stance, and therefore fail to survive. These latter instances are perhaps as common as the simpler versions, the ones in which the mother/analyst starts out with a firmly grasped sense of separateness.

Very often, then, analysts, prior to becoming able to create the kind of separateness that makes it possible to "enter into relation" with their patients as separate presences, must go through a time of embeddedness in the other. If one thinks this way, psychoanalytic treatment (and human relationships altogether, actually) is a series of continuous oscillations taking place across varying lengths of time—from moments to years— between embeddedness in the other and the appreciation of the other's otherness. This to-and-fro is an ongoing feature of the analyst's involvement with the patient, just as it is part of the patient's involvement with the analyst. It is the substance of the interpersonal field. The process is represented in the psychoanalytic litera- ture as the alternation of mutual dissociative enactment and its breach (see, e.g., Bass 2015; Bromberg 1998, 2006, 2011; Davies 2004; Hirsch 2014; Levenson 1972, 1983, 1991; Mitchell 1988; Pizer 1998; Stern 2010, 2015, 2019; Wolstein 1959), or "doer/done to relations" and intersubjectivity or mutuality (Aron 1996; Benjamin 1988, 1990, 1995, 2017).

Analysts who think this way, of course, are hardly relieved of their spe- cial responsibility to grasp and work with their unconscious involvement and the blindness to otherness that is associated with it. But taking this view of their involvement clarifies for these analysts that, among their other tasks, they must repeatedly work their way from their initial, often embedded relatedness to the patient into a state of separateness from which they can think effectively about themselves, the patient, and the analytic relatedness, and then decide with relative freedom how to proceed. An illustration of this process ends this chapter.

Witnessing

I understand witnessing, which goes on throughout life, to originate in the earliest days, as babies begin to grasp themselves via whatever they can take in about the experience of their being that is continuously being created in the people around them, especially the most emotionally salient of those people. But even more significant, in the long run, is the "internal witnessing" that takes place inside minds, as one part of oneself observes, recognizes, and tolerates another (Stern 2009, 2023, Chapter 4). In Chapter 2, I described the idea in these words (see also Stern 2022b):

> Eventually, our initial witnesses from the outside world are internalized and elaborated, so that imaginary witnesses internal to the personality are created—and these internal presences are loving ones to the extent that our earliest witnesses have been. Self-affirmative internal conversation then becomes feasible. One self-state witnesses another, and the result is the formulation of a new and wider experience of oneself—thoughts, yes, but no less, feelings, memories, perceptions. The boundaries of the self expand. Not-self becomes self. For this to happen, there must be a vantage point in one's own mind, a second "location," from which to turn back and "see" or "hear" or "feel" ourselves, and to care about what we see, hear, and feel. We begin to see ourselves through the eyes of others, hear and value ourselves through their ears.
>
> [p. 646]

Often the analyst in the grip of countertransference, which I think about as the analyst's part of mutual enactment, is unable to grasp that neither he nor the patient is able to "back away" from the other far enough for critical review. Each is "buried" in the other, "like the Sphinx in the desert sand" (Becker 1964). Under such circumstances, witnessing is impossible because the states within each participant's mind that must be observed are disconnected from those other states in that same mind that must do the observing (Stern 2004).

And so, to disembed ourselves from the other, to become separate enough from the other to be the other's witness, those who seek the appreciation of otherness—parents, analysts, and so many others—*must find their way back to their own capacity to observe themselves*. It is in witnessing ourselves that we begin or resume the appreciation of the other as a separate person. Witnessing ourselves is the means by which we set the other at a distance, emerge from embeddedness, transform "animal" to "human."

When the analyst, after having lost the capacity to witness himself for a time, emerges from embeddedness and thereby finds a way back to selfrecognition, the patient commonly senses the change in the analyst's state, either by sensing the difference in the analyst's words and conduct, or via some form of communication that remains unconscious, and the patient is then liable to respond with new thoughts and feelings about himself, or about the analyst. Witnessing is a reciprocal process. If the relationship between two people is basically collaborative, as psychoanalysis is, the emergence from embeddedness of one of them tends to arouse a reciprocal emergence by the other. This point is illustrated by the clinical material that appears just below.

Although we can define the problem of creating or regaining separateness from the other, the problem does not come with an instruction manual: we cannot consciously decide to reveal to ourselves the capacity to observe our minds when we have lost track of that capacity. But, of course, often we do nevertheless manage to do this thing that we cannot simply decide to do. What makes it possible?

I believe, on the basis of clinical experience, that we do not free our capacity to set the other at a distance by anything like a process of articulate understanding. That is, we do not solve the problem via the interpretive analysis of transference or countertransference. I believe, and have argued many times (see, e.g., Stern 2004, 2010, 2015, 2022b), that enactment is breached via an unbidden shift in our perception of the other, ourselves, and the nature of the interaction between us. In my experience, this shift is routinely nonverbal: it *happens*.[7] And it is a field process: it is generally provoked (without awareness) by something the other says or does, and that response of course is itself provoked by something one has oneself said or done before that. To find one's way to emergence from embeddedness in the other does require that we immerse ourselves in our experience and let ourselves be saturated with it as thoroughly as possible. Emergence leans heavily on our motivation to do good analytic work, and therefore on our desire to know ourselves and the other. And all those purposes, in turn, require that we be able to think and feel with whatever freedom remains available in such moments. But these things are all that we can do: we cannot *make* ourselves able to think when our minds are clouded by enactive involvement. As the poet Paul Valéry (1952) puts it, *"We have no means of getting exactly what we wish from ourselves"* (p. 102). Often enough, it is only after a period of being suffused with the relevant experience that we even see that we are involved in an enactment at all, and that we need to rediscover the observer of our own experience within ourselves.

When all is said and done, there is a mystery here, lying at the heart of our work, a mystery I believe we can never resolve. There is no technique by which we can summon at will the capacity to set the other at a distance, which we must do if we are to appreciate that person's otherness. We must accept that we cannot know exactly why and how it is exactly *now* that we can breach an enactment. We can make informed guesses about the answer to that question, and we should. But very often, or even usually, we simply cannot know why we could not manage to breach the enactment and free the treatment last month, or why the event happened now and not next week.

I end with a clinical illustration of what I have said, including this mystery that lies at the heart of it.

Clinical illustration

Emma, a single, white corporate executive in her late thirties, very bright and talented, meets with me four times a week.[8] She wants a family more than anything, but is worried that she just can't manage a relationship, with its ceaseless opportunities to disappoint the other person and fall into a pit of shame. She is extraordinarily, and more or less continuously, self-critical, not infrequently to the point of self-hatred. But she is just as continuously honest, courageous, and articulate in trying her level best to tell me what is going on in her mind. I am not going to explain here the roots of all these matters in her early life, although Emma and I know a great deal about that. Along with our examination of present-day life and the events that transpire between us, we speak about her history in most sessions. For the purposes of this chapter I describe only a week or so of our relatedness, an episode in the continuous sequence of embeddedness in one another and emergence from it. During these sessions we discovered yet another way to set one another at a distance, transcend the enactment that bound us, and think anew about our relationship and Emma's life and mind. The sessions took place online during the COVID pandemic.

Friday

On a recent Friday, Emma was especially troubled. I know how distressed she can be about the end of sessions, and this was the last session until Tuesday, and so a few minutes before the session's end, I offered to meet with her the next day, a Saturday. (I do not work on Saturdays, which Emma knew.) I knew that it would be hard for her to say yes to this offer, because she would have to contend with the worry of burdening me (no matter what I said), which she felt she already did too much just by being with me in sessions.

But Emma surprised me this time. She assented, with gratitude, and we parted.

Saturday

The next day's session was unusually productive, and ended on a positive note. We learned a good deal, and Emma felt much better about what had troubled her on Friday. In fact, that issue between us (which I forgo describing for reasons of brevity) was resolved enough to have vanished.

Tuesday

Our next hour was on Tuesday. When Emma came in, she began talking in a highly self-critical vein, eventually concluding that the validity of the positive feelings she had had on Saturday was now in doubt. Listening to Emma build to this conclusion, I felt helpless and stymied. It was clear to me that something was demanded of me in this moment, but I could not imagine a helpful way to intervene. Eventually I said, in regard to the return of Emma's self-hating feelings, "That's too bad," with what I thought was a sympathetic attitude. But I was also vaguely aware, too little aware to formulate for myself at that moment, of a certain annoyance on my part. Looking back at this moment from later on, during the email exchange I will discuss below, I saw that I was annoyed that we were right back in the soup. I felt, perhaps unreasonably, that there was a certain recalcitrance to Emma's misery: did she really have to do this again?

In retrospect, I see that both Emma and I were caught in a kind of fusion, each of us stuck in a single, rigid role relative to the other. I was not able to deal with Emma as a separate person in that moment, but only as the reciprocal part of my own feelings. This is the autocentric world, the world of projection and introjection, in which the other must play the part required by one's own internal drama. My reaction to her therefore had more to do with whatever her refusal to feel good meant to me than it did with the meaning the situation had for her. I did not understand what was happening, but was enough aware that something was the matter to feel vaguely guilty about not being more generous. I could not articulate any of this to myself at the time. (This vague discomfort is what I [Stern 2004] have elsewhere described as "affective snags and chafing," which are mildly uncomfortable emotional alerts that one's unconscious involvement with the patient needs attention.)

Unsurprisingly, Emma reacted to the unmentalized part of my reaction, my annoyance. She became even more unhappy, but she was no more able than I to say why. She, too, was locked into the enactment and could not think. The session ended on that note. I did not understand what had happened. Neither did she. Neither of us was happy about the situation.

Emma often emails me, and I always respond, usually with just a few words, sometimes at greater length. Later that day, she sent me this message.

> Sorry for being so negative.
>
> I don't know how/if I can keep doing this, I mean meeting and talking, because it's so painful in an unpredictable way. I mean, my emotional states are too unpredictable.
>
> I feel in that electrified grip-trapped kind of way—I want to stop meeting and I can't bear to not meet.
>
> I know I always say this—and I don't really want you to agree—but maybe I should stop seeing you for three weeks or so, till maybe January? I can tell it's a little frustrating for you, and that's the part I can't bear the most. Because I feel too ashamed that I can't question better or do it the way you say, so I could feel better. And I don't have enough internal energy to bear quite so much pain, from when I talk about stuff and feel worse and it's my own fault.
>
> I am so sorry.

This message broke through something in me, and I immediately grasped, and could name to myself, the subtle annoyed quality and the impatience with which I had treated Emma during the session earlier in the day. Here, it seems to me, is a small instance of the mystery at the heart of our work to which I have referred: I cannot say exactly what happened in my experience in reading her email, or why that particular moment made the difference. I do believe that my experience reading the email set Emma at a greater distance from me and began to reawaken my appreciation of her otherness— that is, a better sense of what this situation was like for her. I could then grasp what I had felt in her presence. I began to emerge from our mutual embeddedness. I could witness myself internally (i.e., I could observe my own reactions) and aspire to be her witness (i.e., I could hope to serve that same observing function for her). In an attempt to offer her a witnessing presence, I wrote back to her:

> I'm sorry myself, Emma. The last thing I want to do is contribute to your suffering, and I know that sometimes I do. We should talk about what's best for you going forward. I will keep an open mind about it. Clearly, though, whatever we do about the future, as long as we're meeting we need to talk consistently about what's going on in the room—in a way that's helpful to you, not hurtful. It's really no good for you to go home after a session feeling this bad.[9] We have to prevent that, and I think whatever chance we have of doing that has to do with talking openly with one another.

Was Emma angry with me at some level? Perhaps. One day we will need to be able to imagine and discuss such possibilities, but not now—not yet. For now, the important thing for me to attend to was that my attitude, expressed most clearly in my annoyed and slightly sullen "That's too bad," had hurt her, and she had been ashamed. There had been a break in our connection. This was not a transference distortion to be analyzed, but a retraumatization to be recognized and acknowledged. What was required from me, however I could manage it, was the recognition of what had happened, from each of our points of view. It did not at the moment require that I try to connect the incident with her history (although we did get there later—see below). Whatever bits of therapeutic action may have been set into motion in this email exchange depended less on insight than on a kind of straightforward and affirmative relatedness that requires separateness, and cannot take place from within a merger. In setting my own experience at enough distance that I could see and accept that I had been impatient and exasperated, and thereby had been willing to risk hurting Emma, and that I regretted that outcome and could tolerate knowing this about myself, I began to disembed myself from this episode of autocentric fusion with her and to find my way to a more allocentric attitude. It seems that, just as I had apparently done within my own mind when I reawakened my capacity to observe myself, I now set Emma at a distance that made it possible for me to think about her, and about her and me. Emma answered me as follows:

> That makes complete sense about talking openly, I will try my absolute best. Sometimes I start getting confused, and I don't think I even really understand what's happening (I mean, in the room) or what I'm feeling, except confused and then more and more distanced from you. But we can talk about it more tomorrow, I can do that.

When I read this message, I felt that, reciprocally, in response to my attempt to make contact with her, Emma had begun to observe herself and then to breach the enactment from her end of it, thereby at least partially disembedding from me. I felt in her words (and later events confirmed it) that these emotional events had allowed Emma both an explicit awareness of the shame she had felt before, and the beginning of an alternative to it (i.e., maybe her feelings had something to do with my participation and not simply with her own inadequacy). In embracing these experiences as her own, she accepted me as her witness (that is, she listened to me and found something of my experience of her inside her own mind). The process of witnessing is as much the acceptance of witnessing as it is the offer of it.

In response to Emma's email, and before the following session, I responded:

> Yes, I did mean that you need to talk to me. But I also need to try to tell you what my experience of you is. This isn't always easy. But it would make you feel better if I can do it—at least if I can do it in the way I imagine doing it, with an exploratory and curious attitude and without any blaming.

Emma wrote in response:

> Yes, I can imagine it isn't always easy to do that (that's an understatement). And I always want to know your thoughts and reactions. But I

know it's hard because sometimes I unpredictably end up feeling worse in some way when I know intellectually that it's never your intention to do that, in fact your intentions are the opposite, I know that rationally. I get off track when my emotions start to take me in all different directions.

Here we see that Emma is no longer overwhelmed by bad feelings, but she does not yet see that my intentions are not necessarily simply and uniformly good. She does not yet seem to grasp that I can be impatient with her for my own reasons, reasons that have to do with what I want from life (and from her—i.e., in this case, therapeutic success) and not with something "wrong" that she has done. She does not yet accept that I am complicated, as she is herself. She sees me, in part, as she needs to see me: she idealizes me, and in that sense she sees me autocentrically and remains embedded in me. It is worth noting this observation, because it substantiates a point I made earlier: neither embeddedness nor emergence from it—neither fusion nor separation—is absolute. One can be merged with the other to a greater or lesser extent about any issue, and even when one has emerged from the other in some respects, one remains embedded in others.

Wednesday

During this session, in a continuation of the email exchange, and as a further step in our emergence from our embeddedness in one another, I told Emma that I knew that I needed to do my best to tell her the truth as I saw it, whether it was pretty or not—and not just about her life, but about the relatedness between us and my reactions to her. I told her that I know that in her family this kind of attitude is in short supply, because her parents, in different ways, in order to satisfy the images of themselves they each need to preserve above all else, routinely avoid the recognition or acknowledgment of the self-referential nature of their feelings and their relatedness. Their children were, and are, continuously put in the position of having to acknowledge that their parents' feelings arise, without exception, in the service of the parents' intention to serve the children's interests. I told Emma that I had been exasperated and impatient with what seemed to me her insistence on ruining the good feelings of the Saturday session. I told her that I know that it would have helped if I could have found my way to a recognition and acknowledgment of those feelings, but that I was apparently guilty enough to be "stuck," unable to find my way through my feelings at that moment. I explained that her email had helped me in that respect, awakening me to what I had felt. I had the impression that telling her the role of her email made her feel better. She does not often understand her own contribution to our successes.

I thought about why I was stuck at this particular juncture. What was going on with me? I thought it was likely that I had been unconsciously sulking, wanting to be able to see our work as good and productive, and to feel that I was a good and helpful analyst. Like Emma's mother and father, regardless of how Emma felt, I apparently wanted her to cooperate in making me feel like a good analyst. I wanted this outcome badly enough to make me impatient and somewhat intolerant of her expression of unhappiness.

Eventually, in this Wednesday session, I told Emma these speculations. She said that she knows she does do her best to make me feel fulfilled as an analyst—an irony that reveals, despite the fact that Emma granted me permission to use our work as an illustration in this chapter, that presenting this clinical material is itself likely to be an enactment between us, as most clinical presentations probably are in one way or another. Emma said she remembers that when I said, "That's too bad," she felt I was distancing myself from her. When her parents distance themselves, she said, she feels it's her fault and she searches herself for what she could have done "wrong" to provoke their disappointment.

Coda

I have written this chapter largely from the analyst's perspective, because my subject has been the means by which analysts find their way to the freedom to observe their own minds that is the prerequisite for setting patients at a distance, and then for "entering into relation" with them. But I could just as well have written about the same process from the point of view of the patient, with the analyst as the other—and in fact that is the typical perspective in the psychoanalytic literature. I hope I have made clear that Emma had to go through the process of disembedding herself from me, just as, if I were to help her, I had to emerge from my embeddedness in her. I hope it is clear that this disembedding is a collaborative, dialogic process: neither Emma nor I could have changed the nature of our participation without the contribution of the other.

Emma sent the last email I will present several hours after the Wednesday session (i.e., the final session in the account I have just given). I read it as confirmation of the value of analysts (and patients) doing whatever they can to fulfill the aims articulated by Buber and Schachtel.

> I appreciate it so much. All of it, and especially what you said about it being helpful when I feel I'm being told the truth. I'm always anxious and hypervigilant about what the truth is, and whether someone is telling it to me or not. So you hit the nail on the head—it's very comforting when I can tell that you're telling me the truth. And, also as you observed, it's very comforting when you get something right, whether it's "good" or "bad," or whatever it is. When you get it right and it feels true, I always feel a lot calmer and better. (Author's note: I understand Emma to mean here that being told the truth about my impatient reaction to her helped her set me at a distance, to emerge from her embeddedness in me, and to accept being witnessed.)
>
> And when that doesn't happen—and I understand it's just part of life—then sometimes I have meltdowns. And my behavior, or what I say, when that happens is still a little (or maybe a lot) beyond my control. I can't control the freak-outs very well at all. I get ashamed, I freak out, and then I get ashamed about freaking out, and it's a full-on meltdown.
>
> I feel a lot comforted now, pretty much over the meltdown of yesterday. And the meltdown was I think a lot related to my having felt unusually better on Saturday, as we discussed. But it *is* progress, I think, that I can get through/past meltdowns sooner now. I can reconstitute more quickly, so to speak. I'm kind of surprised about that, in a good way.

A week later, Emma reported an astute observation she had made over the weekend. I was delighted with what she said, because her observation involved a creative and frank acknowledgment of her parents' roles in her unhappiness, something it has often been hard for Emma to accept or even see. Emma had come to see, she explained, that the only time her parents, and particularly her mother, said anything sympathetic to her was when Emma expressed self-hatred. When she did that, her mother would question the perception—not because she wanted her daughter to feel better, Emma now observed, but because having a self-hating daughter contradicted her image of the perfect mother she needed to be. She just couldn't bear it. On the other hand, said Emma, if she (Emma) felt good or accomplished, and let her parents know about it, they would immediately question her facts or her perception of the situation, making her feel ashamed. Emma had realized over the weekend that these sequences of events were entirely dependable. They happened this way virtually every time. And therefore, for Emma, feeling miserable and self-hateful came to feel safe, and feeling good or accomplished became dangerous, because it would inevitably be ruined, and she would be devastated. Better, and safer, to do it to herself first. Then, at least, she didn't have to live with the suspense and the shattered hopes. She added that when she became so self-critical on that Tuesday, about the previous session on Saturday, she might have been unwittingly provoking me to reassure her, as she had learned to do with her parents. She said, "So me enacting a relatedness from my childhood in the Tuesday session might also have been a precipitant for you to feel impatient with me." She meant that she had ruined the good feelings, disappointing me, in order to encourage me to try to reassure her. I saw her point immediately, of course. She could not have illustrated more elegantly the principle that it is almost always a fuller picture of what happens in treatment to recognize the analyst's failures to offer provision as meaningful, mutual parts of unconscious enactments, the ways each person is embedded in the other, than it is to describe them, simplistically I think, as nothing but the analyst's regrettable misfires.

I believe this last piece of work—Emma's grasp of an aspect of her relationship with her parents and her extrapolation to her relationship with me—was a direct consequence of a new bit of freedom to think that resulted from our negotiation of the enactment that I have described taking place during the previous week. The entire sequence of events during these sessions was part of the process of this episode of our emergence from embeddedness in one another. There have been, and will be, many more such episodes.

I do not claim that my understanding of my work with Emma, and the way I carried it out, are demanded by the material. There are many valid ways of grasping the events I have described, and of responding to them. I do hope that the ideas I have proposed throughout the chapter, and my reasons for behaving as I did with Emma, are clear, or at least as clear as I can make them. What I hope to have done, as I wrote in introducing this chapter, is to convey an orientation to clinical practice.

Notes

1 The German-language version of the theoretical portion appeared in a special issue of the *Jahrbuch* devoted to the theme of distance in psychoanalysis (Stern 2022a). At the request of the *Jahrbuch*s editor, the German-language version of the clinical illustration that appears at the end of that article was broken off from the rest of the paper and published separately in the following issue (Stern 2023), with several commentaries. I thank the *Jahrbuch* for permission to publish in *JAPA* this very heavily revised, English-language version of the two articles, now reunited in a single chapter.
2 I address later in this chapter the point that one part of oneself can be "other" to another part of oneself, and in fact must be, if one is to know one's own mind. For the moment, I ask the reader to bear with me.
3 Among the many who might be cited here, special mention is due to Winnicott (1971), Loewald (2000), Mahler (Mahler, Pine, and Bergman 1975), Fonagy and Target (1996; Target and Fonagy 1996; Fonagy et al. 2002), Benjamin (2017), and Poland (2018).
4 Ernest Becker (1964) memorably describes something very much like embeddedness in the other: the patient cannot "back away" from transference expectations and examine the analyst critically. "The rules are so inextricably entwined with the concrete object that there is no backing away for critical review, no symbolic dexterity possible. The … patient is as buried in his object as the Sphinx in the desert sand" (p. 179).
5 Note the relation of Winnicott's differentiation of "object relating" and "object usage" (1971) to Schachtel's contrast of autocentric and allocentric perception, or embeddedness and emergence from it; and to Buber's unfortunately named polarity of the "animal" and the "human" aspects of "the principle of human life."
6 During "primary maternal preoccupation" (Winnicott 1956), the infant is merged with the mother, but the mother remains separate enough to allow the high degree of identification that is necessary for her adaptation to the baby's needs. Mother is not *merged* with baby; she is *optimally responsive* to the baby. The same goes for analyst and patient. When the time comes, and "object relating" transitions into "object usage" (Winnicott 1971), the sensitive mother (or analyst) understands that the baby (or patient) needs her to be a "separate phenomenon."
7 This view should not be taken to mean that analysts simply wait around for something to happen. The relevant clinical process, partly described in the following sentences, is what I have elsewhere (Stern 1990) referred to as "courting surprise." That is, while we cannot control such events, psychoanalytic training and experience do teach us how to put ourselves in a position in which liberatory surprise is most likely to occur.
8 Emma has read this chapter and granted permission to publish this description of our work. I have also written elsewhere about work with Emma (Stern 2022b).
9 I do not mean to suggest, in saying this, that it is either possible or desirable, for Emma or anyone else, never to leave a session feeling bad. It was my judgment, in this particular instance, knowing Emma, that the content of her email signified a traumatic level of distress that she would not metabolize, and that would therefore not lead to analytic work, but that would simply overwhelm her until it dissipated.

References

Aron, L. (1996). *A Meeting of Minds: Mutuality in Psychoanalysis.* Hillsdale, NJ: Analytic Press.

Bass, A. (2015). The dialogue of unconsciouses: Mutual analysis and the uses of the self in contemporary relational psychoanalysis. *Psychoanalytic Dialogues* 25:2–17.

Becker, E. (1964). *Revolution in Psychiatry.* New York: Free Press.

Benjamin, J. (1988). *The Bonds of Love.* New York: Pantheon.

Benjamin, J. (1990). Recognition and destruction: An outline of intersubjectivity. In *Relational Psychoanalysis: The Emergence of a Tradition,* ed. S.A. Mitchell & L. Aron. Hillsdale, NJ: Analytic Press, 1999, pp. 183–200.

Benjamin, J. (1995). *Like Subjects, Love Objects.* New Haven: Yale University Press.

Benjamin, J. (2017). *Beyond Doer and Done To: Recognition Theory, Intersubjectivity, and the Third.* New York: Routledge.

Bromberg, P.M. (1998). *Standing in the Spaces: Essays on Clinical Process, Trauma, and Dissociation.* Hillsdale, NJ: The Analytic Press.

Bromberg, P.M. (2006). *Awakening the Dreamer: Clinical Journeys.* London and New York: Routledge.

Bromberg, P.M. (2011). *The Shadow of the Tsunami: And the Growth of the Relational Mind.* New York and London: Routledge.

Buber, M. (1950). Distance and relation. In *The Martin Buber Reader: Essential Writings,* ed. A.D. Biemann. London: Palgrave Macmillan, 2002.

Davies, J.M. (2004). Whose bad objects are we anyway? Repetition and our elusive love affair with evil. *Psychoanalytic Dialogues* 14:711–732.

Foehl, J.C. (2014). A phenomenology of depth. *Psychoanalytic Dialogues* 24:289–303.

FONAGY, P., Gergely, G., Jurist, E., Target, M. (2002). *Affect Regulation, Mentalization, and the Development of the Self.* New York: Other Press.

Fonagy, P., & Target, M. (1996). Playing with reality: I. Theory of mind and the normal development of psychic reality. *International Journal of Psychoanalysis* 77:217–233.

Fromm, E. (1941). *Escape from Freedom.* New York: Rinehart.

Fromm, E. (1947). *Man for Himself.* New York: Rinehart.

Hirsch, I. (2014). *The Interpersonal Tradition: The Origins of Psychoanalytic Subjectivity.* New York: Routledge.

Levenson, E.A. (1972). *The Fallacy of Understanding.* In *The Fallacy of Understanding & The Ambiguity of Change.* New York: Routledge, 2005.

Levenson, E.A. (1983). *The Ambiguity of Change.* In *The Fallacy of Understanding & The Ambiguity of Change.* New York: Routledge, 2005.

Levenson, E.A. (1991). *The Purloined Self: The Interpersonal Perspective in Psychoanalysis,* ed. A. Slomowitz. New York: Routledge, 2016.

Lionells, M., Fiscalini, J., Mann, C., & Stern, D.B., Eds. (1995). *Handbook of Interpersonal Psychoanalysis.* Hillsdale, NJ: Analytic Press.

Loewald, H. (1978). Primary process, secondary process, and language. In *The Essential Loewald: Collected Papers and Monographs.* Hagerstown, MD: University Publishing Group, 2000, pp. 178–204.

Loewald, H.W. (2000). *The Essential Loewald: Collected Papers and Monographs.* Hagerstown, MD: University Publishing Group.

Mahler, M.S., PINE, F., Bergman, A. (1975). *The Psychological Birth of the Human Infant: Symbiosis and Individuation.* New York: Basic Books.

McKay, R.K. (2019). Where objects were, subjects now may be: The work of Jessica Benjamin and reimagining maternal subjectivity in transitional space. *Psychoanalytic Inquiry* 39:163–173.

Mitchell, S.A. (1988). *Relational Concepts in Psychoanalysis: An Integration.* Cambridge: Harvard University Press.

Pizer, S. (1998). *Building Bridges: The Negotiation of Paradox in Psychoanalysis.* New York: Routledge.

Poland, W.S. (2018). *Intimacy and Separateness in Psychoanalysis,* ed. W.F. Cornell. New York: Routledge.

Schachtel, E. (1959). *Metamorphosis: On the Conflict of Human Development and the Psychology of Creativity.* New York: Basic Books.

Schachtel, E. (1966). *Experiential Foundations of Rorschach's Test.* New York: Basic Books.

Slochower, J. (2014). *Holding and Psychoanalysis: A Relational Perspective.* 2nd ed. New York: Routledge.

Stern, D.B. (1990). Courting surprise: Unbidden perceptions in clinical practice. *Contemporary Psychoanalysis* 26:452–478.

Stern, D.B. (1997). *Unformulated Experience: From Dissociation to Imagination in Psychoanalysis.* New York: Routledge.

Stern, D.B. (2004). The eye sees itself: Dissociation, enactment, and the achievement of conflict. *Contemporary Psychoanalysis* 40:197–237.

Stern, D.B. (2009). Partners in thought: A clinical process theory of narrative. *Psychoanalytic Quarterly* 78:701–731.

Stern, D.B. (2010). *Partners in Thought: Working with Unformulated Experience, Dissociation, and Enactment.* New York: Routledge.

Stern, D.B. (2012). Witnessing across time: Accessing the present from the past and the past from the present. *Psychoanalytic Quarterly* 81:53–81.

Stern, D.B. (2015). *Relational Freedom: Emergent Properties of the Interpersonal Field.* New York: Routledge.

Stern, D.B. (2017). Interpersonal psychoanalysis: History and current status. *Contemporary Psychoanalysis* 53:69–94.

Stern, D.B. (2019). *The Infinity of the Unsaid: Unformulated Experience, Language, and the Nonverbal.* New York: Routledge.

Stern, D.B. (2022a). Distanz und Beziehung: Auftrachen aus dem Eingebetettsein im Anderen, Part 1. *Jahrbuch der Psychoanalyse* 85:70–106.

Stern, D.B. (2022b). On coming into possession of oneself: Witnessing and the formulation of experience. *Psychoanalytic Quarterly* 91:639–667.

Stern, D.B. (2023a). Diskussion: Relationale Psychoanalyse: Distanz und Beziehung: Auftauchen aus dem Eingebettetsein im Anderen. *Jahrbuch der Psychoanalyse* 86:189–198.

Stern, D.B. (2023b). Interpretation: Voice of the field. *Journal of the American Psychoanalytic Association* 71:1127–1148.

Stern, D.B., & Hirsch, I., Eds. (2017a). *The Interpersonal Perspective in Psychoanalysis, 1960s–1990s: Rethinking Transference and Counter-transference.* New York: Routledge.

Stern, D.B., & Hirsch, I., Eds. (2017b). *Further Developments in Contemporary Interpersonal Psychoanalysis, 1980s–2010s: Evolving Interest in the Analyst's Subjectivity.* New York: Routledge.

Stern, D.B., Mann, C., Kantor, S., & Schlesinger, G., Eds. (1995). *Pioneers of Interpersonal Psychoanalysis.* Hillsdale, NJ: Analytic Press.

Target, M., & Fonagy, P. (1996). Playing with reality: II. The development of psychic reality from a theoretical perspective. *International Journal of Psychoanalysis* 77:459–479.

Valéry, P. (1952). The course in poetics: First lesson, transl. J. Mathews. In *The Creative Process,* ed. B. Ghiselin. Berkeley: University of California Press, pp. 92–106.

Winnicott, D.W. (1947). Hate in the countertransference. In *Collected Papers: Through Paediatrics to Psychoanalysis.* New York: Basic Books, 1958, pp. 194–203.

Winnicott, D.W. (1956). Primary maternal preoccupation. In *Collected Papers: Through Paediatrics to Psychoanalysis.* New York: Basic Books, 1958, pp. 300–305.

Winnicott, D.W. (1960). Ego distortion in terms of true and false self. In *The Maturational Processes and the Facilitating Environment: Studies in the Theory of Emotional Development.* New York: International Universities Press, 1965, pp. 140–152.

Winnicott, D.W. (1963). Dependence in infant-care, in child-care, and in the psychoanalytic setting. In *The Maturational Processes and the Facilitating Environment: Studies in the Theory of Emotional Development.* New York: International Universities Press, 1965, pp. 249–259.

Winnicott, D.W. (1971). *Playing and Reality.* New York: Basic Books.

Winnicott, D.W. (2016). The use of an object in the context of *Moses and Monotheism.* In *The Collected Works of D.W. Winnicott, Volume 9.* Oxford: Oxford University Press, pp. 33–38.

Wolstein, B. (1959). *Countertransference.* New York: Grune & Stratton.

Chapter 4

Interpretation
Voice of the field

This chapter was originally part of a 2023 symposium in the Journal of the American Psychoanalytic Association *called "Whither Interpretation?". The invitation to contribute was a welcome opportunity to expand the ideas about interpretation and the interpersonal field that I had been developing over the previous decade.*

When former patients are asked to describe the most significant and memorable moments in their psychoanalytic treatments, they virtually never report interpretations made by their analysts. They report events that took place *with* their analysts, yes—but these events are seldom defined by the revelation of new content. I will argue that the most precious analytic moments usually have to do with feeling understood.

Some of these instances of feeling understood, no doubt, are responses to interpretations. But even in these cases, in my experience, as I describe in these remarks, it is often not really the content of the interpretations—their information or truth value—that is responsible for the creation of precious analytic memories. It is instead the way the interpretations made the patient *feel*. Interpretation most commonly works, I will claim, not by making the unconscious conscious (although I will say nothing to question the significance of the content and accuracy of interpretations), but by widening and/ or deepening the patient's sense of being known or recognized by someone who has become emotionally significant, a process that I have elsewhere called "witnessing" (Stern, 2009, 2012, 2022, 2023. For a brief review of the literature on witnessing in psychoanalysis see Stern, 2022, pp. 642–644). Witnessing grows from feeling recognized, but adds to that experience the

DOI: 10.4324/9781032688893-5

element of "coming into possession of oneself" (Stern, 2022), by which I mean not only the sense that one's experience is one's own, but also that

> we know and feel that it is *we who are doing the knowing and feeling*. When these two events co-occur—the knowing and feeling, and knowing and feeling that we are knowing and feeling—we come into possession of ourselves.
>
> (p. 640, italics in original)

Writing in this same vein, McLaughlin (1995) says

> We need to find in the other an affirming witness to the best that we hope we are, as well as an accepting and durable participant to those worst aspects of our ourself that we fear we are ... [We seek to] have what we are become known to and accepted by the other, in whose sum we may more fully accept ourself.
>
> [p. 434]

Of course, I am only one of a virtual army of clinicians who have observed that the analyst's interpretations have relational effects. Some of those writers (Benjamin, 2017; Bromberg, 2011; Bach, 2006; McLaughlin, 1995; see also the 2019 interview of Fonagy by Duschinsky et al.) share my emphasis on recognition. The field of psychoanalysis has been debating for 100 years (Ferenczi & Rank, 1924) the relative influence in therapeutic action of relational effects vs. the insights created by the information value of the analyst's interpretations. And for nearly as long as that—since Strachey's (1934) classic statement of therapeutic action as the introjection of the analyst—it has been considered possible that, as Greenberg (in press) writes, "psychic structure itself can be modified purely on the basis of the experienced relationship." Greenberg goes on to note that "over the years other theorists [i.e., other than Strachey] have suggested ways in which the interpreting analyst provides mutative relational experience in the course of conducting a traditional treatment."

There are any number of examples of this point. Some of these theorists believe that their positions demand changes in the practice of psychoanalysis; others do not. The important point for the present purpose is that all of them believe that traditional analytic interpretation has relational effects. What I have said over the years about the role of witnessing in therapeutic action is one such view, with its own particular emphasis.

The witnessing perspective preserves the most basic claim that psychoanalysts have always made for clinical interpretation: the content and accuracy of the analyst's interpretive interventions are central to therapeutic action. These qualities continue to matter. But often the *reason* that they matter, in this view, is less familiar. Often the primary reason that the content and accuracy of interpretations matter is not that they allow the revelation of unconscious content in consciousness—as in the Kleinian understanding of the interpretation of unconscious phantasy, or the contemporary Freudian understanding of the interpretation of defense and resistance. Neither do content and accuracy matter primarily because they contribute to the visibility and eventual resolution of the transference. Nor are the mutative properties of the truth value of interpretations necessarily most significantly reflected in dynamic changes in the functioning of the patient's mind. Let me be very clear about this point: I do not deny the existence of any of these factors. I do not deny to insight, the heart of what Ogden (2019) calls "epistemological" psychoanalysis, a role in therapeutic action. I do claim, though, that the revelation of unconscious content is often, or usually, not the most important therapeutic impact of interpretation.

Instead, from my perspective, the most important reason that the content and accuracy of the analyst's interpretations matter is that they are contributions to the analyst's growing capacity to serve as the patient's witness. They matter because they mean to the patient that the analyst *knows* the patient. They matter because they are the evidence most available to patients that they have a home in the analyst's mind. I believe, as Bromberg (2009) puts it, that "the primary source of therapeutic action *is* the relationship, not something created *through* it" (p. 356).

Among those who have preceded me in making this point are Guntrip, Winnicott, and Fairbairn. Guntrip, in his deeply felt and moving paper on his analyses with Fairbairn and Winnicott, written right at the end of his life, reported Fairbairn to have said to him, "You can go on analysing for ever and get nowhere. It's the personal relation that's therapeutic." Fairbairn, wrote Guntrip, "held that psychoanalytic interpretation is not therapeutic per se, but only as it expresses a personal relationship of genuine understanding" (Guntrip, 1975, p. 145). Guntrip heartily agreed, and we know that Winnicott did, too.

Let me add immediately the essential point that to feel recognized is not necessarily to believe that what the other recognizes about you is something you like about yourself or are proud of. The most significant interpretations are those that reveal something about which the patient is uncomfortable or anxious or ashamed, or even something that provokes the patient's rage at others, or self-hatred. But in an episode of recognition and witnessing, such things are revealed without provoking shame. The patient feels that the analyst sees something about the patient that the patient may feel awful about but, unlike what began in the patient's experience with parents, and what keeps happening in the patient's contemporary life, the analyst manages to draw attention to these affective events without provoking shame or some other break in the emotional connection. A patient of mine, for example, a woman who is notably self-hateful, said to me, "It's very comforting when you get something right, whether it's 'good' or 'bad,' or whatever it is. When you get it right and it feels true, I always feel a lot calmer and better." I like to describe this kind of episode as "seeing you seeing me": that is, "I (the patient) see you (the analyst) seeing me; and because I *really do* see you seeing me, I also see that there is every reason for me to question that you are feeling what I would have thought you would feel under such circumstances." I will present such an incident at the end of this chapter as a clinical illustration of what I want to convey about interpretation and witnessing.

Who creates interpretations?

I have questioned since the beginning of my career, in the early 1970s, the dictum that therapeutic action is primarily rooted in the information value of the analyst's interpretations. As fascinating as it was to observe that people really did change in treatment, I harbored doubt from the beginning, despite my appreciation of the continuous role of unconscious processes, that change, when it happened, was the result of the light shined on unconscious contents by the interpretations I was being taught to offer those with whom I worked.

My concerns were often represented in what I read. Reading that literature was a relief. Foremost was the work of my psychoanalytic teachers and colleagues, most of whom identified as interpersonal psychoanalysts (Stern et al., 1995; Stern & Hirsch, 2017a, b), but for the most part, despite their acceptance of the significant contribution of the analyst's personal presence, those writers continued to maintain the view that the therapeutic impact of interpretation is to be found in its information value. In the 1960s and early

1970s, these analysts seldom theorized the impact of relational factors in interpretation—with the notable exceptions of Benjamin Wolstein (1959; Bonovitz, 2009) and Edgar Levenson (1972/2005). In the 1970s I began to read Kohut (1971, 1977) and the work of the British object relations writers and other Independents then being discovered in the United States (e.g., Kohon, 1986), and in the 1980s my fellow relational analysts (Mitchell & Aron, 1999) began to contribute. In all three of these latter traditions, the relational effects of interpretation began to be theorized as seriously as the creation of insight had been in the generation before.

What began as a trickle has become a flood. Ogden (2019) notes a shift in psychoanalysis from a more or less exclusive concern with information, knowing, and understanding ("epistemological psychoanalysis") to a greater interest in being and becoming, or process and experience ("ontological psychoanalysis"). Misgivings akin to my own that interpretations create therapeutic action solely on the basis of their information value have come to constitute a trend—

> a movement from a conception of mind as a "mental apparatus" for processing experience (in the work of Freud, Klein, and Fairbairn) to a conception of mind as a process located in the very act of experiencing (in the work of Winnicott and Bion). The evolution of this strand of thinking might be thought of as a movement from a notion of mind as a noun, to a notion of mind as a verb, a living process, perpetually in the act of coming into being.
>
> [Ogden, 2020, p. 219]

To Ogden's citation of Winnicott and Bion as the most basic sources of this seachange, I propose to add Edgar Levenson. While Levenson's work (1972/2005, 1983/2005, 1991/2016, 2017) is not as widely recognized as it deserves to be, he belongs in the company of these innovators. (See Stern, 2006, and Foehl, 2008, for presentations of Levenson's views.) I recently described the heart of Levenson's work in this way:

> One [i.e., the analyst] can't just describe at will one's own unconscious participation in the analytic relationship, even that part of it one can infer well enough to characterize it, because every time one says something, one is interacting from within the same configurations one wishes to name. One plays out the patterns in the relationship as

one describes them. Language is therefore no less a form of conduct than a form of meaning; and so the analyst cannot say anything to the patient that refers to their unconscious patterning without simultaneously enacting it. Therapeutic change comes about, then, not via insight but within a "discourse of action" (Levenson, 1983/2005, p. 83). The therapeutic relationship is a "playground" (Levenson, 1982), and mutative effects are the outcome of spontaneous play on this playground. And the play is unpredictable. Change is what happens by itself once restrictive patterning ceases to structure the relationship (Stern, 2024).

Just as, in Ogden's (2019) words, "Winnicott shifts the focus of psychoanalysis from the symbolic meaning of play to the experience of playing, and Bion shifts the meaning from the symbolic meaning of dreams to the experience of dreaming in all its forms" (p. 661), so Levenson shifts our analytic focus from the symbolic meaning of therapeutic relatedness (transference) to the *experience of the analytic relationship.* Levenson understands psychoanalysis as the attempt to grasp what analyst and patient are up to, and what they are up to in the treatment comes from the shapes and patterns of their early relationships with caretakers. What patterns are being enacted? The question is not asked with the aim of eventually revealing hypothesized unconscious sources of the transference. The intention is not to identify the patient's unconscious fantasies, an aim Levenson (1983/2005) identifies with persuasion and not cure. As Foehl (2008) puts it, for Levenson (1972/2005), even in his early work, "explanation—the search for cause and validation—was relinquished in favor of the description of structure" (p. 1242). The configuration of the analytic relatedness, the patterns themselves, in which the analyst is involved right along with the patient, are the point. Fifty years ago, Levenson (1972) could already say, "Rather than emphasis on the patient as a discrete historical process, interest shifts to the immersion of therapist-patient in their common transformational field and, most important, to their unique creation of each other" (1972, p. 221). Even the analyst's interpretations must be understood, says Levenson, as partially shaped by the very phenomena they are intended to illuminate. In illustration of this point I wrote that,

> without realizing it, the analyst of a masochistic patient makes sadistic interpretations of masochism; the analyst of a seductive patient

who is nevertheless fearful of sexuality makes seductive interpretations of the patient's fear; the analyst of a narcissistically vulnerable patient interprets the narcissism in a way that wounds the patient's self-regard.

(Stern, 2010, p. 171)

A few years later, commenting on this phenomenon, I added:

[I]nterpretation without consideration of its immediate context is seriously incomplete, a "fallacy of understanding" [this is the title of Levenson's first book] that not only does not have curative properties but also serves as one more repetition of the very problem the interpretation is an attempt to address.

(Stern, 2015, pp. 26–27)

Because we analysts are continuously and unconsciously embedded in relatedness we do not and cannot fully understand, we have no choice but to interpret from there, no choice but to accept that our position means that we cannot know all the meanings of what we say (and do). While all analysts are obviously responsible, no matter their theoretical frame of reference, for doing something more with their unconscious involvement than their patients are, they are nevertheless embedded in the interpersonal field in the same way the patient is. What I say in this chapter is an elaboration of this view, a way of understanding clinical interpretation not just as the analyst's conscious creation, and not only as comprehension derived from the analyst's observations of the patient's mind. Interpretations are not even exclusively the products of analysts' own, independent thought processes. And while knowledge about the patient gleaned by analysts from the countertransference is irreplaceable, of course, the point of view I take about interpretation is a field theory, and it therefore not only goes beyond analysts' observations of patients; it also goes beyond their observations of their patients' affective impact on analysts themselves. Interpretation becomes a psychoanalytic contribution to what Ogden references as being and becoming, process and experience. Much less than it used to be is it understood to be a matter of information and knowing. From this vantage point interpretation has always been more a matter of ontology than epistemology. Or as Levenson puts it,

The very breakdown of narrative order, the temporary chaos which is provoked, may, in itself, be vital to a creative process, a reorganization of experience into far more complex and flexible patterns. I am claiming that the real task in therapy is not so much making sense of the data as it is, but resisting the temptation to make sense of the data! [1988, p. 5]

Interpretations, then, are emergent phenomena that do not fully belong to any one person. They are psychic products that issue from the mutual embeddedness that is the interpersonal field. Interpretations that contribute to change do so because they memorialize the appearance of novelty in the field, and thus new freedom, a freedom that, while it is certainly an object of the greatest interest to the analyst, cannot be exhaustively observed, and certainly cannot be created with exclusively conscious purpose, by either the patient or the analyst. While the possibility of new freedom between the patient and the analyst can sometimes be purposefully influenced by one or the other participant, it is not under either's simple control. As Foehl (2014) says,

The content of a communication must be seen in relation to its active participation and context, in relation to a system of relationships that play themselves out in the mutual sensuality of engaged moments of the hour ... [W]e are far more implicated into the other's response in the field of our saying than we typically know or acknowledge[p. 300].

I do not mean for a moment, of course, to suggest that analysts have *no* control over their clinical participation. After all, in one way or another, the conceptualization of the analyst's purposeful clinical influence is the substance of much of the clinical theory of psychoanalysis. As I will describe in a clinical vignette below, while I do believe that analysts must come to terms with being unable to determine all the meanings of their own participations, including their interpretations, I also contend that there is much they can do to learn about these meanings. Over time, the analyst absorbs, and can think about, the regularities of the field created with each patient. Some of these regularities take place within the parts of the field that function with relative freedom, and are therefore not difficult to work with. Often the more important regularities are the subtle affective discomforts in the analyst's experience that suggest the ways in which the field is not free to evolve spontaneously. I have referred to these nuances, which are usually at least slightly uncomfortable, as affective "snags" and "chafing" (Stern, 2004), and I have suggested that they are stimulated by the analyst's unconscious involvement in mutual enactments that are hard to grasp for the time being, either because they are vague and ill-defined, or because there exist powerful reasons for them remain unknown—and often both. The analyst works toward the emergence of these sources of constriction in the field, hoping to illuminate them—including the analyst's own part in them, of course. And so, despite having to recognize that unconscious influence on analysts is more extensive and continuous than used to be believed, clinicians working with this field theory model are hardly left without the means to consciously pursue the therapeutic agenda.

I also want not to be misunderstood to be attempting to do away with the individual unconscious. The field is not a substitute for the individual unconscious, but a supplement to it—or perhaps we could say that the field is the changing context within which the individual unconscious, which we understand to be more firmly structured and less variable over time than the field, expresses itself, or engages with living. The concept of the interpersonal field has that attribute in common with the various concepts of the analytic third (Ogden, 1994, 2004; Benjamin, 2017; Gerson, 2004). The individual unconscious is the more or less predictable and unchanging residue of the past. The field is more complex and unstable than that: it is the conscious and unconscious interaction of two individuals, and unlike the inner world it is inextricably bound up with whatever setting serves as its context in the moment. And yet the field, in the present, is our route of access to the individual unconscious and the past.

I am fond of a relevant metaphor from the work of Ferro (Ferro & Basile, 2009). The field for him is a structure of unconscious phantasy, and so is different from my interpersonal/relational understanding of it (Stern, 2013, 2020), in which it is a largely unconscious but social phenomenon. But I admire the humor and intimacy of Ferro's relationships with his patients, so obvious in his writings, and I have learned much from him despite our differences. Ferro describes the field as a movie made by two directors, the analyst and the patient. If one were to view such a film, one could not pick out which director was responsible for which parts of the film. Nor can we necessarily know who is responsible for any particular detail of the psychoanalytic field. But each of the two "directors," Ferro says, is also simultaneously making *another* movie, their own movie—a movie about themselves making the first movie! And so room is made for both the field and the individual unconscious.

One of my purposes here, to put it provocatively, is to suggest that analysts, because they belong to the interpersonal field, cannot know exactly what they are doing.[1] To a significant degree, their interpretations, however accurate and emotionally responsive they may turn out to be, grow organically and emergently, and generally without the analyst's full awareness of this aspect of their origins, from dynamic shifts in the configuration of the field. The analyst's interpretations, even when they do not directly concern the field, are shaped by it. Interpretations constitute not just the analyst's own thoughts, but the struggle of the analytic couple to know itself. Analyst and patient are always mutually embedded to one degree or another (Stern, 2023), which means that what each usually takes to be their own, internally constructed experience ("endogenous," we have often called it in psychoanalysis) really can't be so simply claimed to be the product of a single mind.

From this perspective, *the analyst's interpretations are the voice of the field*. A shift in the field makes it possible to see and say something differently than before, and the analyst puts it into words. Interpretations are the expressions of the new psychic freedom made available in this way. A tension has relaxed; a frozen place in the joint analytic mind has thawed. New meanings arise in this way from new relational configurations. The availability of a new understanding is an implicit announcement of the very shifts that have made it possible. Interpretations, in the best moments, then create the patient's experience of being recognized.[2]

The analyst (and the patient) can say, do, and feel only within the limits established by the field. The field is like a changing screen that, as the possibilities for experience pass through it, selects which parts of each person's mind can be engaged by this moment in time. I want to emphasize struggle here—not just the field's role in the construction of coherent understanding, but its sometime recalcitrance, its frequent reluctance to know itself.

The analyst's embeddedness in the field should not be understood to imply passivity on the analyst's part. The analyst's interpretations are active creations even if they are not as consciously willed as traditional theory would suggest they are. And even if the content of interpretations is not itself the engine of change but more often the reflection of it (the shifts in the field being the main event), content continues to play a highly significant role. As I have said, the patient's recognition of the truth of the analyst's interpretation is one of the things that tells the patient that the analyst has recognized them. The content of this new recognition also has an effect on the treatment's future, though, because what is said by the analyst participates in the shaping of the analytic field that is to come, and in the shaping of the patient's life.

I have argued for many years that, when the field is spontaneous—that is, when the affective comfort of both partners is relatively uncompromised (affective comfort can never be more than *relatively* uncompromised, of course)—analytic relatedness can assume whatever form is most closely tailored and responsive to the circumstances of the moment. Significant compromises of the freedom of thought and feeling—compromises of the freedom to experience, we could say—are the results of unconsciously mediated regulatory processes growing from participants' unconscious need to maintain some minimum level of mutual affective comfort in one another's presence. It is the field that embodies these affective regulatory processes, partly by bringing some self-states "onstage" from each mind and sending others back into the wings to await their next appearance (various statements of this view can be found in Stern, 2010, 2015, 2019b). The shift of self-states in and out of consciousness on the basis of interpersonal context reminds me, on the one hand, of Bromberg's (1998, 2006, 2011) use of the metaphor of the stage in his dissociation model of the mind as multiple self-states, and on the other, of Ferro's (e.g., 2009) metaphorical embodiment of the changing context of experience as the "casting" of new "characters."

If giving thought and feeling their freedom is letting one's mind go where it will, allowing the action on the stage to take whatever shape suits the moment, then compromised thought and feeling is the rigidly enforced need or desire of one or both analytic participants to write the play in one particular way, with the implied rejection, or at least disregard, of other dialogue, scenes, and characters that might have been created instead. The themes of the play under way in any particular moment, we might say, are announced by the analyst's interpretations—with more or less accuracy and usefulness, and more or less saturated expression, depending on how well the analyst happens to understand the play the two are performing at that moment and the part each is playing in it, and how the analyst senses that the patient will react to an undisguised reference to the themes of the play.

The point I have just made is central enough to what I want to say that I will approach it from a second angle: whenever the field allows patient and analyst a certain degree of freedom, the analyst's capacity to think and feel, and to construct interpretations on that basis, is relatively unhampered. The analyst can be curious, can use the new thoughts and feelings that emerge at such times to construct new understandings, and these understandings, offered to the patient, then contribute to a further relaxation of the field.

But when the field's freedom is compromised—when the field is constricted or rigidified in a way that stifles the requisite degree of spontaneity, allowing a narrower range of experiential alternatives—then only certain parts of the analyst's and patient's minds can be known or felt by the analyst, and the depth and breadth of the understandings available to the analyst for communication to the patient are correspondingly diminished. These episodes of constriction in the field have been referred to for decades now as mutual enactments, especially in the relational literature (Stern, 2004, 2010, 2015; Bromberg, 2006, 2011). Enactment stifles freedom of thought and makes interpretation impossible: the voice of the field is silenced.

It goes without saying that the freedom and compromise to which I have just referred do not constitute a dualism. At any particular moment, the field, and the experience of both analytic participants in it, may exist anywhere along the continuum between the absence of constraint and the tightest control—between what I have elsewhere called curiosity and dissociation (Stern, 1997).

A clinical vignette: Seeing you seeing me

The sequence of moments I have chosen to illustrate the role of interpretation in field theory is prosaic, because I want to leave the impression that the field shifts that open possibilities for new understanding and interpretation are often not dramatic clinical interactions, but ordinary ones. I want to illustrate the point that the analyst may not even explicitly notice such shifts as they are occurring. And yet the moment I will describe, like any moment I could choose, is so complex that the task of fully translating its compact, compressed, procedural presentation into verbal terms is virtually impossible. Verbal meanings must be created and presented sequentially, whereas the multiple, procedurally organized meanings of clinical process are routinely represented and enacted simultaneously. We select what we say, including our interpretations, from a collection of possibilities much,

much larger than we usually realize. We tend to feel, looking backward, that our interpretations were demanded by the material. Sometimes they are. But usually, it seems to me, analytic interpretations are not simply acknowledgments of the elephant in the room. They are part of an active process of charting a course through a sea of meaning that might be traversed in many other ways—and would be, by someone else. Conducting clinical psychoanalysis according to field theory requires a thoroughgoing acceptance of one's personal presence in the work.

I have written this excerpt with more explicit verbal understanding of my own affect than I had as I was going through it. But while I did not have these words for the experience as it took place (we seldom do), what I have written is a representation of what it felt like to be with my patient in these moments, reflected on in retrospect.

Alan, a white professional of about 30 whose 3 sessions per week have been on the phone since COVID (he prefers phone to video image), was talking about a situation at work when my cell phone rang with another call, which I sent to voicemail. Alan's signal reception was momentarily interrupted, though, so he could imagine what had happened. He said, "Another call?"

I said, "Yeah, but I sent it to voicemail," implying that he ought to just go on. There was a brief pause.

"So I guess that's not a problem for you," said Alan.

Alan's remark did not strike me as particularly worthy of note. "Nope," I said.

There was now a longer silence. I began to suspect that something about this moment had affected the flow of Alan's thought, since he'd been talking animatedly and suddenly wasn't. I felt the moment as a field shift, although I didn't label it as such. I experienced a bit of what I referred to earlier as "affective chafing." After a minute or so, sounding thoughtful, Alan said, "You know, I don't think I ever told you that the reason I always call you a couple of minutes late is so I don't do to you what happened just now."

I recognized part of what he was referring to. We had talked about his lateness many times (see the clinical material reported in Chapters 7 and 8), but we had never discussed it from this angle. "Do you mean," I said, "that you're thinking I might still be on the phone with someone else at the very beginning of your session, so you delay calling for a minute or two so you won't interrupt me?"

"Yeah."

Another brief silence, which I broke. "That hadn't occurred to me. Probably it should have." I knew that Alan would understand what I said as a reference to our shared understanding of his worry about being a burden and his efforts to stay out of the way of his parents—and often enough, me, too.

With a sharp little laugh, Alan said, "But I guess I don't have to worry." There was something about the way Alan said this, and the way he laughed, that surprised me and brought me up short, something that communicated more than the literal meaning of his words—chafing again on my part. I had a vague feeling-sense of what this "more" was, but I couldn't yet say anything about it.

"What do you mean?" I asked.

There was a pause. "Well," said Alan hesitantly, "the session on Friday..." [which was the day of the previous session]. He stopped. I thought, immediately and spontaneously, of the way the session on Friday had ended. Alan had been in the middle of a thought, and I had ended the session abruptly. I had forgotten about that until this moment, but now I remembered that I had felt mildly uncomfortable about it at the time. I don't know exactly how I knew, but it was clear to me that it was this incident that Alan was referring to when he mentioned the session on Friday.

I now thought I was a little clearer that Alan's curt laugh a moment earlier, when he said, "But I guess I don't have to worry," had sounded sardonic to me, as if it expressed a certain lowkey bitterness. That was what had surprised me, and was the thing that I did not yet feel ready to address. I could not at that moment formulate the thought, but later on I could see that it was as if I imagined Alan feeling something like, "Why do I go around worrying about *him*! If he wants to end a session, he just does it—no matter what it means to me." But all this was very subtle, nowhere near as definite and intense as I have no choice but to make it sound when I give words to it. Once again, we could say that the field—the atmosphere between Alan and me, and the possibilities for what might emerge from it—shifted very slightly.

I decided to make sure I knew what we were talking about, so I said, "You thinking about how we ended on Friday?"

"Yeah," he said, "I guess." So I was right. That subtle tone was still there. He paused.

I said, "We ended pretty abruptly."

"I guess so," said Alan, sounding a bit reluctant.

I asked him how he felt about that. He said nothing.

"Well," I said, "I was thinking that here you take the trouble to spare me having to end sessions abruptly with other people, but I end *your* session on the dot, in the middle of something you were saying. Could make you wonder why you take the trouble to make sure I don't have to do that with somebody else. Could make you feel a little annoyed with me."

After a few moments, Alan said, predictably, "Well, that wouldn't be reasonable. You were just staying on schedule."

"I'm leaving all that to one side for the moment," I said. "Your feelings about this don't necessarily have a lot to do with what you or I think is reasonable. I'm talking about what you might have felt, whether or not you thought it was reasonable."

There was a minute or two of what felt to me like a contemplative silence. Then, signaling that the field had altered yet again, Alan sighed deeply and said, with feeling, "Yeah, I hadn't really let myself think about it, but I didn't like it."

This moment opened into Alan's slightly new experience of his own feelings, and thus into new perceptions of me (that I can be involved in my own agenda to an extent that his interests suffer) and also of himself (he doesn't like it when I do that). Over the next two weeks Alan began for the first time to experience angry feelings toward his highly narcissistic mother, whom he had tried very hard not to burden (by doing whatever he could to be a good boy). Alan had known that he must be angry with her, because even he could see that any child of hers would have to be, but he had not been able to *feel* it, and he offered endless excuses for her. Also for the first time, Alan began to talk about food differently, beginning to connect eating with being angry. He has always been considerably heavier than he wanted to be, and his mother had routinely shamed him for it. Alan nevertheless ate whenever he could, all day long, and now he suddenly developed a conviction that eating had been a self-destructive expression of rage toward his mother. This was his thought, not mine. He questioned the excuses he had always provided to explain her treatment of him, and he now saw that he had spent his life making sure that she was simply not going to win this battle—he just was not about to stop eating. He had always felt that his appetite was irresistible and outside his control, and for this reason he had not had much to say about it in treatment. It felt like a simple fact of life, like the weather. Now he began to consider that he could choose not to eat for his own reasons, having nothing to with submitting to or resisting his mother. He talked about already noticing that he could bear feeling hungry, and even wanted to bear it, in order to make his body more like what he wants it to be. His anger and shame, and the relevant parts of his relationship with his mother, had become thinkable.

As the weeks went on, Alan expanded the range of his observations, telling me that, "all my life I have avoided taking care of myself." His hurt and angry response to his mother's narcissistic use of him, he came to believe, had led to the lifelong inhibition of anything that would let his mother off the hook. Although he now lived on his own, Alan did not make his bed, wash the dishes, keep his room neat, or get his hair cut when he felt he needed it. He hated his own lax habits about these things, it turned out—but he also refused to give them up. Now he began to do so: in addition to eating differently, he cleaned his room, washed the dishes, bought a rowing machine and began to use it, and kept his hair cut in the way he felt it looked the best.

The moment I have described in the session between Alan and me may actually have been the moment when these themes consciously emerged. I can't be sure of that, of course, since the theme had been playing out between us for years, sometimes with our awareness but often enough under the radar. But I can say with reasonable certainty that, at the very least, the incident I have reported was a contribution to the unfolding of the theme.

A number of the things I said in this excerpt might reasonably be called interpretations. I want to focus on my suggestion to Alan that he might be angry with me. I hope it is clear from my detailed report of the events why and how, in my view, this interpretation was an expression of the field and not simply a thought that I created in my own, separate mind. Note the progression of events. I had conveniently forgotten the abrupt ending of the Friday session, and so I would not, on my own steam, have gone back to it. Neither would Alan have returned to it, if the phone had not rung at a key moment. (Yes, contingency plays a role in creating the field.) And even then, Alan would not have brought to my attention his displeasure with me if I had not noticed the sardonic quality of his laugh. And I would not have had the thought about the laugh unless he had allowed himself the vulnerability to produce it—because, of course, that little laugh was a risk for him.

Alan and I jointly created the circumstances—the context, the field—in which it became possible for me to see and say what was happening between us. This time it was me saying it. It could just as well have been him, though, and often enough it is. All of the emotionally salient meanings of the events I have recounted—and I could go on at much greater length with many more similarly detailed observations of our joint creation of this moment—constituted a preamble to my capacity to say something about the situation. When I offered my thoughts about what Alan might be experiencing, and what he had felt on Friday, what I offered emerged from what had happened between us. A shift in the field between us had led Alan to reveal his feelings and had opened the possibility of me imagining them—along with imagining my part in those feelings, a part that under other circumstances I could easily have missed. It takes a responsive field shift to bring such a thing to the explicit attention of either the patient or the analyst. That is, Alan was as responsible as I was for the emergence of the interpretation I offered him. My words were spoken by the voice of the field.

Witnessing and the unexpected

In ending let me turn to the roles I believe witnessing and the unexpected played in the therapeutic action of this incident, and how my interpretations contributed to that end. Remember Alan's curt little laugh, seeming to me to be bitter or sardonic. This was the only expression of his anger at me that I was able to grasp in that moment, but I did grasp it, and I believe Alan knew I had grasped it. It is very important to my case, though, that I did not, and do not, know why I was open to Alan's criticism on this particular occasion. Why now? Nor do I know why Alan allowed himself this criticism of me in this moment.

Let me tell you what I understand to have happened, keeping in mind that, while I do believe that something like what I will describe took place in Alan's mind, the events were implicit, and so I cannot secure independent confirmation from Alan. But with that proviso, consider this account: Alan heard the sound he made when he laughed; he imagined me hearing that sound (remember we were on the phone); he sensed that I was nonplussed, and he knew (on some level) that I knew he was unhappy with me. *But*—most important—he also could sense that I was not angry with him in response.

Nor was I wounded. And I did not try to shame him for being angry with me. In Winnicott's (1971) terminology, I survived. (Again, though, I don't know why I survived *now*.) I offered Alan an interpretation of his angry feeling:

> [H]ere you take the trouble to spare me having to end sessions abruptly with other people, but I end *your* session on the dot, in the middle of something you were saying. Could make you wonder why you take the trouble to make sure I don't have to do that with somebody else. Could make you feel a little annoyed with me.

The sympathetic affective tone with which I said this grew from the shift in the field that had already taken place when I noted and absorbed the meaning of Alan's bitterness without defensiveness, and so I believe that my interpretation contributed to the impression Alan already had started to form that I knew he was angry with me and was not retaliating. Because Alan saw me seeing him, I think he also felt (not just knew, but felt), for one of the first times, the presence of his own expectation that he would feel ashamed of being angry. He could turn his explicit attention to all of this. The upshot was that the expectation that he would feel he was a shameful, bad boy *this time did not have to remain unformulated, and therefore was thinkable*. Because he *could* formulate it, he could see that his expectation of my reaction went unfulfilled by me.

I believe that, when Alan saw that I saw him expressing anger at me, and saw that I did not react in a way that shamed him, his shame became his own. He could now know and feel that it was *he* who was creating this feeling, and he could think about it. Simultaneously, and equally important, he became able to formulate what had been his unformulated expectation of being shamed for being angry—and because he could now think about that, too, it immediately began to lose its power to stifle his rage.

But while I do believe what I have just said, and I certainly (!) have no interest in abandoning the individual mind (as I have written above), I also want to be sure not to distract from my point by emphasizing traditional intrapsychic dynamics any more than necessary. In my view, interpretations, when they are mutative, encourage change not only because they create insight, but also because of their place in what Levenson describes as the "discourse of action" (1983/2005, p. 83), the context from which interpretations emerge. The interpretations most significant to the change process give voice to a shift in the possibilities between analyst and patient, and therefore they are most important as the evidence of a new way of being. Interpretations that appear to be "epistemological" efforts in Ogden's (2019) terms, that is, may very well be more meaningfully understood to be "ontological," because they are signs that patient and analyst have found their way into a different way of being with one another.

I want the primary emphasis in thinking about this vignette, in other words, to fall squarely on the processes of becoming, on the way Alan did not just understand the past but also came into new being, with me, in the present moment. He came into possession of himself (Stern, 2022). I want the emphasis to be on Alan's and my own joint presence and less-than-fully-conscious relatedness through the episode. It was our presence together, and what we did and felt, that created the new freedom from which novel aspects of experience became accessible, and then emerged between us, partly in the form of an interpretation. In Levenson's view, writes Foehl (2008), "Understanding must give way to *not* understanding, to something new that we can neither predict nor, without being part of the process of its unfolding, describe" (p. 1261). In the same vein, Bromberg (2009) says that "interpersonal novelty is what allows the self to grow because it is unanticipated by both persons, it is organized by what takes place between two minds, and it belongs to neither person alone" (pp. 355–366).

The clinical sequence I have described was mutative *precisely because* neither Alan nor I can say why it happened. *The fact that we did something unexpected together is the point.* Mutative events—unexpected field shifts—spring *de novo* from we know not where, answering a desire that often enough we don't even know we have—a desire that our experience and conduct with our patients will slip the traces of the unconscious patterning that otherwise structures so much of what happens between us.

Notes

1 Here I am reminded of the case made by philosopher Donald Schön (1983) that professional activity of all kinds (law, medicine, psychotherapy, etc.) is defined by what he called "reflection-in-action," by which Schön meant that professionals must decide what to do without knowing the outcome beforehand. Professionals must come to terms with routinely thinking on their feet and acting before being able to know whether the action they have chosen is the best one to take. Schön's observations do not require field theory, but they are certainly consistent with it.

2 Writing these events forces me to present them as if they are steps in a linear process: field shift → new freedom of thought/feeling → the availability of new understanding → interpretation → the patient feels witnessed. In practice, I believe that all of this occurs more or less simultaneously.

References

Bach, S. (2006). *Getting from Here to There: Analytic Love, Analytic Process.* Hillsdale, NJ: Analytic Press.

Benjamin, J. (2017). *Beyond Doer and Done To: Recognition Theory, Intersubjectivity, and the Third.* New York and London: Routledge.

Bonovitz, C. (2009). *Looking back, looking forward: A reexamination of Benjamin Wolstein's interlock and the emergence of intersubjectivity. International Journal of Psycho-Analysis* 90:463–485.

Bromberg, P.M. (1998). *Standing in the Spaces: Essays on Clinical Process, Trauma, and Dissociation. Hillsdale,* NJ: The Analytic Press.

Bromberg, P.M. (2006). *Awakening the Dreamer: Clinical Journeys.* Hillsdale, NJ: The Analytic Press.

Bromberg, P.M. (2009). *Truth, human relatedness, and the analytic process: An interpersonal/ relational perspective. International Journal of Psychoanalysis* 90:347–361.

Bromberg, P.M. (2011). *The Shadow of the Tsunami: And the Growth of the Relational Mind.* New York and London: Routledge.

Duschinsky, R., Collver, J., & Carel, H. (2019). *"Trust comes from a sense of feeling one's self understood by another mind": An interview with Peter Fonagy. Psychoanalytic Psychology* 36:224–227.

Ferenczi, S., & Rank, O. (1924). *The Development of Psychoanalysis*, trans. Caroline Newton. New York: Nervous and Mental Disease Publishing Company, 1925.

Ferro, A. (2009). *Transformations in dreaming and characters in the psychoanalytic field. International Journal of Psychoanalysis* 90:209–230.

Ferro, A., & Basile, R. (2009). *The universe of the field and its inhabitants.* In *The Analytic Field. A Clinical Concept*, eds. A. Ferro R. Basile. New York: Routledge, pp. 5–29.

Foehl, J.C. (2008). *Follow the fox: Edgar Levenson's pursuit of psychoanalytic process. Psychoanalytic Quarterly* 77:1234–1267.

Foehl, J.C. (2014). *A phenomenology of depth. Psychoanalytic Dialogues* 24:289–303.

Gerson, S. (2004). *The relational unconscious: A core element of intersubjectivity, thirdness, and clinical process. Psychoanalytic Quarterly* 73:63–98.

Greenberg, J.R. (in press). *Therapeutic action.* In *The Textbook of Psychoanalysis, 3rd Edition*, eds. G. Gabbard, B. Litowitz, & P. Williams. Washington, DC: American Psychiatric Association Press.

Guntrip, H. (1975). *My experience of analysis with Fairbairn and Winnicott— (How complete a result does psycho-analytic therapy achieve?). International Review of Psychoanalysis* 2:145–156.

Kohon, G. (1986). *The British School of Psychoanalysis: The Independent Tradition.* New Haven: Yale University Press.

Kohut, H. (1971). *The Analysis of the Self.* New York: International Universities Press.

Kohut, H. (1977). *The Restoration of the Self.* New York: International Universities Press.

Levenson, E.A. (1972). *The Fallacy of Understanding.* New York: Basic Books.

Levenson, E.A. (1982). *Playground or playpen. Contemporary Psychoanalysis* 18:365–372.

Levenson, E.A. (1972/2005). *The Fallacy of Understanding.* In *The Fallacy of Understanding & The Ambiguity of Change.* London and New York: Routledge.

Levenson, E.A. (1983/2005). *The Ambiguity of Change.* In *The Fallacy of Understanding & The Ambiguity of Change.* London and New York: Routledge.

Levenson, E.A. (1988). *The pursuit of the particular—on psychoanalytic inquiry.* *Contemporary Psychoanalysis* 24:1–16.

Levenson, E.A. (1991/2016). *The Purloined Self: The Interpersonal Perspective in Psychoanalysis*, ed. A. Slomowitz. New York and London: Routledge.

Levenson, E.A. (2017). *Interpersonal Psychoanalysis and the Enigma of Consciousness*, ed. A. Slomowitz. London and New York: Routledge.

McLaughlin, J.T. (1995). *Touching limits in the analytic dyad. Psychoanalytic Quarterly* LXIV:433–465.

Mitchell, S.A. & Aron, L., Eds. (1999). *Relational Psychoanalysis: The Emergence of a Tradition.* Hillsdale, NJ: The Analytic Press.

Ogden, T.H. (1994). *The analytic third: Working with intersubjective clinical facts. International Journal of Psychoanalysis* 75:3–20.

Ogden, T.H. (2004). *The analytic third: Implications of psychoanalytic theory and technique. Psychoanalytic Quarterly* 73:167–195.

Ogden, T.H. (2019). *Ontological psychoanalysis or "What do you want to be when you grow up?" Psychoanalytic Quarterly* 88:661–684.

Ogden, T.H. (2020). *Toward a revised form of analytic thinking and practice: The evolution of analytic theory of mind. The Psychoanalytic Quarterly* 89:2:219–243.

Schön, D.A. (1983). *The Reflective Practitioner: How Professionals Think in Action.* New York: Basic Books.

Stern, D.B. (1997). *Unformulated Experience: From Dissociation to Imagination in Psychoanalysis.* London and New York: Routledge.

Stern, D.B. (2004). *The eye sees itself: Dissociation, enactment, and the achievement of conflict. Contemporary Psychoanalysis* 40:197–237.

Stern, D.B. (2006). *Introduction to a new edition of The Fallacy of Understanding* and *The Ambiguity of Change* by Edgar A. Levenson. Hillsdale, NJ: The Analytic Press.

Stern, D.B. (2009). *Partners in thought: A clinical process theory of narrative. Psychoanalytic Quarterly* 78:101–131.

Stern, D.B. (2010). *Partners in Thought: Working with Unformulated Experience, Dissociation and Enactment.* London and New York: Routledge.

Stern, D.B. (2012). *Witnessing across time: Accessing the present from the past and the past from the present. Psychoanalytic Quarterly* 81:53–81.

Stern, D.B. (2013). *Field theory in psychoanalysis, Part 2: Bionian field theory and contemporary interpersonal/relational psychoanalysis. Psychoanalytic Dialogues* 23: 630–645.

Stern, D.B. (2015). *Relational Freedom: Emergent Properties of the Interpersonal Field.* London and New York: Routledge.

Stern, D.B. (2019a). *How I work with unconscious process: A case example. Contemporary Psychoanalysis* 55:336–348.

Stern, D.B. (2019b). *The Infinity of the Unsaid: Unformulated Experience, Language, and the Nonverbal.* London and New York: Routledge.

Stern, D.B. (2020). *Field theory and the dream sense: Continuing the comparison of interpersonal/relational theory and Bionian field theory. Psychoanalytic Dialogues* 30:538–553.

Stern, D.B. (2022). *On coming into possession of oneself: Witnessing and the formulation of experience. Psychoanalytic Quarterly* 91: 639–667.

Stern, D.B. (2023). *Distance and relation: Emerging from embeddedness in the other. Journal of the American Psychoanalytic Association* 71: 641–668.

Stern, D.B. (2024). Interpersonal psychoanalysis. In *The Textbook of Psychoanalysis*, 3rd Edition, eds. G. Gabbard, B. Litowitz & P. Williams. Washington, DC: American Psychiatric Association Press.

Stern, D.B., Kantor, S., Mann, C., & Schlesinger, Eds. (1995). *Pioneers of Interpersonal Psychoanalysis*. London and New York: Routledge.

Stern, D.B., & Hirsch, I., Eds. (2017a). *The Interpersonal Perspective in Psychoanalysis, 1960s–1990s: Rethinking Transference and Countertransference*. London and New York: Routledge.

Stern, D.B., & Hirsch, I., Eds. (2017b). *Further Developments in Contemporary Interpersonal Psychoanalysis, 1980s--2010s: Evolving Interest in the Analyst's Subjectivity.* New York: Routledge.

Strachey, J. (1934). *The nature of the therapeutic action of psychoanalysis. International Journal of Psychoanalysis* 15:127–159.

Winnicott, D.W. (1971). *Playing and Reality*. London and New York: Routledge, 2005.

St Wolstein, B. (1959). *Countertransference*. New York: Grune & Stratton.

Chapter 5

Feels like me

Formulating the embodied mind

*Unformulated experience is not always given form in the kind of symbolic
representation that allows explicit, conscious thought, and I learned long
ago from Merleau-Ponty to think of unformulated experience as embodied. But despite holding those views, I had not made the explicit leap to
imagining what part, exactly, the embodiment of unformulated experience
might play in clinical process until I was invited to contribute to an issue of*
Psychoanalytic Inquiry *on embodiment in psychoanalysis. This chapter is
the beginning of such an exploration.*

I have only rarely written about embodiment, at least in so many words
(but see Stern 2010, Chapter 1, "The embodiment of meaning in relatedness"), nor have I made a thorough study of the literature on psychosomatic
processes or somatic knowing. In this chapter, I do my best to reveal how
the theme of embodiment has always been reflected in my work on unformulated experience, dissociation, enactment, and the interpersonal field.
Merleau-Ponty's (1945/1962) thought is never far from what I say in this
chapter. What I say, in a sense, is a gloss on his view of the experience of
each of us: "(Q)uite simply he is his body and his body is the potentiality
of a certain world" (p. 106). For the most part, though, I do not relate my
views in the present context to other views of psychosomatics, somatiza-
tion, and embodiment than my own. I select for emphasis only those few
entries that seem to me to fall within my area of immediate interest, from
the vast literature on these topics that exists in psychology, psychiatry, psychoanalysis, and the literatures of other psychotherapeutic traditions.

Symbolic representation and procedural meaning

Although the body plays a central formative role in the ongoing creation
of experience, this bodily experience is not necessarily the outcome of

DOI: 10.4324/9781032688893-6

consciously registered and self-reflective bodily sensations. That is, while most of what we experience in psychoanalytic work—what we *need* to experience if we are to find our way to effective clinical intervention— is created via our bodily presence in the world in general, and with our patients in our consultation rooms in particular, we do not necessarily know those experiences in the separate and definable terms of language.

That can make it difficult to think, write, or talk about the nature of embodiment. Embodiment resists verbal description in the same way that unconscious process does. In both cases (which overlap, of course), while we are utterly convinced of the existence of our objects of study (we cannot make sense of our conscious experience without inferring them), they very often defy explicit description. They are frequently invisible, even usually, and even when we do sense them, they may remain impenetrable to our conventional means of establishing reflective meaning—i.e., we often cannot *say* them. And so when it comes to studying these "phenomena," we must accept that, as the sage put it, you can't get there from here. And yet, of course, when it comes to making sense of these things, *there* is exactly where we must get.

Take our affective reactions, which may be simultaneously our most significant clinical data and the part of our experience that we are most likely to describe as bodily processes. And yet, despite their somatic origins, we do not necessarily experience them as bodily. They *can* be experienced in that way, of course. When we are enraged, our "gorge rises"; sadness "wells up" in us; we can be "racked" with guilt or find ourselves in an "agony" of suspense or despair. But affects also may not be experienced that way—even when we believe that they are the kind of phenomena that do arise in the body. When I sense that the person sitting in the chair facing me is sad, for example, I have every reason to believe that I come to this perception through the elaboration of processes that reach me via my senses, my body's creation of responses to those sensory processes, and my transformation of those responses into reflective experience. But those sensory and perceptual processes, and our responses to them, have little, if anything, to do with the kind of symbolic representations, verbal or nonverbal (visual imagery, for instance), that we have conventionally considered as meaning in psychoanalysis.

But there exist an increasing number of conceptions of other kinds of meaningful unconscious psychic phenomena than the verbal-symbolic or visual imagery. While these other conceptions are different from one another in many important respects, they have in common the intention to describe mental contents and processes not composed of explicit significations or symbolizations, neither verbal nor nonverbal—i.e., unrepresented states (Levine et al., 2013). I do not have the space here to say anything substantive about these models. I can only supply some of the relevant references: Bion, 1962/1977; Botella & Botella, 2005; Green, 2005; Laplanche & Pontalis, 1968, 1973; Lombardi, 2015, 2016; Matte Blanco, 1975; Scarfone, 2015; Stern, 1983, 1997, 2019; Winnicott, 1971.

None of the unrepresented states described by these writers is meaning that we can "point at." It is present in the mind—it is *there*—and in each case it seems reasonable to characterize it as somatic in some sense. What else could it be? And yet we do not necessarily feel something explicit or specific in our bodies that we know corresponds to it. In the case of my reaction to my sad patient, I *just know* the sadness, I simply find myself in possession of this knowing. We usually pay little or no attention to *how* we know at such moments, and often enough we do not necessarily even pay explicit attention to the fact *that* we know. It is unlikely that we would say the word "sad" to ourselves at this moment, for instance—as in, "Oh, she is sad." We are much more likely just to have a sad "sense" of the things transpiring in the consulting room at this moment. This "sensing" then affects our ongoing experience and conduct.

Here is the point: we must somehow be in touch with the nonverbal/ somatic if we are to be able to think reflectively about ongoing relatedness, but this being-in-touch is frequently not something we can say in words, or that even occurs to us to say.

I think we all accept that we have no means of directly representing this mysterious kind of meaning (after all, that is why we refer to it as "unformulated experience," "unrepresented states," and so on), and therefore we have no way to actively and purposefully reflect on it. Yet we continue our attempts to conceptualize it—to describe in words what we can infer about it. The very presence of so many accounts of unrepresented states demonstrates that we can at least offer speculative theoretical descriptions of it.

We can think of this kind of knowledge (or sensing, or psychic presence, or whatever expression you prefer to use) as *procedural*, i.e., not given symbolic representation in the mind, but represented instead in something like sensory excitations of various kinds, global perceptual responses, or the kinds of somatic action patterns that are analogous to body-memories. In this latter case, the common example is knowing how to ride a bicycle. What we know about riding a bike is hardly organized in linear fashion, and it cannot be given verbal representation. You can't tell someone how to balance on a bike. The *doing* of it, the riding of the bike—or, to expand our range to the therapeutic situation, the affect-charged exchanges that make up human interaction—just happen.

We *occupy* this kind of knowing, or *it* occupies *us*. We do not reflect on it, we live it. In many cases, it will never be possible to reflect on it; in other cases, it may be possible to give it at least partial symbolic representation at some point. The important thing for my present purpose is that there is no difference between this kind of psychic phenomenon and what it concerns. It is thing-like. It is not a representation: what you see is what you get. It is of a piece with living.

So much of life, and especially our social experience, conscious and unconscious, including psychoanalytic and psychotherapeutic work, is meaning of this kind. In clinical practice, procedural meaning emerges in our experience continuously and ceaselessly—and much more often than not, without attracting our explicit attention. One might say that procedural meaning is the medium of the treatment (e.g., Clyman, 1991; Herzog, 2011; Rosenblatt, 2004). Or one might take a further step and say, with (among others) the Boston Change Process Study Group (2010), that procedural meaning *is* the treatment.

Language and the body: A dialectical relation

In either case, whether procedural meaning is the medium in which the treatment takes place or whether it actually composes the treatment, it can be tempting to believe that nonverbal meaning, including the procedural, inevitably precedes symbolic representation. In this commonly held view, often more an unexamined assumption than an explicitly embraced position, the nonverbal is what the verbal represents. The nonverbal, from this perspective, is the "what" to which words conform, or the mental and perceptual stuff that words label, and it follows from this view that the nonverbal/procedural is therefore the more basic form.

Actually, though, the question of whether the nonverbal (and therefore the body) precedes language is more complicated than we are used to thinking it is.[1] It turns out, for instance, that it is quite possible to grasp some particular content in symbolic terms, even verbal-symbolic terms, and only *thereafter* to be able to give it a nonverbal, procedural, somatic meaning. That is, under certain circumstances, *verbal meaning not only precedes the nonverbal, but also makes the nonverbal form possible.* In an example I have used before (Stern, 2019, pp. 80–81), a man from the Brazilian rain forest, a member of a tribe that had had no previous contact with outsiders, was played a recording of a Viennese waltz by one of the first visiting anthropologists. The man was utterly baffled; he could find no meaning at all in the experience. The anthropologist then explained that these sounds were, in the anthropologist's world, a version of the kinds of sounds made in the man's village for ceremonial purposes. As the anthropologist spoke, you could see recognition dawning on the man's face, and eventually he smiled and enthusiastically nodded his head: he *understood*. Thereafter, presumably, this man, without having to explicitly remind himself of the anthropologist's verbal explication of his bodily experience ("*that* is *music!*"), could harvest sense from other sounds of European cultural origin that he now was able to experience as part of a category with which he was familiar, a sensorial category that had been defined in verbal terms. He no longer had to give explicit thought to the matter to have a meaningful experience of these sounds. Verbal thought redefined the world in such a way that not only words changed; nonverbal experience itself became different.

And so, in contradiction to the assumption that the nonverbal comes first, it can be argued that it is language that determines the possibilities for *all* meaning—not only that which can be articulated in words, but also nonverbal and nonsymbolic meaning. This view is what has been called the "expressivist" or constitutive theory of language (see especially Charles Taylor, 2016): meaning-systems, or semiotics, establish the webs of meaning that are the stuff of culture. In these terms, it is language in the broadest sense (that is, not just verbal language but all semiological systems of symbols) that determines what can be meaningful in any sense at all, and so the meaningfulness of nonverbal psychic representations, such as visual imagery, and even procedural meanings, which have no symbolic representation, can be understood to be conditioned by their relationship to language (Stern, 2019; Charles Taylor, 2016).[2]

And therefore, I want to be clear that I do not intend the message of this chapter—that embodiment is foundational for psychoanalytic practice—to suggest that I, any more than Merleau-Ponty, to whom language was as centrally important as the body, relegate language to a secondary status (always keeping in mind that what I mean by language is semiotics, not verbal language alone). I do not agree with those psychoanalytic writers (e.g., Boston Change Process Study Group, 2010; Bucci, 1997) who have portrayed the nonverbal and the nonsymbolic as more basic to human experience than language.

Language and the nonverbal across psychoanalysis

I have just begun to consider these problems (see, Stern, 2019). The questions are deep and thorny, and they have a long history in psychoanalysis. In Freud's (1900) first metapsychology, usually referred to in North America as the topographic theory (system Ucs, system Pcs, system Cs), the unconscious is composed of *thing-presentations*, nonverbal and unknowable. These meanings, understood to be psychic elements, primitive representations one step removed from things-in-themselves, are impossible for consciousness to apprehend until they are cathected by the preconscious and linked with language, thereby becoming *word-presentations*. Ever since this early conceptualization by Freud, and helped along by the intellectualistic conception of language favored by Lacan, the broader theory of language that comes to us from semiotics has been given short shrift. The absence of emphasis on semiotics in psychoanalysis is understandable, because for Freud the nonlinguistic forms always precede the verbal ones, and therefore language is a paler form of meaning than nonlinguistic forms (his thing-presentations). In the first metapsychology, the topographic theory, the unconscious is the inevitable source of the truth, which can never be apprehended directly. The unvarnished truth of the unconscious precedes its (diluted) representation in verbal terms. Significant dissenters from this view, most of whom are philosophers and linguists, and who take the constitutive or expressivist view of language I have already introduced (e.g., Charles Taylor, 2016), include Loewald (1978) and Merleau-Ponty (1945/1962), and see Vivona (2009, 2012), who presents dramatic empirical research findings that support views such as Loewald's.

Contributors within psychoanalysis to a broader view of language include a group of writers grappling critically with Lacan's influential conceptualizations, in which affect is largely denied significance in the process by which linguistic meaning comes into being. Living within a psychoanalytic world dominated by Lacan's views, a significant contingent of French psychoanalytic writers have been especially aware of the limitations of a purely verbal conception of language. These writers have had to contend with what Green (2005) calls the "intellectualist conception" of language (p. 208) that Lacan adopted from Saussure. Green, describing such a conception of language as "homogenizing" (because meaning is forced into a single, "intellectualist" form), broke with Lacan over this issue, among others, and thereafter favored the linguistic views of semioticians such as Sebeok and Peirce, whose models are "heterogeneous," allowing verbal language to be composed of "rhetoric-hermeneutic" forms that are not strictly "logico-grammatical." (That is, some aspects of language operate in ways that are not verbal at all, but affective. For Green's [2005] use of these terms, see pp. 202–211.) Psychoanalytic proposals of this sort, according to Green, include Aulagnier's *pictogram*, Rosolato's *demarcation signifier*, Anzieu's *formal signifier*, and Laplanche's *enigmatic signifier* (later to take more widely recognized form as the *enigmatic message)*. Many other writers, some of them reacting to Lacan and others writing outside his immediate influence, have contributed in various ways to our recognition that affect, and therefore the life of the body, contributes to the process by which linguistic meaning comes into being, and to our appreciation of the role of the linguistic in parts of experience we tend to ghettoize within the nonverbal (e.g., Bion, 1962/1977; Kristeva, 1997; Laplanche, 2011; Lecours & Bouchard, 1997; Lombardi, 2015, 2016; Matte Blanco, 1975; Scarfone, 2015; Roussillon, 2011; Winnicott, 1971).

I must be satisfied in this chapter with the mere statement of this large problem. I do hope that this brief introduction to the issue, though, at least makes it clear that to focus on the role of the body in psychoanalysis and psychotherapy does not have to suggest that language is secondary. The body and its processes, like everything else in human experience, can be understood to become meaningful via processes that are linguistic in the broadest, semiological sense. And yet it is also true that the preservation of a fundamental, even foundational, role for language does nothing to contradict the traditional psychoanalytic understanding that, as Green (2005) puts it, "the psychic can be conceived as emerging from the somatic" (p. 170). The two positions, that is, that the body precedes language, and that language—the symbol systems that compose culture—is the source of the meanings we give to somatic events, constitute a dialectic that needs to be consulted in any consideration of the sources of mind and the nature of clinical process.

Formulation of the procedural

The question remains: how does the body contribute to experience? What is the channel of translation (Laplanche) or transformation (Bion, Green) from the somatic to the psychic? This is a question asked by contemporary psychoanalysts with some frequency and urgency. My own form of the question is this: how should we understand the *formulation* of embodied experience?

What do I mean by *formulation*? During the first decades of my work (Stern, 1983, 1997) I defined formulation as the capacity to create reflective meaning by articulating unformulated experience in verbal language. This model works when the unformulated experience in question can be represented in words. But it will be immediately obvious that such a conception does not comport with what I have just said about the nonverbal symbolic and the procedural: in many instances, that is, nonverbal and procedural meaning cannot be articulated in words, and therefore cannot be reflected upon in the way I described in my initial presentations of the theory of unformulated experience.

For these reasons, and with these issues in mind, I recently revised the model of unformulated experience (Stern, 2019). I reconceptualized the nature of the process that results in the transformation from unformulated experience to something that deserves to be described as formulated. I replaced the process of articulating unformulated experience in verbal language with the more general and commodious process of creating any kind of meaning at all. Unformulated experience should not be most basically understood as unarticulated in words; it should instead be understood not to be effectively, personally meaningful. The question is not the presence or absence of verbal language, then, but the presence or absence of *personal meaningfulness*. To formulate experience is to create greater meaningfulness than existed before, to make one's own something that has not been before, to transform not-me into me (Bromberg, 1998, 2006; P.M. Bromberg, 2011; Stern, 2010, 2015, 2019), to "come into possession of oneself" (see Chapters 2–4); it is to transform "what was foreign, external, threatening, and *unheimlich* into a part of oneself" (Shalgi, 2021, p. 107).[3]

Some unformulated experience can be represented in verbal language, and therefore the process of formulation in these cases continues to be well described as *articulation*. Other unformulated experience, however, when it becomes meaningful, participates in the life of the mind as visual-symbolic or procedurally organized psychic elements. As Suzanne Langer (1942) recognized long ago, these things "are not necessarily blind, inconceivable, mystical affairs; they are simply matters which require to be conceived through some symbolic scheme other than discursive language" (p. 82). In these cases, the transition or transformation from unformulated to formulated experience is not well described as articulation. I prefer to describe the process of formulating this kind of unformulated experience as *realization*, a word that I hope conveys Langer's attitude. As meaning of this sort becomes *useable* by the mind, as it is *formulated*, it goes through just as great a metamorphosis as do those meanings that are articulated in words, but the nature of the metamorphosis, and its product, are different.

The burden of this chapter is, therefore, to describe that metamorphosis in the case of procedural meaning, much of which is embodied. The transformation in the case of reflective meaning is easy to imagine in a general sense, even if the details remain mysterious: all we have to do is imagine the absence of language giving way to the presence of language. That may not be an easy thing to visualize, but it is at least an unmistakable change in state. We can also imagine the formulation of nonverbal-symbolic meaning: we create visual images, which, like words, are possible to experience consciously. We can even imagine such images being unconscious.

It is much more difficult, though, to give a convincing account of what it could mean to refer to the formulation of the procedural. We cannot turn to the same kind of easily imagined endpoint of the process that we have in the creation of reflective meaning, anchored as it is by the phenomenologically apprehensible creation of meanings in words. Nor can we turn to visual imagery. In the case of procedural meaning, we do not even know what the endpoint of the process of formulation looks like.

Here I turn to the way I have solved the problem elsewhere (Stern, 2019). Remember that I have modified the criterion for the formulation of experience. Where once I used the presence or absence of verbal-reflective articulation to differentiate formulated meaning from unformulated experience, I now differentiate the two according to the presence or absence of meaningfulness. I now want to add that meaningfulness can be understood phenomenologically. For experience to be meaningful means, for me, that I *accept* it. It is part of my world. I *accept*, that is, that it *feels like me*. And if I *accept* experience in this way, if it *feels like me*, it becomes possible to *use* that now-meaningful experience in the spontaneous construction of creative living. If I cannot accept it, it remains unformulated to one degree or another, its meaningful possibilities for my life unconsidered, or partially so. These rejected possibilities for experience are *not-me* (Stern, 2010). This kind of dynamically enforced unconscious refusal to interpret, or to interpret fully, is what I refer to as *dissociation* (Stern, 1997). Note that all these mental elements and actions—*acceptance, feels-like-me, use, the spontaneous construction of creative living, not-me, and dissociation*—are largely matters of affect, and thus of the body. From this perspective, then, the formulation of experience is simultaneously a relational event, an affective one, and an encounter between psyche and soma.[4]

Some examples of each of these phenomena can be given expression in verbal language, but many others cannot. Perhaps the most important thing to say, for the purposes of the present discussion, is that only rarely are these processes and elements created or deployed by conscious decision. They happen "by themselves," outside the relevance of rationality or conscious decision. They are thoroughly dynamic expressions of the mind: none of them can happen unless they are affectively tolerable or bearable, and the judgment of whether or not a psychic content or process is bearable, while it is sometimes the outcome of deliberation, usually goes on outside consciousness. From this collection of processes a path is charted, and then re-charted, in every moment, from unformulated to formulated experience, from body to mind. In fact, a convenient way to contain this entire collection of processes is a word we also use to refer to the outcome of these processes: mind. The formulation of experience is the creation of mind.

The formulation of the procedural possibilities for meaning takes place when they change status from *not-me* to *feels-like-me*.[5] This shift in status is, in its turn, dependent on the configuration of the interpersonal field, and it is this feature of the theory that defines its interpersonal/relational orientation. In Freud's model and the ego psychological one that followed it, particularly in North America, the creation of consciousness was an intrapsychic process carried out via various compromises of drive and defense, in combination with the demands of the external world. In the theory of unformulated experience, the process of formulation (which should not be simply equated with the creation of consciousness, since, as we have seen, procedural material, when it is formulated, is not necessarily accessible to conscious thought and memory in the same way that symbolic representations are) is equally dynamic, since the interpersonal field is largely unconscious. Just as the contents of consciousness are determined by the compromise of drive and defense in the most traditional theories, the process of formulation is a product of the interaction of the possibilities brought by each participant to the relatedness with the field they jointly create between them. What each person can experience in the presence of the other (an internal and/or external other, who may be conscious and/or unconscious) depends on the nature of what can transpire between them. This point has been a cardinal feature of the theory since its inception (Stern, 1983, 1997, 2010, 2015, 2019). Note that the interpersonal/relational way of conceptualizing the creation of meaning is no less dominated by the nonrational parts of living than is the traditional, more intrapsychic conception. Unconscious relational processes, that is, are no more or less likely to be rational than drive; rationality is simply irrelevant to both.

Clinical illustration

Any clinical material I have published in the past, or any description of my work in the present, could be used to illustrate what I have said. The case I have chosen was published a number of years ago (Stern, 2009; pages reproduced here are pp. 84–87). There may be an advantage in using a previously published report, because rather than writing it with the purpose of revealing one thing or another, one notes instead that the illuminating material is already present—and that perspective may create conviction, because it is itself a demonstration that embodied experience always lies at the heart of clinical experience, for both patient and analyst, even when, as in an illustration originally written for a different purpose, we have paid no particular attention to it. The clinical report begins with background and a bit of history. I interrupt the presentation several times to provide commentary. The original case material is indented in regular type; the commentary is not indented and is printed in italics.

[My patient was] an unusually attractive, charming, socially adept, intelligent, and well-educated woman who, despite always having assumed that she would marry and have children, could not seem to make relationships take that direction. Now approaching the age of 40, she was worried about her future. To begin with, I was baffled at her lack of success, and despite myself, I began to wonder if perhaps her problem was that her positive attributes threatened most of the men she met. (I did not yet understand that she threatened me.) But this explanation did not seem to me to be a very good explanation, because it seemed unlikely that she could have threatened *all* the men she met. And besides, that interpretation would ignore whatever her own contribution might be. At this point, though, I could do no more than refer to "her contribution" in the abstract. Nevertheless, I pointed out to her, somewhat dutifully, that only if she could discover ways in which she was unconsciously creating and maintaining her own distress would there be realistic hope that she could change this part of her life.

Abstract principles hardly motivate people to enter psychoanalysis. That is doubly true for those patients, such as this woman, whose capacity for self-observation is limited. (I was later to find, happily, that this impression needed to be revised.) The analyst needs to be able to cite a concrete example of some way in which the patient unconsciously undermines herself. More than that, the analyst needs to believe the example he cites. With this woman, I could neither cite nor believe. I was struggling with the thoroughly nonrational perception that she was flawless. I knew better, of course. I was even able to refer back to the example of her lack of psychological mindedness as an illustration, but, unsurprisingly, I could not convince myself: the perception that dogged me was a feeling, not a reasonable perception.

I did not yet see that her perfection was itself the point: she was like the perfect princess who lived at the top of the glass mountain. Like the suitors who tried to ride their horses up the mountain to reach the princess, I could find no point of purchase, no way to talk to her that would create some kind of sense of relatedness with her. It was easy for me to feel inadequate in her presence.

I was reduced to hashing and rehashing with her the end of the relationship that had finally brought her into treatment. She was in genuine pain about this, and she appreciated my suggestion that her pain was less about the man himself than about her worry that her hopes for the future were dimming fast. But this idea was hardly sufficient to carry the treatment. I could sense that, unless I found a way to help her deepen the work—which is to say, unless I found a way into a discussion of the less than perfect parts of her experience, but without shaming her about them—the treatment was going to end shortly. She would feel better, at least temporarily, and if I had nothing more to offer, she would leave.

I had ceased anticipating this patient's visits with pleasure soon after we had started meeting, and at this juncture, two or three months in, I was becoming quite familiar with the feeling that I was not a very competent analyst for her. My rehashing of her recent relationship seemed vapid, superficial, and intellectualized to me, and while it was not difficult for me to connect my feelings of inadequacy with her impenetrability, I also imagined, with moderate discomfort, that she agreed with my assessment ofmy efforts.

This sense of inadequacy was not a thought; it was a feeling, and not a specifiable feeling, not something I could point to, not something I even had words for at that time. When I think back on it, I think it was more a sense of heaviness and threat that weighed on me like a heavy blanket.

Actually, it is not true to say that I could observe nothing beyond this woman's perfection. I have mentioned being impressed with her impenetrability. I had also noticed the defensive quality of her continuous, brittle good cheer. She could cry about her pain, and she could be angry, but only if some objective situation in the outside world merited it. I had the sense that sadness or anger under any other circumstances would feel unjustifiable to her, and would probably represent a weakness in her eyes. It would shame her. She could not be vulnerable to me, in other words, and I felt sure that I was not the only one with whom she felt this way. As a matter of fact, I imagined that this might be exactly the problem she was encountering in maintaining a romantic relationship. I could not just offer the patient that observation, though, not unless I had something to say that would help her make use of it in a way that did not potentiate the shame I could sense in the wings.

I don't think I thought of the word "shame" for what I sensed in my patient until later. I certainly couldn't have referred to what I eventually understood as my shame. Shame was not-me for both the patient and me at that time. It was something to which I reacted without realizing I was reacting. It was part of the continuous mutual influence that passed between us, and not something I could have said was there, and if I didn't know it was there, I surely didn't know I was reacting to it. We routinely call this unconscious. We might as well also call it embodied.

Time was running out. This was not a person who could discuss her frustration with the treatment or with me in a productive way. To do so would seem unacceptably hostile to her, rather like criticizing her marvelous parents (one of many attitudes that had made it difficult to get the treatment moving). Or rather, even if she *were* able and willing to talk about her frustration, it would do her no good unless I could say something that would give that frustration a different or broader meaning than it had now, something that would bring some life into the work for her. If I could not do that, then talking about her frustration would simply be a prelude to her departure.

And so one day, having failed to come up with the perfect (!) interpretation, and with the time left in the treatment swiftly draining away, I took a deep breath and stumbled into an attempt to say something authentic to this woman about my reaction to her presentation of herself. I did not know where I was going, or exactly what I would say when I got there.

I know I felt I had nothing to lose. I was trying to see if I could say something coherent to my patient about what we were doing. We can imagine that the doing was embodied. It's not just that the meaning of what we were doing was hidden away somewhere. Rather, that meaning did not exist in any way we could think about. It was unformulated. It was right there in what we were doing and feeling together, embedded in it. I was hoping that I would find a way to accept *the relevant but unknown, invisible, embodied parts of the relatedness between us so that they could* feel *like me. I was hoping, I think, to formulate experience that I imagined I was dissociating (one cannot know such a thing, only imagine it), and in that way, to make an emotional connection to her. I was hoping to be able to understand her well enough, and her and me together, to become her witness (I mean more than I can explain here. For presentations of the process of witnessing, see Stern, 2009, 2012, Chapters 2–4). But I did not even really know at that point what creating and occupying such a role would look like.*

I talked to her for a couple of minutes about feeling that there must be parts of her that she was not pleased about, that maybe she didn't even like, because everyone has parts like that. Yet (I told her), I didn't seem to be able to get to know her that way. I told her that I felt she was having a very hard time being vulnerable with me, letting me really know her. I told her that, while vulnerability could be uncomfortable for anyone, I thought it must be particularly uncomfortable for her. I could see, I said, that unless we were able to move what we were doing in the direction of me getting to know her in a way that would no doubt make her feel vulnerable, the treatment was going to end, because she was going to cease seeing any value in it. I told her I knew how frustrated she must be with what we were doing, and, like me, how little she must be able to figure out how to make things different between us.

There are many thoughts contained in what I have just said. They do qualify as formulated. But I was using them to try to find my way to something else, something I had no idea how to look for, something embodied, and perhaps dissociated.

These thoughts did not come smoothly, nor did I express them that way. I struggled with them. And of course I was watching her reaction. She seemed interested in what I had to say about vulnerability, and she agreed outright with my estimation of her frustration. These things were good, but still I could not see how I was going to identify something in her experience, something that she could see at least as well as I could, that would open what we were doing into a psychoanalytic treatment.

At some moment, as I was talking, she appeared to me to change. It was quite subtle. She seemed softer and more open. That description, though, "softer and more open," was not available to me in the moment, only later on, when I thought back on it. In fact, I was not even aware of the presence of my new perceptions until, in retrospect, I tried to understand what had happened in the moments before I finally found myself able to say what occurred to me next, which was something new about her experience, something that I thought she would recognize and that might just help us into a more analytic kind of relatedness.

The tiny events I have just described are, to me, the heart of what happened that day. I had no idea how important "softer and more open" was until much later. But at that later point, I recognized that something physical had happened. The field shifted here, in those infinitesimal moments in which the patient became softer and more open.[6] I had unlocked something in her, and she then unlocked something in me. These were nearly, or literally, physical releases. It is as if some of the tension and meaning I had been been casting about for had been "held" (a word frequently used by bodyworkers) in my patient's facial muscles, and from there had had a constraining or inhibiting effect on me. I don't want to be too concrete about this, though: I don't want to say that the affect was literally present in the patient's muscles. I want to imagine something looser than that, something that leaves room for subtle and shifting relations between psyche and soma. I want to say that I became her witness.

The thought formed itself as I was speaking. Actually, I am quite sure that its possibility was created by the prior subtle change in my perception of her, which was, in turn, created by some change in her own affective state. As I spoke, I think that my novel perception was also helped along by my patient's facial expressions, through which she expressed a frank, friendly, and inquisitive interest in what I was saying.

But I am describing these moments with more precision than I experienced at the time. The truth is that I surprised myself—I didn't know what was coming until I was in the process of uttering it. I said, "I think you must be lonely. I think you must always have been lonely." Seeing her shock and recognition, and the tears welling in her eyes, I was encouraged to continue: "I wonder if you have ever felt really known by anyone."

She wept, but this was not the hard crying that had accompanied her angry descriptions of the way her boyfriend had treated her. She hid her face in her hands. After a minute or two of silence she looked up at me and said simply and sadly, "I *am* lonely. I've always been lonely." After another silence, she confirmed that, indeed, she had never felt that anyone had known her, not even her parents, who were so very proud of everything she had accomplished, but equally eager not to know more than that about her. Her mother had actually physically turned away from her, she told me, on the few occasions when the patient had tried to talk to her about less than sunny matters. (Over the next months she revealed, unsurprisingly, that there actually had been quite a few unsunny matters.)

The session ended. It was obvious to both of us that we had started to do something quite different. As she walked in the door for her next session, she said as she sat down and smiled at me, "Now we have something to talk about." It was unnecessary to say it.

Commentary

The unformulated, embodied meaning that had been embedded in the relatedness between this woman and me was liberated by a shift in the field. What had been *not-me* became *feels-like-me*, at least for now (these events happen over and over again in successful treatments); that is, what had been dissociated—i.e., unformulated for unconscious defensive reasons—was unfrozen and became meaningful. This is the process by which I became my patient's witness, and perhaps she became mine. We were each able to *accept* something about ourselves and our relatedness that allowed us each to *use* it in the *spontaneous construction of creative living*. This is a small example of the way that therapeutic action is always intricately entwined with embodied meaning.

What I am claiming is that the embodied parts of the relationship between the patient and me were either responsible for, or at least deeply involved in, the new thoughts I conveyed to the patient. Simple as those thoughts were, they were unavailable to me until I was "loosened up," so to speak, by her becoming "softer and more open." I am specifically denying that the availability of my thoughts had anything to do with theoretical understanding, however crucial that understanding is to the mind-set I bring to the consulting room. (And it is crucial.) But our work, as we conduct it, depends not on ideas, but on our *use* of ideas, the ones that migrate from our minds to our bones, and that allow us to create an emotional connection with the patient. Relatedness embodies mind.

Whenever we can create a connection with someone where there was not a connection before, something good is liable to happen. As true as I believe this simple point is, though, it is less than obvious how we should construct a psychoanalytic understanding of it. "Connection" can seem quite simple and innocent in colloquial usage, but that is deceptive. After all, not every good feeling between patient and analyst is a source of therapeutic action. Connection clearly has something to do with one's feeling of being accepted, and accepting the other. Mutual recognition is another key ingredient. So is understanding the other and being understood. And we know that the process of creating new connection is often identical to successful work with enactments—in which case a new intimacy replaces the old, stuck relatedness, just as happened between me and my patient in my illustration.

But this is not the place for a sustained discussion of these points. What I want to say for the present purpose is that any psychoanalytic account of the idea of connection and intimacy—along with recognition, acceptance, and being understood—will need to include a link with the body. The physicality represented in the meaning of the word—connection—suggests embodiment right off the bat. New connection, as we saw, grows from the formulation of embodied meaning.

Notes

1 Vivona (2009, 2012) presents extensive and coherent empirical evidence that the nonverbal does not precede language, and that there is therefore no "preverbal" period in development. Rather, language (not semantic meaning, of course, but the roots of language nevertheless) is present from the very beginning of life, even in the womb.
2 By "semiotics," I mean to refer to the study of signs and symbols and their use. A symbol system is any collection of meanings that take their significances from their relationship to one another. So "red" in semiotic terms is not defined as a particular wavelength of light, but as the color that is not green, blue, yellow, orange, pink, and so on. Semiotics contains verbal language, which is no doubt the primary symbol system, but semiotics is a much broader category, including within it much that should be considered nonverbal.
3 The process is described in the French literature as "subjectivation" (e.g., Casoni et al., 2009; Wainrib, 2012) or "subjective appropriation," although very few of the key references are yet available in English translation.
4 Others, probably many others, have argued for the link I have drawn here between relatedness, affect, and embodiment. Some of those writers are Loewald (1978), Harris (2014), and Vivona (2014).
5 When I coined this term—feels-like-me—I inadvertently featured the role of embodiment, since how something "feels" is an embodied phenomenon.
6 Let me make sure I leave the correct impression: the field did shift here, and in a very important way. But shifting in the field is expectable; flux is the field's usual, continuous state. The relatively unusual state is the frozen or rigidified relatedness—enactment—that results from dissociation. Dissociation has the effect of shutting down the field's spontaneity. And so under most circumstances there is nothing unusual about a shift in the field. But between this particular patient and me, about this particular part of our relatedness, a shift in the field marked a return to spontaneity of a part of the field that had been dissociatively frozen.

References

Bion, W. R. (1962/1977). Learning from experience. In *Seven servants: Four works by Wilfred R. Bion* (pp. 1–111). Jason Aronson, 1977.

Boston Change Process Study Group. (2010). *Change in psychotherapy: A unifying paradigm.* W. W. Norton & Co.

Botella, C., & Botella, S. (2005). *The work of psychic figurability.* Routledge.

Bromberg, P. M. (1998). *Standing in the spaces: Essays on clinical process, trauma, and dissociation.* The Analytic Press.

Bromberg, P. M. (2006). *Awakening the dreamer: Clinical journeys.* The Analytic Press.

Bromberg, P. M. (2011). *The shadow of the Tsunami: And the growth of the relational mind.* Routledge.

Bucci, W. (1997). *Psychoanalysis and cognitive science: A multiple code theory.* Guilford Press.

Casoni, D., Gauthier, M., Brunet, L., & Bienvenu, J. (2009). The work of René Roussillon: An overview of his major concepts. *Canadian Journal of Psychoanalysis, 17,* 108–130.

Clyman, R. B. (1991). The procedural organization ōf emotions: A contribution from cognitive science to the psychoanalytic theory of therapeutic action. *Journal of the American Psychoanalytic Association, 39S* (Supplement), 349–382.

Freud, S. (1900). The interpretation of dreams. *Standard Edition, IV,* ix–627. Hogarth.

Green, A. (2005). *Key ideas for a contemporary psychoanalysis: Misrecognition and recognition of the unconscious.* Routledge.

Harris, A. (2014). Curative speech: Symbol, body, dialogue. *Journal of the American Psychoanalytic Association, 62*(6), 1029–1045. https://doi.org/10.1177 /0003065114557863

Herzog, B. (2011). Procedural interpretation: A method of working between the lines in the nonverbal realm. *Psychoanalytic Inquiry, 31*(5), 462–474. https://doi.org/10.1080 /07351690.2011.552050

Kristeva, J. (1997). *New maladies of the soul.* Columbia University Press.

Langer, S. (1942). *Philosophy in a new key: A study in the symbolism of reason, rite, and art.* Harvard University Press.

Laplanche, J. (2011). *Freud and the sexual: Essays 2000–2006* (Trans. J. House, J. Fletcher, & N. Ray). The Unconscious in Translation.

Laplanche, J., & Pontalis, J.-B. (1968). Fantasy and the origins of sexuality. *International Journal of Psychoanalytic Psychotherapy, 49,* 1–18.

Laplanche, J., & Pontalis, J.-B. (1973). Deferred action; deferred. In D. N. Smith (Ed.), *The language of psycho-analysis* (pp. 111–114). Norton.

Lecours, S., & Bouchard, M. (1997). Dimensions of mentalisation: Outlining levels of psychic transformation. *The International Journal of Psycho-Analysis, 78,* 855–875.

Levine, H. B., Reed, G. S., & Scarfone, D. (Eds.). (2013). *Unrepresented states and the construction of meaning: Clinical and theoretical contributions.* Karnac.

Loewald, H. (1978). Primary process, secondary process, and language. In *The essential Loewald: Collected papers and monographs* (pp. 178–204). University.

Lombardi, R. (2015). *Formless infinity: Clinical explorations of Matte-Blanco and Bion.* Routledge.

Lombardi, R. (2016). *Body-mind dissociation in psychoanalysis: Development after Bion.* Routledge.

Matte Blanco, I. (1975). *The unconscious as infinite sets: An essay in bi-logic.* Duckworth.

Merleau-Ponty, M. (1945/1962). *The phenomenology of perception (C. Smith, trans.)*. Routledge & Kegan Paul.

Rosenblatt, A. (2004). Insight, working through, and practice: The role of procedural knowledge. *Journal of the American Psychoanalytic Association, 52*(1), 189–207. https://doi.org/10.1177/00030651040520011901

Roussillon, R. (2011). *Primitive agony and symbolization.* Karnac Books, Ltd.

Scarfone, D. (2015). *The unpast: The actual unconscious.* The Unconscious in Translation.

Shalgi, B. (2021). Between mythos and logos: Surrender, vitalization, and transformation. In A. S. Cooney & R. Sopher (Eds.), *Vitalization in psychoanalysis: Perspectives on being and becoming* (pp. 101–121). Routledge.

Stern, D. B. (1983). Unformulated experience: From familiar chaos to creative disorder. *Contemporary Psychoanalysis, 19*(1), 71–99. https://doi.org/10.1080/00107530.1983.10746593

Stern, D. B. (1997). *Unformulated experience: From dissociation to imagination in psychoanalysis.* Routledge.

Stern, D. B. (2009). Shall the twain meet? Metaphor, dissociation, and co-occurrence. *Psychoanalytic Inquiry, 29*(1), 79–90. https://doi.org/10.1080/07351690802247286

Stern, D. B. (2010). *Partners in thought: Working with unformulated experience, dissociation, and enactment.* Routledge.

Stern, D. B. (2012). Witnessing across time: Accessing the present from the past and the past from the present. *Psychoanalytic Quarterly, 81,* 53–81.

Stern, D. B. (2015). *Relational freedom: Emergent properties of the interpersonal field.* Routledge.

Stern, D. B. (2019). *The infinity of the unsaid: Unformulated experience, language, and the nonverbal.* Routledge.

Stern, D. B. (2022). On coming into possession of oneself: Witnessing and the formulation of experience. *Psychoanalytic Quarterly* 91:639–667.

Stern, D. B. (2023). Distance and relation: Emerging from embeddedness in the other. *Journal of the American Psychoanalytic Association* 71: 641–668.

Taylor, C. (2016). *The language animal: The full shape of the human linguistic capacity.* Harvard University Press.

Vivona, J. M. (2009). Embodied language in neuroscience and psychoanalysis. *Journal of the American Psychoanalytic Association, 57*(6), 1327–1360. https://doi.org/10.1177/0003065109352903

Vivona, J. M. (2012). Is there a nonverbal period of development? *Journal of the American Psychoanalytic Association, 60*(2), 231–265. https://doi.org/10.1177/0003065112438767

Vivona, J. M. (2014). Speech as the confluence of words, body, and relationship: Discussion of Harris, Kirshner, and Spivak. *Journal of the American Psychoanalytic Association, 62*(6), 1081–1086. https://doi.org/10.1177/ 0003065114558922

Wainrib, S. (2012). Is psychoanalysis a matter of subjectivation? *The International Journal of Psychoanalysis, 93*(5), 1115–1135. https://doi.org/10.1111/j.1745-8315.2012.00645.x

Winnicott, D. W. (1971). *Playing and reality.* Tavistock.

Chapter 6

How does history become accessible?

Reconstruction as an emergent product of the interpersonal field

Richard M. Gottlieb was a prominent American psychoanalyst who died prematurely, leaving behind him an essay, "Reconstruction in a Two-Person World May Be More about the Present than the Past: Freud and the Wolf Man," published posthumously (Gottlieb, 2017). Gottlieb had proposed a panel to take place at the meetings of the American Psychoanalytic Association (APsaA). It was to be called "The Past in the Present, the Present in the Past," and it was to be focused on the topic of historical reconstruction in psychoanalysis in general, and on his paper in particular. The plan was for Gottlieb's paper to be the focus of comment by colleagues from the fields of North American ego psychology (represented by Harold Blum), relational psychoanalysis (me), and the neuroscience of memory (represented by Richard Lane). Gottlieb's intention was fulfilled at a panel presentation, intended to be a memorial to him, at the Winter Meetings of APsaA in New York in 2018, and the papers were published in the Journal of the American Psychoanalytic Association *in that same year.*

Historical reconstruction has been central to both clinical process and therapeutic action in psychoanalytic ego psychology (e.g., Blum, 2005), and Harold Blum has been not only one of the primary contributors to North American ego psychology, but also probably the foremost contributor to the psychoanalytic literature on historical reconstruction. Gottlieb had known that I would take a different perspective than Blum's, and I feel sure that he hoped that the differences between our views would be highlighted by our commentaries. They were.

This chapter is the commentary I wrote for that occasion. I portray as outcomes of the interpersonal field what the patient can know about their own past life, and what the analyst can infer and imagine about it. When new historical material becomes available during the treatment, I take the

DOI: 10.4324/9781032688893-7

position that it is because of a shift in the field that has already taken place,
resulting in a new relational freedom (Stern, 2015), a freedom that broad-
ens the limits of what analyst and patient can experience in one another's
presence, thus making new thoughts, feelings, perceptions, and memories
accessible and available. What the analyst and the patient can know in any
particular moment about the patient's history, and what they can feel about
it,depends on the configuration of the field in that moment.

  Although I have not addressed the point in this chapter, the accessibility
of the analyst's own history and feelings about it are just as dependent as
the patient's on the configuration of the analytic field. The analyst, that is, is
no different in this respect. And so, for example, in his classic articles about
the personal reminiscences that arise in the course of working with enact-
ments, Jacobs (1991) takes the perspective that he believes he is revealing
the private paths he took to understanding his patients: his elaborations of
his own history, that is, allowed him to grasp the unconscious meanings of
his patient's experience. I am inclined to believe instead that the arousal
and accessibility of these new, and newly relevant, memories in Jacobs's
mind were indications of shifts in the field that freed Jacobs to think and
feel differently about his own life in the patient's presence.

I am honored to be part of this panel created in the memory of Richard
Gottlieb. Given the panel's purpose, I had to decide how to approach his
contribution to it (Gottlieb 2017). The best way, it seemed to me, is to react
to the paper just as I would if he were living. I will be straight-forward in
disagreeing with Gottlieb when that's how I feel, and I will be using the
paper, and the topic of historical reconstruction in general, as a springboard
for my own perspective on the subject.

  I was surprised to read the first sentence of Gottlieb's abstract: "The
psychoanalytic process of reconstruction has yet to be reexamined from the
perspective of today's two-person psychologies." This statement certainly
does not square with my reading of the literature. Gottlieb himself cites
Edgar Levenson's work, in which the story of the patient's life that comes
into being in the treatment is understood to be shaped in part by the analytic
relatedness, especially its unconscious aspects—just as the relatedness, of
course, is significantly shaped by the history. But Levenson is hardly alone.
As far as I know, every writer whose theoretical orientation can be described
as interpersonal, relational, or intersubjective has taken a view of this general variety, frequently described as constructivist or hermeneutic.[1] These

writers haven't necessarily addressed the matter of historical reconstruction explicitly, but that's because the question of reconstruction just isn't crucial to their view of therapeutic action. Their general views, though, leave us no doubt about what they would have to say about reconstruction were they to write about it.

Reconstruction as unbidden thought

In the hermeneutic view, all experience, including historical reconstruction, is constructed via interpretive activity in the here and now. By "interpretive activity" philosophers such as Hans-Georg Gadamer (1960) refer not to interpretations of the specifically psychoanalytic variety, but rather to the much more generic, moment-to-moment interpretations that, in the hermeneutic perspective, constitute our ongoing sense of every moment of our lives. The ceaselessly interpretive nature of our experience is usually unbidden, carried out without an awareness of our participation, so that routinely we treat our spontaneous thoughts and feelings as if they are simply features of the natural world—or, sometimes, as if our conscious intentions are more responsible for them than they are. We overestimate the conscious purposefulness of any number of experiential phenomena. I will argue here that some of our most significant historical reconstructions belong in this category.

In the hermeneutic view, both memory and historical reconstruction are jointly constituted by two influences, one of them from the past and the other from the present. Each of these influences ceaselessly participates in shaping the effects of the other. The past contributes the conservative influence: the relevant, previously constructed experience brought to the present moment by the one who constructs history or remembers it. This conservative influence is an expression of the psychodynamic significance and memorial representation that has already structured this piece of history in earlier times. The conscious and unconscious organization the experience already has in our minds contributes stability and familiarity to our sense of our lives.

The contribution of the present, on the other hand, is unpredictable and therefore carries the potential for novelty, and for that very reason the present moment always threatens stability—or, depending on your point of view, holds out the promise of instability. The present moment, that is, is affected by contingencies that exceed our control. We never know what influences will come to bear in the immediate future, or what those unexpected influences may draw from us, and so each moment, despite the conservative influence of the past, contains seeds for a change not only in the future, but in our experience and understanding of the past as well. In interpersonal and relational thinking, this potentially destabilizing present context is conceptualized as the interpersonal field, a social or two-person phenomenon shot through with conscious and unconscious affect.

While all psychoanalysts believe that any kind of unconscious influence, including the continuous interpretive or hermeneutic influence I have described, should be consciously grasped as thoroughly as possible, the existence and impact of the field's influence, from a relational or interpersonal perspective, are also considered to be an ongoing, continuous part of the way life is ordinarily known, and therefore as something that cannot always be explicitly understood. The nonrational parts of the field do not function by creating a subjectively rooted divergence in the present from a past that has an objective existence. The idea of an objective account of the past seems increasingly mythical.

As I read Gottlieb's paper, the influence of the unconscious parts of the relatedness between Freud and the Wolf Man encourages misrepresentation by Freud of the patient's history, or at least a picture of that history that is so selective that it approaches misrepresentation—as if, in other words, the unconscious influence of contemporary relatedness on historical reconstruction is liable to be distorting and therefore regrettable—just as countertransference was for so long understood to be a distorting influence.

In contrast to this view (and, parenthetically, in agreement with contemporary views of countertransference), those many analysts who share some variety of my general perspective take the position that the continuous, unconscious influence of the field is a perfectly valid and expectable source of meaning. This influence is just as expectable in the case of the analyst's reconstructions of the patient's history—and of the patient's historical reconstructions of his own life, for that matter—as it is in any other aspect of experience. The field does not obscure meanings that exist apart from it, as if field processes were distorting influences from outside a memory that would otherwise be objectively correct; rather, the field actually participates in shaping and constituting meanings that could not come into being without it (see Gadamer 1960). It's just that we aren't, and can't be, as fully in control of that shaping and constituting function as most of us grew up believing we could be.

In the terms of the theory of unformulated experience, a frame of reference I have been developing over several decades (see, e.g., Stern 1983, 1997, 2010, 2015, 2018), each person's experience is re-created in every moment. Experience has an emergent quality that we sense in the continuous reformulation that is consciousness. That is the contribution of the present to experiential novelty, to which I have referred. But that emergent quality is not the most significant influence on the construction of each moment's experience. The most significant influence is the conservative one, to which I have also made reference: the experience of all the moments that have come before the present moment. Each moment is rooted in its own history, in other words, in the succession of moments that has preceded it.

New historical reconstructions—novel experiences of the past, in other words—are frequently examples of emergent reformulations, and when they are, they are unbidden reworkings of previous memories and previous psychodynamic significances according to the conscious and unconscious influences of the present moment. These new reconstructions are possible because of the potential for disruption or deconstruction introduced by the interpersonal field. That disruption, or novelty, is a matter of locating and using the "wiggle room" in the way the last moment becomes the next one—all of which tends to happen outside awareness.

But lest I leave the wrong impression, let me make it clear that the perspective I am presenting is not relativistic, as it sometimes has been described by my critics. Analysts are not simply free to say whatever they like. Reconstructions, to be valid, must observe the constraints supplied by reality. I have often presented the case for this view in scholarly and clinical detail (Stern 1997, 2010, 2015, 2018). Here I must be satisfied with simply making reference to it.

Historical reconstruction and therapeutic action

In contemporary psychoanalysis we tend to locate therapeutic action more in what happens in the here and now and less in what we used to conceptualize as an objectively accurate rendition of the patient's history. But we do continue to respect the role of reconstruction in the change process, of course, and perhaps the most distinguished representative of that view is a member of this panel: Harold Blum. I agree with the claims Blum makes in his Freud lecture of 2002 (published as Blum 2005) about the therapeutic impact of historical reconstruction. He observes that transference guides reconstruction. As you will see, I agree in broad outline with this position; I think every psychoanalyst does.

While I accept these points, though, my own view is different in certain respects. I think it fair to say that for Blum it is always the analyst's *conscious and deliberate understanding* that guides reconstruction. The analyst uses his theory and his rational judgment to create the particular understanding of the patient's history that is most meaningful and useful under current circumstances.

I cannot and do not wish to take issue with the view that this kind of interpretive work is very common: we know perfectly well that we create historical reconstruction on the grounds of both logic and theory. But—and here is the difference I want to introduce—I think that this common practice is *not* the case with the reconstructions that matter most in therapeutic action. *Those* reconstructions, while our theories may make them more *expressible* and even more "knowable" than they would otherwise be, are not available or accessible to us simply *because* of our theory or logic; *those* reconstructions come about for reasons other than the analyst's expert application of theory and rational judgment to the interpretive task.

I don't believe that the most important events in therapeutic action have to do with a consciously constructed interpretive process. Conscious construction of an interpretation works only when what is to be understood already lies within the range of thought that can exist within the interpersonal field as currently constituted. But meanings that already exist under present circumstances, or at least meanings that *could* exist if our attention were drawn to them, are not highly controversial, and are seldom highly important. They are examples of what Merleau-Ponty (1945) calls "empirical speech," which cannot birth new meaning. Speech, says Merleau-Ponty, is an "institution," by which he means that we possess "ready-made meanings" for what is already within the range of our thought. These matters arouse in us only what he calls "second order thoughts; these in turn are translated into other words which demand from us no real effort of expression and will demand from our hearers no effort of comprehension" (p. 184).

The creative use of language, on the other hand, in Merleau-Ponty's frame of reference, requires an experience of *seeing or perceiving differently*, and one must *be* different to *see* differently. In my terms, that means that the field must change in order for certain new meanings to arise. Given this view, while I am very interested in the new psychic contents created as a result of a new capacity to think, it is not new contents per se but the newly available capacity to create them that is evidence of therapeutic action. The growth of mind, which is a matter of increasing our range of access to the psychic possibilities available to us, takes place via interpersonal field processes.

This view is held by interpersonal and relational analysts such as Lewis Aron, Jessica Benjamin, Philip Bromberg, Jody Davies, Darlene Ehrenberg, Adrienne Harris, Irwin Hirsch, Irwin Hoffman, Edgar Levenson, and Stephen Mitchell, but it is held also by analysts otherwise as different from me and other relational analysts (and from one another, for that matter) as Sheldon Bach, Madeleine and Willy Baranger, Antonino Ferro, André Green, César and Sára Botella, and Wilfred Bion. All of these analysts, among many others, consider themselves and their patients to be jointly, ceaselessly, and both consciously and unconsciously embedded in a field of mutual influence. For me, the ceaselessly changing, self-organizing (Galatzer-Levy 2017) configuration of that field is responsible for determining which psychic contents can be symbolized, thought, or formulated in any particular moment. New thought is possible when the field is relatively free to develop spontaneously—that is, when the reciprocal influences of analyst and patient on each other can unfold with a reasonable degree of comfort. The spontaneous formulation of experience and thought is prevented or inhibited, though, when the therapeutic interaction encounters rigid or frozen parts of the field—what are called enactments in my language (Stern 2004, 2010, 2013) and "bastions" or "bulwarks" in the language of the Barangers and their collaborators (Baranger, Baranger, and Mom 1983). At these times the immediate future of therapeutic relatedness becomes stilted and/or uncomfortable, taking on a compulsive or stereotyped quality that may not be apparent until later. Spontaneous thought ceases.

These frozen places in the field are phenomena not only of interaction, but also of mind. From this vantage point, mind is not contained within the confines of one skull, but is instead what I have described as "distributed" (Stern 2010). Mind is a field phenomenon. I share this perspective not only with my interpersonal and relational colleagues but also with Bionian field theorists, represented most prominently by Antonino Ferro (see, e.g., Ferro 2009; Ferro and Basile 2009; Ferro and Civitarese 2016) and Giuseppe Civitarese (see, e.g., 2013, 2014).

The unconscious rigidities of the field lock the therapeutic couple out of certain kinds of thought, feeling, and experience. Conceptualized in this kind of theory, therapeutic action is understood to be the sensing of frozen places in the field and then the application of whatever effort can be mobilized to melt or free them. To free the field is to create the possibility of new meaning.

Remember that in the view articulated by Blum in his Freud lecture of 2002 (Blum 2005) it is the analyst's conscious and deliberate understanding of the transference that guides historical reconstruction. I hope it is clear already that I accept this view under many circumstances. But I differ with it in the case of most of the new clinical understandings that really matter, including historical reconstructions that pack a wallop, the ones that have a substantial impact on the patient, the analyst, and the course of the treatment. These reconstructions are not simply the result of the application of theory and clinical judgment; they are instead the organic expressions of a change in the analytic relationship, and they cannot come about without a shift in the field, a new freedom, a release from an inhibiting or stereotyping influence on patient and analyst that may very well have been unsuspected to that point in the treatment. The new construction itself has therapeutic effects, of course, effects that are described clearly by Blum, but in my frame of reference the new construction is possible only because of the shift in the field that preceded it, and so it is actually *that* event that seems to me to lie at the heart of therapeutic action. It is not the analyst's interpretation that is most significant in creating the change, in other words; it is the shift in the field that made that new interpretation—in this case, that new historical reconstruction—come together in the analyst's mind. The interpretation is therefore at least as much a sign that the important change has already occurred as it is the engine of the change (Stern 2009). The analyst's new thought, like the patient's, is a spontaneous, emergent product of the interpersonal field. This process generally happens in a way that feels sufficiently natural that we do not notice it or question it.

I want to be clear, though, that I do embrace in my work my knowledge about the patient and my preferred clinical theory. I have in my bones an ongoing appreciation of the transference and countertransference, an appreciation that is as much a matter of affective resonance as abstract thought. I have a conscious, intentional grasp of the patient's history. And I carry with me, again probably more meaningfully in the bones than in the brain, the insights of the developmental and clinical theories that have most influenced me.

But I do not sit with my patients and figure out the reconstructions that matter most. Rather, I "find" them in my mind; they "arrive," they "come to me." They are unbidden, just like the words I use to convey them to the patient. We never know exactly what we are about to think, feel, or know. When our experience as analysts is productive, it emerges as a fulfillment of our deepest clinical and personal intentions, while simultaneously contributing to the shaping of those intentions as they grow into the future.

While many psychoanalytic writers do not take the perspective I have just outlined, I am hardly alone in embracing it, and those who agree with me are not limited to interpersonal or relational writers. Madeleine Baranger, for instance, wrote in 1993 that "the 'intersubjective field' underlies as something unsaid or unsayable both the analysand's material as presented and the analyst's formulations; in the latter, it determines both the content of the interpretation and the feeling-conviction that the interpretation must be formulated" (pp. 306–307).

Before turning to a clinical illustration, let me emphasize my belief that in any creative endeavor there is a time for spontaneity and a time for deliberation. That is, I hardly mean to claim that treatment is, or should be, nothing but spontaneity and emergence. We all make careful judgments about what is best to do, and those judgments must be consciously considered, taking into account all that we know about our patients and the course of their particular treatment. What I do intend to say is that, when it comes to historical reconstructions that have not yet appeared in the treatment, it is often the case that "you can't get there from here." Some historical reconstructions are actually *inaccessible* to both patient and analyst until the interpersonal field shifts in some significant way that allows them to exist, to come together, in the mind of one participant or the other. The accessibility of the material that makes this work effective, in other words, is not necessarily controlled by the conscious intentions of patient or analyst.

Clinical illustration

For several years I have been seeing a brilliant, accomplished, and attractive middle-aged woman I will call Laurie. A positive affective atmosphere has been the rule between us. I have long known that she was sexually abused as a child by a man whose job frequently brought him into her building, and often enough into her apartment, where she was apparently assaulted repeatedly over a fairly long period. On each of these occasions, her mother, the only other person living in the apartment (the parents were divorced and the father lived elsewhere), took advantage of the presence of another adult to step out for a break, or to run an errand, leaving the child alone with the handyman. The patient believes she probably tried to tell her mother what was happening, but doesn't actually remember doing so; she imagines, however, that her mother did not believe her. The mother, though a warm person, was neglectful and oblivious under the best of circumstances, and often teased the patient about being a dramatic complainer, a "Sarah Heartburn." The patient imagines that given all these factors she would not have persevered in trying to convince her mother had she professed doubt about the abuse—which is what the patient imagines her mother did. And so things continued on in this miserable vein.

The patient had never offered much detail about any aspect of the abuse. She wasn't deeply disturbed about her lack of curiosity; she just couldn't remember much and felt there wasn't much she could do about it. Nor, I must admit, was I especially disturbed about the fact that the patient could say so little about this, or about what I now see, looking backward, as the relative absence of my own curiosity.

In fact, I didn't understand my own attitude as a lack of curiosity at all. It seemed obvious to me that I would have been interested had Laurie been able to report more details surrounding these events, but I accepted what she said about not being able to remember much. I did consider her lack of curiosity an effect of the dissociation attendant on the trauma, but despite thinking I was open to this material, it didn't occur to me to imagine that she and I might proceed differently in the treatment. I wonder whether I would have been able to approach this part of the patient's experience more effectively had I been able to question more fully my attitude toward the relative absence of curiosity in both of us. I doubt it, actually. My best guess is that the blunting of our curiosity was an essential enough aspect of the field that merely noticing it would not have been enough to destabilize it. A real change in the field was probably necessary. But of course I don't really know the answer to this question. At any rate, I wasn't as frustrated, concerned, or interested in this state of affairs as, in retrospect, I might expect to have been. This kind of clinical process, incidentally, in which patient and analyst are both blithely unaware of what later appear to have been obvious oversights, is one of the forms of relatedness that seems to me emblematic of mutual dissociative enactments. We can say that the field was rigidified, frozen, in this respect, and that what I have referred to elsewhere as "relational freedom" (Stern 2015) was compromised in ways that neither the patient nor I understood, or even noticed.

The patient had been in a long analysis earlier in her life. There was not much affective depth in that treatment, though, and the patient felt very different this time around. She began the treatment while living in New York, where we both lived at the time. She came twice a week, less than either of us would have liked, but she had a job with an enormous degree of responsibility, and it was difficult for her to manage even that frequency. When she relocated to another city and took on even more responsibility, she wanted to continue with me by telephone, but within a few months it became clear that it was simply impossible for her to keep up even two sessions a week. We agreed to meet once a week, but again, before much more time had passed, the patient told me, reluctantly, that she thought she should stop treatment altogether because she simply could not commit to the same time every week.

This was a strange situation. But however we were to understand it, I didn't feel that it should simply be described as a lack of commitment or as resistance (a concept I actually don't use). I still felt strongly the patient's interest in the treatment and the depth of her involvement with me. So I did something I had not done with anyone before: I told her that I remained aware of her involvement with me and the treatment, and that I knew she had not ceased to feel that our work was helpful. She agreed with these assessments. Given my sense of these things, I told her, I thought that her willingness to give up the treatment reflected the absence of an appropriate sense of entitlement to what was good for her—in the service of her need to satisfy the demands of the many people who wanted her time and atten-tion. She and I both knew that she was prone to set aside her own wishes and feelings in favor of the needs of others, and so my remark made sense to her. I told her I would be willing to schedule her sessions one week at a time, once a week, until we could manage a better schedule.

She was relieved and moved, and accepted my proposal with gratitude. We began to work this way about a year and a half ago, and sessions have often taken place on the phone from airports and hotel lobbies, although Laurie attends sessions in person whenever she can manage to be in New

York. She takes responsibility for making sure that we have time set aside each week, usually scheduling sessions a month or so at a time.

Soon after I challenged the patient's decision to end treatment and we began this ad hoc schedule, the patient suddenly began to find herself with new memories of the sexual abuse in virtually every session. This part of her history began to get much more specific and disturbing. It turned out, however, that the patient's distress in the face of her new memories was much less pronounced than the relief she felt at being able to know and think about what had happened to her. New memories are still appearing, along with reconstructions, offered by each of us at different moments—reconstructions regarding the abuse itself, and others about why and how no adults ever knew about it. It is not only the patient's curiosity that is aroused now; I, too, have become more curious, and my curiosity is reflected in more frequent, fully detailed, and incisive reconstructions about the abuse, who should have known about it and why, its impact on the rest of the patient's life, how she must have felt, and the dynamic situation in her mind and in her life that made it possible for all of this to unfold as it did.

The schedule of the treatment is now regular again, and we are in the midst of discussing what you, the reader, no doubt have already imagined: the frequency of our meetings, while it can reasonably be argued was demanded by special circumstances, also reflected the patient's anxiety—based on the unreliability of her parents, but especially her mother—about being as deeply involved with me as she would be if she let herself go. The patient is also working on establishing a New York office for her company. She has a number of reasons to want to live in the city again, but a significant one is her wish to resume attending her sessions in the usual way.

Now, I must admit this is a bit of a shaggy dog story, because I am just now reaching my point, which is this: one day, soon after the new memories started appearing, the patient said spontaneously, "I think I'm remembering these things now because you didn't just let me leave." She added, "I feel even more confident in you and in our relationship than I used to." I knew immediately that she had heard my offer to schedule meetings infrequently and ad hoc as evidence that I took her hopes and fears—and the realities of her life—seriously, even when she herself didn't, and I knew that this had made a difference to her—a difference not only between us in the relationship, but in her capacity to think. It also occurred to me that the difference this made to *her* had made a difference to *me*: this was when I began to note the expansion of my curiosity that I have noted, and my more frequent and thorough reconstructions. Yet until Laurie's revelation of the difference it made to her that I didn't accept her decision to leave, the shift in the nature of my own participation had not really occurred to me. I was unaware of what apparently had happened in my mind. Rather, as I have already quoted Madeleine Baranger, the field had "determine[d] both the content of the interpretation and the feeling-conviction that the interpretation must be formulated."

And so it was not only the patient's mind, but also my own, that grew in response to the new freedom between us; I, too, was able to think more curiously and deeply about the abuse, and over the following months I have been able to offer reconstructions of these events and their meaning to the patient that I have every confidence would never have entered my head had the field not changed as it did. But let me also emphasize that I do not believe the reconstructions were themselves the primary curative factor, though of course they were helpful; what was primarily therapeutic was the new freedom in the field that *set in motion* these reconstructive events— among other things.

Could I have accomplished the same thing if the field had not shifted as it did? I have no way of knowing the answer to that question, but I am inclined to answer that it would have been unlikely, because there is no reason to think that I would have been able to feel the nature of the problem of my absent curiosity in a way that would have remedied it. In any case, in this particular field, the one this patient and I created, I didn't have the choice to proceed that way, because I had available to me neither an interpretive strategy nor even the thought that there was something I was not paying sufficient attention to, and it seems to me beside the point to ask whether I somehow *should* have done something that it did not occur to me to do.

I believe that the impact I had on the patient required a "spontaneous gesture" on my part (Winnicott 1963). In this case, that spontaneous gesture emerged from my recognition of the patient's attachment to me, and from my sense that she needed to be protected from her willingness to leave behind something precious. For her part, the patient was able to be open to what I said in a way that allowed what I offered to become what we might call an effective therapeutic reply to the obliviousness and lack of caring in her history. I am quite sure that if I had done the same thing deliberately, as a corrective—that is, if I had done it to have a transferential impact "on purpose"—the intervention would have been useless, or worse. What I did was a spontaneous manifestation of the same field that it influenced, and the result has been not only the recovery of memories and the construction of what cannot be remembered, but also an expansion and deepening of the patient's entire history. Could there be a more eloquent testament to historical reconstruction as an emergent product of the interpersonal field?

Note

1 Perhaps the first writer to take a view that is at least somewhat related to Gottlieb's was Jung (1955), who argued that sexual memories of infancy and childhood are largely created later in life, via a process of fantasy, so that our histories are symbolic representations of our current states of mind. In taking this view, Jung was not adopting a hermeneutic perspective, but rather a view that presaged Gottlieb's—that the effect of the present on the past is distorting, not merely constructive. Freud, of course, contested Jung's doctrine (*Zarückphantasieren*, or retrospective fantasy), which deemphasized (but did not fully disavow) the roles of infantile sexuality and infantile and childhood sexual trauma. As is well known, Freud could not tolerate Jung's disagreement on these issues, and the split between the two was in this way set in motion. Interestingly enough, it is generally accepted (Laplanche and Pontalis 1967) that it was in the Wolf Man case (Freud 1918), which Gottlieb uses as the clinical illustration of his thesis, that Freud most clearly rebutted Jung on these points by suggesting that his concept of *Nachträglichkeit* allowed him to preserve the developmental and etiological significance of infantile sexuality and "real" infantile sexual trauma while also taking into account the impact of the present on the past.

References

Baranger, M. (1993). The mind of the analyst: From listening to interpretation. In *The Pioneers of Psychoanalysis in South America,* ed. N. Lisman- Pieczanski & A. Pieczanski. New York: Routledge, 2015, pp. 306–320.

Baranger, M., Baranger, W., & Mom, J. (1983). Process and non-process in analytic work. *International Journal of Psychoanalysis* 64:1–15.

Blum, H.R. (2005). Psychoanalytic reconstruction and reintegration. *Psychoanalytic Study of the Child* 60:295–311.

Civitarese, G. (2013). *The Necessary Dream: New Theories and Techniques of Interpretation in Psychoanalysis,* transl. I. Harvey. London: Karnac Books, 2014.

Civitarese, G. (2014). *Truth and the Unconscious in Psychoanalysis,* transl. A. Elgar, I. Harvey, & P. Slotkin. New York: Routledge, 2016.

Ferro, A. (2009). Transformations in dreaming and characters in the psycho-analytic field. *International Journal of Psychoanalysis* 90:209–230.

Ferro, A., & Basile, R. (2009). The universe of the field and its inhabitants. In *The Analytic Field: A Clinical Concept,* ed. A. Ferro & R. Basile. New York: Routledge, pp. 5–29.

Ferro, A., & Civitarese, G. (2016). Psychoanalysis and the analytic field. In *The Routledge Handbook of Psychoanalysis in the Social Sciences and Humanities,* ed. A. Elliott & J. Prager. London: Routledge, pp. 132–148.

Freud, S. (1918). From the history of an infantile neurosis. *Standard Edition* 17:7–122.

Gadamer, H.-G. (1960). *Truth and Method,* rev. transl. J. Weinsheimer & D.G. Marshall. London: Continuum, 2015.

Galatzer-Levy, R. (2017). *Nonlinear Psychoanalysis: Notes from Forty Years of Chaos and Complexity Theory.* New York: Routledge.

Jacobs, T. (1991). *The Use of the Self: Countertransference and Communication in the Analytic Situatio*n. New York: International Universities Press.

Jung, C.G. (1955). The theory of psychoanalysis: 7. The aetiology of neurosis. In *The Collected Works of C.G. Jung: Vol. 4.* Princeton: Princeton University Press, 1970, pp. 157–180.

Laplanche, J., & Pontalis, J.-B. (1967). *The Language of Psycho-Analysis,* transl. D. Nicholson-Smith. New York: Norton, 1973.

Merleau-Ponty, M. (1945). *Phenomenology of Perception,* transl. C. Smith. London: Routledge & Kegan Paul, 1962.

Stern, D.B. (1983). Unformulated experience: From familiar chaos to creative disorder. *Contemporary Psychoanalysis* 19:71–99.

Stern, D.B. (1997). *Unformulated Experience: From Dissociation to Imagination in Psychoanalysis.* New York: Routledge.

Stern, D.B. (2009). Partners in thought: A clinical process theory of narrative. *Psychoanalytic Quarterly* 78:101–131.

Stern, D.B. (2010). *Partners in Thought: Working with Unformulated Experience, Dissociation, and Enactment.* New York: Routledge.

Stern, D.B. (2013). Relational freedom and therapeutic action. *Journal of the American Psychoanalytic Association* 61:227–255.

Stern, D.B. (2015). *Relational Freedom: Emergent Properties of the Interpersonal Field.* New York: Routledge.

Stern, D.B. (2018). *The Infinity of the Unsaid: Unformulated Experience, Language, and the Nonverbal.* New York: Routledge.

Winnicott, D.W. (1963). The development of the capacity for concern. In *The Maturational Processes and the Facilitating Environment: Studies in the Theory of Emotional Development.* London: Hogarth Press, 1965, pp. 73–82.

How I work with unconscious process, part 1

A case example

Chapters 7 and 8 are illustrations of how my field theory understanding of the nature of unconscious process leads me to work clinically. Both chapters present my work with the same man, two episodes separated by a period of something like two years. Chapter 7, "How I work with unconscious process: part 1–A case example," was written as my contribution to a panel, "The Royal Road: Where Are We Now? Conceptualizing and Engaging the Unconscious: Three Analytic Perspectives," presented by the New York University Postdoctoral Program in Psychoanalysis and Psychotherapy on May 2, 2019. The panel was designed to reveal what is characteristic about the way clinicians with differing theoretical orientations (contemporary Freudian, Lacanian, and interpersonal/relational) work with unconscious process.

Unformulated experience and the events of the field

For Freud (1895, 1915), unconscious contents are fully formed. These contents—that is, thing-presentations—cannot be directly grasped by the mind, so we cannot tell what they are except by inference. This is the eternal problem faced by psychoanalysis: given that we are locked out of unconscious process, how can we know its nature? Freud seems to take it for granted that the intimations we do have of thing-presentations—word-presentations—refer to fully formed meanings. Unconscious phantasy, that is, while it cannot be directly perceived, is "there." It pre-exists our acquaintance with the word-presentations we use to try to grasp it.

I don't think unconscious process is best conceived as fully formed meaning. For me, unconscious process is *potential* experience, what conscious experience *might become; and* for that reason, I (2010a, 2014) do not accept that the contents of the unconscious are aptly described as

DOI: 10.4324/9781032688893-8

unconscious phantasy. I describe the potential meaningfulness that, for me, is unconscious process as "unformulated experience," and I describe it as states that are vaguely organized, primitive, global, nonideational, and affectively saturated. I take the position that conscious experience is not static, but instead is continuously in the process of coming into being—of being formulated and reformulated—over and over again (Stern, 1983, 1997, 2010b, 2015, 2018).

I hope it makes sense, then, that in my frame of reference, the most crucial clinical events from moment to moment—both inside and outside the consulting room—are those that resolve the ambiguity of unformulated experience into some sort of explicit, conscious shape. In my thinking, the most significant influence on the shape taken by conscious experience is the current configuration of the interpersonal field. That is, the nature of the analytic relatedness is largely responsible for what the analyst and the patient can consciously experience in one another's presence. To the extent that the field is free to develop spontaneously, the conscious thoughts and feelings of both analyst and patient are free to do the same, and to the extent that the field is frozen or constricted, the depth and spontaneity of the participants' conscious experience is compromised. The appearance of novel conscious experience, therefore, depends on a change, or shift, in the field.

And so, in my frame of reference, the revelation of unconscious content is not really the point, and interpretation is not necessarily the means of therapeutic action. Taking this point of view is hardly equivalent to dismissing interpretation, of course, because what we say to our patients is an important influence on the next generation of clinical events. But more important, from where I sit, is the spontaneity and freedom of the field. For me, when the analyst is capable of knowing or feeling something new toward or about the patient—that is, when the analyst becomes capable of a new experience, or of making a new interpretation—the particulars of what the analyst says to the patient (the interpretations) play a lesser role in therapeutic action than the newly available freedom in the field that made the interpretation possible in the first place (Stern, 2009, 2013, 2017). Thus, I try to focus my clinical attention on the ways that the field is constricted, ways in which what I have called "relational freedom" is compromised. I generally don't think about my interventions as consciously chosen interpretations, even though they may take that form, but as participations that grow from my conscious and (especially) unconscious involvement in the field (Stern, 2015; Chapters 2–6). I judge the success of my interventions by asking myself whether they contribute to the field's spontaneous unfolding, or instead, reinforce some kind of interpersonal constriction.

Clinical illustration

Now let me introduce you to Alan, a 26-year-old patient of mine. He is sweet, emotionally generous, charming, warm, as honest as he can be, and self-effacing. His self-effacement can be misleading, though. It's sincere, but it does come and go. Alan is often viciously self-critical, to the point of being self-hateful, but in certain significant respects he also has a very high opinion of himself. He has an MBA, a powerful interest in being successful and wealthy, and is highly intelligent. He should probably be called brilliant. Alan came to me through a colleague from another state. I see him three times a week, and we have worked together for about a year. Recently a series of events took place between us that I hope will illustrate my thoughts about working with unconscious process.

Alan is in treatment because of anxiety and depression that have often become severe enough to be debilitating, making it more or less impossible for him to get out of bed. This, of course, has been a challenge for him in many ways, and certainly in his career. (More about that in a moment.) But when he can work, he takes advantage of the fact that he is unusually knowledgeable and intuitive about finance for someone his age. He has started working for several hedge funds, and in each, he is almost immediately recognized as a *wunderkind*, and is given a surprising amount of responsibility. And each time he fails, because, after starting by firing on all cylinders—enthusiastic, impressive, and full of energy—Alan simply cannot get himself out of bed and into the office. The prospect of success has seemed only to worsen this problem.

Each time this happens, Alan finds a way to pick himself up, to rebuild his hopes and try again. Each time, he has been able to use his father's considerable influence in the world of finance to gain a new toehold and to create high expectations among his older colleagues. As things deteriorated in his most recent job (the only one I have been around to witness), and for a time thereafter, he was overcome with despair, suicidal feeling, and crushing self-hatred. And yet it seems that no one, not even those he has disappointed, reviles or blames him. Alan tends to inspire warm feeling in those around him, and that includes me. So when he fails, it seems to his coworkers that it's just a real shame that he couldn't make it work. He has quite a few close, longstanding friends, young men he has known since the very beginning of his life, a fact that bodes well for the future.

Alan is the oldest of four and has two sisters and a brother. They are all close with one another. The siblings are allies who depend on one another in many ways, and especially in dealing with their parents.

Alan's relationships to father and mother are more complicated. I would say that he is devoted to them, but I would also say that he and they all need to see him that way. His father, who pays a portion of his treatment bills and living expenses, seems to me to be sincerely concerned about his son, and calls me for advice now and then, which I have been unwilling to give him. I tell him that I understand that he feels he must do what he can to motivate his son, but that this is between the two of them, and that he must do what he believes is best. I have recently found that the fact I've taken these calls at all is problematic for Alan, who said, up to that point, that I should feel free to talk to his father. Alan is nothing if not obliging—often to his detriment. Now he agrees with me when I tell him that I think that talking with his father may be making him feel that the treatment belongs just a little less to him. Alan experiences his father as loving and generous, but also as demanding, self-centered, and incapable of seeing Alan's point of view.

Mother has been diagnosed as bipolar and she drinks too much. Alan grew up with her frequent tantrums, during which she screamed at the children in a way that often frightened him. Sometimes these episodes took place in public, which was humiliating for him; sometimes Alan was reduced to tears and terror, hiding for hours in a dark closet. Mother and father are, and always have been, very taken with Alan's talents, especially his intelligence, which mother described to her friends and acquaintances in great detail, sometimes in front of him. Alan tells me he was very well behaved as a boy, and I believe him. His mother helped to create this attribute and then exploited it by displaying him in front of her friends like a show pony. Alan can say that he resented this repeated scenario, but he did not refuse to participate, nor does he now, when the occasion arises.

Alan grew up feeling that he owed it to both his parents to be a good son, which meant that he needed to be obedient and grateful. He seldom if ever talked back to them, and he felt bad on those occasions when he did. It seems to me, when I listen to him, that both his parents insist on, and feel entitled to, continuous devotion from him, and any deviation from that attitude results in either rage or terribly hurt feelings on their parts. Today, the hurt feelings and disappointment feel worse for Alan than the rage, but I can imagine that it was often different when he was younger. Alan and his three siblings talk frankly, with a degree of maturity that I find a little jarring, about how to handle their parents' needs. It often seems to me that the children are the parents.

When Alan was eight, he had an experience that he considers formative. In his own mind, he was what he refers to as a "magnificent" baseball player. One day he had a bad accident on the field. His mother pooh-poohed the injury, and left the baseball diamond to do some errands. It turned out that Alan had a serious compound fracture. His athletic career was over, he says; he was all washed up. He has told this story to me a number of times, and each time, along with the trauma, I sense a smile hovering just behind his face, conveying what I imagine to be a secret pleasure in being able to *really nail* his mother on this one.

This history is impossibly condensed, but as sketchy as it is, I'm sure that it suggests some of what has happened in his relationship with me. Soon after Alan and I began working together, I spoke to his former analyst (who was the referring out-of-state colleague I mentioned before), someone I like and respect. I told her that I liked Alan. She responded, "Me, too. I just wish he would've come to treatment more often." So here we go. At that time, Alan was missing a session with me now and then.

He was absent more often than most of my patients, but not enough to be a serious problem for the treatment. Things were going well for him then: he had just moved into his new apartment with his oldest friends, and he was soaring in his new job.

Then, as he seemed to be on an upward trajectory at work, Alan began missing sessions more often than he came to them. First, he missed one or two per week (out of three); then, within a month, he was missing most of them. Eventually he was missing almost every one. He was depressed, yes, but that wasn't even close to being the whole story. As I began to know his difficulty just getting himself out of his apartment, I started calling him when he was late, having a pretty good idea that he was still at home. Sometimes he picked up his phone, often he didn't. He always had long, complicated explanations for missing the session, and he kept insisting that he would get there if he could. But something always stymied him. I've often heard explanations like these; we all have. But Alan is a champion explainer. Over and over again something happened that seemed unavoidable.

Here's a typical example: one day at the time of his appointment he texted me to say that he was nauseous and dizzy, but hoped to talk to me on the phone. (He texted me quite often, usually between sessions, and, as we shall see, he often did valuable work in these texts, even when he didn't come to sessions.) However, that day I didn't hear from him and he didn't answer his phone. He wasn't actually sick, it turned out. He had fallen asleep and slept through the ringing phone. I do believe that his text was sincere, and I believe he really did fall asleep and that he managed not to hear the phone. He doesn't lie.

Eventually I asked him if he wanted to continue in treatment. I told him that it wasn't necessary to force himself to do something he really didn't want to do, and that I thought that, if he didn't want to be there, he'd have a terrible time telling me. I also told him that I knew he felt he was wasting my time and his father's money, and that he hated that. This was a theme for him. He wanted to be able to support himself, but couldn't control his expenses, often feeling that just about the only thing in the world that would comfort him was very good food.

But Alan insisted that he did want to come, that he wanted and needed to be in therapy, and that his difficulty getting to me didn't reflect the wish not to be there. He agreed with me when I responded that I thought that he and I got along pretty well, and I told him that this fact made his claim that he did indeed want to continue our work seem plausible. It seemed that he wasn't avoiding treatment in order to avoid me—although, as you'll see, this was not at all the whole story.

Eventually I began spending a significant part of our time together offering Alan interpretations of this problem of getting to his sessions. I communicated my message in many different forms. The most common was to refer to two different parts of him, one that wanted to come and another that didn't. It wasn't hard to connect this little model to Alan's situation with his parents: his wish to be a good boy and his resentment about it. I told him that the ideal solution was to refuse to be a good boy—in this case, being a good patient—without feeling that he bore responsibility for it, because his absences were due to acts of god, not something he chose.

As time passed, I felt increasingly that what I was saying was stale and intellectualized, that, rather than finding what I wanted to say emerging in myself, in the way I generally feel the arrival in my mind of interventions that are vital and affectively alive, I was resorting to stereotyped interpretations. I told Alan more than once that I was unhappy with myself in this respect. I told him that it seemed that we had to make some kind of sense of his capacity to come to his sessions, but that I felt like I was hitting him over the head with my interpretations. Predictably, Alan was reassuring. I knew he would have liked this reassurance to be sincere, but I also knew it wasn't.

What do you suppose happened in response to all my intellectualized argumentation? How could Alan maintain good- boy status while continuing to carry out his revenge? He did it by finding it impossible to understand what I said. My interpretations, as simple and stereotyped as they were, baffled him. He was genuinely puzzled. He struggled dutifully. But he just couldn't get it. Then, finally, Alan not only didn't come for his sessions, he stopped answering the phone. This went on for a number of sessions, longer than I had been out of touch with him before. I was concerned. At that point I received the following text. It is long even in this abbreviated version, from which, for reasons of confidentiality, I have cut about half.

> Hi Dr. Stern, I'm safe in the Hamptons [where his family has a vacation house]. You probably know I feel terrible that I haven't responded to you. To be fully transparent I haven't listened to your voice messages because as you might suspect it kinda makes me feel worse. I was feeling on Friday like I was just getting pulled in every direction socially and therefore bound to let everyone down. So anxiety kinda kicked in and said, "Escape to the Hamptons." I wanted to speak to you on the phone this morning during my session time.

What comes next is a long and detailed explanation of what stopped him from calling on that particular morning. Alan continues:

> I've been continually ruminating on our conversation last Wednesday [that Wednesday was the last time we had actually talked], and I think I've finally got some understanding of it through my head, but it's still sort of fuzzy. But it didn't help. I just couldn't do what it felt like other people expected me to do … It was like I was telling myself to fuck off because I had already worked so hard in that session. [He meant that he hated himself for working so hard to satisfy his own expectations, and mine, in that session.] I might be making this up, but perhaps I'm starting to understand what you were getting at when you asked me

if I "wanted" to continue working with you. I hesitated and resolved yes, but when I really reflect on it now, I think that during that hesitation the answer is probably more nuanced. In my conscious self, yes, I want to work with you because I want to change my life on my own terms, to be happier. But no, I don't want to work with you, because I feel like I'm doing it to make my parents and friends happy. And it's really dark, actually, it's almost like I want to kill myself but I feel like I need to go to therapy because that's what people think I should do. Changing the perspective to a bit more meta, I think I finally realized what you're trying to get me to understand to get out of this trap. That it's possible that I don't have to be a lazy, selfish person for letting myself feel that I don't want to do something. I really want to talk to you about all that but I'm getting in my own way, like this neurosis is fighting for its life.

Alan had written me many texts as thoughtful as this one. I can't tell you why this particular text unlocked my capacity to think, but it did. I didn't recognize that at the time, though. In the terms I am using in this chapter, the field shifted, but shifts in the field are so much of a piece with living that they are seldom consciously knowable until later on, if at all. Often, until that later time, the events just happen, without being submitted to the rest of the mind for thoughtful consideration.

In my answering text, I said this to Alan:

> I have a thought about how we might proceed that might just make it unnecessary to keep pulling on the Chinese finger trap[1]—at least between you and me, and then maybe elsewhere as well. Please see if you can come to the session tomorrow and we'll talk about it.

My new thought was very simple. (It seems to me that the most important analytic events usually are.) I saw that I had to back off my insistence on understanding the problem Alan had in getting to his sessions.

Alan did show up for the next session—he had apparently "heard" something compelling in my text, as I had in his. I told him that, from now on, I thought we ought to ignore everything except what was in his head in the session, whether that made sense or not, and whether it was connected to something obviously meaningful or not. We needed to stop going over and over his attendance issues.

What was important about this, I think, was that I meant it. I felt that I just couldn't stand to keep hitting him over the head and feeling intellectualized. Of course, my suggestion was hardly radical. It was nothing more than a restatement of free association, although I didn't think of that at the time. I thought that what I said came completely from me. And I think I was right, actually, even though of course I probably could not have thought of this particular alternative without being a psychoanalyst. I took this step with the sense that I really didn't know if it would work, but the decision came with a certain serenity. If you will permit me to use a very big expression for a very small event, it was what Neville Symington (1983) called "an act of freedom," what Emmanuel Ghent (1990) described as "surrender," or what many of us, including me (Stern, 2010b, 2014), understand as the breach of a mutual unconscious enactment.

When a frozen place in the field melts, the changes that take place are seldom as dramatic as they were in this case. The text exchange took place six months ago. Alan has not missed a session since then. In the week following the exchange, Alan started talking about what he calls a "hurt little boy" inside him, a part of him responsible for both his compliance and amiability and his resentment about complying. The metaphor may be a cliché in the broader culture, but it's not when someone really means it, as Alan does. He also began articulating in much more detail the ways in which he doesn't want to come to sessions. When he talks now about not wanting to come, he identifies it as his own desire, not just something that happens to him.

Why exactly does this vignette deserve to be called work with unconscious process? What exactly was unconscious here? I think that the fact that Alan has started talking directly, and with agency, about his reluctance to come to sessions points the way. Alan could not tolerate being someone who would refuse to do what was expected of him by those he loved, and who loved him. He could not be a bad boy. If he refused expectation, he would have to suffer self-hatred, and if he agreed to go along, he would be (unconsciously) rageful. Not to mention dishonest. That's another story, but one Alan is starting to tell. The sacrifice of integrity that has been required for all these years in order to comply has been painful for him.

Alan enacted all this with me by missing more and more sessions, all the while feeling he had no other choice. Until now, this aspect of his identity—the boy who wanted to refuse his parents—was dissociated. What has finally come into awareness is the possibility of being the bad boy without being monstrous—or rather, the possibility of being the good boy and the bad boy at the same time, and able to negotiate between them.

Although I am sure we will have to go through various iterations of all this, I also think that Alan is no longer limited to toggling dissociatively back and forth between these two states of being, inhabiting just one of them at a time. Now, I hope and believe he is on the road to mourning the good boy he can never really be, and to accepting the bad boy in him without having to feel that he (that is, the "whole" Alan) is not worthy to live.

We charted jointly the route to this outcome. As Alan was accomplishing the breach of his own dissociation, I was doing the same: I gave up what I now see as the attempt to enforce his obedience, like his parents, all the while trying to convince myself (and doing a pretty good job of it) that I was doing nothing more than trying my damnedest to be a good analyst. What happened was not an episode of insight, a packet of information passed from me to him. What I offered him (or perhaps I should say what he offered me—because there's a case to be made that he was as much responsible for the outcome as I was) was a shift in relatedness, an expansion of "relational freedom" (Stern, 2015), and that shift then made it possible for each of us to feel, speak, and think differently.

Note

1 Alan had described his predicament in life more than once by reference to this childhood toy, which I remember from my own childhood. The Chinese finger trap is a woven wicker cylinder into which you insert your index fingers, one on either end. If you try to pull your fingers out, the cylinder tightens, trapping your fingers. The more you pull, the tighter the trap gets. The only way to get out of the trap is to give up and allow the trap to return to its original state. The solution to our dilemma had always been there in the form of this excellent metaphor. We understood the part about getting caught in a trap that wouldn't let go, but I think that neither of us saw, until later on, the further implication that we needed to stop trying to force the matter. This is not a thought that the field yet gave us the freedom to formulate.

References

Freud, S. (1895). Project for a scientific psychology. *The standard edition of the complete psychological works of Sigmund Freud. Volume I (1886–1899): Pre-psycho-analytic publications and unpublished drafts* (pp. 281–391). London: Hogarth Press.

Freud, S. (1915). The unconscious. *The standard edition of the complete psychological works of Sigmund Freud, Volume XIV (1914–1916) On the history of the psycho-analytic movement, papers on metapsychology and other works* (pp. 159–215). London: Hogarth Press.

Ghent, E. (1990). Masochism, submission, surrender— Masochism as a perversion of surrender. *Contemporary Psychoanalysis, 26*(1), 108–136. doi:10.1080/00107530.199 0.10746643

Stern, D. B. (1983). Unformulated experience: From familiar chaos to creative disorder. *Contemporary Psychoanalysis, 19(1),* 71–99. doi:10.1080/00107530.1983.10746593

Stern, D. B. (1997). *Un formulated experience: From dissociation to imagination in psychoanalysis.* New York, NY and London: Routledge.

Stern, D. B. (2009). Partners in thought: A clinical process theory of narrative. *The Psychoanalytic Quarterly, 78*(3), 701–731. doi:10.1002/j.2167-4086.2009.tb00410.x

Stern, D. B. (2010a). Unconscious fantasy versus unconscious relatedness: Comparing interpersonal/relational and Freudian approaches to clinical practice. *Contemporary Psychoanalysis, 46*(1), 101–111. doi:10.1080/00107530.2010.10746041

Stern, D. B. (2010b). *Partners in thought: Working with unformulated experience, dissociation, and enactment.* New York, NY and London: Routledge.

Stern, D. B. (2013). Relational freedom and therapeutic action. *Journal of the American Psychoanalytic Association, 67*(2), 227–255. doi:10.1177/0003065113484060

Stern, D. B. (2014). A response to LaFarge. *The International Journal of Psychoanalysis, 95*(6), 1283–1297. doi:10.1111/1745-8315.12291

Stern, D. B. (2015). *Relational freedom: Emergent properties of the interpersonal field.* London and New York, NY: Routledge.

Stern, D. B. (2017). Unformulated experience, dissociation, and *Nachträglichkeit*. Journal of Analytical Psychology, *62*(4), 501–525. doi:10.1111/1468-5922.12334

Stern, D. B. (2018). *The infinity of the unsaid: Unformulated experience, language, and the nonverbal.* London and New York, NY: Routledge.

Symington, N. (1983). The analyst's act of freedom as agent of therapeutic change. *International Review of Psycho-Analysis, 10,* 283–291.

How I work with unconscious process, part 2

The emergence of meaning from unformulated experience

There was a lapse of something like two years between the writing of Chapter 7 and Chapter 8. Chapter 8, "How I Work with Unconscious Process, Part 2: The Emergence of Meaning from Unformulated Experience" picks up the thread of the work with the same young man who was the subject of Chapter 7. This piece was written for the annual meetings of the International Association of Relational Psychoanalysis and Psychotherapy (IARPP), which was scheduled to be held in Los Angeles in 2020. Like Chapter 6, it was intended to be an illustration of the clinical consequences of thinking as I do about unformulated experience and the field. But the annual IARRP meetings were cancelled that year because of COVID, and the meetings were postponed again, and for the same reason, in 2021. In 2022 the meetings did finally go forward, in Los Angeles, in person, as originally planned.

I see in retrospect that, although I did not set out to do it, I have illus-trated in these two accounts of enactments the fact that successful treatment requires us and our patients to work repeatedly with enactments that play out similar themes. Psychoanalysts have known that working through is an essential part of treatment since near the beginning of the discipline. But from an interpersonal/relational view there is a twist: analysts often cannot reasonably be held accountable for knowing, during the enactment, that they are involved with the patient in unconscious themes similar to those that animated previous enactments with the same patient. That is, analysts cannot always necessarily see that a repetitive state of affairs is coming, or even understand that it has actually arrived. The "grip of the field" (Stern, 1989), an unconscious impact, often prohibits one's observation of one's own experience in a way that prevents, at least temporarily, thoughtful engagement with it. We are all well-acquainted with feeling vaguely the

DOI: 10.4324/9781032688893-9

repetitive theme, but without consciously recognizing the nature of the involvement, or its familiarity, until a period of unconscious immersion in it has elapsed.

My most recent book, published in 2019 (Stern, 2019), is a revision of some of the content of my first one, published in 1997. In the first book, I defined the formulation of experience in the terms of language. I intended a broad, semiotic view of language, but I often wrote in that first book in a way that made it sound as if I limited "formulation" to the articulation of experience in verbal language. I wrote the recent book to counter that impression. It has always been clear to me that much of experience, perhaps most of it, goes on outside verbal language, and I wanted in the recent book to conceptualize how that experience could be formulated in its own, nonverbal terms—that is, without being given verbal articulation.

Here is a very brief summary of the ideas I developed in that recent book to deal with this problem: I now define the boundary between formulated and unformulated not as the line between words and wordlessness (Stern, 2001), but as the boundary separating personally meaningful psychic contents from those that are not (or not yet) personally meaningful. Experience is personally meaningful, in my terms, when we can identify our role in creating it. We do not sense such experience as alien, intruding on our minds; instead it "feels like me." The process by which experience comes to "feel like me" I call "coming into possession of oneself" (see Chapter 2). When we come into possession of ourselves, we "accept" a meaning and can thereafter "use" it in the ongoing construction of spontaneous, creative living. We may be able to give symbolic representation to experience that "feels like me" and that therefore qualifies as meaningful, but often we cannot. That is, meaningfulness is often procedural in nature, and procedural knowing, like knowing how to ride a bicycle, does not necessarily require either articulation in language or realization in nonverbal imagery (Stern, 2019).

Dissociated experience very often can be cognitively known but not felt—that is, not affectively known. It is abstracted, stereotyped, intellectualized, the psychic equivalent of a dry recitation. In an important sense, as we might say on the basis of Merleau-Ponty's (1945) understanding of the mind, unformulated experience is disembodied (see Chapter 5). We don't have the sense that it belongs to us. It doesn't feel as if it *expresses* us, as if it *manifests* us (Taylor, 2016). Personally meaningful experience, on the other hand, *is* embodied in Merleau-Ponty's terms; it *does* express or manifest us (Stern, 2019).

It can be hard to digest these ideas in the abstract, especially when I must present them so schematically. I hope that the following clinical material will tie these ideas to the ground.

I had been seeing Alan for three years, three times per week, at the time of writing the first version of this chapter. In Chapter 7 I wrote about events that took place earlier, after a year and a half of treatment, and I briefly review those events here. This episode in the treatment, like the earlier one, is focused around Alan's problem with attending his sessions. In the first installment Alan was 26 years old. There was a period of months at that time during which he missed more and more of his sessions, until he was missing most of them, making only sporadic contact by phone and text. He was anxious and depressed much of the time, the same problems that had led him to enter treatment in the first place. I asked him if he wanted to keep coming, making it clear that I was ready to accept his departure from treatment if that's what he wanted. But he insisted that he wanted and needed to be in treatment, and to see me in particular.

I believed he meant that. Yet he continued missing sessions. He would prepare himself to leave his apartment, but then would fall asleep, or he would sleep through several alarms he had set. Then he would contact me later, full of shame and self-criticism, mystified by his own behavior.

Over several months, I responded to all this by interpreting whatever I could understand about Alan's motives. I wasn't happy with this way of proceeding, but I really didn't know what else to do. I didn't feel that I was *choosing* interpretation; I felt I was *resorting* to it. Increasingly, I sensed that the clinical process—Alan's missed sessions and my interpretations, which could themselves be plausibly interpreted as disguised ways of saying, "Cut it out!"—was a mutually compulsive replication of some of the most problematic circumstances of Alan's relationship with his parents, especially his mother.

Mother drank too much, and was often angry at Alan when he was a child, most often when he failed to fulfill her narcissistic expectations of him. Her extreme berating of him, and her disregard of his feelings, qualified as what Philip Bromberg (2006, 2011) would have called developmental or relational trauma. Alan was sometimes reduced to cowering in the back of a closet, hoping to avoid discovery. Mother sometimes took Alan and his three sisters for trips on cruise ships on which they were the only children and their care was entrusted to unfamiliar servants hired for the duration of the cruise. The children saw their mother only during cocktail hour, when they were brought to the party and displayed to the other guests, who marveled at their maturity and good behavior. In those days, with the same warmth, charm, and notable intellectual gifts that characterize him today, Alan was proud of his capacity to arouse this response in the adults. He now feels drastically different. Looking back in time, he now imagines that, along with his pride in being able to arouse admiring reactions in the adults, he harbored angry feelings.

I interpreted all of this in relation to our sessions—what seemed to me to be the inevitable resentment that Alan would feel about pleasing his parents and me by expending the considerable effort it took him to commute to our sessions (this was before COVID). But I felt increasingly clumsy and ham-handed about this interpretive theme, because I began to see that I was telling Alan (not in so many words, but by implication) that he needed to do a better job of pleasing me, and Alan, reluctant to be the angry, bad boy, was finding a plethora of ways to fail me passively, so that he didn't have to face his hostile intentions or his wish to disappoint me.

One day, in response to a long, emotionally alive text from Alan after he missed yet another session, I felt that I suddenly knew how to proceed, and I texted Alan that I thought I knew what we might do. I asked him to see if he could manage to get to his appointment the next day. Apparently sensing something different in my text, Alan did show up the next morning. I told him that I thought we had to stop focusing on the matter of his attendance and just focus on whatever it was that was in his mind. I told him I wanted him just to talk about whatever came to mind, whatever happened to matter to him at that moment. I didn't notice at that moment that I was asking Alan to free associate.

But whatever it was I was asking, it had the effect I had felt it would. Alan came to his next session and talked freely, and he came to the one after that, and then the one after that. He didn't miss a session over the next year. We settled into a new rhythm, and we got back to work in a serious way. I knew that it wasn't a renewed commitment to free association that had helped. Instead, I understood the change as a shift in the field that had allowed my development of new thoughts and feelings about Alan, and my communication of this sense of things to him—which then resulted in a corresponding expansion in his own capacity to formulate what we were doing. By intervening as I did, I broke up the stale and stereotyped pattern of missed sessions and interpretation in which we had been caught. I didn't convey what I did out of a consciously created intention; I certainly didn't "figure something out." I just suddenly knew what needed to be done. What I said moved us from embeddedness in a narcissistically organized enactment to a greater sense of relational freedom (Stern, 2013; see also Chapter 3). Interventions successful in melting a frozen place in the field always seem to me to occur to me spontaneously, as this one did.

Before I go on to tell you the next part of my story, let me take a moment to consider how we might think about the outcome I have just described in the terms of the formulation of experience that I described previously in this chapter. What was it that became meaningful? What had been without meaning? I would say that whatever was not meaningful, it was not a particular experience; the problem could not be assuaged by the revelation of a particular content. No, what Alan and I would not allow to become meaningful was an aspect of our identities—both of us. Alan felt stifled by the expectation that he attend sessions, but he could not tolerate being the bad boy, and so he managed to miss his sessions while feeling utterly helpless to do otherwise. And from my end: I didn't want to believe I was trying to persuade or coerce him to attend his sessions, and so preserved my image of myself as a good analyst by expressing myself in interpretations that were manifestly about his unconscious motives, but which probably also conveyed to him the message that he should cut it out.

I have less and less interest in insight—the creation of particular thoughts—as the agent of therapeutic change, and more and more interest in the expansion of relational freedom (Stern, 2013, 2015). I think that coming to his sessions and talking to me had ceased to "feel like me" to Alan. Being in sessions had come to feel dead to him, meaningless, a dissociative performance of the sort he put on for his mother. His unconsciously mediated refusal to attend was, in a sense, a stand of integrity, a poorly understood and self-destructive attempt to live his own life. His sessions came to feel as if they belonged to someone else, as so much of his life has always felt. What I said to Alan about talking about whatever was in his head had the effect of helping him to formulate his experience with me, awakening his capacity to feel that his sessions were his own, so that the experience came to "feel like me." The experience became meaningful and alive once again, and Alan thereafter could use it in the spontaneous creation of living—in this case, in the spontaneous living of his sessions themselves.

Now let me turn the clock forward about a year and a half and tell you about another episode between Alan and me, again about his attendance at sessions. In the 18 months since the last episode, Alan missed only a handful of sessions, and those only in the most recent 6 months. He did have the same kinds of difficulties getting out of bed and temptations to get back into bed, and at those times we had held sessions on the phone (again, it was prior to COVID). Sometimes Alan called me at the time of the session, sometimes I called him. But we almost always held sessions, and we both felt that, despite this continuing problem, Alan's life was moving forward. During this last year and a half Alan had initiated and then deepened his first romantic relationship. He and his girlfriend were close, quite emotionally intimate, and looked to one another for support and understanding. He began a new job, and he managed it without the unbearable anxiety that had plagued him in earlier years of the treatment.

But despite this improvement, Alan's anxiety frequently remained intense, and he continued to have problems with what he now called his "anxious sleepiness," an intense weariness that overcomes him even now, often quite suddenly, and knocks him out, even in the middle of the day, and can lead to him being late to work or missing work altogether, letting down his girlfriend, and missing his sessions with me. While I have always been convinced by its meaningful timing that the sleepiness is a psychological symptom, we have done the due diligence: sleep studies proved negative for anything physiological.

A couple of weeks prior to the events I am about to recount, Alan, who had sessions on Monday, Wednesday, and Thursday, missed Thursday. By text he apologized and said he would see me Monday. Then, Saturday night, he texted me again, writing that, "I seem to have really upset Susan [author's note: his girlfriend] and I'm terribly worried about it." I texted back asking if he wanted to talk, and he said, "If you could find a moment I would really appreciate it." I knew that the fact that he'd missed the Thursday appointment meant that texting me now, and answering me directly about wanting to talk, especially since it was a Saturday night, came at a cost to him. I knew that he worried (and not unreasonably) that he was disturbing me.

I have seldom felt that Alan's texts were intrusive, and I didn't feel that way this time. Alan had texted me outside sessions, but he had never asked me to call him, so I understood this to be a significant event. I called him and we talked for 15 or 20 minutes. I listened to the problem and helped him give shape to his thoughts. It turned out Alan had slept through an important occasion, disappointing Susan and embarrassing her, because she couldn't answer the questions of friends and family who asked where he was. When Alan woke up and called her in a panic, Susan had told him angrily that she didn't want to talk to him. I suggested that, if he wanted to communicate with her about this, it might be easier for her, because she was angry, if he texted her instead of calling. When Alan and I hung up, he thanked me with particular emphasis. He wanted me to know he really appreciated it. Then, half an hour later, he sent me the text he had sent to Susan and asked me, "Do you think I'm communicating the right thing?" I saw no point in doing anything other than trying to be directly helpful, feeling that anything else would shame him unnecessarily, so I texted simply, "Very beautiful, Alan." And it was. It was deeply felt. In that text, one of the things Alan said to Susan, referring to the temptations of his anxious sleepiness, was this: "My doctor is more confident than I am that he and I can make progress on this issue, so I work to make headway as hard as I am able." I said in my return text, "You're right, I do believe you can make headway on this, even though I also understand that you are mystified about the why and how of it."

That was Saturday night. On Monday morning, contrary even to *my* expectation, Alan missed his appointment. He called me later in the day, so desperate with shame that he could hardly speak to me. He just couldn't believe he'd overslept again, especially after having asked me to speak to him on Saturday night. We spoke briefly and agreed to meet at our regular time on Wednesday.

When Wednesday rolled around, Alan arrived, lay down on the couch, and began to tell me with real sorrow that he was "completely pathetic." Trying to be a collaborative patient, he told me that he knows there must be reasons he didn't want to come to sessions. He knew that it's not just happening *to* him, but that it's him doing this, and that he must not be doing everything he can to get here.

I, of course, have often said such things to him—in interpretive, noncritical form. There was a time, during the first long episode of Alan's problems with getting to his sessions, when his absences sometimes provoked me, and I'd be irritated. But not now. I did explicitly recognize that there might very well be a hostile intention buried somewhere in all of this, but I trusted that the absence on my part of an affective response to such an intention (I did not even feel the kind of uncomfortable "snag" or "chafing" (Stern, 2004) that I associate with the presence of an enactment as yet invisible) was a good reason not to make that the focus of my intervention. Instead, I now found myself identified with the part of Alan who really was disappointed in himself and felt like he was a failure, what he had just described as "completely pathetic." Without giving the matter a great deal of thought, other than to turn my attention inward and reassure myself that I believed I was speaking in support of the treatment and Alan himself, I said, "You know, Alan, actually I think that you always do as much as you can to get to your sessions." I meant this, despite my recognition of the possibility that we might eventually complicate our picture of such events with the recognition of provocation on Alan's part. I believed that, within the limits imposed by his unconscious involvement, which were (by definition) outside his ken, Alan was indeed doing his best to come, and was as baffled as I was by his difficulty.

There was a long silence, perhaps two or three minutes. Then Alan sighed deeply and said mournfully, "I think I don't take very good care of myself."

I didn't know yet all of what this meant (it turned out to mean a great deal), but I did get the clear sense that Alan was conveying something in saying this that was very different from the shame and self-criticism of the moments before, something that came from a place more compassionate to himself, and I also felt clearly that this communication had to do with Alan's understanding of what I had just said to him. He had heard or felt in what I said something that had allowed him to let up on himself a bit. Let me state the obvious: it would not have had the same effect for me to have suggested to him that he cultivate greater compassion for himself, or for me to have made the observation that he was being pretty hard on himself. Comments like that would not have rung quite true. They aren't exactly what I meant. There wasn't any good reason, after all, for him *not* to feel critical of himself about this. It's just that self-criticism wasn't really to the point. And so I didn't say anything that attempted to make him feel better. I did believe what I said, though, and I think Alan could feel all this. He sensed that I was speaking spontaneously. In retrospect, this was a moment, I think, when Alan expected, without exactly knowing that he expected it, that I would react in a way that would shame him about his absence, but I did not react that way, and he saw that, and believed in my sincerity. It was a moment in which Alan had an experience of what I have referred to as "seeing you seeing me" (see Chapter 4).

The main thing here to which I want to draw attention is what I believe was the sudden shift in how Alan was able to think and feel, apparently as a result of what I said to him. I want to underline, that is, that the range of what can be thought and felt broadens when a frozen part of the field thaws. When Alan said that he thought he didn't take very good care of himself, and said it so sadly, we can see that the range of his thoughts and feelings about himself had widened and deepened. Alan moved from the perception that he was a bad guy and a failure to the feeling that perhaps his internal demands were somehow unreasonable, because they amounted to insisting that he do something (always get to his sessions) that, for reasons he and I didn't understand, he couldn't do. I think he suddenly found himself think-ing that perhaps he deserved more understanding than he had imagined. Maybe his desire for nurture wasn't merely pathetic. Maybe that desire for nurture could actually "feel like me." The main thing I am trying to do here is to present Alan's new freedom to think and feel as an outcome of what took place between us, and not simply as an interpretation, a piece of new information that I imparted to him. It was a change in the course of our relationship, in the field between us. If there was revelation of content, it followed from the change between us (see Chapter 4).

I asked Alan what he meant when he said that maybe he didn't take good care of himself. Again, a long silence. I did already know something about what I had asked him. I knew about a character in Alan's inner life we called "the little boy," who wanted to be loved and taken care of, and about whom grown-up Alan feels deeply ashamed. Alan wanted not to feel like the little boy, and not to be identified with the little boy by anyone else. Another relevant thing I knew: when Alan missed sessions, he felt appreciative of the calls I made to try to reach him. They made him feel well cared for, and he was ashamed of the pleasure he took in that. He had even imagined (reasonably enough, to me) that provoking me to behave this way could be one of the many reasons he missed sessions. One more thing I knew: when he was growing up, Alan looked forward on weekend mornings to being able to go to his parents' room and "cuddle" with them in bed. This meant a great deal to him. At some point, when he was perhaps seven or eight, the parents, involved in a divorce, stopped sleeping together and suddenly curtailed the cuddling, telling him he was too old for it. For the "little boy," this felt awful, especially what Alan had taken to be the suggestion that he was a horribly needy baby.

It was I who broke the silence that followed my question to Alan about what he thought he meant when he said that maybe he didn't take very good care of himself. I asked him if not being taken care of might have something to do with the little boy. He said yes, of course it did, and we talked about the little boy for a few minutes. I don't remember exactly what was said then, but I did find myself in possession of a new impression of the little boy as a dissociated presence within Alan—not as concrete as an alter, but certainly a presence. And so I asked Alan whether maybe the little boy could talk to me directly.

Alan seemed uncertain. He said he wasn't sure that could ever happen. Why? Because it would require that the situation feel completely safe, and Alan didn't know exactly how it could feel that way. A few minutes earlier, Alan had begun talking about the part of him that he felt most comfortable with as "the dominant part of me." And so now, I said yes, of course it didn't feel safe, because the reason Alan was there, at least according to his dominant part, and probably according to most of the rest of the world, as well (at least in Alan's mind), including me, was to get rid of the little boy. Yes, he said, again sadly. After a minute or two he began to talk about the little boy; he didn't yet allow the little boy to speak for himself, but he talked about him in a different way, and in more depth, than he had before.

"Did I ever tell you about the parts of my personality?" asked Alan. I told him he hadn't. Well, he said, he had always imagined that he had three parts: his central nervous system, through which everything had to pass; the right side of his body; and the left side of his body. The right side of his body contained all of what he felt was physically and emotionally strong: it was thoroughly level-headed and in control, brilliant, unflappable, athletic, dependable, cheerful, polite, and grown up. The right side was self-contained and needed nothing from anyone. And then there was the left side— physically and emotionally weak (by which Alan meant pathetic, needing nurturance and hoping for love), poorly coordinated, unable to cope with disappointment (especially in matters of love and nurture), and sometimes irrationally angry.

We didn't need to make the obvious connection, although one of us may have done so: the left side was the little boy; the right side was the part of him he had grown up trying to feel that he was, the side of him on display for the world to admire, especially his parents' worlds. Privately, I began to think about the consequences of Alan's dissociated identifications, or self-states:[1] it made Alan humiliated and disgusted with himself to be the reviled left side, although that side, being the imagined site of his most vulnerable feelings, also needed his protection; and to be the right side made him feel expansive, powerful, and desirable, while carrying the risk of being grandiose, full of himself, and feeling better than other people, ways of being he decried.

Alan now returned to his history, telling me once again a story I knew, but that he told, and I heard, with a new sense of its meaning. He was in seventh grade and had already put on the weight that has tortured him ever since. In PE class, the boys were required to run a mile. Alan was the slowest, and so when he neared the end of the mile, all the rest of the boys, having finished their runs, were crowded together, watching and jeering him. Alan decided to deal with the situation by clowning. He turned around, intending to run the last hundred yards backwards, and he grinned and waved at his gathered schoolmates. But he miscalculated and ran into a wall along the side of the track, sprawling awkwardly on the ground. His schoolmates laughed so hard some of them fell on the ground holding their sides. This is a humiliation that still cuts deeply, and it is the quintessential experience of the left side of Alan's body.

It turned out that the sides of Alan's body were part of a larger left/right mythology, which now began to come to light. Alan asked me if he'd told me about the way he had to climb stairs in the subway. Again, he hadn't. It turns out that, when he arrives at a set of stairs, Alan must calculate in a split second which foot to use on the first step. The point is to set the foot on the first step that will result in the right foot stepping first onto the next floor. This protects him, because the side of the body that first touches the next floor is identified with that floor. It is a safer and better world for Alan for any floor to be part of the right-side world and not the left-side one.

I have ranged far afield in telling you these details of what happened between Alan and me that day and soon after. I have done that for a reason. I want to illustrate the point that is my reason for writing this chapter: what can be formulated in the minds of analyst and patient is determined by the state of the interpersonal field. To the extent that the field is unconstricted— which is to say, to the extent that it is not dominated by compulsive, dissociative enactments—there is relative freedom for analyst and patient to formulate their experience in whatever way allows the treatment to proceed as spontaneously as possible. Under these circumstances, analyst and patient are each able to accept and use their experience in the ongoing construction of creative living.

But to the extent that the field is frozen, constricted by enactment, experience remains dissociated and therefore unmeaningful and unformulated. It doesn't "feel like me." I am making the case that, in the illustration I have just offered, my very simple, spontaneous suggestion that Alan did his best to attend his sessions had the effect of melting a frozen place in the interpersonal field and made possible, in that spot in the field, the replacement of constriction with spontaneity, and the development of meaningfulness from material that had not been meaningful before. This event took place at a tipping point in the clinical process that grew out of the ongoing relatedness between Alan and me in ways that we can imagine in retrospect but that we cannot necessarily know with any certainty.

After the intervention, like water suddenly turning to ice at 32 degrees, certain material that had been without an alive sense of meaning in the minds of both Alan and me became meaningful. This material was not limited to the meanings of his missed sessions, but included also material he told me about during the rest of that session, and on into the following week: the meanings of the right and left sides of his body, walking up the steps in the subway, and other things that I have not reported here.

That is, while I don't know exactly why my suggestion that Alan did his best to get to his sessions had the effect of helping Alan to allow these matters to attain formulation, I do believe that is what happened. Alan had always "sort of" known some of these things, but they were shameful and quite private—private not only to others, such as me, but in an important sense private to Alan himself. He had never thought to tell anyone about them; he had not even formulated them in verbal language. They had lived a shadow life in his mind. Now, though, these meanings came to "feel like me" in the new interpersonal context created between us; new relational freedom came into being. And the consequence was that all these matters, the absence of which had not even been registered prior to my intervention about getting to sessions, were now explicitly welcomed to the interpersonal field. New meaning emerged from unformulated experience.

Note

1 "Dissociation" here does not mean that the psychic material in question is completely unavailable. Alan knew all about the right side and the left side. "Dissociation" here refers to the fact that Alan must *be* only the right side or the left side; they cannot co-exist in his experience of himself in the moment.

References

Bromberg, P.M. (2006). *Awakening the Dreamer: Clinical Journeys*. New York and London: Routledge.

Bromberg, P.M. (2011). *The Shadow of the Tsunami: And the Growth of the Relational Mind*. New York and London: Routledge.

Merleau-Ponty, M. (1945). *The Phenomenology of Perception*, trans. Colin Smith. New York: Routledge & Kegan, 1962.

Stern, D.B. (1989). The analyst's unformulated experience of the patient. *Contemporary Psychoanalysis* 25:1–33.

Stern, D.B. (1997). *Unformulated Experience: From Dissociation to Imagination in Psychoanalysis*. New York and London: Routledge.

Stern, D.B. (2001). Words and wordlessness in the psychoanalytic situation. *Journal of the American Psychoanalytic Association*, 50: 221–247.

Stern, D.B. (2004). The eye sees itself: Dissociation, enactment, and the achievement of conflict. *Contemporary Psychoanalysis*, 40: 197–237.

Stern, D.B. (2013). Relational freedom and therapeutic action. *Journal of the American Psychoanalytic Association*, 61: 227–255.

Stern, D.B. (2015). *Relational Freedom: Emergent Properties of the Interpersonal Field*. New York and London: Routledge.

Stern, D.B. (2019). *The Infinity of the Unsaid: Unformulated Experience, Language, and the Nonverbal*. London and New York: Routledge.

Taylor, C. (2016). *The Language Animal: The Full Shape of the Human Linguistic Capacity*. Cambridge, MA: Harvard University Press.

Part II

Dissociation

Chapter 9

Dissociation and unformulated experience

A psychoanalytic model of mind

This chapter is an overview of my understanding of the processes of dissociation and unformulated experience, with the aim of illustrating how these ideas can be understood as the basis for a psychoanalytic model of mind. The chapter was first published, in an earlier form, in an encyclopedic presentation of dissociation: Dissociation and the Dissociative Disorders:DSM-V and Beyond, *edited by P.F. Dell and J.A. O'Neil in 2009. The version of the chapter printed here is a revision prepared for the second edition of that book. This summary includes a brief overview of most of the revisions in the theory of unformulated experience that I wrote long after the original presentation of the idea (Stern, 1983, 1997). These revisions were presented in my most recent book (Stern, 2019), and largely have to do with expanding the theory in a way that allows the conceptualization of two kinds of formulation of meaning: not only verbal, as in the original form of the theory, but also nonverbal.*

While dissociation is conceived in many ways in the trauma literature, theories of dissociation tend to center around the idea of a self-protective process that takes place when the events of life are beyond tolerance. We leave ourselves, so to speak; psychically, we turn away.

In the particular way I use the term, these meanings are preserved, but expanded. Dissociation is not only a fallback position. It is also part of a psychoanalytic understanding of the nature of experiencing, a means of understanding both the unconscious and the defensive processes, on the one hand, and consciousness on the other. Thus, dissociation is one of the most significant components of a psychoanalytic model of mind. When I first presented my ideas (Stern, 1983), my inspirations were both psychoanalytic (Levenson, 1972/2005, 1983/2005, 1991/2016, 2017; Schafer, 1976,

DOI: 10.4324/9781032688893-11

1983, 1992; Schachtel, 1959; Spence, 1982; Sullivan, 1940, 1953) and philosophical (Fingarette, 1969; Gadamer, 1965/2004, 1966; James, 1890; Merleau-Ponty, 1945/1962, 1964; Taylor, 2016). I have sought to develop a relational perspective on mind that is at once clinically useful, hermeneutically grounded, and phenomenologically recognizable.

I came to dissociation via the influence of Harry Stack Sullivan (1940, 1953). Sullivan differed from the classical analysts of his day in seeing the origin of "problems in living" (a term he preferred to "psychopathology") not in the clash of drive and defense, as was the dominant view in his time, but in what had actually happened in relationships with significant others. Relationships and the need for them replaced drive and defense as the stuff of life. For Sullivan, dissociation, not repression, was the primary defensive maneuver, because he understood the primary danger to be the revival of intolerable experience, not the breakthrough of primitive endogenous fantasy. (Sullivan's conception is distinguished from Freud's theory of repression in the following section.) From a modern perspective, we could say that, for Sullivan, the great threat was retraumatization. Eventually, Sullivan's views formed the basis for what became interpersonal psychoanalysis (see Lionells et al., 1995; Stern, et al., 1995, Stern & Hirsch, 2017a, b), and Sullivan and interpersonal thinking then became one of the primary springboards for relational psychoanalysis (e.g., Mitchell, 1988, 1993, 1997, 2000; Mitchell & Aron, 1999). For the most part, I will be able to credit in this short account only the most immediate sources of my views.

The brevity necessary in a summary chapter such as this one precludes several subject matters I would like to be able to include, but cannot. The first is clinical illustration. This I particularly regret, because the ideas were created in the attempt to make a clinical contribution (see my work in the reference list, which contains many clinical illustrations). The second is the body of work that has been devoted to the dissociation of self-states from one another, pioneered especially by Bromberg (1998, 2006, 2011). I have often written about dissociation and mutual enactment in the treatment situation as the defensively motivated separation of self-states. While that view is easily integrated with the views I present here, and has been (Stern, 2010, 2015), I will only be able to consider it in passing. This subject deserves a chapter of its own.

In recent years, I have been particularly interested in the comparison and contrast of the theory of unformulated experience, in which dissociation plays a prominent role, with Bionian field theory (e.g., Ferro, 2009; Ferro & Civitarese, 2016; see also Stern, 2015, Chapters 3 & 4), and also with theories in which, as in the theory of unformulated experience, states of mind are inaccessible not because they are repressed but because they cannot be given psychic representation at all (Bion, 1962/1977; Green, 1975, 1999; Laplanche, 1999, 2011; Botella & Botella, 2005; Levine, Reed & Scarfone, 2013; McGleughlin, 2015, 2020). I must be satisfied in this chapter merely to make reference to the many links between this material and the phenomena and theory of dissociation and unformulated experience.

Assumptions underlying the repression model

In order to contextualize dissociation as a defensive process, I begin by outlining the ideas from which I depart. I start with certain assumptions underlying the repression-based classical psychoanalytic model of mind, and then contrast that perspec- tive with a dissociation-based view. I do not intend my description of repression and the primary and secondary processes to be an authoritative account; rather, this description of the primary elements of the traditional psychoanalytic theory of mind serves as a foil against the background of which I clarify my own views and highlight major differences in emphasis of the two ways of thinking.

Mental representations due to be repressed, wrote Freud (1915a), are both repulsed by consciousness and attracted by previous repressed contents in the unconscious. Once repressed, representations can be cognized only via the primary process, Freud's (1895, 1900, 1915b) term for the means by which he believed the unconscious (or later in his work, the id) continuously sought to reinstate the perceptions associated with the original satisfactions of drive. The primary process seeks hallucinatory wish fulfillment. Except for certain nonlinguistic functions (such as the use of words as simple labels), language appears in the primary process only in a regressed and primitive form.[1]

But Freud also believed that, for those aspects of subjectivity that could be represented in language, consciousness was the natural state. These aspects of mental functioning, the secondary process, had been traditionally described in the psychology of the day: waking thought, attention, judgment, reasoning, and controlled (consciously chosen) action. On one hand, the secondary process regulates the primary process, inhibiting hallucinatory wish fulfillment (at least during waking life) and heedless observance of the pleasure principle (which would bring even greater unpleasure in its wake). It might also be said, though, that the secondary process is merely an *indirect* route to drive satisfaction, one shaped by a respect for the complexities of reality (Freud, 1895, 1900, 1915b).

In Freud's thinking, there is an insistent pressure for drive to be represented in awareness. All repressed representations, in the form of what Freud (1915a, b) called "derivatives" of the repressed or the unconscious, press for expression; derivatives "want" to be released, to be satisfied, just as drive itself does. And so we have the doctrine of the return of the repressed, the continuous pressure toward consciousness exerted by contents that have been repressed (Freud, 1915a). In turn, this urgent pressure is the origin of the necessity for the development by the ego of unconscious defenses: because the sudden appearance of certain drive-related material in consciousness would arouse intolerable anxiety (that is, in the end there would be more unpleasure than pleasure), there come to be processes in the mind that, when unconsciously deployed, prevent that kind of sudden eruption. Although the repressed does continuously come back in the form of "a *compromise* between the repressed ideas and the repressing ones" (Freud, 1896, p. 170; italics in original), the ego turns out to be a worthy adversary.

Despite being the prize over which the battle between drive and defense is fought, however, that part of the ego which we know as consciousness is itself a fairly passive aspect of the mind in Freud's scheme. The contents of consciousness are not specifically selected. Rather, they are what can be tolerated by the defenses, what remains when the smoke of battle has cleared, the outcome, an epiphenomenon, a byproduct, of the clash of drive and defense. Consciousness is not the main event; it is what remains after the great events have taken place. Just as symptoms or dreams are the effects of parts of the mind beyond themselves (i.e., the unconscious), and in that sense, consciousness, too, is a passive record in Freud's work. In Freud's terms, we can imagine consciousness as the most superficial layer of an archeological dig—a fascinating, essential record we must study if we want to appreciate the events that, in disguised fashion, are sedimented in it—but the record of a compromise nevertheless.

Like other writers of his day, Freud accepted without reservation the idea that the mind—and therefore, the unconscious—is composed of fully formed contents. This unconsidered belief derives from the deep and culture-wide assumption, explicitly accepted by Freud (Schimek, 1975), that perception is a sensory given, and that experience is therefore rooted in mental elements that come to us already fully formed. Freud's era took place long before the development of the "New Look" in perception research (Bruner & Klein, 1960; Bruner & Postman, 1949), in which perception was reconceptualized in constructivist terms. Even today, and especially in everyday life, we are seldom aware that we construct our own experience. We are much more likely to feel as if everything we experience was already there, fully formed, merely awaiting our registration of it. The view I present later directly contradicts this view.

Following in the wake of the assumption that perception is merely a matter of registering fully formed sensory stimuli is an equally crucial corollary just as unconsidered and widely accepted in psychoanalysis today as the first point was in Freud's era: if we are unaware of some aspect of experience, it is because we have made ourselves unaware. That is, because the elements of thought are always already present in our minds, defense is necessarily a matter of unconsciously refusing to acknowledge fully formed and pre-existing mental content. Lack of awareness is unconsciously purposeful. Most psychoanalysts still accept these postulates about consciousness and the unconscious in an unquestioning way—that is, without considering that they represent only one of the alternatives. Later in this chapter I will champion one of those neglected alternatives.

These points, of course, amount to Freud's hypothesis of repression, the foundation for virtually every model of unconscious defensive processes since Freud. In the terms of repression, to keep contents unconscious requires effort, what Laplanche and Pontalis (1973) call "a complex interplay of decathexes, recathexes and anticathexes [of] the instinctual representatives" (p. 394). These "instinctual representatives" are not "bound," as is the secondary process, and so it is their inclination to occupy the entire mind. In this "barbarians-at-the-gates" sense, consciousness is part of their "natural" domain, a land they would overrun immediately without the intervention of defense. It would probably be more accurate, actually, to say that the id is continuously trying to convert the rest of subjectivity into a version of itself, a land run by the rules of the primary process. In the imagery of a less military metaphor, it is as if the repressed were a beach ball we are trying to keep underwater by sitting on it. Unless we balance ourselves with the greatest care, expending a good deal of energy in the process (and even then we may be unsuccessful), the beach ball explodes out from under us and shoots up to the surface.

And so, in this view, unless defense interrupts the process, understanding ourselves and the world around us ought to be natural and effortless. In Freud's view, we already contain the knowing we need. It is there inside us, formed and ready: *"the essence of repression lies simply in turning something away, and keeping it at a distance, from the conscious"* (1915a, p. 147; italics in original). Except when we are genuinely ignorant, the thoughts and feelings we need in order to make sense of our lives would come into our minds if we would but allow them to do so. It seems that understanding should arise by itself; the process of coming to understand does not seem to require any particular explanation. *Mis*understanding, on the other hand, is an anomaly, *mis*understanding is the event we need to explain. We can misunderstand out of ignorance, of course. But with that single exception, misunderstanding is anomalous in the perspective associated with the repression hypothesis: when we do not understand, it can only be because the natural unfolding of comprehension has been interrupted by unconscious defensive processes.

Notice that this view implies yet another assumption, one much more open to question now than even 30 or 40 years ago, and still taken for granted in many quarters: if we accept that the truth impresses itself upon us, then we are (usually without realizing it) taking the position that truth is singular and objectively verifiable. In this view, the unconscious is made up of the truths we will not accept—fully formed feelings, thoughts, and mental "objects" that have the kind of invisible, objective existence of a stage set behind a curtain. The goodness or fullness of our understanding is judged by reference to whether we accept the truth, which, in turn, is defined as the mental representation of objective reality.

The question, then, is whether what we understand corresponds to objective reality. For this reason, the position I am describing often has been described as the "correspondence" view of truth: we judge that we have reached the truth when our understanding "matches" or "corresponds to" the supposedly objective reality that we are trying to grasp.

One might think that the respect for psychic reality (i.e., inner reality, the mind's own reality) in classical psychoanalytic views is inconsistent with the correspondence view. After all, in Freud's theory and the theories of those who followed him, psychic reality is the entirely *subjective* foundation of motivation, and therefore of psychic life. You cannot understand someone else's motives without first understanding the subjectively based intrapsychic fantasies that underlie them. In this sense, it is true that psychic reality is hardly an objective phenomenon. However, this subjectivity can still be *understood* in objective terms. As non-rational as it is, psychic reality can still be seen as a singular, predetermined phenomenon that allows only one objective understanding. In most cases, classical analysts do write, as a matter of fact, as if the proper psychoanalytic understanding of psychic reality is an objective understanding, as if the nature of subjectivity (psychic reality) is objectively verifiable. Nor does the existence of multiple subjective truths about the same mental contents necessarily contradict the correspondence view, because each of these multiple truths can still be understood to have an objective existence.

Note that the correspondence view implies that any influence on understanding besides objective reality must be misleading; this implication leads directly to our usual definition of bias or prejudice as a predisposition or preconception that distorts knowing by reducing our capacity to allow reality simply to register itself. (We shall find a different view in hermeneutics and the dissociation view associated with it.) From the correspondence perspective, understanding is absolute and noncontextual: the nature of truth in one circumstance is the same as it is in another. These points uniformly underline the correspondence view's tendency to portray understanding as passive and unidirectional, a straightforward inscription of world on mind. The only effort required by the process of knowing is expended in the removal of impediments to a natural unfolding. Thus, we understand by clearing away the obstacles that prevent mind from following its inclination to shape itself in reality's image.

But what if things are otherwise?

Unformulated experience: A dissociation-based psychoanalytic model of mind

In point of fact, almost everyone these days agrees that things *are* otherwise. Almost no one accepts the correspondence view anymore—neither psychologists, psychoanalysts, philosophers, nor cognitive neuroscientists. Virtually no one would argue today, at least not in the most traditional way, that truth is defined simply by objective observation. Knowing and understanding are constructed, not merely registered.

And yet many classical psychoanalysts still accept a modified version of the older view. Lawrence Friedman (2000), for instance, one of the most influential of Freudian theorists, champions objectivity as an ideal, describing objective observation as a construction built up from many small observations, each of which, in and of itself, may be subjective.

The particular dissociation-based view I am describing, rooted in the concept of unformulated experience, grew from the same soil that nurtured the move away from correspondence theory, and so it contradicts many of the assumptions underlying the repression-based view. I address these differences in the same order I presented the assumptions discussed above.

Perception is *not* a sensory given in the dissociation model; instead, perception is constructed from a less fully formulated state: there is an ongoing process of emergence in perception, thought, and feeling, from vagueness to clarity. Mental contents therefore are not necessarily fully formed, especially unconscious contents. Instead, they are *unformulated*, less clearly actualized than they will be when they are formulated. The unconscious is composed of *potential* experience, contents that do not yet have an explicit, knowable shape, and that may take any one of several or many possible shapes when eventually they are formulated.

To begin with, my position was that the formulation of meaning takes place exclusively in language (e.g., Stern, 1983, 1997). I took that position because my purpose at that time was limited to charting the path of experience from its unformulated beginnings to the explicitly meaningful shape it takes in reflective awareness. I believed that only when experience is formulated in verbal language could it be consciously, explicitly reflected on, and of course the creation of a capacity to reflect in areas of our lives in which we could not reflect before has always been a hallmark of psychoanalysis.

I have not changed my view about the nature of explicit reflection, although I do now consider therapeutic action to be less a matter of reflection, or understanding, than of greater freedom in the interpersonal field (which then allows greater understanding). Recently, I have expanded the theory of unformulated experience to include formulated *nonverbal* meaning (Stern, 2018). In keeping with that expanded purpose, I now believe we should recognize two varieties of unformulated experience. Some unformulated experience, when its potential is formulated, tends toward *articulation as verbal-reflective meaning*; this is the kind of formulation I have described before, the kind of formulation that allows explicit reflection. But a second kind of unformulated experience, when its potential is formulated, tends toward *realization as nonverbal meaning*. Some nonverbal meanings, once they are realized, can then be articulated as verbal-reflective meaning and enter explicit, reflective awareness. But many nonverbal meanings— procedural meanings are a good example—are not necessarily amenable to articulation in verbal language, and therefore cannot be reflected on. These latter meanings do participate in the creation of living, but in their nonverbal form, not in a verbally articulated one.

Let me offer a brief, simple example of what I mean by realized nonverbal meaning. Let us say that a particular (fictional) patient is highly anxious about sexual arousal, so anxious that he can allow himself only a very pale version of the sensory pleasure of sex. The unformulated experience of a sexual encounter contains myriad affective and sensory possibilities, only some of which are realized in anyone's experience. In the case of our fictional patient, the possibilities that are realized—the nonverbal sensory and affective meanings that he derives from the sexual experience—are notably muted. The man can reflect on these muted realizations, but only to a certain extent. Because language is not an adequate means of symbolizing the nuances of sensory experience, our patient can reflect on only a portion of even that part of his unformulated sexual experience that has been realized as nonverbal meaning.

Perhaps the most significant role played by realized nonverbal meaning is its part in ongoing relatedness. Imagine my fictional patient in a social situation in which flirtation is a possibility. Flirtation, we shall say, has been infected by the patient's anxiety about sexuality. My patient is therefore hobbled in such a context. He is unlikely to have access to the experience that he would need in order to make ongoing, intuitive sense of the other person's flirting, or to participate in a natural way in the flirting himself. He is overcome with anxiety, both because of what he does grasp (again, nonverbally) about this kind of relatedness, and because of what his anxiety prevents him from comprehending.

All of us bring with us into each moment an unformulated "way of being" from which we unconsciously select and develop the meanings that become our verbal and nonverbal experience of that moment. The parts of our ways of being that we cannot tolerate are not selected; we can say that these possibilities are dissociated, verbal and nonverbal alike. The parts of our ways of being that we can tolerate, on the other hand, are either articulated (in verbal-reflective meaning) or realized (in nonverbal meaning). We are able to use the articulated and realized parts of experience in the ongoing negotiation of relatedness with others. But to the extent that we do not articulate or realize our ways of being in any particular moment, our flexibility and freedom to relate to the other in that moment are compromised.

In the case of both verbal-reflective articulations and nonverbal realizations, then, consciousness is not a passive outcome, but a creation, an achievement that demands the expenditure of effort. We understand only what we formulate, and that process of construction requires mental work. If experience has a "natural" state, it is neither articulation nor realization, but lack of formulation. Without the application of attention and effort, unformulated experience stays just as it is. The contents of consciousness are therefore *not* merely what is left over after an internal battle. They are specifically and actively selected according to our (conscious and unconscious) interests and values, in interaction with the contexts in which the formulation of our experience takes place. The metaphor of the beach ball hurtling up from the depths as soon as it is no longer held down is replaced by a symbol of effort, perhaps something like a heavy adjustable lens that must be pointed in a particular direction and then wrested to a new setting in order to bring an unconsciously chosen view into clarity. Consciousness is an active creation, an accomplishment, not a leftover.

If unconscious mental contents are unformulated, it no longer makes sense to conceive of defense as a refusal to acknowledge a truth that already exists in parts of our minds to which we have no access. Instead, defense becomes the prevention of the formulation of unformulated experience— the prevention of the very existence of articulations and realizations. If we define dissociation as the inability or unconscious unwillingness to formulate experience in symbolic form (and most of us do define it that way), it follows that to prevent experience from being shaped into verbal-reflective or nonverbal meaning is to dissociate.[2] The primary defense is therefore dissociation. In this way of thinking, it is not fully formed mental contents that must be controlled (because they are not "there" to *be* controlled). What must be controlled by defense is instead the effort that we would need to expend in order to formulate the unformulated. The willingness to make this effort, to try to open ourselves to what is questionable, and therefore to what it is possible to formulate, is what I refer to as "curiosity." In this frame of reference, defense, or dissociation, can be defined either as the unconscious refusal to formulate experience or as the unconsciously motivated refusal to be curious.

Remember that in the repression model, understanding is the natural state of affairs, interrupted only by the distortions of defense. It is probably clear by now that this cannot be true of the dissociation model I am presenting. If understanding always remains to be constructed, then it is not the *presence* of understanding, but its *absence* that is the natural state of affairs. Understanding does not happen "by itself"; it is an outcome of some kind of effort. *Lack* of understanding is what happens "by itself." And therefore the mystery that surrounds not-knowing in the repression model is transferred to the process of understanding—that is, to the process by which meaning is formulated.

What is understanding?

I have already said that dissociation is the unconscious refusal to be curious; I have also said that curiosity is what makes understanding possible; and finally, I have said that understanding, not the absence of understanding, is now the mysterious event requiring explanation. And so, if we are to understand dissociation, we must understand the nature of understanding itself. What process is it that dissociation interrupts? How should we understand understanding?

According to hermemeutic philosopher Hans-Georg Gadamer (1965/2004, 1976), we can never perceive reality itself; that is, we can never perceive reality in any absolute or unmediated sense.[3] Instead, we construct reality according to the various traditions sedimented in our languages and cultures. Reality is mediated to us by the meanings that have currency in our time and place. Language and culture are the lens through which our understanding of the world and ourselves comes into being. And so in Gadamer's work we have a view that is neither objectivist nor relativist, but that charts a course between the two (Bernstein, 1983; Sass, 1988). On the one hand, truth is constrained by reality, but on the other, each of our formulations is only one of the possibilities, potentiated by its context. Reality is manifold; truth is multiple.

Gadamer redefines "bias" and "prejudice," arguing that our "preconceptions," the meanings that our cultures predispose us to find, are what make it possible for us to make any meaning at all. We depend on bias and prejudice. They are crucial: "It is not so much our judgments as our prejudgments that constitute our being" (Gadamer, quoted by Linge, 1976, p. xvii). Elsewhere Gadamer (1966) says, "Prejudices are biases of our openness to the world.

They are simply conditions whereby we experience something – whereby what we encounter says something to us" (p. 8). And yet, Gadamer (1965/ 2004) also tells us that learning something new is a matter of transcending these prejudices: "Every experience worthy of the name runs counter to our expectation ... Insight is more than the knowledge of this or that situation. It always involves an escape from something that had deceived us and held us captive" (pp. 319–320). Prejudices are both the ground on which we can experience anything at all and the blinders we must manage to reflect on and disconfirm if we are to experience anything new.

For hermeneuticists, including Gadamer, the process by which we bring our prejudices into play and then disconfirm them is the hermeneutic circle. The idea arises from a paradox. We can understand only those communications that we can locate in their proper contexts. Unless an utterance can be placed in the appropriate configuration of tradition, its meaning remains obscure. Imagine trying to understand certain passages in Freud without knowing that he was taking issue with Jung; or trying to understand a dream without knowing the events of the day preceding it, or the patient's associations to it; or trying to understand a patient's barely supportable characterization of a co-worker as greedy without knowing that the patient himself is terribly afraid of being greedy.

We comprehend by means of continuously projecting complete understandings into communications from the other, communications we actually understand only partially. We extrapolate complete understandings on the basis of the partial understandings we already have. And where do the partial understandings come from? They are in turn stimulated by the complete understandings we project. Thus is the circle closed. But of course, something else must happen, or else comprehension would be nothing more than self-reference. All comprehension is a process of projecting partial understandings into fully rounded ones, and then modifying these projections on the basis of what we actually come into contact with in conversation with the other person.[4] In other words, when we have understood, we have been able to treat our projections like hypotheses, and when we have not understood, we have not managed to adopt this degree of uncertainty. The problem is clear: how do we avoid seeing nothing more than we expect to see? Under what circumstances can projections be hypotheses rather than givens? Dissociation is the condition under which we see what we expect to see. Novelty does not speak to us; we are ruled by our preconceptions, which remain invisible to us. We are not able to be curious about what faces us and instead are satisfied, even insistent upon, limiting ourselves to what is familiar. Curiosity is the active attitude of openness that allows us to disconfirm our preconceptions and substitute new meanings for them.

In emphasizing curiosity as an active attitude of openness, I mean to be going far beyond the everyday meaning of the word. I intend to refer to an openness to what is unbidden in life, to what comes to us if we are able to allow ourselves to accept the uncertainty of the experience we will have in the next moment. Curiosity is *not* the asking of questions, or at least not merely the asking of questions. Because it is a kind of acceptance (to be differentiated from approval) of whatever arrives in one's mind, a surrender to one's own capacity to construct the unexpected, curiosity may, in fact, appear to be a passive state of being. But if it is passive, it is a very actively maintained kind of passivity. Unfettered curiosity is the polar opposite of dissociation.

Perhaps the greatest divergence of Gadamer's hermeneutic view from correspondence theory is Gadamer's insistence that truth is always accomplished in dialogue. It can never be created in isolation. Uncertainty about preconceptions, and the consequent possibilities for the perception of novelty, can be created only when one's own projections are met by the attempt of the other to speak (or act) back, to converse. Truth is a mutual creation forged in dialogue.

In these points Gadamer unwittingly shares a view that has developed over many decades in interpersonal and relational psychoanalysis: the most important context in the creation of understanding or meaning is the interpersonal context, or the interpersonal field. Harry Stack Sullivan (1940) wrote that "Situations call out motivations" (p. 191), reversing the usual polarity. He means that any particular moment's experience is heavily influenced by the people with whom we are relating at the time (by "people," I mean both real, flesh-and-blood beings in the outer world and the internal objects of the inner world). The contents of consciousness are a function of one's predispositions, in interaction with the nature of the interpersonal field. And so we come to the conclusion, very different from the conclusion of early Freudian psychoanalysts, that what is true depends, within the significant constraints provided by reality, on the interpersonal situation in which that truth is formulated. The interpersonal field determines, to a large extent, the explicit shape taken by unformulated experience, or even whether it will take any shape at all. The interpersonal field is the single most significant of the contexts that continuously participate in the creation of experience and the decision about what is true.

To insist (unconsciously) on keeping experience unformulated is to dissociate; to be open to formulating it, and to grasping the preconceptions that help give it shape, is to be curious. Therefore, dissociation, too, exists relative to the interpersonal field. In fact, any particular interpersonal field can be said to be defined by the particular relationship of curiosity and dissociation within it. Think of it this way: the explicit experience it is possible to formulate (be curious about) in one field (that is, in the presence of one particular person, or a particular internal object) differs from the experience that can be formulated in another. And reciprocally, the experience that *cannot* be formulated (is dissociated, outside the range of curiosity) in one field also differs from the experience that cannot be formulated in another. Dissociation and curiosity define one another; each gains its meaning only in the context of the other. Curiosity is the absence of dissociation; dissociation is the absence of curiosity.

The role of language

The capacity to make new meaning, either linguistically or nonverbally, is one way to describe the process of effective curiosity, the absence of dissociation. Dissociation is an insistence on the creation of familiar experience, conventional forms that cannot contain novelty and that signify, as Mallarmé puts it, only as "the worn coin placed silently in my hand" (cited by Merleau-Ponty, 1964, p. 44). Conventionalization, of course, obscures novelty, which disappears into the familiar. We hardly notice what is being signified.

Gadamer's work is part of the linguistic turn in philosophy that began, in different ways, with Heidegger and Wittgenstein. Language is not a tool that we use as we please, as if words were clothing for meanings that exist independent of them. Instead, to the extent that we allow language to give us all it can, *it* controls *us*. In fact, it constitutes us. Language is the sum total of a culture's traditions, and tradition is the culture's collection of the prejudices and preconceptions that we must have if we are to make any meaning at all. Language does not simply label meanings, it creates their very possibility. Language has a life of its own, an unruly and generative life that Merleau-Ponty (e.g., 1964, 1968, 1973) has described particularly well.

Here is an interesting and significant conclusion suggested by this view of language: meanings made possible by language are not limited to those in the verbal-reflective mode. Among the possibilities created by language are the possibilities we have for *nonverbal* meaning—even the kind of non-verbal realizations that are not necessarily amenable to verbal-reflective articulation! This point is perfectly consistent with Gadamer's thought, because for Gadamer, as for his mentor Heidegger before him, it is lan-guage that creates the architecture of experience, and it is that architecture that makes *any* meaning possible. Therefore, and ironically enough, espe-cially for those who think of the verbal and the nonverbal as independent modes of representation, the hermeneutic perspective holds that language plays a significant role in defining the possibilities for nonverbal meaning.[5]

If we give ourselves over to the "wild-flowering mind" (Merleau-Ponty, 1964, p. 181), we frequently experience ourselves as conduits for the mean-ings that arise in us. Despite feeling that meanings arrive in our minds unbidden at such times, we are liable to feel that it is just this experience that is most our own, and that it is in just such moments that we are most ourselves. We are at our best as conversational partners: it is at these times that we can most fully create in our own minds the world of the other, and thereby grasp what the other is conveying to us. It is at these times that novelty reveals itself to us. And because we give ourselves over to curiosity and the world of the other in the same instant that we give ourselves over to language, it is also at such moments that we are most fully imaginative and least dissociated.

Two varieties of dissociation

Experience is a narrative process. We are attached to the stories we tell our-selves about our lives. We are so attached, as a matter of fact, that myriad possibilities in life remain unformulated simply because we experience in habitual ways, insistently telling our particular stories. We continuously burn bridges to meanings we might otherwise have formulated. These unconsidered alternatives are not necessarily meanings we would actively turn away from if we knew them; we miss the opportunity to actualize them only because of our focus elsewhere. This very common kind of dis-sociation I refer to as *passive dissociation*, or *dissociation in the weak sense* (Stern, 1997, Chapter 6; 2010). We can often be helped to see some of these meanings simply by having our attention drawn to their possibility.

But there are also meanings, of course, that we actively avoid, that we turn away from with unconscious purpose. This is experience that we maintain in an unformulated (unconscious) state for defensive reasons. The pain such experience would create in us is simply more than we will bear. The worst of such pain is caused when we are unable to avoid the formulation of experience that we cannot even acknowledge belongs to us; such experience is what Harry Stack Sullivan calls "*not-me*," and it feels as if it exists outside the bounds of what we can accept as "self." Trauma, of course, falls into this category. If we are to maintain an acceptable degree of comfort and psychic equilibrium, *not-me* must be maintained as unformulated experience. We develop a quite specific unconscious refusal to articulate or realize these aspects of our subjectivity. This defensive process I refer to as *active dissociation* or *dissociation in the strong sense* (Stern, 1997, Chapter 7; Stern, 2010).

Now let me go back a step: remember that the contents of consciousness are heavily influenced by the nature of the interpersonal field. To make this claim, it turns out, is to arrive at the very same theory of dissociated self-states that has become highly influential in relational psychoanalysis in recent years (e.g., Davies & Frawley, 1994; Mitchell, 1993; Bromberg, 1998; Pizer, 1998; Stern, 1997, 2010, 2015). One merely has to reverse the lens and, instead of looking at the self-state (i.e., the current configuration of the interpersonal field) as a significant part of the context that determines the shape of the experience to be formulated, look at the particular selection of experience that can be formulated as what defines a self-state. A self-state, if we think about it this way, is defined by the experience that can be formulated within it. And therefore, dissociation in the strong sense (the unconscious refusal to formulate certain content) is synonymous with the dissociation of self-states from one another. Unconsciously refusing to formulate certain mental content, that is, is equivalent to unconsciously enforcing the defensive isolation of the self-state in which this content could be known (Stern, 2010, 2015).

From dissociation to imagination: The question of psychopathology

But I am not suggesting that dissociation in the strong sense is necessarily pathological. Every *me* is accompanied by a *not- me*, and all of us, therefore, dissociate in the strong sense, at least sometimes. The differentiation of "normal" and pathological dissociation is more complicated than that (for definitions and descriptions of "expectable" and "pathological" dissociation, see Bromberg, 1998).

It is usually taken for granted that the aspects of psychic functioning most affected by dissociation are those we think of as the building blocks of experience: affect, thought, perception, and memory. In the largest sense, though, dissociation is not fully described as a failure of any of these functions. Dissociation is a failure to allow one's imagination free play. In many instances one can think of the failure of imagination as the collapse of transitional space (Winnicott, 1971) into deadness or literalness. Merleau-Ponty (1964, 1968, 1973), who has captured the sense of what I mean by imagination as well as anyone, writes that "speech takes flight from where it rolls in the wave of speechless communication" (p. 165). He tells us that creative speech, which is the domain of imagination, "tears out or tears apart meanings in the undivided whole of the nameable, as our gestures do in that of the perceptible" (1964, p. 17). Imagination is our capacity to allow meanings of both kinds, what Merleau-Ponty refers to as the nameable and the perceptible, and what I have described as the verbal and the nonverbal, to come to fruition within us as they will. If we wish to do so, we can use Lacan's terms here: imagination takes place in the realm of the Symbolic, dissociation in the Imaginary. Just as in the Imaginary, dissociation is the insistence on denying that life is in continuous, unpredictable flux. In order to prevent the eruption of *not-me*, the next moment must be completely (and falsely) predictable, at least in certain important respects. Experience must be forced into conventional, stereotyped shapes that are not necessarily the best fit for it.

Experience should not be categorized as simply "present" or "absent," formulated or unformulated. That way of thinking would be a simple-minded dualism. I have already defined the absence of dissociation as (relatively) unfettered curiosity. I can now expand that point: experience ranges from highly imagined to highly dissociated, with all the implied variations in between. It is by now a clinical truism that experience dissociated in the strong sense—dissociated with unconscious defensive purpose—does not simply disappear into some untended part of the mind, but is instead repetitively externalized, unconsciously enacted in relationship (Davies, 1996, 1997, 1998, 1999; Davies & Frawley, 1994; Bromberg, 1998, 2006, 2011; Stern, 1997, 2010, 2015, 2018; Pizer, 1998). Enactments are more or less stereotyped, rigid, constricted, and highly selective ways of behaving and experiencing. They require a dampening of curiosity and imagination. During an enactment, what one does not understand is precisely the dissociated meanings one is simultaneously bringing into play in the relationship. It follows logically, and turns out to make good clinical sense, too, that therapeutic action is a matter of breaching these enactments (Stern, 2010), thereby creating more "relational freedom" (Stern, 2015). When that happens, which requires the recognition, by either the patient or the analyst, of the dissociative constriction, the field shifts in a way that allows greater freedom of thought in both minds. New understanding arises at such moments, but the new understanding is more a signpost or landmark of the really significant change—the shift in the field that created the new freedom in the first place—than it is the primary engine of therapeutic action.

One conclusion that all this leads to is that there is no particular intrinsic *variety* of dissociation that we should define as pathological. We all dissociate in the same way for defensive purposes, and we all unconsciously enact the dissociated meanings. On the other hand, the degree of people's insistence on maintaining a dissociative enactment, and the degree of their difficulty in thinking about (understanding, interpreting) the enactments in which they are involved, varies considerably. The more inaccessible the dissociation is to interpersonal negotiation, the more rigid and unyielding is its enactment. In the case of particularly rigid enactments, one's capacity to be curious about them is severely curtailed. On the basis of this way of thinking, pathological dissociation should be defined according to the frequency and thoroughness of impairment in the capacity for imagination.

The fact that pathological dissociation must be identified contextually and not absolutely means that, in this scheme, there can be no objective determination of abnormality. Selecting the point on the continuum between dissociation and imagination that separates normal and pathological dissociation is a contextual, clinical matter, and therefore the problems that bring people for treatment are better understood, as I suggested in the beginning of this chapter, as what Sullivan (1940) referred to as "problems in living" than as psychopathology.

Concluding remarks

I have addressed throughout my work the matter of working clinically with unformulated experience, dissociation, and enactment. I have only been able to gesture in the direction of that work here. I recommend the interested reader to Bromberg's and Davies's work on the topic, as well as my own (see reference list).

The field of trauma and the field of psychoanalysis have grown closer in recent years (Bromberg and Chefetz, 2004; Chefetz, 2015; Howell, 2006, 2020; Howell & Itzkowitz, 2016). In closing, I want to express my hope that the psychoanalytic model of mind I have described, in which dissociation plays such a central role, contributes to this *rapprochement*.

Notes

1 But see Loewald's (1978) brilliant reformulation of the theory of the primary and secondary processes, in which language can partake of the primary process without being schizophrenic, as in poetry or free association. In fact, for Loewald language is not really alive *unless* it is in contact with the primary process. Freud's account of the primary process and secondary process changed and developed over his lifetime. Gill (1967), though, feels that in the end Freud offered "nothing like a comprehensive metapsychological treatment" (p. 265) of these ideas. Interested readers should consult Gill's (1967) careful study.

2 The "inability" to formulate experience is a consequence of massive psychic trauma, and is not my primary subject. I address primarily the "unconscious unwillingness" to formulate in this chapter, a defensive process. But I do mention both inability and unwillingness in this sentence. I make that choice because I want to emphasize that most of us, as I say in the text, define dissociation of *any* kind as the prevention of symbolic representation.

3 In addition to Gadamer's (1965/2004) magnum opus, *Truth and Method*, a collection of his seminal papers is presented in Gadamer (1976), which is accompanied by a useful introduction to his work (Linge, 1976). Numerous secondary sources are also available (e.g., Bernstein, 1983; Warnke, 1987; Weinsheimer, 1985; Scheibler, 2000).

4 Gadamer applies his conception of understanding most often to the grasp of the meanings of cultural products such as art, drama, and literature. But he does also write about the kind of understanding that goes on between two people. I am limiting my discussion here to the attempt of two people to understand one another.

5 Space restrictions do not allow me to make this argument in the detail it deserves. Elsewhere (Stern, 2018) I have made a more complete presentation.

References

Bernstein, R. J. (1983). *Beyond objectivism and relativism: Science, hermeneutics, and praxis*. Philadelphia: University of Pennsylvania Press.

Bion, W. R. (1962/1977). *Learning from experience*. In *Seven servants: Four works by Wilfred R. Bion* (pp. 1–111). New York: Jason Aronson.

Botella, C. & Botella, S. (2005). *The work of psychic figurability: Mental states without representation*. New York: Routledge.

Bromberg, P. M. (1998). *Standing in the spaces: essays on clinical process, trauma, and dissociation*. Hillsdale, NJ: The Analytic Press.

Bromberg, P. M. (2006). *Awakening the dreamer: Clinical journeys*. Hillsdale, NJ: The Analytic Press.

Bromberg, P. M. (2011). *The shadow of the tsunami: And the growth of the relational mind.* New York: Routledge.

Bromberg, P. M. & Chefetz, R. A. (2004). Talking with "me" and "not-me": A dialogue. *Contemporary Psychoanalysis, 40,* 409–464.

Bruner, J. S. & Klein, G. S. (1960). The function of perceiving: New Look retrospect. In S. Wapner & B. Kaplan (Eds.), *Perspectives in psychological theory.* New York: International Universities Press.

Bruner, J. S. & Postman, L. (1949). Perception, cognition, and personality. *Journal of Personality, 18,* 14–31.

Chefetz, R. (2015). *Intensive psychotherapy for persistent dissociative processes: The fear of feeling real.* New York: Norton.

Davies, J. M. (1996). Linking the pre-analytic with the postclassical: Integration, dissociation, and the multiplicity of unconscious processes. *Contemporary Psychoanalysis, 32,* 553–576.

Davies, J. M. (1997). Dissociation and therapeutic enactment. *Gender and Psychoanalysis, 2,* 241–257.

Davies, J. M. (1998). The multiple aspects of multiplicity: Symposium on clinical choices in psychoanalysis. *Psychoanalytic Dialogues, 8,* 195–206.

Davies, J. M. (1999). Getting cold feet defining "safe- enough" borders: Dissociation, multiplicity, and integration in the analyst's experience. *Psychoanalytic Quarterly, 78,* 184–208.

Davies, J. M. & Frawley, M. G. (1994). *Treating the adult survivor of childhood sexual abuse.* New York: Basic Books.

Ferro, A. (2009). Transformations in dreaming and characters in the psychoanalytic field. *International Journal of Psychoanalysis, 90,* 209–230.

Ferro, A. & Civitarese, G. (2016). Psychoanalysis and the analytic field. In A. Elliot (Ed.), *The Routledge handbook of psychoanalysis in the humanities and the social sciences* (pp. 132–148). New York: Routledge.

Fingarette, H. (1969). *Self-deception.* London: Routledge and Kegan Paul.

Freud, S. (1895). Project for a scientific psychology. *Standard Edition, 1,* 295–387.

Freud, S. (1896). Further remarks on the neuro-psychoses of defence. *Standard Edition, 3,* 162–185.

Freud, S. (1900). The interpretation of dreams. *Standard Edition,* 4–5.

Freud, S. (1915a). Repression. *Standard Edition, 14,* 146–158.

Freud, S. (1915b). The unconscious. *Standard Edition, 14,* 166–204.

Friedman, L. (2000). Are minds objects or dramas? In D. K. Silverman & D. L. Wolitzky (Eds.), *Changing conceptions of psychoanalysis: The legacy of Merton Gill* (pp. 146–170). Hillsdale, NJ: The Analytic Press.

Gadamer, H.-G. (1965/2004). *Truth and method.* Revised translation, by J. Weinsheimer & D. G. Marshall, from the 2nd edition in German. London: Continuum.

Gadamer, H.-G. (1966). The universality of the hermeneutical problem. In D. E. Linge (Ed.), *Philosophical hermeneutics* (pp. 3–17). Berkeley, CA: University of California Press, 1976.

Gadamer, H.-G. (1976). *Philosophical hermeneutics (D. E. Linge,* Trans. Ed.). Berkeley, CA: University of California Press.

Gill, M. M. (1967). The primary process. In R. R. Holt (Ed.), *Motives and thought. Psychoanalytic essays in honor of David Rapaport* (pp. 260–298). Psychological Issues, Vol. 18–19. New York: International Universities Press.

Green, A. (1975). The analyst, symbolization, and absence in the analytic setting. *International Journal of Psychoanalysis, 56*, 1–22.

Green, A. (1999). *The work of the negative* (A. Weller, Trans.). London: Free Association Books.

Howell, E. F. (2006). *The dissociative mind.* New York: Routledge.

Howell, E. F. & Itzkowitz, S. (Eds.). (2016). *The dissociative mind and psychoanalysis: Understanding and working with trauma.* New York: Routledge.

Howell, E. F. (2020). *Trauma and dissociation-informed psychotherapy: Relational healing and the therapeutic connection.* New York: Routledge.

James, W. (1890). *Principles of psychology.* New York: Henry Holt and Co., 1899.

Laplanche, J. (1999). *Essays on otherness.* New York: Routledge.

Laplanche, J. (2011). *Freud and the sexual: Essays 2000–2006.* New York: International Psychoanalysis Books.

Laplanche, J. & Pontalis, J.-P. (1973). *The language of psycho-analysis (D. Nicholson-Smith, Trans.).* New York: Norton.

Levenson, E. A. (1972/2005). *The fallacy of understanding.* In *The fallacy of understanding G the ambiguity of change.* New York: Routledge.

Levenson, E. A. (1983/2005). *The ambiguity of change. The fallacy of understanding.* In *The fallacy of understanding G the ambiguity of change.* New York: Routledge.

Levenson, E. A. (1991/2016). *The purloined self: The interpersonal perspective in psychoanalysis* (A. Slomowitz, Ed.). New York: Routledge.

Levenson, E. A. (2017). *Interpersonal psychoanalysis and the enigma of consciousness* (A. Slomowitz, Ed.). New York: Routledge.

Levine, H. B., Reed, G. S. & Scarfone, D. (Eds.). (2013). *Unrepresented states and the construction of meaning: Clinical and theoretical contributions.* London: Karnac.

Linge, D. E. (1976). Editor's introduction. In D. E. Linge (Ed.), *Philosophical hermeneutics* (pp. xi–lviii). Berkeley, CA: University of California Press.

Lionells, M., Fiscalini, J., Mann, C. M. & Stern, D. B. (Eds.)-. (1995). *The handbook of interpersonal psychoanalysis.* New York: Routledge.

Loewald, H. W. (1978). Primary process, secondary process, and language. In *Papers on psychoanalysis* (pp. 178–206). New Haven & London: Yale University Press, 1980.

McGleughlin, J. (2015). Do we find or lose ourselves in the negative? *Psychoanalytic Dialogues, 25*, 214–236.

McGleughlin, J. (2020). The analyst's necessary nonsovereignty and the generative power of the negative. *Psychoanalytic Dialogues, 30*, 123–138.

Merleau-Ponty, M. (1945/1962). *The phenomenology of perception* (C. Smith, Trans.). New York: Routledge & Kegan Paul.

Merleau-Ponty, M. (1964). *Signs* (R. McCleary, Trans.). Evanston, IL: Northwestern University Press, pp. 3–35.

Merleau-Ponty, M. (1968). *The visible and the invisible* (C. Lefort, Trans.). A. Lingis. Evanston, IL: Northwestern University Press.

Merleau-Ponty, M. (1973). *The prose of the world* (C. Lefort, Ed., J. O'Neill, Trans.). Evanston, IL: Northwestern University Press.

Mitchell, S. A. (1988). *Relational concepts in psychoanalysis.* Cambridge, MA: Harvard University Press.

Mitchell, S. A. (1993). *Hope and dread in psychoanalysis.* New York: Basic Books.

Mitchell, S. A. (1997). *Influence and autonomy in psychoanalysis.* Hillsdale, NJ: The Analytic Press.

Mitchell, S. A. (2000). *Relationality*. Hillsdale, NJ: The Analytic Press.

Mitchell, S. A. & Aron, L. (Eds.). (1999). *Relational psychoanalysis: The emergence of a tradition*. Hillsdale, NJ: The Analytic Press.

Pizer, S. (1998). *Building bridges: The negotiation of paradox in psychoanalysis*. Hillsdale, NJ: The Analytic Press.

Sass, L. A. (1988). Humanism, hermeneutics, and humanistic psychoanalysis: Differing conceptions of subjectivity. *Psychoanalysis and Contemporary Thought*, *12*, 433–504.

Schachtel, E. (1959). *Metamorphosis*. New York: Basic Books.

Schafer, R. (1976). *A new language for psychoanalysis*. New Haven: Yale University Press.

Schafer, R. (1983). *The analytic attitude*. New York: Basic Books.

Schafer, R. (1992). *Retelling a life*. New York: Basic Books.

Scheibler, I. (2000). *Gadamer: Between Heidegger and Habermas*. Lanham, MD: Rowman & Littlefield.

Schimek, J. G. (1975). A critical re-examination of Freud's concept of unconscious mental representations. *International Journal of Psycho-Analysis*, *2*, 171–187.

Spence, D. P. (1982). *Narrative truth and historical truth: Meaning and interpretation in psychoanalysis*. New York: Norton.

Stern, D. B. (1983). Unformulated experience. *Contemporary Psychoanalysis*, *19*, 71–99.

Stern, D. B. (1997). *Unformulated experience: From dissociation to imagination in psychoanalysis*. Hillsdale, NJ: The Analytic Press.

Stern, D. B. (2010). *Partners in thought: Working with unformulated experience, dissociation, and enactment.* New York: Routledge.

Stern, D. B. (2015). *Relational freedom: Emergent properties of the interpersonal field*. New York: Routledge.

Stern, D. B. (2018). *The infinity of the unsaid: Unformulated experience, language, and the nonverbal*. New York: Routledge.

Stern, D. B., & Hirsch, I. (Eds.). (2017a). *The interpersonal perspective in psychoanalysis, 1960s–1990s: Rethinking transference and countertransference*. New York: Routledge.

Stern, D. B. & Hirsch, I. (Eds.). (2017b). *Further developments in contemporary interpersonal psychoanalysis, 1980s–2010s: Evolving interest in the analyst's subjectivity*. New York: Routledge.

Stern, D. B., Mann, C., Kantor, S. & Schlesinger, G. (Eds.). (1995). *Pioneers of interpersonal psychoanalysis*. New York: Routledge.

Sullivan, H. S. (1940). *Conceptions of modern psychiatry*. New York: Norton, 1953.

Sullivan, H. S. (1953). *The interpersonal theory of psychiatry*. New York: Norton.

Taylor, C. (2016). *The language animal: The full shape of the human linguistic capacity*. Cambridge, MA: Harvard University Press.

Warnke, G. (1987). *Gadamer: Hermeutics, tradition and reason*. Stanford, CA: Stanford University Press.

Weinsheimer, J. C. (1985). *Gadamer's hermeneutics: A reading of truth and method*. New Haven, CT: Yale University Press.

Winnicott, D. W. (1971). *Playing and reality*. London: Tavistock.

Chapter 10

Unformulated experience, dissociation, and *Nachträglichkeit*

The first part of this chapter is an interpersonal/relational psychoanalytic account of some relationships between dissociation, time, and unformulated experience. Trauma, and the dissociation to which trauma leads, freezes time, which makes it impossible to formulate certain kinds of new experience.

Instead, potential new meanings remain unformulated. The route of clinical access to frozen time is the interpersonal field: to thaw time and allow new experience, the ways in which the interpersonal field is itself frozen need to be addressed. This part of the chapter was originally written for a 2016 plenary panel at the Winter Meetings of the American Psychoanalytic Association.

The second part of the chapter presents and explores a point of confluence between the views in the first part of the chapter and certain aspects of French psychoanalysis, with particular reference to the concept of Nachträglichkeit *in the work of Jean Laplanche and Haydée Faimberg. This part of the chapter was first delivered as a plenary lecture to the annual meetings of The* Journal of Analytical Psychology *on April 22, 2017.*

I have had an interest in dissociation since the beginning of my career. Over the last few years I have also developed an interest in the matter of time in psychoanalysis (Stern 2012, 2015b). That second interest led me to the concept of *Nachträglichkeit,* first in the work of Modell, and eventually in the thinking of Laplanche and Faimberg. The combination of those interests led to the thoughts I am about to convey to you.

DOI: 10.4324/9781032688893-12

Part 1: Time, unformulated experience, and dissociation

In his review of a novel in a recent issue of the *New York Times Book Review*, Gregory Maguire, a novelist himself, notes that "the linear nature of narrative can impose frustrating constraints on a story" (2016, p. 10). Maguire quotes the following words from a character in the novel he is reviewing: the character objects to what she calls "the tyranny of text … Like getting born, living your life, dying. You know. Text only has one direction. Frustrates me" (p. 10).

Linear time, or *chronos*, a Greek word, is the time of text, and also the time of science. *Chronos* flows forever forward, is regular, and can be measured. But the time of human living, unlike the time of text and science, is not limited to forward motion. Living stories, the meanings of lives, are not governed by those narrative constraints that force written stories to move from beginning to end. In a famous passage, William Faulkner's character Quentin in *The Sound and the Fury*, who thinks often and deeply about time, remembers his father saying this: "Clocks slay time … Time is dead as long as it is being clicked off by little wheels; only when the clock stops does time come to life" (1929, p. 104). Time that is not clicked off and measured (not imprisoned, we might say, with Quentin's father) is the kind of time called *kairos*, a word also taken from the Greek. *Kairos* is imprecise, unmeasurable, and much more humanly significant than *chronos*, because *kairos* flows both forward and backward, retracing its own path. *Kairos* is the time of human experience, the kind of time in which not only does the past create the present, but the present also creates the past. *Kairos* is the time of Freud's (1895, 1897) *Nachträglichkeit*—first translated by Strachey as "deferred action," but given a more accurate English rendering by Laplanche (1998) ('afterwardsness') and by Thomä and Cheshire (1991) ('retrospective attribution'), and commonly referred to—first by Freud (1896), but also, memorably, in the work of Arnold Modell (see especially Modell 1990)—as "retranscription."[1] This is the kind of time in which what Laplanche and Pontalis (1968, 1973) called the "already there," a "something" from the past that may never have had an explicit meaning, takes on significance, sometimes for the first time, because of events in the here and now.

Faimberg (2007) argues for a broader concept of *Nachträglichkeit*, suggesting that we invoke the concept whenever our experience of the past is revised, created, or elaborated by an event in the present. We might understand in this way, for example, the effect of psychoanalytic interpretations.[2] My own thinking goes even further in the direction Faimberg explores, making *Nachträglichkeit* into something like an ongoing feature of mind (see also Puget 2006, Marion 2012, Foehl 2014, LaFarge 2014, Loewenberg 2015). For me, our reflective experience is re-created in every moment, from what I understand to be that pre-existing "something" noted by Laplanche, which I call "unformulated experience" (Stern 1983, 1997). Unformulated experience is potential experience, what experience might become; it is vague, primitive, global, and affectively charged. In each moment, from my perspective, we reformulate the experience that has come before. While the last moment's contents of mind are the greatest influence on the contents of the next moment, there is also always wiggle room, so that no experience is fully predetermined. Each moment's experience becomes the unformulated experience of the next moment's actuality.

Time, dissociation, and the interpersonal field

I think of mind—the formulation of experience—as an expression of *kairos*, by which I mean that mind continuously renews itself, re-creating its own contents in every moment as long as it is alive. Past and present, in this view, are ceaselessly in the process of constructing and reconstructing one another. The interchange of present and past, in one sense, *is* the mind, because it is our means of creating and understanding the significances of our lives.

But the unfettered expression of *kairos*, the spontaneous linking of past and present, in both directions, is the ideal of the mind's functioning. In real life we never see or experience this kind of pure spontaneity, because our capacity to let our minds have that degree of freedom is always compromised by the disappointments, losses, and humiliations we all suffer early in life, and then again along the way. To one degree or another, depending on the severity of the compromise, the natural link between present and past is always threatened, and sometimes severed.

What do I mean by "compromise" here? I mean dissociation.

Dissociation in my understanding is the primary defensive or self-protective psychic process (Bromberg 1998, 2006, 2011; Stern 1997, 2010, 2015b). If we think in terms of time, dissociation is what happens when the experience that would be formulated in our minds if *kairos* proceeded spontaneously is intolerable. The influences of past and present on one another simply do not take place, or rather, we unconsciously shy away from them—they are not "allowed" to take place. And in this way, the experience that would have resulted from that mutual influence of past and present (and our anticipation of the future) on one another just does not come to be. Under these circumstances, we can say that subjectivity is maintained in its unformulated state for unconscious defensive reasons, prevented from change, growth, and articulation. *Kairos* is stymied, and the mind is frozen.

I am not talking about repression here, at least not in the traditional understanding. Dissociation is not a matter of ejecting from consciousness an experience that is already created and then distorting it or hiding it away somewhere in the mind. Dissociation means *not creating the experience in the first place* (Stern 1983, 1997). The most significant dividing line in the mind, for me, is not between symbolically realized experience that can be known, on the one hand, and on the other, symbolic experience that cannot be known. Rather, the most important differentiation of the mind's contents is between subjectivity that can be used in the creation of authentic living and subjectivity that cannot be used in that way.

The use of experience in the creation of living requires symbolization. If we cannot symbolize it, it cannot contribute to the emergence of the next moment's living, or the next week's or the next year's. Often, readers of my initial formulations in this area (e.g., Stern 1983, 1997) took me to mean that symbolization was synonymous with verbal representation, and they objected that to take such a position would be to exclude music, dance, and visual art (among many other human phenomena) from that part of experience that allowed creative living. They would have been quite right to object if that is what I had meant. But that was not what I intended at all, and so recently, in work I have not yet published, I have tried to be explicit about how the formulation of experience is not limited to the verbal register. At this point in time, the idea that unconsciousness can be understood as unrepresented states or unrepresented subjectivity, rather than only as a container of rejected, fully formed experience, has become well known, via the work of Bion (1962), André Green (1975, 1999), César and Sára Botella (2005), and others (e.g., Levine et al. 2013).

Returning to the topic of dissociation, what I want to say is that dissociation is a kind of monkey wrench tossed into the works. The continuous process of experiential renewal, ceaselessly underwritten under favorable circumstances by the free circulation of *kairos*, grinds to a halt. However long it lasts, dissociation interrupts—in that part of the mind affected by it—our capacity to notice that "this" (in the present) feels like "that" (in the past), thereby stifling our capacity to create what Arnold Modell (1990, 2003, 2005, 2009) calls new "emotional categories." The spontaneity of mind is hampered; the experience of novelty suffers; curiosity is shut down.

Conscious experience, though, simply steers around such potholes. Meaning continues to be created and attributed, but only along familiar, unobstructed paths that, simply because they are so very familiar, have lost their capacity to surprise us, and therefore their vitality. By being constrained in this way, potential experience can remain dissociated—that is, unformulated for defensive reasons—sometimes just for moments, but sometimes for years, sometimes even for a lifetime. Past, present, and future are decoupled. Possibility is shut down. *Kairos* is frozen (see also Stern 2012).

What can we do about this as clinicians? We have no direct route of access to time: we have no procedures to influence it; we can only observe its influence on us. Time has its own mind. Or in Gregory Maguire's words: "Memory obeys only the rules it chooses" (2016, p. 10).

Kairos *and the interpersonal field*

But the thinking in this chapter rests on the position that we do have a route of access to a phenomenon closely linked to *kairos*. This phenomenon is linked to *kairos* in a way that sometimes allows us to affect time in the lives of our patients (and ourselves). That *kairos*-linked phenomenon is the interpersonal field, which I understand to be the medium in which dissociation, and therefore also time, is expressed.[3]

What I mean when I refer to the concept of the field, and what I believe is implicit in most, and perhaps all, interpersonal and relational writings, is simply that the analytic situation is defined in terms of its relatedness. Analyst and patient are continuously and inevitably, and consciously and unconsciously, in interaction with one another. This interaction has to do with what they experience in one another's presence, and how they behave. The field also determines what each participant can experience in the presence of the other, especially the affective aspects of experience. The field is, on one hand, the sum total of all those influences, conscious and unconscious, that each of the analytic participants exerts on the other. On the other hand, the field is the outcome of all those influences, the relatedness and experience that are created between the two people as a result of the way they deal with one another (Stern 2015a, 2015b).

In my frame of reference, it is the nature of the interpersonal field, conscious and unconscious, that determines which possibilities attain symbolic form and which others never take shape (Stern 1997, 2010, 2015b). It is the changing configuration of the field that determines which of the potentials in unformulated experience are articulated as the experience of the next moment and which others are dissociated—laid aside, passed over, discarded, remaining unformulated, never to appear in the conscious mind.

We can think of the field as the means by which *kairos*—which is, after all, something other than a concrete presence—becomes meaningfully embodied in human living. When *kairos* is free, in other words, the field is free, and when the field is free, meaning can be freely and explicitly formulated; patient and analyst can each harvest meanings from their pasts—from their pasts prior knowing one another, of course, but also from their past together in the treatment—to reflect on their experience with one another. In dissociation, though, when *kairos* is frozen, the field, too, is frozen, and the clinical relatedness cannot be given symbolic representation; it cannot be thought, only enacted.

Understood in this way, *kairos* is a relational phenomenon, and it has its effects on human life via the living history of the interpersonal field. It is through the medium of the field that the present retranscribes the past and the past shapes the present. And it is also through the field that, in dissociation, the past is denied its effect on the present, and the present is prevented from reshaping the past (see Stern 2012). To the extent that the field is frozen, it is our clinical intention to melt it, and in this process of addressing dissociation we melt time itself, allowing *kairos* to circulate freely once again.

The field, kairos, and spontaneity

Field theory shares with the conception of time as *kairos*, and with the conception of unformulated experience, the ideal of spontaneity. Whether we are talking about Sullivan's "interpersonal field" (e.g., Greenberg & Mitchell 1983; Levenson 1972, 1983, 1991, 2017; Stern 2015a), Mitchell's "relational field" (1988), or the "intersubjective field" of unconscious phantasy (e.g., Baranger & Baranger 1961; Ferro 2009; Civitarese 2012; Ferro & Civitarese 2016), the ideal is the freedom of the field to evolve spontaneously—which includes, in my understanding, the spontaneous development of *kairos*. But of course this ideal, because of the same losses, disappointments, and humiliations I have already mentioned, is never fully actualized. Neither the field nor *kairos*, in other words, can ever be absolutely free: there are always rigid and unchanging configurations of relatedness, parts of the field paralyzed in such a way that dissociated experience cannot attain symbolic representation, sequestering past and present from one another.

If the interpersonal field is to remain spontaneous, then, *kairos* must be free to create spontaneous links between past, present, and the anticipation of the future (Modell 1990, 2003, 2005, 2009), thereby renewing, revising, and elaborating the possibilities of relatedness. To stifle *kairos*, to deaden time into nothing more than the literality and linearity of *chronos*, is to freeze the field. Novel relatedness, and novel *meanings* of relatedness, become impossible, and life with others is restricted to what is already familiar, however painful it may be. To deaden *kairos*, in other words, is to make relatedness blindly transferential. I mean "transferential" now in the original sense, as a variety of the repetition compulsion. That is, the deadening of *kairos* leads to stereotypic relatedness that is less a variety of vital, soulful living than a defensively motivated way to manage life, a way to do nothing more than keep on keeping on.

Enactments

It is the very heart of much of contemporary clinical psychoanalysis to attend to these compromises of intersubjectivity (e.g., Benjamin 1990, 2004, 2017), these frozen places in the field. In contemporary interpersonal and relational psychoanalysis, the frozen parts of relatedness are referred to as "enactments" (Bromberg 1998, 2006, 2011; Stern 1997, 2010, 2015b). Enactments are not necessarily represented in the minds of either the patient or the analyst. Because they exist in this unsymbolized, unformulated state, they are both invisible and mute, and can therefore be devilishly elusive. One cannot even point at something that has no symbolic representation in the mind at all.[4] In the similar conception of the Barangers (1961–62/2008), these same frozen parts of the analytic relationship are described as "bastions" or "bulwarks," requiring what the Barangers call a "second look" from the analyst who wishes to see more clearly his or her own participation in them. The Barangers suggest, though, that a simple review of their clinical participation with the patient—that is, the "second look"—is sufficient to bring to attention interactions that interpersonal and relational analysts are more likely to believe cannot necessarily be so simply and straightforwardly observed, and perhaps cannot be observed at all, no matter how hard the analyst looks.

But whether, like the Barangers, we think that enactments are observable if the analyst pays close attention or, like interpersonal and relational writers, we are more skeptical of this degree of transparency in the clinical interaction, believing instead that enactments often must be learned about over a period of time via the analyst's searching introspection of her own affective experience with the patient, all field theorists in psychoanalysis can agree on the following point: if our goal as clinicians is to breach dissociation—that is, if it is our aim to free *kairos* to circulate with greater spontaneity, and to allow our minds the moment-to-moment opportunity to renew experience—then our immediate clinical aim must be to do what we can to relax the paralyzed parts of the analytic relatedness, what I have elsewhere called the creation of "relational freedom" (Stern 2013, 2015b). If the frozen parts of the interpersonal field can be thawed, time is liberated and the mind becomes more of what it can be. The parts of experience that have been defensively maintained in an unformulated state are given symbolic form and used in thought, and then in the construction of ways of living that had not been conceivable before.

I repeat the point I have just made to give it special emphasis: *the interpersonal field is our route of access to frozen time.*

The case of George

I turn now to a clinical example. Almost any episode of successful clinical work would illustrate what I want to say, and it is clear to me that the ideas I have laid out to this point are hardly the only conceptions one could use to understand the material I will present. I do hope, though, that this illustration helps to ground my point of view.

George is a successful, married artist in his seventies with adult children. I have seen him for several years three times a week, and I have written about our work before (Stern 2015b, Chapter 1). The session I will describe was our last one prior to my two-week vacation just before Labor Day a couple of years ago. On this day, George, always on time for his appointments or a few minutes early, was ten minutes late. I decided to call him.

Rewind to June of the same year, about two months earlier. As in most summers, George left to spend two months with his wife at a remote cabin they own on a beautiful piece of land in the mountains of the West, a hundred miles from the nearest large town. This year, as usual, neither George nor I liked the idea of suspending the treatment this long, especially when the two months of George's absence were added to the two weeks right at the end of it, when I would be on vacation. Both of us felt that we were right in the middle of the work, and George felt, too, his usual warm attachment to me, an attachment that often touched me and which I returned. And so, again as in past years, we decided to continue our usual schedule of sessions on the phone.

That was why, on that morning, I decided to call. When George picked up the phone, and I answered his hello by identifying myself, he said, "Oh lord, I completely forgot! I was thinking I'd be talking to you later, and then it just slipped my mind." I said that I figured he'd forgotten, and that since it was our last session for a couple of weeks I thought it made sense to call. George thanked me and said he would have felt awful if he'd missed our last session before the break. He said he supposed he ought to think about why he forgot. And then, with a sigh of what sounded to me like resignation, as if he were dutifully succumbing to what a good patient was supposed to do, he said, "Maybe it has something to do with today being the last session before you leave." This kind of dutiful way of feeling and talking was familiar to me.

And so, keeping my ear to the ground for other resonances, I told George that I certainly wanted us to attend to his feelings about the impending separation but that it sounded as if his response had been a matter of duty. In response George reminded me of a significant part of our history: "Well," he said, "it's true, I don't really feel so much about you going away, but that's what always happens. Then you leave, and I end up feeling bad while you're gone and having no idea why."

George was right. He was referring to the fact that this had happened before—a sad and sometimes depressed mood that often came over him when I went to a conference or was on vacation. His mood was usually clarified as a reaction to my departure only when I returned. I didn't realize it at the time, but the fact that, this time, George was able to think about the depressed mood that came over him when I left—the fact that he could formulate it and wanted to tell me about it beforehand—was an indication that something was thawing in the field. It is not uncommon in my experience for the first identifiable contribution in such a thaw to come from the patient and not from me.

George's mother was a cold, unaffectionate woman; his father, highly narcissistically vulnerable, could be warm, but he had little to do with George. In George's early years his care was left to an *au pair*, Wilma, a young woman who lived in the house. When George was four or five, Wilma quite suddenly left the family and moved to another state to marry her boyfriend. Wilma was not replaced—although a replacement would hardly have comforted George, who was devastated.

If either of his parents understood George's unhappiness, they did nothing to show it. George was alone, and he hated himself. He hated his vulnerability. He still has an image of himself lying in the center of his bed, as if he were observing himself from the ceiling. The little boy feels utterly bereft and despairing, and is curled into a fetal position. This image arouses George's contempt: he describes himself as a "fat-thighed little piece of shit."

At about the same time Wilma left, George believes he was sexually abused in the cellar of his house, probably repeatedly. It is our work around this material that I have written about before. Sometimes George suspects his father was the perpetrator, sometimes others. He readily grants that there is no reliable evidence that sexual abuse took place, but given a great deal of other material from George's life, I tend to believe it did. In any case, George and I have spent many, many hours "in the cellar," living through scenarios of sexual events that may have taken place there. Sometimes George is a passive, relatively affectless participant; sometimes he feels loved by the shadowy man. It is impossible to know whether any of this is memory or whether it is all fantasy. Often I am a disembodied observing presence over his shoulder, sometimes I am scarcely there at all.[5]

The end of these cellar events came about when the shadowy man somehow conveyed to George that there would be no more meetings, that he was through with George. Despite the frightening, traumatic impact of these episodes, this rejection feels as devastating to George, as he experiences it today in our sessions, as the loss of Wilma. In one of the oft-repeated scenes in the cellar, George, overcome with despair at the rejection, retreats to a crawlspace halfway up the wall of the cellar, kneels on the gravel floor and suffers alone for hours.

During that last phone session before Labor Day, when George and I had begun to talk about me leaving for my vacation and about his worry that he would suffer a depressive episode, the history I have told you passed through my mind. I told George that I thought the emotional atmosphere of our sessions was often a reassurance to him, because he could tell that I wanted to be there. But, I went on, it seemed to me that when I went away, this reassurance often couldn't survive until I returned, so that, after a time, my absence served as a confirmation of what he feared about himself. I said, "The faceless man, Wilma, me—and you: we all agree, at bottom, that you're a fat-thighed little piece of shit. Otherwise why would we leave you?"

George murmured that I was right, then was silent. I found my thoughts turning to George's tendency to discount his significance to those he is close to, especially his wife and children. He is reliably generous and helpful to them, yet always reverts to the belief that they—and others—don't really care about or value him. He often takes it for granted that I don't either, and he wryly denigrates himself more or less routinely, making sure he does it before I can. George seldom feels angry about feeling unappreciated. He does not feel deprived. He feels instead sadly resigned.

Thinking about George's image of the "fat-thighed little piece of shit," I said something to him about his incapacity to grasp the esteem and affection in which he is held by others, including me, and he then talked for a while about his relationships with his wife and children, adding detail, feeling, and depth to the point.

As George talked, I began to hear another theme. Maybe, I thought, feeling unappreciated *protects* George. If he doesn't really depend on being loved, he can't be as badly let down, hurt, or humiliated. Eventually I told him that I thought he was afraid to depend on my connection to him, and that maintaining the sense of his own unworthiness, as painful as that was, and as vulnerable as it left him to depression when I go away, at least protected him from the even more devastating disappointment he would feel if he let himself depend on my feelings about him, and *then* I didn't come through. George laughed when I said that he wasn't fool enough to believe in *that*. What I didn't say—but I did think it—was that it is better to disparage yourself than to lose confidence in the goodness of those you love.

It seemed the most natural thing in the world for me to add, after a pause, "Well, but maybe it isn't so foolish to believe in that, after all. Maybe you could imagine that I'll come back. Maybe you could even imagine that I'll *want* to come back."

With quiet amazement, George said slowly, drawing out the words, "Maybe I *could* think that. Maybe I could." We ended the session on this note. The next time I saw him was in my office after Labor Day. He had not suffered a depressive episode.

I hope it goes without saying that it was the relatedness George and I had made between us over a long period of time that allowed these events to take place. In the end what happened was really very simple, even if what led up to it was not. As is most often the case in analytic work, the moments of greatest impact are shaped by, and take their significance from, the context of the relationship in which they take place. At any earlier time in the treatment, it would have been worse than useless for me to suggest to George that maybe he could imagine that I wanted to come back. It would have been either Pollyannism on my part, or intellectualization.

It so happened that this session revolved around the dissociation and retrieval of attachment and love, and the experience between George and me on this occasion was therefore not particularly hard for either of us to bear, but other sessions with George have been dominated by intense shame and other painful affects. The following point should also go without saying, but let me make sure: sensing and explicating the interpersonal field was just as crucial in those less comfortable situations as it was in the kind of process I have just presented.

I think that, in the treatment up to this point, George and I had not really known and felt certain aspects of his attachment to me, most especially his desire to believe that he had an existence in my mind even when I was away from him. The desire to be significant in this way had been dissociated for most of his life, understandably, and the consequence had been that relatedness for him had been constrained to exist within certain narrow bounds of possibility. The interpersonal field, in other words, was frozen in important respects. *Kairos* was paralyzed, and so novel affective and relational configurations could not come about; only repetitions were possible. This narrowness, of course, affected not only his desires for others to be connected to him, but his own connections to them—what he could and would offer them.

For the present purpose, I merely offer that broad observation, with this minor elaboration. The tragedy took place in both directions: just as George's traumatic relationships in his early life deprived him of the confidence that he continued to exist in the minds of those who loved him when he was not present, so, too, did this traumatic impact deprive him of the means to awaken, through his love, whatever loving possibilities might have been possible for those he loved, especially his parents.

With all his resentments and disappointments, though, George was as loving a son as he could manage. He took care of each of his parents through their terminal illnesses, for example. I can see in George's accounts of those times of illness that he did more than he had to do—and no one else did much of anything. George, though, can take no pleasure or satisfaction in having treated his parents lovingly at the end, insisting that he only did it out of duty—one more sad, dissociative outcome of his early family life, one more way in which the present was forced into the past's lifeless, stereotypic form.

I want to draw your attention to the fact that prior to this session George and I had never discussed the depressed moods that overtook George when I went away. That is, in this session we were thinking about something for the first time, and that means to me that the process that eventuated in George's acceptance that I might actually want to come back probably began long before the words to that effect were spoken, near the end of this session. The appearance of George's foresight, in other words, was a sign that the process of melting dissociation and freeing *kairos* was already well along. The fact that George was the one to draw our attention to it is interesting—although as I have said already, it is not unusual for the patient's experience or conduct to reflect a thaw in the field before the analyst's does. The field is a mutual construction, and that means that, when the field is developing relatively spontaneously, without notable constriction, and new relational configurations are possible—when dissociation is in retreat and *kairos* is free—it is often very complicated to know whether any particular outcome begins with one participant or the other. What George and I did and said in this session emerged from the moment at hand in a way that I find virtually impossible to specify.

Part 2: Unformulated experience and Nachträglichkeit

I promised earlier that I would return to the matter of *Nachträglichkeit* (or in French translation, *après coup*). I want to spend the remainder of this chapter exploring the nature of time in the relationship between, on one hand, *Nachträglichkeit*, and on the other, what I have already said about time, unformulated experience, and dissociation. I hope to stake out some common ground in two otherwise rather disparate views of time in psychoanalysis—the interpersonal/relational and the French. Common ground between interpersonal-relational analysts, for whom *après coup* is just beginning to signify as an interesting subject matter, and the French, for whom the idea has had great significance for decades, can be as difficult to discover as hen's teeth. This is especially true from the point of view of the French (see Waintrater 2012).

I believe that all psychoanalysts belong to a single field, though, and that our views are so much more closely related to one another's than they are to anyone else's that it is absurd for us not to embrace one another as colleagues, even when we pointedly disagree. And so it seems to me that if I can link my interpersonal-relational view of time with the French perspective, it is worth doing so.

Freud (1895) devised the idea of *Nachträglichkeit* as part of his seduction theory, which preceded his later and (in the long run) more influential theory of drive. The physical part of the seduction was, to begin with, said to have taken place in the infancy or childhood of every person suffering hysteria or obsessive-compulsive neurosis, but because the sexual instincts had not matured at such an early point in life, the sexual meaning of the incident was impossible for the child to represent in its mind. The incident remained a mere "something" (this is Laplanche's [Laplanche & Pontalis 1968, 1973] much later way of putting it), present but without any particular meaning. Then, in adolescence, or whenever the relevant sexual instinct matured, the historical seduction suddenly took on meaning as a sexual event, and the "something" that had heretofore been without any particular meaning becomes explicitly sexual and therefore traumatic. The sexual trauma, that is, which at that time Freud thought was ubiquitous in neurosis, literally *does not take place* until the sexual instincts mature enough to make it possible to understand that earlier "something" as a seduction. This conversion of the "something" into a sexual trauma is Freud's initial version of *Nachträglichkeit*.

Although he invented the concept of *Nachträglichkeit*, Freud devoted little attention to it, never devoting any single written statement to its development. To track the idea, according to Faimberg (2005), requires following threads throughout Freud's work. Nevertheless, the concept of *Nachträglichkeit* has accrued great importance, especially in France, as I have already mentioned. It was Lacan (1953), in the 1950s, who drew new attention to it, although he really focused only on Freud's (1918) case of the Wolf Man; Lacan applied *Nachträglichkeit*, that is, primarily to psychosis. It remained for Laplanche and Pontalis (1973), in their classic 1960s French dictionary of Freud's terms, *The Language of Psychoanalysis* (*Vocabulaire de la Psychanalyse*, [1967]), to lend the idea something of its present-day significance for French psychoanalysis.

Laplanche (1998) and others took issue with Strachey's translation of *Nachträglichkeit* in the *Standard Edition* as "deferred action," arguing that this translation wrongly suggested that the meaning that came about later on was there all the time, just waiting for the right stimulus to actualize it, like a time bomb. Instead, said the critics, the meaning was never really there at all; all that existed in the child's mind was that vague "something" to which I have already made reference. A better translation of *Nachträglichkeit* into English, according to Laplanche (1998), is based on the French translation *après coup* (in French, literally "afterwards"), a term that has become famous in France, and increasingly, elsewhere as well. Laplanche proposed that *Nachträglichkeit* be translated as "afterwardsness," because this neologism refers not only to time but also names a special and particular *quality of experience* that has to do with meaning coming into being at a later moment.

I mentioned that for the French *après coup* has become a central term. The concept behind the term—that is, afterwardsness—is sometimes cited as the idea that most meaningfully differentiates French and British psychoanalysis (e.g., Birksted-Breen 2003, Faimberg 2007, Green 2002).[6] The idea could serve just as well to differentiate French from American psychoanalysis, although, as I have noted, many French analysts have so little respect for much of American psychoanalysis that they wouldn't bother to note the differentiation. For many French analysts, the British are wrong about many things, but it cannot be ignored that they have Winnicott and Bion. The Americans, especially the ego psychologists but continuing in the work of many contemporary Freudians, including conflict theorists, are not just wrong, but not really psychoanalytic, and if the French feel this way about American Freudians, they feel it in spades about object relations, interpersonal, and relational analysts, self psychologists, and—no doubt—Jungians, for all of whom, to the extent that the French know the thinking of these groups (and, according to Waintrater [2012], few French psychoanalysts do know these literatures), they have no patience at all.

I am no expert on French psychoanalysis, but I do see that the issue is in some ways fairly straightforward. For most French analysts, psychoanalysis is always, and only, about the unconscious. For this reason, they do not believe that therapeutic action emerges from work on developmental issues, adaptational demands, the historical impact of trauma, the psychology of the ego, the self and its vicissitudes, or even the historical aspects of transference and countertransference. They do not believe in the value of the negotiation of transference-countertransference binds between patient and analyst, verbal communication leading to mutual understanding, or the analyst's affective responsiveness to the patient. But it is not that they deny that these things exist. Rather, they are not things that psychoanalysis is properly understood to concern. Instead, psychoanalysis should concern the workings of the unconscious, and analysts should listen and intervene only on the basis of their grasp of the nature of unconscious process. The French—and not only the French but also many Kleinians and Bionians—take very seriously the principle that, because mental life is dominated by unconscious process, attending to anything else is a distraction—or worse, a betrayal of psychoanalysis.

I am under no illusions: even if I think I can define an area of overlap between my own views and views in which *Nachträglichkeit* is central, there is every reason to believe that, when it comes to the opinions held by many French, Kleinian, and Bionian analysts about the kind of psychoanalysis I have written and practised, I am spitting into the wind. I am going to proceed nevertheless, for two reasons: first, because the clinical and intellectual issues interest me; and second, because, despite being an interpersonal and relational analyst, I have a certain sympathy with these other views. I do feel strongly that we are not in any simple way the masters or mistresses of our fates, but are instead witnesses to the creation of our own psychic lives by the unconscious aspects of our minds.

So how does afterwardsness come into this? What does it mean to be interested only in the unconscious?

This is what I think it means: it means being interested in how the unconscious makes the mind what it is, and for the analyst that means being interested in following the influence of the unconscious on the rest of the psyche, as best one can. One infers these influences, of course; one can never actually see them. That is the nature of unconscious process, from every psychoanalytic perspective.

Thus "afterwardsness" is a concept well designed for the theoretical appreciation of psychoanalytic process defined exclusively by unconscious influence. The mind is not constructed on a linear, forward-looking basis in time, the way developmental theories would have it. I have already claimed that *chronos* is not the kind of time most relevant to psychoanalysis. This is perhaps especially true for the French, for whom, in the course of psycho-analytic process at least (the issue is slightly different in the realm of theory, in which certain historical influences are acknowledged), the mind is not to be grasped in any way as a developmental outcome, but as a continuously reformulated product of unconscious influence. It is constructed, and then reconstructed, over and over again, by the impact of the unconscious. The patterns in which it is constructed are probably similar over time, but the process of construction goes on in the present tense.

Let me offer a very brief illustration of this kind of thinking in the terms of Laplanche. Bear with me: Laplanche's thinking is abstract and philo-sophical, and it may be hard to understand.[7] Keep in mind that I am trying to use the thinking of Laplanche to illustrate what I am saying about the centrality of the present-day influence of the unconscious on psychic life.

Laplanche tells us that what is specifically human about the mind is the capacity to create new meaning, and the creation of new meaning is a process emerging from the necessity to "translate" the "enigmatic com-munications" of the other (these are terms used throughout Laplanche's work), communications that can be difficult or impossible to make mean-ingful ("translate") because of the infantile sexuality that imbues them. In other words, he views infantile sexuality as a special kind of meaning that uniquely resists symbolization, requiring enormous effort and creativity to comprehend—and even then, "comprehension" is a clunky word for what Laplanche intends. By "translation," he doesn't really mean understanding; he means any kind of symbolization at all. He is no more limited to con-ventional intelligibility in describing his process of translation than is Bion (1962), for instance, when he refers to alpha elements or waking dream thoughts, which may be quite non-rational images. They do not need to be comprehensible in any conventional sense; they need only become *sym-bolic representations of some kind*, thereby becoming something more than things-in-themselves. The human aspect of mind, which is the only part of the mind that for Laplanche should concern psychoanalysis, is the special kind of capability to think that comes into being as a result of the necessity to respond to being inhabited by the enigmatic message of the other. The message itself is not necessarily unconscious—but the part of the message that cannot be translated (and no message can be completely translated) does become the repressed unconscious.

If you are lost here, let me offer this: it is the ongoing struggle to translate the leftover portion of the other's enigmatic message, as well as all those messages that were received but never translated at all,[8] that constitutes psychic life. And psychic life should be the exclusive concern of psychoanalysis: psychoanalysis is the study of psychic life, defined in this way. The remainder of life—all the cognitive, historical, emotional, characterological, developmental, and adaptational dimensions of everyday living, including everything that we would refer to as the personality—fall outside the proper purview of psychoanalysis. And here, even if I have lost you, I think it is possible to re-board the train, because we come full circle, to the conclusion with which I started: psychic life for Laplanche is a matter of the present-day influence of the unconscious.

This way of understanding the psychoanalytic view of mind, then, is well described by the concept of *après coup*, or afterwardsness. Think of Laplanche's enigmatic message: such messages are first implanted in the mind by the other during infancy, and then throughout life. The implantation corresponds to that first sexual experience in Freud's original, abbreviated conception of *Nachträglichkeit*. Remember that the significance of that initial experience cannot be known, because the child does not have the relevant instinctual life yet. Just as Freud tells us that the adolescent, with his newly developed instinctual life, suddenly becomes able to look back and give some kind of symbolic representation to the sexual nature of that initial infantile experience, so each of us, according to Laplanche, must first register the message of the other and then, later on, struggle to translate (and re-translate) it. The creation of new meaning is always a two-stage process: for meaning to come about, the implantation of the message must be followed, sooner or later, by its translation. Faimberg (2005, p. 1), referring not specifically to Laplanche's thinking but to *Nachträglichkeit*, describes these "two inseparable phases" as *anticipation* (the appearance of a "something" that may eventually attain symbolic representation) and *retrospection* (the act, undertaken in the future, of retroactively giving meaning to the "something").

For Laplanche, and for many other French writers as well, the significance of the concept of *après coup* is that psychic life is ceaseless creation and revision, always carried out from within the present. The past—at least that part of the past that is relevant to psychoanalysis—is not really built up and memorialized in the mind in the way it is in many varieties of the much more developmentally oriented North American theory. Instead, the past is contained in what happens now.

And so the focus in this kind of psychoanalysis is on what the mind and its contents are becoming at any particular moment as a result of unconscious influence, and the idea of *après coup* can be read as a statement of this kind of theory. We observe the meanings created in the patient's mind, moment to moment, and try to work backwards to what those meanings indicate about the active unconscious processes we cannot observe. All we can know directly is what conscious experience becomes; we can never know what it was before that.

Think of the example of the birthday of a famous person. That date has no particular significance until the person gains fame, and then, in retrospect, the date takes on a new meaning. This skeletal example is a highly simplified metaphor for daily psychic life in the French perspective—with the reservation, of course, that while we can *observe directly* why the date of the birthday gains significance, we can only *infer* why consciousness becomes what it does. All we can know directly is what conscious experience becomes; we can never know what it was before that. In the words of the English historian, C.V. Wedgwood, who was commenting on how we grasp history but might just as well have been talking about *Nachträglichkeit*, "We know the end before we know the beginning and we can never know what it was to know the beginning only" (quoted by Atlas 1995, p. 1).

Faimberg (2007) suggests that the concept of *Nachträglichkeit* be broadened so that it refers not just to the narrow range of life Freud described when he introduced the idea as part of his seduction theory but to a much wider range of phenomena—wider even than Laplanche envisions. For Faimberg, *Nachträglichkeit* encompasses all those events in which some contemporary event—a psychoanalytic interpretation, for instance—shifts unconscious influences in the present in such a way that new meanings come about in the past; old meanings change.

Here is the key point: whereas much of North American psychoanalysis—interpersonal, relational, self-psychological, and Freudian—emphasizes that psychic life is the developmental outcome of the impact of the past on the present, the French perspective (and to a significant extent, the Kleinian and Bionian) lays relatively more emphasis on the idea that psychic life is the outcome of the influence of the present on the past. This is an important difference. It is not absolute, of course, which is why I have portrayed it as a matter of emphasis. But the difference exists.

Jung, of course, made a significant contribution to this issue, one that decidedly does not fall on the North American side of the problem. It was partly to contest Jung's doctrine of *Zurückphantasieren*, or retrospective phantasy, that Freud (1918), in the Wolf Man case, offered one of his few statements of *Nachträglichkeit*. Jung had held that sexual memories of infancy and childhood were largely created later in life, via a process of phantasy, so that our histories are symbolic representations of our current states of mind (e.g., Jung 1912). According to Laplanche and Pontalis (1973, p. 112):

> The adult reinterprets his past in his phantasies, which constitute so many symbolic expressions of his current problems. On this view reinterpretation is a way for the subject to escape from the present "demands of reality" into an imaginary past.

The roles of infantile and childhood trauma, along with that of infantile sexuality, were thereby de-emphasized (although Jung did not fully disavow them). Freud was unwilling to grant this degree of formative influence to contemporary fantasy, nor was he willing to sacrifice a concept as central to his work as infantile sexuality. The concept of *Nachträglichkeit* was a solution to that problem because, by portraying early sexual trauma as having been laid down in memory traces without being experienced as sexual at the time—only becoming sexually traumatic later in life—it allowed Freud to continue to claim a certain degree of emphasis for the role of "real" childhood trauma in the etiology of adult psychopathology. As is well known, Freud could not tolerate Jung's disagreement on these issues, and the split between the two men was in this way set in motion.

Some may justly feel that what I have just said about Laplanche and Faimberg, and also about French psychoanalysis in general, runs roughshod over parts of French thinking that I don't understand. I can only hope that I have characterized the concept of afterwardsness well enough that the comparison I am about to make is reasonable: I want to suggest that the raw material of Faimberg's broadened conception of *Nachträglichkeit*—that which corresponds to what Laplanche calls that "something" from which the process of afterwardsness creates meaning—bears a relationship to what I have described as unformulated experience (Stern 1983, 1997).

To anchor this, let me repeat here my earlier definition of unformulated experience: it is potential experience, what experience might become; it is vague, primitive, global, and affectively charged. In each moment, we reformulate the experience that has come before. While the last moment's contents of mind are the greatest influence on the contents of the next moment, there is also always wiggle room, so that no experience is fully predetermined. Each moment's experience becomes the unformulated experience of the next moment's actuality.

What I want to draw attention to is this: while in many psychoanalytic theories, especially those centered on development, life is portrayed from beginning to end, in a linear way that evokes *chronos*, in other psychoanalytic theories (in particular the theory of unformulated experience, Faimberg's expanded conception of *Nachträglichkeit*, and Laplanche's theory), meaning is created retroactively, along the lines of *kairos*. All these conceptions, while differing in other respects, have in common the point that meaning in the present is assigned to a "something" that already exists in the mind, but without explicit shape.

Now, in the context of this discussion it seems *apropos* to ask whether there is a correspondence between dissociation in my thinking and whatever it is that is responsible, in Faimberg's and Laplanche's theories, for the fact that the new meanings that come about via *afterwardsness* did not come about earlier than they did. In other words, is there sometimes a defensive aspect to the postponement of new meaning in French theory, a defensive aspect that we could understand to prevent new meaning in Faimberg's and Laplanche's work in the same way that dissociation sometimes prevents new meaning in my own? Would it be reasonable to say, from my frame of reference, that Laplanche's "something" exists in a state of dissociation until it becomes subject to what Laplanche calls translation? Could we say that all those enigmatic messages in the *enclave*—that is, the messages that have never been subject to translation at all—are dissociated?

It is probably misleading to be very precise in our application of terms here. "Dissociation," after all, does not really signify in Laplanche's work.

But with that proviso, it does seem to me that the answer is probably that there is indeed a relationship between his theories and mine. Only a small portion of unformulated experience is dissociated, after all. Unformulated experience, like Laplanche's "something," is potential experience that has not yet been articulated. Only some portion of that potential experience is actively dissociated—i.e., is refused articulation for psychodynamic reasons. The largest portion of unformulated experience merely awaits the arrival in the mind of a relevant intention, often in the form of a state of being that is given current relevance by the interpersonal field. When that happens, the unformulated experience that is possible to create from that newly relevant self-state is given a shape without much difficulty. These are the smoothly accomplished self-state shifts—for both patient and analyst, who more or less effortlessly maintain at such moments a comfortable responsiveness to one another—that I have described in clinical terms as "continuous productive unfolding" (Stern 2010, pp. 116–118).

Conclusion

Let me end by returning to my patient George. Recently, a year or so after the episode I recounted earlier, George had a dream in which he was looking across a meadow. He had the spooky sense that something was out there in the meadow, something was buried, something terrible, something he *should have known* was there for a very long time—but somehow he had not known until now.

I listened for quite a while without saying anything. I had my own associations about what this "something" was, but I was reluctant to impose a shape on it. After some time, though, I did say that "something terrible buried in a field" reminded me of a body. Yes, George said, he had thought of that. He continued talking, but without adding anything about the nature of what was buried.

Now, as you already know, I believe that the patient's experience and my own are part of a field created between us, so that while I might not be able to know exactly *how* my experience is related to the patient's, I do have the confidence that, during a session, whatever is going on in my mind is linked to the patient's experience in one way or another. And so I said to George that I didn't know what was buried in the ground, but that I couldn't help thinking of the cellar, because of the ominousness of the situation and the eerie feeling he was having about it. You remember the cellar: that was where the sexual abuse of George, if it actually happened, took place when he was a small boy. George responded to this comment with a spark of recognition. Yes, he said, it was indeed the cellar feeling he was having. I will not go into the details of what emerged at this juncture, but I will say that suddenly we were able to talk about what this buried thing was.

Dissociation is not a process that applies directly to psychic products such as memories, thoughts, feelings, and so on. Instead, for most interpersonal and relational analysts (e.g., Stern 1997, 2010, 2015b; Bromberg 1998, 2006, 2011), dissociation applies to aspects of identity, states of being that perhaps bear a relationship to what Jung would call complexes. What is dissociated is the possibility of being the person who *would have had* certain memories, thoughts, and feelings. When a dissociation is breached, a piece of one's being that had been sequestered, available only in the form of an enactment—and therefore unformulated, outside the range of symbolization—is suddenly accessible as a state of self, and this state of self is defined by the experience that can be formulated from within it.

The enactment in this instance was very mild: George did not start out occupying the state of being in which he could know that the buried thing in the dream-field was affectively connected to the cellar, but it took no more than me mentioning that possibility for him to be able to shift into a state in which the thought and feeling were readily available. The dissociation involved here is an example of what I (Stern 1997, pp. 129–145) have called "dissociation in the weak sense." There was very little emotional pain associated with breaching it, and the experience it allowed was not especially aversive. The part of subjectivity from which this thought could be accessed, in other words, was already part of the self. It was already "me"; we were not contending with the kind of much more difficult and troubling situation that often comes about when the sequestered part of subjectivity is not part of the self—what Sullivan, Bromberg, and I all call "not-me."

And yet, even if it was a mild dissociation, this does seem to have been a moment in which a dissociation was breached, a different self-state came to the fore, and a new experience was formulated. We might also say that this was a moment in which the kind of "already there" that Laplanche and Pontalis (1968, 1973) describe as the raw material of *Nachträglichkeit* was given an explicit shape for the first time. George even chose the word "something" to describe the thing that was already there, the very word Laplanche and Pontalis selected to represent unshaped meaning.

Notes

1 Along with Modell (1990), D. N. Stern (2004) has addressed the roles of *chronos* and *kairos* in psychoanalysis.
2 For other recent perspectives on *Nachträglichkeit* that, like Faimberg's, complement the perspective I offer here, but without explicitly recognizing the distinction between *chronos* and *kairos*, see Birksted-Breen (2003) and Dahl (2010).
3 For the history of the concept of the interpersonal field, and discussions of its current significance, see Stern 2013, 2015a, 2015b.
4 Expanding on Michael Fordham's (1974) work on "Defences of the self" and Leopold Stein's (1967) earlier conception of the "immunological" disfunction of the self, Donald Kalsched (2013b, 2015) is in the process of integrating interpersonal and relational views of trauma, including the ideas about enactment I have just referenced in the text, into the Jungian literature. Kalsched (1996, 2013a) has also addressed the role of trauma in general in the contemporary Jungian perspective.
5 Was I also sometimes the shadowy man? I often wondered, of course. I might even say that I found it hard to imagine otherwise. But in those days, however plausible that understanding was, clinical events did not seem to me to confirm it. More recently, though, good clinical evidence of this aspect of the relatedness has come to light. Regrettably, I do not have the space in this chapter to go into that aspect of the case.
6 Neither Birksted-Breen (2003) nor Faimberg (2007) suggests that this distinction is unproblematic. In fact, both papers are written in a way that questions it.
7 For those unfamiliar with Laplanche, good secondary sources are Fletcher (2007) and Scarfone (2013). I found that the primary sources to start with are *New Foundations for Psychoanalysis* (Laplanche 2016) and *Freud and the Sexual* (Laplanche 2011).
8 They are stored, or better, lodged, in what Laplanche refers to as the *enclave*.

References

Atlas, J. (1995). 'Pinpointing a moment on the map of history'. *New York Times,* Section 4 ('Week in Review'), Sunday, March 19.
Baranger, M. & Baranger, W. (1961–1962/2008). 'The analytic situation as a dynamic field'. *International Journal of Psychoanalysis,* 89, 795–826.
Benjamin, J. (1990). 'Recognition and destruction: Ān outline of intersubjectivity'. In *Relational Psychoanalysis: The Emergence of a Tradition,* eds. S.A. Mitchell & L. Aron. Hillsdale, NJ: The Analytic Press, 1999.
Benjamin, J. (2004). 'Beyond doer and done to: An intersubjective view of thirdness'. *Psychoanalytic Quarterly,* 73, 5–46.
Benjamin, J. (2017). *Beyond Doer and Done To.* New York: Routledge.
Bion, W.R.R. (1962). *Learning from Experience.* London: William Heinemann.
Birksted-Breen, D. (2003). 'Time and the *après-coup*'. *International Journal of Psychoanalysis,* 84, 1501–1515.
Botella, C. & Botella, S. (2005). *The Work of Psychic Figurability: Mental States without Representation.* Trans. A. Weller & M. Zerbib. Hove: Brunner-Routledge.
Bromberg, P.M. (1998). *Standing in the Spaces: Essays on Clinical Process, Trauma, and Dissociation.* Hillsdale, NJ: The Analytic Press.
Bromberg, P.M. (2006). *Awakening the Dreamer: Clinical Journeys.* Hillsdale, NJ: The Analytic Press.
Bromberg, P.M. (2011). *The Shadow of the Tsunami: And the Growth of the Relational Mind.* New York: Routledge.

Civitarese, G. (2012). *The Violence of Emotions: Bion and Post-Bionian Psychoanalysis.* London: Routledge.

Dahl, G. (2010). 'The two time vectors of *Nachträglichkeit* in the development of ego organization: Significance of the concept for the symbolization of nameless traumas and anxieties'. *International Journal of Psychoanalysis,* 91, 727–744.

Faimberg, H. (2005). 'Après-coup'. *International Journal of Psychoanalysis,* 86, 1–6.

Faimberg, H. (2007). 'A plea for a broader concept of *Nachträglichkeit*'. *Psychoanalytic Quarterly,* 76, 1221–1240.

Faulkner, W. (1929/1946). *The Sound and the Fury & As I Lay Dying.* New York: Modern Library.

Ferro, A. (2009). 'Transformations in dreaming and characters in the psycho-analytic field'. *International Journal of Psychoanalysis,* 90, 209–230.

Ferro, A. & Civitarese, G. (2016). 'Psychoanalysis and the analytic field'. In *The Routledge Handbook of Psychoanalysis in the Social Sciences and Humanities,* ed. A. Elliot & J. Prager. London: Routledge.

Fletcher, J. (2007). 'Seduction and the vicissitudes of translation: The work of Jean Laplanche'. *Psychoanalytic Quarterly,* 76, 4, 1241–1291.

Foehl, J.C. (2014). 'Rays of the world: Depth and the reversibility of time'. *Rivista Psicoanalisi,* 60, 481–496.

Fordham, M. (1974). 'Defences of the self'. *Journal of Analytical Psychology,* 19, 2, 192–199.

Freud, S. (1895). 'The hysterical proton pseudos (case of "Emma")'. In 'Project for a scientific psychology'. *SE* 1.

Freud, S. (1896). 'Letter 52. Extracts from the Fliess papers'. *SE* 1.

Freud, S. (1897). 'Letter 75. Extracts from the Fliess papers'. *SE* 1.

Freud, S. (1918). 'From the history of an infantile neurosis'. *SE* 17.

Green, A. (1975). 'The analyst, symbolization, and absence in the analytic setting'. *International Journal of Psychoanalysis,* 56, 1–22.

Green, A. (1999). *The Work of the Negative,* trans. Andrew Weller. London: Free Association Books.

Green, A. (2002). *Time in Psychoanalysis: Some Contradictory Aspects.* London: Free Association Books.

Greenberg, J.R. & Mitchell, S.A. (1983). *Object Relations in Psychoanalytic Theory.* Cambridge, MA: Harvard University Press.

Jung, C.G. (1912). 'The theory of psychoanalysis'. *CW* 4.

Kalsched, D.E. (1996). *The Inner World of Trauma: Archetypal Defenses of the Personal Spirit.* London: Routledge.

Kalsched, D.E. (2013a). *Trauma and the Soul: A Psychospiritual Approach to Human Development and Its Interruption.* London: Routledge.

Kalsched, D.E. (2013b). 'Encounters with "dis" in the clinical situation and in Dante's *Divine Comedy*'. Psychoanalytic Inquiry, 33, 5, 479–495.

Kalsched, D.E. (2015). 'Revisioning Fordham's "Defences of the self" in light of modern relational theory and contemporary neuroscience'. *Journal of Analytical Psychology,* 60, 477–496.

Lacan, J. (1953/1966). 'The function and field of speech and language in psychoanalysis'. In *Écrits: A Selection,* trans. A. Sheridan. London: Tavistock.

LaFarge, L. (2014). 'On time and deepening in psychoanalysis'. *Psychoanalytic Dialogues,* 24, 304–316.

Laplanche, J. (1998). 'Notes on afterwardsness'. In *Essays on Otherness,* eds. J. Fletcher & L. Thurston, trans. P. Slotkin & L. Hill. London/New York: Routledge.

Laplanche, J. (2011). *Freud and the Sexual,* trans. J. House & N. Ray. New York: Unconscious in Translation.

Laplanche, J. (2016). *New Foundations for Psychoanalysis,* trans. J. House. New York: Unconscious in Translation.

Laplanche, J. & Pontalis, J.-B. (1967). *Vocabulaire de la Psychanalyse.* Paris: Presses Universitaires de France.

Laplanche, J. & Pontalis, J.-B. (1968). Fantasy and the origins of sexuality. *International Journal of Psychoanalytic Psychotherapy,* 49, 1–18.

Laplanche, J. & Pontalis, J.-B. (1973). *The Language of Psycho-Analysis,* trans. D. Nicholson Smith. New York: Norton.

Levenson, E.A. (1972). *The Fallacy of Understanding: an Inquiry into the Changing Structure of Psychoanalysis.* New York: Basic Books.

Levenson, E.A. (1983). *The Ambiguity of Change.* New York: Basic Books.

Levenson, E.A. (1991). *The Purloined Self: Interpersonal Perspectives in Psychoanalysis,* ed. A. H. Feiner. New York: Contemporary Psychoanalysis Books. Republished in 2016 by Routledge.

Levenson, E.A. (2017). *Interpersonal Psychoanalysis and the Enigma of Consciousness.* New York and London: Routledge.

Levine, H.B., Reed, G.S. & Scarfone, D. (eds.). (2013). *Unrepresented States and the Construction of Meaning: Clinical and Theoretical Contributions.* London: Karnac.

Loewenberg, P. (2015). 'Time in history and in psychoanalysis'. *Journal of the American Psychoanalytic Association,* 63, 769–784.

Maguire, G. (2016). 'Spirits and sinners: Review of *Mr. Splitfoot,* by Samantha Hunt'. *New York Times Book Review,* January 10, 2016.

Marion, P. (2012). 'Some reflections on the unique time of *Nachträglichkeit* in theory and clinical practice'. *International Journal of Psycho-Analysis,* 93, 317–340.

Mitchell, S.A. (1988). *Relational Concepts in Psychoanalysis: An Integration.* Cambridge, MA: Harvard University Press.

Modell, A. (1990). *Other Times, Other Realities.* Cambridge, MA: Harvard University Press.

Modell, A. (2003). *Imagination and the Meaningful Brain.* Cambridge, MA: MIT Press.

Modell, A. (2005). 'Emotional memory, metaphor, and meaning'. *Psychoanalytic Inquiry,* 25, 555–568.

Modell, A. (2009). 'Metaphor – the bridge between feelings and knowledge'. *Psychoanalytic Inquiry,* 29, 6–17.

Puget, J. (2006). 'The use of the past and the present in the clinical setting'. *International Journal of Psychoanalysis,* 87, 1691–1707.

Scarfone, D. (2013). 'A brief introduction to the work of Jean Laplanche'. *International Journal Psycho-Analysis,* 94, 3, 545–566.

Stein, L. (1967)-. 'Introducing not-self'. *Journal of Analytical Psychology,* 12, 2, 97–113.

Stern, D.B. (1983). 'Unformulated experience: from familiar chaos to creative disorder'. *Contemporary Psychoanalysis,* 19, 71–99.

Stern, D.B. (1997). *Unformulated Experience: From Dissociation to Imagination in Psychoanalysis*. New York: Routledge.

Stern, D.B. (2010). *Partners in Thought: Working with Unformulated Experience, Dissociation, and Enactment*. New York: Routledge.

Stern, D.B. (2012). 'Witnessing across time: Accessing the present from the past and the past from the present'. *Psychoanalytic Quarterly*, 81, 53–81.

Stern, D.B. (2013). 'Relational freedom and therapeutic action'. *Journal of the American Psychoanalytic Association*, 61, 227–255.

Stern, D.B. (2015a). 'The interpersonal field: Its place in American psychoanalysis'. *Psychoanalytic Dialogues*, 388–404.

Stern, D.B. (2015b). *Relational Freedom: Emergent Properties of the Interpersonal Field*. New York: Routledge.

Stern, D.N. (2004). *The Present Moment in Psychotherapy and Everyday Life*. New York: Norton & Company.

Thomä, H. & Cheshire, N. (1991). 'Freud's concept of *Nachträglichkeit* and Strachey's "deferred action": Trauma, constructions and the direction of causality'. *International Review of Psycho-Analysis*, 18, 407–427.

Waintrater, R. (2012). 'Intersubjectivity and French psychoanalysis: A misunderstanding?' *Studies in Gender and Sexuality*, 13, 295–302.

Chapter 11

Dissociative multiplicity and unformulated experience

Chapter 11 was written as a commentary on an article by Diamond (2020), "Return of the Repressed: Revisiting Dissociation and the Psychoanalysis of the Traumatized Mind." In that article, Diamond takes the point of view that dissociation has been unnecessarily and unfairly excluded from psychoanalytic thought for reasons that are primarily political, not clinical or intellectual. It is Diamond's intention to undo this wrong by contributing a way of thinking in which repression and dissociation can both be accommodated—that is, in which the two conceptualizations are complementary.

One of the questions I am most often asked is whether dissociation and repression can co-exist. Usually the questioner, like Diamond, believes that they can and do co-exist, and that this "fact" should simply be acknowledged. This is not my perspective. My understanding is that dissociation and repression imply different models of the mind (see Stern [1983, 1997] and Chapter 9 of this book), and that they therefore cannot really co-exist.

This commentary on Diamond's article offered me an opportunity to address this problem. In writing this piece, while I obviously had to present Diamond's arguments in summary form, I explained his points fully enough to allow the commentary to stand alone. What I want to say about repression and dissociation can be understood without consulting Diamond's article.

Diamond's model is simple and straightforward, two characteristics that recommend it. He aims to integrate the two broad categories of unconscious defense in psychoanalysis, dissociation and repression, and then add splitting to the model. On repression, he takes the usual view: repression is the unconsciously motivated removal of mental contents from awareness that have already attained verbal-symbolic form. Dissociation, by contrast, is

DOI: 10.4324/9781032688893-13

the "segregation" (a word Diamond often uses and that I like) or sequestration of mental contents that have not yet attained verbal-symbolic representation. Because these contents cannot be worded, they cannot become conscious (at least not in Diamond's model, in which, as in Freud's (Breuer and Freud 1893; Freud 1895, 1915), consciousness requires verbal-symbolic representation) and therefore cannot be forgotten. Such psychic contents were never conscious, really, in the first place. They are registered only on the somatic level, and so when they threaten the stability of the mind, segregation is the only way to deal with them.

Diamond recognizes two different kinds of dissociation. *Primary dissociation*, the conception often used by trauma theorists, who are often not identified with psychoanalysis, comes into play in response to trauma, and is an "unconscious protective autoregulation that keeps psychic experiences separated from consciousness while obliterating the sense of personal agency" (p. 852). Primary dissociation, in other words, is "automatic" (i.e., not the outcome of psychodynamic processes, but a survival mechanism). It is not unconsciously motivated, and should not be understood to be deployed like a defensive process. Rather, it takes place apart from agency; it happens.

But, saying he is taking a page from contemporary interpersonal/relational writers, Diamond wants also to recognize *secondary dissociation*, a dynamically meaningful defensive process that he portrays as "originating in unconscious experiences of internal conflict, particularly when unacceptable object representations and fantasies are activated" (p. 852). As in primary dissociation, contents are dealt with by segregating them, but unlike primary dissociation, this segregation is not an automatic, nondynamic survival mechanism but an unconsciously motivated defensive process. What repression is to verbal-symbolic meaning, secondary dissociation is to somatically represented meaning. Diamond cites my work and that of Philip Bromberg as part of his inspiration for secondary dissociation.[1] But Diamond leaves out what differentiates our models from his. If he had cited those distinctions, he could not have used Bromberg's work and mine to support his view. I take up these distinctions below.

To top off his model, in a neatly thought out point, Diamond defines his fourth defensive category, splitting, as the segregation of verbal-symbolic meanings. In Diamond's terms, then, we might describe splitting as the dissociation of verbal-symbolic meanings. Both verbal-symbolic meanings (via secondary dissociation) and somatic meanings (via splitting), then, can be sequestered for defensive reasons.

Comparing dissociation and repression across theories

Diamond believes that the fact that dissociation and repression have seldom, if ever, been integrated into a single theory of defense has been due to an unnecessary commitment to the belief that the theories in which these two ideas originate clash with one another (or at least that they clash in this particular way) and therefore cannot co-exist. Janet's thinking (1889; Ellenberger 1970), the hypnoid states theory of hysteria of Freud and (especially) Breuer (Breuer and Freud 1893), and Ferenczi's model of mind (e.g., 1931), too, writes Diamond, were unnecessarily vilified in the mainstream psychoanalytic literature of most of the twentieth century. They were portrayed as contradictions to the concept of repression that Freud developed as he moved into a theory in which the mind derives not from relations with the outside world (as in Janet's thinking, or Freud's seduction theory) but from relations with the inner one. Dissociation, in other words, was thought to contradict the theory of mind shaped by drive theory, the topographic model, and eventually the structural model.

Diamond believes that this rejection of dissociation was unnecessary, a theoretical development motivated politically for the most part. The same kind of politically fueled rejection of dissociation by North American Freudians, Diamond believes, was the consequence of the theoretical chasm that opened early in the twentieth century between their theory, which employed repression, and interpersonal and relational psychoanalysis, which were (and still are) often grounded in dissociation. As a result of these underlying schisms, what Diamond believes is the simple fact that dissociation and repression co-exist has gone largely unrecognized, and psychoanalysis has been denied important clinical and theoretical ideas.

It is time, Diamond tells us, to understand the underlying pairs of theories (seduction theory and drive theory; Freudian theory and relational theory) as complementary, not contradictory. If we rethink repression and dissociation without what Diamond considers unnecessary theoretical "baggage"— that is, if we understand them from the bottom up, avoiding a theory-driven definition of the issues involved—Diamond believes we will be able to give a coherent account in which repression and dissociation (and splitting) can each be accommodated. Diamond's desire to bring repression and dissociation together is an attempt to create unity where he believes its absence is a political matter, an accident of intellectual politics.

I hardly disagree with the pursuit of parsimony. But dissociation as it was used by Janet, Breuer, and Ferenczi, and then by interpersonal and relational writers, simply isn't dissociation as Diamond employs the term. (I address the details of this problem of definition just below.) One can't just pluck dissociation and repression from their contexts in their theories of origin and then simply use them in different contexts, the way one might take a plain white button off one shirt and sew it onto another. What the terms *dissociation* and *repression* mean is shaped by the roles they play in the theories in which they function. If dissociation and repression were each separately fungible—that is, if each way of using the terms were interchangeable with alternative versions—Diamond's argument for parsimony would work. But that's not the case in our field today. One of the great bugaboos for comparative psychoanalysis is the embeddedness of ideas in their larger theoretical surrounds: often, even usually, we can't depend on what appears to be a relationship of identity, or even similarity, between two ideas drawn from different theories (Stern 2013).

I want to be clear that I am not rejecting Diamond's ideas in and of themselves. While writers may or may not agree with Diamond's characterization of dissociation, his way of using the term can at least be accommodated by any theory in which dissociation is used in a model of the mind as unitary (e.g., Blass 2015; Lombardi 2016). Diamond's thinking, that is, does not contradict the underlying premises of such theories. But, as we shall see in a moment, Diamond's way of defining dissociation does contradict the defining aspects of contemporary psychoanalytic views in which dissociation leads to the multiple self. In particular, it contradicts the interpersonal/relational understandings of dissociation that Bromberg and I have proposed over the last several decades.

Dissociative multiplicity

In a recent article, O'Neil (2018), addressing what he calls the "polysemy" of the term *dissociation*, offers three different definitions of the phenomenon. The first two are helpful in defining the issues I want to bring up about dissociation as Diamond discusses it. Here are the three definitions.

1. *Dissociative multiplicity*, or the hypnoid view, goes back "at least" to the nineteenth century and the views of Janet. This is the oldest definition, and the original one. In this kind of dissociation, trauma results in the fragmentation of consciousness itself, and each piece of the personality, or self, comes to have an independent existence. In extreme cases, this form of dissociation results in dissociative identity disorder (DID). This earliest form of dissociation remains the basis today for psychoanalytic theories of the multiple self (Bromberg 1998, 2006, 2011; Stern 1997, 2010, 2015).[2] Sounding very much like Bromberg, O'Neil writes that "autohypnotic [i.e., hypnoid] defenses mobilized against threat and overwhelming experience may facilitate immediate survival, but then linger long after the threat has passed, and become the core of subsequent mental structure" (p. 264).

O'Neil's second definition is *dissociation of mental faculties of a given consciousness*: "Sensation, emotion, intention, thought, action, etc., are disconnected from the central consciousness" (p. 264). In this definition, dissociation is not fragmentation of consciousness itself, or of the personality. Instead, experience in the various faculties (sensation, emotion, and so on) is separated from consciousness, which is conceptualized as unitary.

Only recently, and controversially, says O'Neil, has the third definition, *depersonalization and derealization*, been accepted by clinicians as a designation of dissociative phenomena. For the present purpose, this third definition may be disregarded.

In Diamond's paper, dissociation is understood according to the second of these definitions, "dissociation of mental faculties of a given consciousness." Diamond's dissociation, that is, takes place in a mind or self conceptualized as unitary. Both Diamond's primary dissociation and his secondary dissociation are forms of this way of thinking: psychic contents (memories, fantasies, and so on) are segregated from awareness by being denied verbal-symbolic representation.

Theories of the multiple self, on the other hand, such as Bromberg's and my own, are ways of accounting for O'Neil's first form of dissociation, "dissociative multiplicity." Let me quote Bromberg (2003), who offers in the following passage an overview of this way of understanding dissociation:

> Interestingly, dissociation, in human beings, is fundamentally not a
> defense but a normal hypnoid capacity of the mind that works in the

service of creative adaptation. It is a normal *process* that can become a mental *structure*. As a process, it can become enlisted as a defense against trauma by disconnecting the mind from its capacity to perceive what is too much for selfhood and sometimes sanity to bear. It reduces what is in front of someone's eyes to a narrow band of perceptual reality ("Whatever is going on is not happening to *me*"). As a defense against the *recurrence* of trauma, it creates a mental structure that serves as an early warning system. Its key quality is its ability to retain the adaptational protection afforded by the hypnoid separateness of incompatible self states, so that each can continue to play its own role, unimpeded by awareness of the others.

[p. 560]

And so in dissociation as a hypnoid phenomenon, or as what O'Neil calls dissociative multiplicity, trauma results in the creation of states of mind, being, or self that are, in important respects, independent of (dissociated or sequestered from) one another. Trauma, from this perspective, is not limited to terrifying or life-threatening experiences. Indeed, in Bromberg's frame of reference (1998, 2006, 2011) each of us experiences as we grow up, in various ways, "developmental" or "relational trauma," which may be deeply distressing but is not life-threatening. And so all of us dissociate along the way. As a consequence, we have all created multiple, structuralized states of mind.

Diamond cites Bromberg and me as writers whose contributions he wishes to integrate into a unitary theory of dissociation and repression. Either Diamond doesn't recognize the conflict between his theory and ours, or he believes that our views can simply be folded into the model he proposes—as if his model is commodious enough to contain our ideas, as well as those of Janet, Breuer (who championed the hypnoid view in his early work with Freud), and Ferenczi. If we were to accept this perspective, "dissociative multiplicity" would simply disappear as a separate point of view, absorbed by "dissociation of mental faculties of a given consciousness." This outcome, of course, is unacceptable to those of us who think of the self as multiple, as a dynamic amalgam of states of mind. While I accept that Diamond's model is a viable model of dissociation if the mind is taken to be unitary, I cannot accept that it either replaces or contains dissociative multiplicity.

Symbolization and unformulated experience

There is another aspect of Diamond's thinking that, if I were to accept it, would require me to sacrifice my own point of view. This contradictory aspect has to do with the role of symbolization in Diamond's views, on the one hand, and, on the other, in my theory of unformulated experience (Stern 1997, 2010, 2015, 2018). I am often asked whether dissociation and repression can co-exist in my frame of reference. I reply that, no, they cannot. This commentary offers me an opportunity to explain why I see things that way.

In most psychoanalytic models, when experience that has reached verbal-symbolic form is too anxiety-provoking, it must be removed from consciousness. It must be repressed, that is, forced out of consciousness into the dynamic unconscious. Sometimes such experience is removed after it has become conscious; more often its impending appearance in awareness sets off signal anxiety, and that anxiety in turn sets defensive processes in motion even before the experience becomes the focus of awareness. In either case, though, defense in the repression model is a matter of preventing access to meanings that already exist in symbolic form, and that, even when they are banished from consciousness, continue to exist, fully formed, in another, unconscious part of the mind.[3] This, as we shall see, is not the case when experience is maintained in its unformulated state for unconscious defensive reasons.

When I began to write about unformulated experience (Stern 1983), I was deeply impressed by a brief remark made by Harry Stack Sullivan:

> One has information about one's experience only to the extent that one has tended to communicate it to another or thought about it in the manner of communicative speech. Much of that which is ordinarily said to be *repressed* is merely unformulated.
>
> (Sullivan 1940, p. 185)

This passage linked in my mind with my conviction that the process by which contents arrive in consciousness is not best described as the uncovering or revelation of previously shaped meanings, but as the emergence of new experience, as the creation of fully formed meanings and experiences from vaguer, more global, and affectively saturated precursors. I called this vaguely structured state "unformulated experience" and found evidence for it in experimental cognitive psychology, philosophy, literary criticism, and psychoanalysis. Unconsciousness, I proposed then (Stern 1983), is not composed of fully formed meanings. It is instead *potential meaning*. Unformulated experience is the pre-existing, unconscious, raw form of what consciousness can, or might, become.

Then and now, my understanding of moment-to-moment psychic life is that consciousness is always in process, continuously being reshaped and reborn. Consciousness, that is, is in a ceaseless process of formulation and reformulation, in which each moment's formulations are the heaviest influences on the nature of the formulations that come about in the moment after that. And yet there is always "wiggle room." Never is the next moment's conscious experience fully predetermined. Novelty is ensured, but the significance of history is unquestioned.

Defense, in this way of thinking, needed to be reimagined. Certain formulations could not be allowed to come into being, because they were what Sullivan (1953)—and later, Bromberg and I—referred to as "not-me." Not-me, if it were to shape awareness, would lead one to feel that one was what one *will not, cannot, must not* be. If one were forced to accept the presence of not-me in consciousness, one would not be recognizable to oneself. Such an outcome is aversive for anyone, of course, but for highly traumatized people, it can provoke a psychotic episode.

The process by which consciousness is ceaselessly renewed should not be understood as a spontaneous, unfettered thing. The formulation of experience, that is, is hardly the result of idealized, pristine inner promptings. Rather, it is continuously compromised by the defensive avoidance of certain formulations, motivated by our need and demand for emotional safety. Some formulations must simply not be made. These "not-me's" habitually go unformed; they remain unsymbolized. They have no shaped or structural presence in the mind. They are like the white spaces in a painting: they have no actual presence, and yet their absence gives shape to other presences. These white spaces—unformulated experience that, in an ongoing way, is continuously denied formulation for unconscious defensive reasons—are what I describe as "dissociated experience," and the process by which their formulation is habitually prevented is my understanding of "dissociation."

Experience is formulated, in other words, along familiar paths that tend to guarantee that conscious experience will continue to be safe—recognizable as one's own. States of being that are emotionally safe in this way "feel like me" and can be "accepted" and "used" in the spontaneous construction of creative living (Stern 2018). Other states of mind, not- me, that do not promise this kind of safety are dissociated, maintained in an unsymbolized, defensively unformulated, dynamically unconscious state. This is a hypnoid view of dissociation, a model that, along with Bromberg's, falls within O'Neil's "dissociative multiplicity." In these models, dissociation is not the enforced separation of particular experiences from a central consciousness, but the sequestering of states of mind from one another and the consequent fragmentation of the mind or self.

To maintain psychic stability in models of dissociative multiplicity is to make inaccessible, via unconscious defensive processes, portions of one's own mind, or possibilities for one's own identity. It is as if the doors of certain rooms in a mansion were locked, so that one could never go there. And yet the possibilities for other, different lives stay alive in those locked rooms.

The potential experience that is dissociated in this way cannot be interpreted in psychoanalytic treatment, because it is not symbolically realized. It would take far too long to offer an adequate description here of what this conceptualization means for the conduct of psychoanalytic work (see Stern 1997, 2010, 2015, 2018). Suffice it to say that therapeutic action has to do with "thawing" the "frozen" places in the interpersonal field, rigid forms of relatedness that have the function, and create the effect, of locking one into familiar forms of thought, feeling, and relatedness. These "frozen places" in the field manifest as enactments between patient and analyst, and enactments, in turn, are "the interpersonalization of dissociation" (Stern 2004, 2010). When we work successfully with enactments, the field thaws and some part of previously dissociated not-me becomes available for use in the creation of ongoing living.

Dissociation, as I envision it, is the defensive prevention of symbolization. That much Diamond and I have in common. Diamond does acknowledge that dissociation can have to do with the defensive prevention of symbolization (at least verbal symbolization). That is what he means by "secondary dissociation."

But for Diamond, secondary dissociation is only one possibility. Another is repression, the banishment of formulated verbal experience to the unconscious. In my model, there is no place for repression—or for splitting, for that matter—because those two processes are understood, by most of those who use the terms, including Diamond, to operate on previously accessible, symbolically realized experience, which continues to exist in the unconscious after the event of repression.

In my frame of reference, by contrast, previously formulated experience that must be rejected for dynamic reasons is (we could say) "shredded" in the continuous process of reformulation, as all experience is fated to be, and then is simply not created again in the next moment. Defense, in other words, is not the banishment of pre-existing meaning to a mythical psychic geography, the unconscious, but the unconscious refusal to create those meanings in the first place. The same previously symbolized meanings that are repressed in Diamond's model, that is, simply disappear, in my way of thinking, in the ongoing process of casting and recasting that is the continuous reconstruction of awareness. This part of the mind once again becomes unformulated, as it was before its initial construction. It may then become available for reformulation at some later time, if and when the interpersonal field changes in such a way that the meaning no longer feels intolerably alien. But in the meantime it is not simply "there" in the unconscious, like repressed meaning; it is not awaiting a relaxation of the grip of the defensive process that "put it there," ready to emerge in the same form it had before its disappearance from consciousness.

Concluding thoughts

I cannot accept Diamond's portrayal of dissociation for two reasons: I would need to sacrifice dissociative multiplicity, which would invalidate both Bromberg's theory and my own; and I would have to jettison my theory of symbolization, unformulated experience. While theoretical integration can be valuable under some circumstances, bringing conflicting ideas under the same roof can also run roughshod over differences that are better maintained and studied. The accounts of dissociation contributed by Bromberg and me cannot be used to support Diamond's integrative project.

In the interest of considering Diamond's perspective on its own terms, I have not even broached yet what is the most substantial difference between Diamond's point of view and my own, and I want to do that briefly before ending this response to his paper. Diamond's thinking is rooted in the longstanding tradition of North American psychoanalytic ego psychology, in which clinical work centers around knowing (insight), the achievement of symbolization, largely verbal symbolization, accomplished via the analyst's interpretive activity. Diamond's integration of repression, dissociation, and splitting is his account of how to conceptualize as mechanisms our difficulties in accessing certain mental contents, and how to reverse or otherwise deal with those mechanisms, thereby promoting awareness.

I respectfully disagree with the underlying assumptions of this portrayal. All analysts, of course, make interventions that qualify as interpretations. But for those who work as I do, even when we do interpret, the new thoughts we grasp and then convey to our patients are events in an ongoing, emergent process of unconscious, affect-laden, non-rational relatedness that has gone on for a substantial period before the new thought becomes available, and will continue to unfold as the present stretches into the future. The analyst's interpretation is a way station, a location on the path. Much of therapeutic action, on this view, does not depend upon making unconscious meaning accessible in words, and very little of it has to do with the creation of rational understanding of what has been unconscious.[4]

Let me hasten to say that this hardly means that those of us who think this way discard interpretation, or even that we would know how to do so. That is, it goes without saying that verbal symbolization not only retains great analytic value, but also is unavoidable when two people sit down together to tackle the analytic task. But any new understanding is the outcome of the shifts in the interpersonal field that made the new thought (or feeling, or perception) possible. Interpretation, in other words, is not simply an intervention the analyst consciously decides to employ. When it does happen, new understanding is a sign that the important change—the change in the analytic relatedness that made the new understanding possible in the first place—has already transpired (Stern 2015, 2018). And therefore, when we are trying to think about the processes that prevent symbolic realization, or the formulation of experience, processes such as dissociation, we focus more than Diamond does on the nature of what transpires in the analytic relatedness, and less on the rational assessment of mental contents and what to do with them.

Notes

1　Other than her early work with Frawley (Davies and Frawley 1994), Diamond does not cite the work of Jody Davies (1996a,b, 1997, 1998, 1999, 2001a,b, 2003, 2004, 2005, 2006, 2013, 2015) in this regard, but he might have done so. Davies's thinking is as relevant as Bromberg's and mine to the issues of dissociation considered by Diamond. Other significant contemporary contributors to dissociation theory from the interpersonal and relational psychoanalytic traditions include Howell (2005, 2020; Howell and Itzkowitz 2016) and Chefetz (2015).

2 However, neither Bromberg's conception of the multiple self nor my own should be understood to be anchored in DID, as Freud's was anchored in hysteria. Instead, both Bromberg's thinking and mine were deeply influenced by Harry Stack Sullivan (1940, 1953), for whom dissociation was primary for everyone. See Bromberg (1998, 2006, 2011) and Stern (1983, 1997, 2018).

3 This characterization applies to repression as it is understood in Freud's model, and in the North American, ego-psychological versions of repression that were directly inspired by Freud (including Diamond's). It does not apply to certain other uses of the term "repression"—for example, that of Laplanche (2011).

4 Views of this kind are shared today by analysts from a wide variety of theoretical positions. My own position, which I cannot present here, is available in recent publications (e.g., Stern 2010, 2015, 2018).

References

Blass, R.B. (2015). Conceptualizing splitting: On the different meanings of splitting and their implications for the understanding of the person and the analytic process. *International Journal of Psychoanalysis* 96:123–139.

Breuer, J., & Freud, S. (1893). On the psychical mechanism of hysterical phenomena. *Standard Edition* 2:1–17.

Bromberg, P.M. (1998). *Standing in the Spaces: Essays on Clinical Process, Trauma, and Dissociation*. Hillsdale, NJ: Analytic Press.

Bromberg, P.M. (2003). Something wicked this way comes. *Psychoanalytic Psychology* 20:558–574.

Bromberg, P.M. (2006). *Awakening the Dreamer: Clinical Journeys*. Hillsdale, NJ: Analytic Press.

Bromberg, P.M. (2011). *The Shadow of the Tsunami and the Growth of the Relational Mind*. New York: Routledge.

Chefetz, R.A. (2015). *Intensive Psychotherapy for Persistent Dissociative Processes: The Fear of Feeling Real*. New York: Norton.

Davies, J.M. (1996a). Dissociation, repression and reality testing in the countertransference: The controversy over memory and false memory in the psychoanalytic treatment of adult survivors of childhood sexual abuse. *Psychoanalytic Dialogues* 6:189–218.

Davies, J.M. (1996b). Linking the pre-analytic with the postclassical: Integration, dissociation, and the multiplicity of unconscious processes. *Contemporary Psychoanalysis* 32:553–576.

Davies, J.M. (1997). Dissociation, therapeutic enactment, and transference-countertransference processes: A discussion of papers on childhood sexual abuse by S. Grand and J. Sarnat. *Gender & Psychoanalysis* 2:241–257.

Davies, J.M. (1998). Multiple perspectives on multiplicity. *Psychoanalytic Dialogues* 8:195–206.

Davies, J.M. (1999). Getting cold feet defining "safe-enough" borders: Dissociation, multiplicity, and integration in the analyst's experience. *Psychoanalytic Quarterly* 78:184–208.

Davies, J.M. (2001a). Back to the future in psychoanalysis: Trauma, dissociation, and the nature of unconscious processes. In *Storms in Her Head: Freud and the Construction of Hysteria,* ed. M. Dimen & A. Harris. New York: Other Press, pp. 245–264.

Davies, J.M. (2001b). Erotic overstimulation and the co-construction of sexual meanings in transference-countertransference experience. *Psychoanalytic Quarterly* 70:757–788.

Davies, J.M. (2003). Falling in love with love: Oedipal and postoedipal manifestations of idealization, mourning, and erotic masochism. *Psychoanalytic Dialogues* 13:1–27.

Davies, J.M. (2004). Whose bad objects are we anyway? Repetition and our elusive love affair with evil. *Psychoanalytic Dialogues* 14:711–732.

Davies, J.M. (2005). Transformations of desire and despair: Reflections on the termination process from a relational perspective. *Psychoanalytic Dialogues* 15:779–805.

Davies, J.M. (2006). The times we sizzle, and the times we sigh: The multiple erotics of arousal, anticipation, and release. *Psychoanalytic Dialogues* 16:665–686.

Davies, J.M. (2013). My enfant terrible is twenty: A discussion of Slavin's and Gentile's retrospective reconsideration of "Love in the afternoon." *Psychoanalytic Dialogues* 23:170–179.

Davies, J.M. (2015). From oedipus complex to oedipal complexity: Reconfiguring (pardon the expression) the negative oedipus complex and the disowned erotics of disowned sexualities. *Psychoanalytic Dialogues* 25:265–283.

Davies, J.M., & Frawley, M.G. (1994). *Treating the Adult Survivor of Childhood Sexual Abuse*. New York: Basic Books.

Diamond, M.J. (2020). Return of the repressed: Revisiting dissociation and the psychoanalysis of the traumatized mind. *Journal of the American Psychoanalytic Association* 68:839–874.

Ellenberger, H.F. (1970). *The Discovery of the Unconscious: The Evolution of Dynamic Psychiatry*. New York: Basic Books.

Ferenczi, S. (1931). Child-analysis in the analysis of adults. *International Journal of Psychoanalysis* 12:468–482.

Freud, S. (1895). Project for a scientific psychology. *Standard Edition* 1:295–397.

Freud, S. (1915). The unconscious. *Standard Edition* 14:166–215.

Howell, E.F. (2005). *The Dissociative Mind*. New York: Routledge.

Howell, E.F. (2020). *Trauma and Dissociation-Informed Psychotherapy: Relational Healing and the Therapeutic Connection*. New York: Routledge.

Howell, E.F., & Itzkowitz, S., Eds. (2016). *The Dissociative Mind in Psychoanalysis: Understanding and Working with Trauma*. New York: Routledge.

Janet, P (1889). *L'automatisme psychologique*. Paris: Felix Alcan.

Laplanche, J. (2011). *Freud and the Sexual: Essays 2000–2006*, transl. J. House, J. Fletcher, & N. Ray. New York: The Unconscious in Translation.

Lombardi, R. (2016). *Body-Mind Dissociation in Psychoanalysis*. New York: Routledge.

O'Neil, J.A. (2018). Hypnosis and psychoanalysis: Toward undoing Freud's primal category mistake. *American Journal of Clinical Hypnosis* 60:262–278.

Stern, D.B. (1983). Unformulated experience: From familiar chaos to creative disorder. *Contemporary Psychoanalysis* 19:71–99.

Stern, D.B. (1997). *Unformulated Experience: From Dissociation to Imagination in Psychoanalysis*. New York: Routledge.

Stern, D.B. (2004). The eye sees itself: Dissociation, enactment, and the achievement of conflict. *Contemporary Psychoanalysis* 40:197–237.

Stern, D.B. (2010). *Partners in Thought: Working with Unformulated Experience, Dissociation, and Enactment*. New York: Routledge.

Stern, D.B. (2013). Why is comparative psychoanalysis so difficult? Response to commentaries by Foehl and Troise on "Field theory in psychoanalysis, Part I: Harry Stack Sullivan and Madeleine and Willy Baranger." *Psychoanalytic Dialogues* 23:523–527.

Stern, D.B. (2015). *Relational Freedom: Emergent Properties of the Interpersonal Field.* New York: Routledge.

Stern, D.B. (2018). *The Infinity of the Unsaid: Unformulated Experience, Language, and the Nonverbal.* New York: Routledge.

Sullivan, H.S. (1940). *Conceptions of Modern Psychiatry.* New York: Norton, 1953.

Sullivan, H.S. (1953). *The Interpersonal Theory of Psychiatry.* New York: Norton.

Chapter 12

Dissociative enactment and interpellation

This brief presentation on the relation between Jacques Derrida's decon-struction, on the one hand, and trauma/dissociation in clinical psychoa-nalysis, on the other, was written for a panel, "The Traumatic Field: Psychoanalytic Growth and the Growth of Psychoanalysis," one of a num-ber of such panels that composed a conference, "Unknowable, Unspeakable and Unsprung: Psychoanalytic Perspectives on Truth, Scandals, Secrets, and Lies," held on October 5, 2013, in New York City. The panel was con-vened to consider the question of whether psychoanalysis itself might be understood as a symptom of the traumata of those who created it. The pres-entation you are about to read was therefore situated, as you will see, as a contribution to thinking about this possibility.

Some of the things I say here about systemic or structural racism have become much more widely recognized in the years since then, so that if I had the piece to write again, I would probably feel less need to explain what I mean by the binary relation of Black and white. I would more readily take it for granted that my audience would know what I meant.Sadly, though, while the concept of systemic racism is more widely recognized,and while there is simply no reasonable argument that racism is anything other than a continuous presence in American life, I don't have the impression that the idea of systemic racism is today necessarily more widely understood or accepted than it was then. My greatest dissatisfaction with the field of psy-choanalysis today, including my own work, is the relative absence of seri-ous considerations of race. We should be asking, as Derrida did, how our theories reflect structural racism. That is, we should be asking ourselves not only how we can incorporate race into our ideas (that's good, but not enough), but also how psychoanalytic ideas actually embody racist ideol-ogy. How could they not?If racism is baked into American life, why would

DOI: 10.4324/9781032688893-14

it not be baked into American theories? We should be prepared to sacrifice our ideas, or at least modify them appropriately, whenever we manage to see deeply enough into them to grasp whatever racism exists there. Seeing that deeply into ideas we use every day is very difficult—just consider how hard it is, for example, to make a precise formulation of the nature of Nazi influence on Heidegger's philosophy. But it is essential that we make the effort. The part that race plays in our lives is more important than preserving cherished ideas.

As I thought about the question of whether psychoanalysis might itself be considered a symptom of trauma, I found myself drawn to the role of linked pairs of terms in Western thought, and especially to the thinking of Jacques Derrida, one of the most influential twentieth-century philosophers, who devised and described what has become widely known as the deconstruction of meaning. I am going to try to combine the sweep of Derrida's ideas with the contribution of another French philosopher, Louis Althusser; I am then going to connect these ideas about ideology with ideas about dissociation and enactment; and eventually, I am going to arrive at a thought about the practice of psychoanalysis.

I am not thoroughly grounded in Derrida's work, but I know enough about it to understand that it is a variety of the kind of dialectic analysis that I have been thinking and writing about for many years. In a deconstructive analysis, meaning is shaped not only by what it is, but also by what it is not. This principle applies to any writer's work, and for that matter, to all other art or scholarship; in fact, although deconstruction is most commonly applied to verbal language, the principles of deconstruction apply to any human experience that is given symbolic form—not only language, but dance, painting, and so on. For example, we might think of our experience of bodies this way. We might ask about the ways that belonging to our particular time and place leads us, without awareness, to emphasize certain perceptions and meanings of our bodies, and just as unconsciously to de-emphasize others. To which bodily experiences do we grant special significance, and what other such experiences do we tend to keep in shadow?

The structural linguist Saussure long ago put forward the idea that the units of language are defined by means of what he was the first to call "binary oppositions." One cannot understand either term in a binary opposition without also understanding the other, and the relation between the two. Think of "good" and "bad." Some decades later, Derrida added to this account in an important way, arguing that certain highly significant binary oppositions are organized hierarchically and violently, so that one of the two terms dominates and governs the other. I'll offer an example of this phenomenon in just a moment.

In an article in the popular press, written as a kind of intellectual obituary for Derrida and published just a few days after the philosopher's death, the scholar Mark C. Taylor (2004) concisely describes Derrida's principal idea:

> The guiding insight of deconstruction is that every structure – be it literary, psychological, social, economic, political or religious – that organizes our experience is constituted and maintained through acts of exclusion. In the process of creating something, something else inevitably gets left out.

Through Derrida and others, we have become familiar over the last several decades with the harm binary oppositions lead to when our minds are created in their images. A classic example is race in the United States. In the white/black binary opposition, no longer consciously acceptable but nevertheless unconsciously influential on us all, blackness is not only "other" to whiteness, but also defined in a way that devalues blackness. Whiteness is not necessarily actively idealized, but it doesn't need to be, because it is drained of "bad" qualities, which tend to be assigned to blackness, leaving whiteness to occupy the position of standard, uncontroversial decency, without much edge or definition—in a word, normality. Thus white people don't often characterize their own whiteness. They don't need to. It's like physical health: health is what is expectable, and so we understand disease as a deviation from it. Whiteness, especially for white people—although also for people of color under some circumstances—is the "normal" standard from which blackness deviates. Blackness, on the other hand, tends to be characterized in more detail, and often more negatively, and so both white people and black people are inclined to be much more aware of meanings for blackness than for whiteness. We have become familiar over the last decades with similar analyses for many other identity categories defined by binary oppositions: male/female, young/old, straight/gay, and so on. It is not accidental that all these examples have moral or political implications, because, as I've already said, for Derrida binary oppositions always involve power differentials. One term always dominates the other.

As I thought more about these connections, and although I recognized that Derrida was not thinking about trauma when he described the domination of one term in a binary opposition by the other, the conceptual links between deconstruction, psychic trauma, and dissociation fairly leaped out at me. Let me explain.

Consider what happens when trauma leads to dissociation: the outcome is the separation, or sequestration, of states of being from one another. Each exists in isolation from the other, and yet each part of the experience is the missing part of the other, and so each state is the reason that the other is meaningful.[1] I am the familiar "me" only as long as I can keep my dissociated experience—that is, "not-me"—at bay. And "not-me" only continues to exist as long as "me" cannot allow it to become part of itself. We might even say that it is the exclusion of not-me that creates the boundaries of what feels like me. That is why it is so hard for the self to change. To allow not-me to become part of the self is to be a different me.

One could say, using poststructuralist language, that dissociation results in "either/or" experience—me or not-me—and that the challenge in psychoanalytic treatment is to create "both/and" experience. We might say, actually, that our readiness to construct binary oppositions is itself the problem. In fact, although I can't explore this more fully here, this point has been made for decades by relational psychoanalytic writers. Jessica Benjamin (e.g., 1990), in particular, describes the shift to intersubjectivity from the "doer-done-to" dynamics of reversible complementarity. Her work is a meditation on the movement from "either-or" to "both-and."

What I want to suggest is that dissociated states of being, the outcome of trauma—me and not-me—constitute a kind of binary opposition. We see this in dissociative enactments, in which the other person in the interaction is treated as if s/he were manifesting one's own dissociated state. The interaction is commonly structured as something like this: "*I'm* not bad (or narcissistic, hateful, envious, contemptible, and so on). No, *you're* bad." One has access only to a portion of experience, the part that's tolerable; the remainder is assigned to the other, and the two parts must be kept separate. It is a case of either/or: one can occupy *this* state of being or *that* one, but the both/and alternative, which would be to occupy the two states simultaneously, is not feasible until, if things go well, the treatment makes it possible. And notice, just as in the case of the binary oppositions I have already mentioned, that the pole of the dissociative enactment that one characterizes negatively—that is, the experience and conduct of the other—is defined in more detail than the pole that one characterizes positively—the part of the experience attributed to, and experienced as, oneself. In a dissociative enactment, in other words, just as "black" is characterized by those who are white more completely than is "white," in an enactment of my dissociated experience, *you* are characterized more completely than *I* am. *You* are very often some very particular kind of bad (sadistic, or unreasonable, or impossible), but *I* am simply what you are not—good or reasonable in some fairly generic way.

All right: all this may be interesting to think about, but why does it matter to link dissociation/enactment theory and deconstruction? Here we reach the points I most want to make. For Derrida, binary oppositions and their implications for theorizing come about through a social process that we might characterize as more or less impersonal—impersonal, that is, in the sense that the process affects all of us, not just those of us from certain backgrounds or who have suffered certain traumatic experiences. In the United States we are all implicated, to go back to my example, in the continuing existence and reproduction of the identities of "black" and "white," identities that participate in shaping our minds.

Binary oppositions, in other words, tend to be expressions of ideology, the kinds of influences that a large collection of Marxist (e.g., Gramsci) and postmodern (e.g., Foucault) theorists have taught us have the effect, when we acknowledge them (as we all do, like it or not), of constituting our subjectivities. Ideology constitutes us by a process that Louis Althusser (2000/1969), adopting a term and an idea already in circulation at the time he wrote, labeled "interpellation." In Althusser's famous example, when the policeman "hails" us, shouting, "Hey, you!," in the very act of turning around to acknowledge the hail we are shaped into subjects in society's image. In their work on the relation between interpellation and recognition, Guralnick and Simeon (2010) describe the outcome of the policeman's hail this way: "We immediately morph into *self-as-criminal*, thereby revealing where the force of the State and our identity as individuals meet" (p. 407). Our subjectivity congeals in such a moment: we are now *a person who can be hailed in that way by a policeman*; we are subject to that authority; we feel guilty of something. This kind of influence is well-nigh unavoidable.

In interpellation we have the structure of the binary opposition: the two poles, and the dominance of one by the other, all instantiated in a way we might call automatic—or better for our psychoanalytic purposes, unconscious. In the process of interpellation there is no conscious inter-vention on the part of any of the individuals involved. The process is not individually motivated; the subjection of the individual is a social matter.

When we are treated as black or white, we are "hailed," in a sense, and when we acknowledge that treatment, which we do frequently without giv-ing the matter conscious thought, we are in that very moment constituted as participants in the world of black and white, but without the opportunity to consider whether this is what we want, or even approve of. That is what ideology does. Binary oppositions, it seems, are built into the very process by which subjectivity is constituted.

We usually think of dissociative enactments in clinical psychoanalysis and psychotherapy quite differently than that. For one thing, we think of these enactments as personal exchanges, not impersonal ones. But consider what dissociative enactment and interpellation have in common. In both, one person treats another in a way that assigns a certain shape to both sub-jectivities: in Althusser's hail, I am a policeman and you are subject to my authority; in a dissociative enactment, I am a reasonable person and you are not. Often enough, in a dissociative enactment, precisely because the attempt of the other to control the interaction is unconscious to both parties, the one accused, like the person hailed by the policeman, is affected with-out knowing it. Unthinkingly, the accused one takes on the attribution—by which I *don't* mean that the one who is accused of being unreasonable (for example) necessarily accepts that she *is* unreasonable. Actually, the unthought part of the interaction is most often simply that the one who is accused takes part in it in a natural, reciprocal way. What comes naturally, for instance, might be the feeling that *I'm* not unreasonable—no, *you're* unreasonable for accusing me in this crazy way. The effect of the dissocia-tive accusation on the one who is accused, that is, often comes about even if the accused one *disputes* the attribution, because denying influence doesn't necessarily dispel it. In fact, denial, especially if it is defensive in nature, is as much a participation in the enactment as blind acceptance of the attribu-tion would be. Denial can even make the influence less visible and therefore more insidious. In psychotherapy, when the patient unconsciously pres-sures the analyst to assume an uncomfortable role, the shaping effect on the analyst's experience can come about even if the analyst responds with no more than the quiet defensiveness that we would all agree is probably unavoidable when one person floats an accusation against another.

And so we might say that the analyst is "hailed" by the patient in the transference (and sometimes, of course, the patient is hailed by the analyst in the same way), and presto!—there is the countertransference! We might even go so far as to say that in a dissociative enactment one party is *interpellated* by the other. That is similarity number one between interpellation and dissociative enactment: a transformation of subjectivity takes place as the result of the unconsciously motivated treatment of one person by the other.

Now, similarity number two, about which I will be briefer: both interpellation and dissociative enactment result in the establishment of either/or binaries: I am being reasonable; you are not. Complexity vanishes. Similarity number three: in both the case of binary oppositions and dissociative enactments, either/or phenomena are defined by the domination of one term by the other. Derrida makes this point explicitly about the binaries he describes. Dissociative enactments, too, tend to be adversarial, because these interactions are created by the attempt of one person to foist an unconsciously refused and unformulated part of his or her subjectivity on to another.[2]

Where does this leave us? We are brought full circle, back to the question of whether clinical psychoanalysis itself might sometimes be a symptom of trauma. Through our interaction with patients, this view would have it, we sometimes participate in interpellations that call aspects of identity into being—in ourselves and the other; and in this way, outside our awarenesses, these events, the dissociative outcomes of trauma, shape the subjectivities we adopt with particular patients.

I may perhaps be offering a new way to express this point, but the thought itself is hardly new. We've long taken it for granted, after all, that countertransference comes about without our awareness. That's the *point* of countertransference. I'm merely adding that who we are with each of our patients, those states of our being that are called into existence from outside our ken, may come about in a way that bears a similarity to interpellation: there exists a continuity, in other words, between the process of dissociative enactment and the process of interpellation.

Let me finish my remarks by asking about the upshot of this relation of dissociation and interpellation for the aims of our clinical work. I think about this question by first reminding myself what we psychoanalysts seek to accomplish: we try to bring into clinical relatedness what has been excluded from it, and thereby broaden and deepen the field between patient and analyst so that it evolves more freely than it could before. Our work with enactments—which are, after all, rigidities in relatedness, what the Barangers (2009) call "bastions" or "bulwarks" in the field—is primary in this respect. Our work with enactments is where new relational freedom (Stem, 2013) comes from. We try to grasp what eludes us, remembering that the unconscious is two things at once: yes, that which is unknown to us— absences that may even be impossible to symbolize; but also that which is a matter of blind belief, i.e., that which is so present that it's absent: we don't see it or feel it or think it. Unconsciousness of either sort is the absence of curiosity—which means that to be unconscious is not only not to know, but even more importantly, not even to know that we don't know. The roles taken by analyst and patient in a dissociative enactment are frequently so thoroughly taken for granted that, like racism, the meaning or significance of the enactment, of the interpellation, however deeply felt and intensely expressed it may be, remains stubbornly invisible to those living it out. Under these circumstances, the best we can do to avoid being indefinitely mired in the aftermath of trauma—the trauma of the patient, the trauma of the analyst, and all that other trauma suffered by earlier generations and sedimented in our theories and practices—is to embrace uncertainty at every opportunity. We need to recognize in our own rigidity an opportunity for the creation of a new freedom. We often need to wait and watch, accepting that we are not transparent to our own scrutiny, and that we therefore may very well be deeply and unwittingly involved in just the problems in relatedness that we think we are learning to know. It is often the case that, to paraphrase John Lennon, psychoanalysis is what happens while you're busy making other plans.

Derrida agreed with all this. He believed that wisdom, in the words of Mark Taylor (2004), whom I quoted earlier, is "knowing what we don't know so that we can keep the future open." We need to respect the tenacity and insidiousness of ideology. In psychoanalysis, that means not only that we must attend to all those same unconscious effects of identity, such as race, that also take place routinely in the other parts of our lives; we must also maintain a respect for the tenacity and insidiousness of enactment in the clinical situation, while simultaneously tuning ourselves to the pitch of freedom. That's easier said than done, as I have tried to say. It's a hard-won and fragile vision, and every time we locate it in the clinical process, we lose it; it disappears, so that we're constantly in the process of refinding and recreating it. But as hard-won as this vision may be, it is a sound basis for moral and political life—for all human relatedness, for that matter, which is always at risk of collapsing into the kind of interpellative interaction that transmits trauma. It's certainly a sound basis for psychoanalysis.

Notes

1 A colleague pointed out to me that readers who are not familiar with relational disso-ciation/enactment theory may wonder why the use of the concept of dissociation adds anything to the more familiar idea of splitting. For a discussion of these issues, see Stern (2004, 2010).

2 In my conception, all the subjectivity that exists outside the range of consciousness, including the part of subjectivity that is dissociated, is unformulated. By "unformulated experience" I mean to refer to *potential* conscious experience, not fully formed content hidden in the mind or distorted in a way that makes it unrecognizable. Unformulated experience is a vaguely organized, primitive, global, non-ideational, affective state. For an explication of this way of conceptualizing unconscious process and dissociation, see Stern (1997, 2010).

References

Althusser, L. (2000). Ideology and state apparatus. In S. Zizek (Ed.), *Mapping Ideology* (pp. 100–140). New York: Verso. (Original work published 1969.)

Baranger, M. & Baranger, W. (2009). *The Work of Confluence: Listening and Interpreting in the Psychoanalytic Field*. London: Karnac Books.

Benjamin, J. (1990). Recognition and destruction: An outline of intersubjectivity. In S. A. Mitchell & L. Aron (Eds.), *Relational Psychoanalysis: The Emergence of a Tradition*. Hillsdale, NJ: The Analytic Press, 1999, pp. 183–200.

Guralnick, O. & Simeon, D. (2010). Depersonalization: Standing in the spaces between interpellation and recognition. *Psychoanalytic Dialogues,* 20: 400–416.

Stern, D. B. (1997). *Unformulated Experience: From Dissociation to Imagination in Psychoanalysis*. Hillsdale, NJ: The Analytic Press.

Stern, D. B. (2004). The eye sees itself: Dissociation, enactment, and the achievement of conflict. *Contemporary Psychoanalysis,* 40: 197–237.

Stern, D. B. (2010). *Partners in Thought: Working with Unformulated Experience, Dissociation, and Enactment*. New York: Routledge.

Stern, D. B. (2013). Relational freedom and therapeutic action. *Journal of the American Psychoanalytic Association,* 61: 227–255.

Taylor, M. C. (2004). What Derrida really meant. *New York Times,* October 14.

Chapter 13

From interpersonal field to mind in the work of Philip Bromberg

In this chapter I describe in a very condensed way what is, to me, the heart of Philip Bromberg's work: the creation of the mind from the affectively charged events of the interpersonal field, and the rootedness of therapeutic action in the analyst's emotional responsiveness to the enactment of the patient's structuralized dissociations. As I said in the introduction of this book,Philip and I have each tried, over our careers, to contribute in our different ways to the view that problems in living, as well as the practices of creation and repair of mind that compose psychotherapy and psychoanalysis, are processes of the interpersonal field.

However important Philip's ideas are to me—and they are—Philip himself was even more important. Because I am writing about Philip's thought here, though, I will say no more about this empty place in my life than that I miss my friend of 40 years. It has been a brief enough period of time since his death that it has required a certain dissociation for me to focus my attention on writing this condensed statement about his ideas, ideas that have become ever more thoroughly thought out, soulful, and deeply satisfying over the years. From the beginning, Philip held an interpersonal view of the individual mind or self, a view in which it made no sense to think about the mind and the interpersonal field as separate. In interpersonal views, mind is inextricably embedded in the field. Philip added brilliantly to our understanding that the analyst's personal, affectively saturated, unconscious responsiveness to the patient is ceaseless, inevitable, and unavoidable. For him, the negotiation of this mutual responsiveness is the key to therapeutic action (Bromberg, 1998, 2006, 2011).

Remember that Philip grew up in a different psychoanalysis than the one in which many readers of this journal did. (I'm old enough that it was

DOI: 10.4324/9781032688893-15

not so different from the psychoanalysis in which I grew up.) When he was young, the emphatically dominant psychoanalysis of North America was Freudian ego psychology, in which analysts were expected to be authorities who knew what was in their patients' minds before patients themselves did, and who were then expected to tell patients about this truth. These analysts could believe that they had these powers because they imagined that they existed outside the patient's influence, or at least that they *should* exist outside the patient's influence, in a realm defined by objective knowledge and expertise. Philip, like all interpersonal psychoanalysts, and then, later, relational analysts, took issue with this way of understanding our work, our identities, and what it is to be human. We didn't accept that relationships were largely matters of projection, and in particular we didn't accept that transference was exclusively given shape from the inside of the mind. We thought, instead, that relationships, from the beginning of life to those in psychoanalysis, were inevitably two-way streets, and that mind is therefore not so simply sourced in the internal world. Philip took us further in that direction. Harry Stack Sullivan, like the experimental psychologists of his day, and such a significant influence on Philip, felt that the mind was a "black box"—unobservable—and therefore should not be theorized. Philip had no such reticence. He laid out, with his customarily compelling style, a way of understanding that mind is composed of interpersonal relations that have become structuralized. (Being compelling was not something he did only in print—he was the most compelling of human beings.)

Philip took his interest in dissociation from Sullivan's understanding of anxiety. For Sullivan, dissociation is understood as the defensive response to intense anxiety, which in its most extreme forms Sullivan described as "uncanny affect." Anxiety was defined by Sullivan in a way that is still not widely understood. Sullivan's anxiety theory was foundational for Philip: and although he didn't often address it explicitly after those first papers in the 1980s, it is baked into all of his work. And so I will say a few words about it.

In Freud's account, anxiety is a signal of internal danger. "Danger" generally means that drive representations threaten to break through defensive measures. Sullivan's understanding, on the other hand, is what he called a "contagion" theory: we "catch" anxiety from our caretakers. We are extremely sensitive to what, in our behavior or feelings, causes anxiety in our caretakers. That happens because, when they become anxious, we lose affective access to them. At best, at such times, they distance themselves from us; at worst, they hurt us or shame us in one way or another. Philip referred to this kind of relatedness as "developmental trauma." To take a very simple example: if, for reasons that have to do with their own early relationships, a parent is anxious in a dependable way about the child's expression of anger, the child very soon absorbs the lesson that feeling or acting angry deprives them of the parent's relaxed warmth, tender ministrations, and positive regard, and exposes the child to what Sullivan called the parent's "forbidding gestures," most of which create shame. The child embarks on a life in which the unformulated experience that could become anger provokes the child's anxiety. If the anxiety is not too intense, our grown child, while never feeling comfortable with being angry, may be able to stay in touch with their affective experience some of the time. This way of being—that is, the part of oneself that feels angry—remains part of what Sullivan, and then Philip, Richard Chefetz (Chefetz & Bromberg, 2004; Chefetz, 2015), Elizabeth Howell (2005, 2020), I (Stern, 2010, 2015, 2019), and others, have all referred to as "me." This part of the grown child's experience is uncomfortable, but the anxiety responsible for the discomfort does not reach an intensity that demands dissociation. But if the anxiety is intense enough—that is, if it is either massive and/or abusive, or "developmental trauma"—then angry feelings simply do not appear in the child's awareness when they otherwise would have. These parts of experience, because of the intensity of the anxiety, are dissociated and therefore remain unformulated, and for that reason they cannot be experienced as "me." They are what Sullivan, Philip, Rich, Elizabeth, and I (see citations above) have all called "not-me."

"Not-me" doesn't just disappear from consciousness: this is crucial in Philip's model of the mind. In the Freudian scheme, the fate of repressed material actually *is* something like disappearance, because traditional defensive processes are phenomena of the inner world, operating only inside the mind. The meanings that could become dangerous, if they became conscious, are parked in some secret mental corner, or they are distorted, fragmented, or denied. The point is that the mind, in the traditional Freudian scheme, takes action internally, inside itself, to keep dangerous content out of awareness.

But that is exactly what cannot happen in any interpersonal or relational theorization, and Philip's work is at the head of that list. For Philip, each of us (and in Philip's work, this is no less true for the analyst than the patient) will do whatever we can to prevent not-me from controlling consciousness. We have all been that child who lost access to the caretaker's warmth, tender ministrations, and positive regard, and all of us have dissociated whatever it was that we believed provoked that withdrawal of love. And so we avoid allowing into consciousness, at almost all costs, the states of self or mind within which we would be in danger of experiencing that dreaded experience, "not-me," which does not even feel like it belongs to us. In my little example, "not-me" is angry feeling, because the caretaker, in the presence of this feeling, could not stay connected to the child.

What we do to prevent the arrival of "not-me" in consciousness lies at the heart of interpersonal life. In fact, what we do to regulate affective consciousness, by unconsciously controlling, to the extent that we can, which states of being structure it is for Philip one of the most significant influences on the configuration taken by any particular interpersonal field. Here, I will not discuss more about these unconscious preventive measures; let me just say that they fall under the rubric of enactment. I recommend that, if you've not already done so, you study Philip's seminal writings on the subject. In my made-up example, we would expect that, when this child goes into treatment as an adult, their analyst, in one way or another, will unwittingly play out with them the caretaker's intolerance of the child's angry feeling. Philip insisted that this response of the analyst was not in some way extracted by the patient, or part of a collusion of some kind on the part of the analyst. Rather, he said, it was to be understood, by both the patient and analyst, as the analyst's own, personal affective responsiveness.

Philip, then, offers us a view of mind thoroughly imbricated with interpersonal relations. As the configuration of the field continuously shifts and changes, each configuration makes certain affectively defined states of mind relevant to the present moment. Those newly relevant states then take on the function of shaping consciousness, only to be displaced themselves as the field changes yet again, bringing other states to relevance, and thereby changing the possibilities for the contents of consciousness. Usually, with significant exceptions, all of this happens "by itself." That is, our minds and the fields in which we are involved carry out these activities without coming to explicit notice.

I think you can see that, for clinical purposes, perhaps the most significant part of the influence wielded by each newly relevant self-state is *to bring to new relevance a state of mind in the other.* The most significant influence of a state of mind, in other words, may be to select the states of mind in the other that will co-determine what the field is in the process of becoming. And simultaneously, the same thing is happening in reverse: that is, whatever state is aroused in the mind of the other turns around immediately and becomes an influence on the states that now become most relevant in the mind of the first participant.

Philip was very clear that there can be no moment in which each party is not influencing the other. He always credited this basic understanding to the work of Edgar Levenson. For Philip, the mind is many things, of course, but perhaps most significantly, it is the organ of mutual affective influence. The analyst is no more able than the patient to escape this process of becoming, and the states of mind brought to awareness in the analyst's mind by the states of the patient are just as personal for the analyst as the patient's states are for the patient, and just as likely to be "not-me"—and therefore unformulated, painful, and troublesome. There can be no moment, then, in which either the patient or the analyst exists apart from the influence of the other. There can be no moment in which the individual mind can be separated from the broader field.

One of the great strengths of Philip's work is that he embeds everything he has to say in clinical material, and so you can dip into his writing anywhere at all and find Philip helping you understand clinical practice. I end with an extremely brief statement of what I think Philip would like to see us do as psychotherapists and psychoanalysts. Here it is: our patients come to us having suffered traumatic experience that has been dissociated and structuralized. We must make an analytic relationship with them, devoted to understanding, that is as deep, spontaneous, and affectively vibrant as we can. If we do that, we will eventually find our way, never with conscious purpose, to the enactment between ourselves and our patients of those structuralized, dissociative aspects of relatedness that brought our patients to treatment in the first place. When this happens, we must do our best to find a way to be adequately and personally responsive, and thus to contribute to melting the rigid, frozen places in the field, diminishing the patient's shame, and restoring spontaneity and vitality.

I have always believed in the primary significance of my affective experience of, and with, my patients. Philip gave me compelling ways to think about that, thoughts I use every day, probably every session. In this way he helped me develop in my work a degree of internal freedom and expressive participation that I would not otherwise have had.

References

Bromberg, P. M. (1998). *Standing in the spaces: Essays on clinical process, trauma, and dissociation.* The Analytic Press.

Bromberg, P. M. (2006). *Awakening the dreamer: Clinical journeys.* The Analytic Press.

Bromberg, P. M. (2011). *The shadow of the tsunami: And the growth of the relational mind.* Routledge.

Chefetz, R. (2015). *Intensive psychotherapy for intensive dissociative processes: The fear of feeling real.* Norton.

Chefetz, R. A., & Bromberg, P. M. (2004). Talking with "me" and "not-me. *Contemporary Psychoanalysis, 40*(3), 409–464. https://doi.org/10.1080/00107530.2004.10745840

Howell, E. (2005). *The dissociative mind.* Routledge.

Howell, E. (2020). *Trauma and dissociation informed psychotherapy: Relational healing and the therapeutic connection.* Routledge.

Stern, D. B. (2010). *Partners in thought: Working with unformulated experience, dissociation, and enactment.* Routledge.

Stern, D. B. (2015). *Relational freedom: Emergent properties of the interpersonal field.* Routledge.

Stern, D. B. (2019). *The infinity of the unsaid: Unformulated experience, language, and the nonverbal.* Routledge.

Part III

Comparative studies

Chapter 14

Field theory and the dream sense

Continuing the comparison of interpersonal/relational theory and Bionian field theory

I have always been drawn to thinking about the emergent quality of experiencing, a state that we identify with dreaming, a feeling that we are all suspended in the midst of the processes of creation, watching the world come into being in front of our eyes and all around us, without knowing what will happen next. This compelling, lifelong experience perhaps has become even more vitalized for me under the influence of the central role of dreaming in Bion's work—dreaming in the broadest sense, i.e., dreaming as thinking, "waking dream thoughts." I live most fully in the moments when I can feel that I am being "taken" by this emergent quality in clinical work, moments in which the patient and I relate effortlessly, deeply involved in the moment, fully engaged together in something to which we surrender (Ghent, 1990), but without necessarily knowing exactly what that "something" is, or what it is becoming. I know at these times that I am doing what I most want to do, and that the outcome, whatever it is, will be good—not necessarily pleasant but productive. The "dream sense" is the term I coined for this feeling, and in this chapter I use this idea to try to continue charting in words the emergent quality of life in general, and of clinical process in particular.

This chapter is a continuation of the comparison of interpersonal/relational theory and Bionian field theory that I began in two articles that appeared in Psychoanalytic Dialogues in 2013 (Stern, 2013 a, 2013b) and that were reprinted in a slightly longer form in my book, Relational Freedom: Emergent Properties of the Interpersonal Field (Stern, 2015). Several commentaries accompanied those articles when they appeared in Dialogues, including one coauthored by the primary exponents of Bionian field theory, Antonino Ferro and Giuseppe Civitarese (Ferro & Civitarese, 2013). I wrote this chapter with the intention of continuing not

DOI: 10.4324/9781032688893-17

only the comparison of our two kinds of field theory but also the dialogue between us.[1]

The chapter has two sections. In the first part I discuss differences between Bionian field theory, on one hand, and interpersonal and relational psychoanalysis, on the other. I take up two points: (1) the significance of the analyst's subjectivity in the co-creation of the analytic field; and (2) the significance of trauma. In the second part, I turn to what the two schools of field theory share, focusing largely on the phenomenon of emergence and what I call "the dream sense."

Part 1: The analyst's subjectivity

Although the concept of the field is recognized much more frequently in psychoanalysis than it once was, most psychoanalysts still ground their views of clinical process in the individual mind: the analyst studies the patient's experience, looking for its unconscious roots, and offers such understanding to the patient when it becomes possible to do so. In recent years the analyst's experience with the patient has become more important in Freudian and Kleinian conceptions than it used to be; the analyst's experience with the patient may even be acknowledged as what makes the depth of the analyst's understanding possible (see, for example, the work of Madeleine and Willy Baranger (1961–1962/2008, 2009). But despite this acknowledgment, for most Freudian and Kleinian analysts the patient's experience nevertheless remains rooted in unconscious phantasy—the shaping of the outer life by the inner one (e.g., Blass, 2017; LaFarge, 2014). The analyst's responsibility is to grasp this shaping influence *inside the patient's mind*. These analysts do today accept their subjectivity as informative; they accept that their experience may indeed hint at new meanings in the patient's mind.[2]

But even in the work of Antonino Ferro and Giuseppe Civitarese, who have done more than any other contemporary Bionians to recognize the joint participation of patient and analyst in shaping the clinical situation, the analyst's personal presence and subjectivity are not understood to be *formative* influences on the experience that eventually comes into being between patient and analyst, and in the patient's mind. In Ferro's and Civitarese's thinking, the analyst and the patient, that is, are not conceived as *symmetrical parts of a mutually constructed field*. The field of play is not level. This point contrasts with interpersonal and relational thinking, which not only acknowledge the subjectivity of the analyst in the co-creation of the clinical process; these ways of conceiving the analytic situation are actually anchored in that view. Patient and analyst contribute exactly the same kind of influence on the shape of clinical relatedness.

That the field is not level in Bionian field theory—that is, that analyst and patient contribute to the field in quite different ways—is thoroughly understandable from Ferro's and Civitarse's perspective because their work grows from a different understanding of the analytic situation than the interpersonal/relational one: Bion's (1962, 1963) model of the container and the contained.

Given constraints of space, I have no choice but to be considerably more concrete about defining container/contained than I would like. I do recognize that whether a particular mental phenomenon is container or contained is a relative matter, determined by the dynamics of the moment (Bion, 1963). For today's purpose, however, even though I recognize that container/contained is more subtle than I will be able to acknowledge, it will have to suffice for me to say that the container is the analyst's mind and the contained is comprised of the patient's projective identifications. The patient sends, in phantasy, projective identifications into the analyst's mind, just as the child sends projective identifications into the mother's mind. These raw or primitive psychic elements, which Bion (1962) terms *beta elements*, are projected because they cannot be tolerated by the patient or child and therefore cannot be thought. They are not symbolically realized; that is, they are not psychic representations but something much closer to things-in-themselves, and so they cannot be used to construct experience, or thought, which requires the psychic manipulation of symbolic elements.

Beta elements, in the course of their sojourn in the analyst's (or mother's) mind, a process Bion describes as reverie, are transformed into *alpha elements*. *Alpha* elements *are* a form of representation, and are therefore thinkable, so that when they are returned to the child or the patient—again, in phantasy—they can be strung together in sequences, creating thoughts, a process Bion describes as "dreaming." By internalizing this process, patients eventually become more able to carry out the transformation of *beta* elements into *alpha* elements within their own minds. The impact of successful treatment is that the patient can dream more of that which before had remained undreamed.

In Ferro's and Civitarese's version of this model, the functions of container and contained, performed within individual minds in interaction with one another in Bion's original description, are instead taken on by the field, which is understood as a jointly constructed unconscious phantasy. The patient continues to supply projective identifications, but to the field now, not directly to the analyst's individual mind, and the analyst continues to contain and transform the patient's projective identifications but, like the patient, not only within his individual mind but also via his participation in the field.

But despite Ferro's and Civitarese's partial interpersonalizing of the analytic situation, the contributions to the field made by analyst and patient, while reciprocal, remain asymmetrical in the same way they are usually understood by Freudian and Kleinian analysts, just as they were in Bion's original formulation of the container and the contained.

This observation of the difference between Ferro's Bionian field theory and interpersonal/relational field theory is my own. Ferro and Civitarese have not explicitly characterized the difference between their views and mine in this way. I do think, though, that they would agree with the way I have characterized the relationship of our views to one another. As evidence that this is the case, consider the following two quotations from a recent article of theirs. First, consider a quotation that states very clearly the parts of our views that overlap. What Ferro and Civitarese have said here seems to me to be entirely consistent with an interpersonal/relational view:

> [I]t is a matter not so much of "giving interpretations" as of laying the foundations for a joint search for meaning. Analysis consists in an exchange of reveries. The impression may be gained that even when not talking about himself the analyst is making arbitrary pronouncements, for instance, if he uses certain metaphors or permits himself to be creative, but this is not the case if his inner life too is deemed to be one of the places of the field.
>
> (p. 136)

This expression—"an exchange of reveries"—makes it sound as if there is a certain symmetry in the analytic relationship, just as there is in interpersonal/relational thinking, and describing the analyst's inner life as "a place in the field" sounds entirely interpersonal to me.

Now compare this statement to another passage from the same article, which makes it clear that symmetry in the analytic relationship is definitely not intended:

> [T]the direction of "pathological" projective identifications is normally from patient to analyst. Temporary reversals of this flow, however, can be observed, and are referred to "negative reverie" or "reversal of the flow of projective identifications." That is not a bad thing, but is a fact of life—but the analyst must eventually become aware of the situation so as to put the system of analysis back in working order so that it can properly serve its original purpose.
>
> (p. 145)

It seems clear in this passage that the field, as it is described by Bion, and in turn by Ferro and Civitarese, is *intended* to be reciprocal and not symmetrical: projective identifications, that is, are intended to flow in one direction only. Interpersonal and relational analysts, on the other hand, take the position that the analyst, while of course usually deferring to the patient in the selection of what is discussed, and exercising analytic restraint and discipline, nevertheless inevitably contributes to the field in exactly the same way that the patient does. The analyst shares responsibility, continuously and unconsciously, for shaping the field, which is, of course, always in flux. One might say that there is an acceptance by interpersonal and relational analysts that projective identifications travel in *both* directions, not just one. But these analysts would also say, of course, that being an analyst comes with a special responsibility to study these phenomena—not only those of patients but their own, as well, to the extent that they can grasp them.

Because analyst and patient in the interpersonal and relational conception are each directly involved with the other, disclosure of the analyst's experience in the field, or what I would prefer to call expressive participation, is not only acceptable in the interpersonal and relational models but often crucial to successful therapeutic outcome. The level playing field makes the nature of the analyst's subjectivity just as relevant to both participants, and to the treatment, as the patient's, and so the question of whether the analyst offers his experience as part of the inquiry is not decided by a principle, as it is in many other schools of thought, including even Ferro's interpersonalized Bionian approach. Instead, the question of whether the analyst's experience is revealed to the patient is decided by the analyst's estimation of the relational context of the moment. There ceases to be a good reason to enforce analytic anonymity as policy—although the desirability of analytic restraint, of course, remains.

Ferro and Civitarese feel emphatically otherwise. In that same article from which I have been quoting (Ferro & Civitarese, 2016), they write that, "In the clinical practice of Antonino Ferro and his followers there is no trace of the self-revelation that is, instead, the hallmark of North American relational psychoanalysis" (p. 144). This position makes sense, if you accept that the container/contained model is the structure of the analytic situation, because within such a theoretical scheme, analysts are understood to be risking damage to their own containing function if they participate expressively. Furthermore, there is no good reason for Bionian field theorists to participate in this way, because the patient's and the analyst's subjectivities are not conceived to be continuously, inevitably, and unconsciously interlocked in the same way they are in interpersonal/relational theory. For the interpersonal/relational analyst, because the unconsciously interlocking participations of patient and analyst (Wolstein, 1959) are unavoidable, not to use them would require not being aware of them, or refusing to acknowledge them, and that would be not only impractical but also undesirable, a misguided commitment to "discipline," tantamount to agreeing in advance to do nothing more than enact them.

The question of trauma

Before I move on to what I believe the two kinds of field theory share, I want to address one more important point about their differences: their approach to trauma. It will come as no surprise that, given my interpersonal/relational commitments, I cannot accept positions in which all clinical process is understood to be the outcome of unconscious phantasy. Ferro (2009) presents this privileging of phantasy in the form of the "oneiric principle"—the principle of dreaming—according to which psychoanalysis should, and can, be concerned *only* with psychic reality—which, of course, in Kleinian/Bionian terms, means unconscious phantasy. We must approach any experience, including trauma, Ferro says, by treating it as a dream.

Ferro is not taking an epistemological position here: he does not question the reality of trauma. Rather, Ferro is saying that all experience, trauma included, is *useful in an analytic process* only to the extent that it can be understood as an expression of unconscious phantasy. The position is that it is only this meaning of trauma—as the expression of unconscious phantasy—that has the special significance that we call psychoanalytic. Ferro and Civitarese believe that trauma needs to be acknowledged in human terms, of course, and they do indeed acknowledge it in that way. But if psychoanalysis is concerned only with the unconscious, as Ferro and Civitarese believe, then we must see, say these writers, that while psychoanalytic treatment can sometimes reveal psychic reality and heal the mind, it cannot heal the world outside the mind. Therefore, Bionian field theorists try routinely to read the significance of trauma through the lens of unconscious phantasy.

In the interpersonal/relational account I favor, on the other hand, the unconscious part of the field is comprised not by unconscious phantasy but by dissociated, affect-laden, unformulated relational configurations that cannot be thought, and therefore must be enacted. I will discuss this further below. For the moment, though, this difference means that interpersonal/relational analysts view trauma, both in the present and in the past, not as an expression of unconscious phantasy, but as something that may indeed have great unconscious significance, but that only comes alive in the treatment via the forms taken by analytic relatedness. Dissociated trauma can be known only through enactment in the analytic situation.

Despite these differences, though, trauma is hardly unknown in Bionian field theory. Bion himself is said to have developed his theories under the influence of, among other things, his experience as a tank commander in France during World War I, when he was psychically assaulted over a significant period of time by carnage and death, a trauma that apparently haunted him for the rest of his life (e.g., Soffer-Dudek, 2015). Referring to the Battle of Amiens, Bion (1982) wrote, "Oh yes, I died on August 8th 1918" (p. 265). It is not infrequent for the severely traumatized to say that they "died" on the occasion of the traumatic events (e.g., see Leed, 1979, who documented war trauma in World War I).

The theme that runs through Bion's work is the creation or prevention of the capacity for thought, and mental processes that encourage and facilitate that capacity or reduce and inhibit it. Thought, said Bion, is the only thing that makes psychic pain manageable, and the mind is the means by which we manage to transform things-in-themselves into thought. If the pain of things-in-themselves is too great, though—and when that happens, we call it trauma—then the creation of the mind is interrupted or prevented. Bionian treatment is therefore devoted to the creation and repair of the capacity for thought, and it is understood to take place in the psychic interchange between patient and analyst—in the projective identifications created by the patient, passed to the analyst, and then reintrojected in a more tolerable form by the patient. And trauma, we can say, is implicated at each step, because the entire point of Bionian treatment is to transform that which was experienced as unbearable, which can be characterized as trauma, into manageable experience.

But in Bionian theory, including Bionian field theory, all of this goes on in unconscious phantasy. Psychoanalytic treatment, from this point of view, is not a joint, patient-analyst consideration of the literal significance of trauma. Trauma or psychic pain is, from this perspective, what makes it so difficult for the patient to allow himself to think, and it is, therefore, pain that makes the patient projectively identify the source of the pain, evacuating it into the analyst. The oneiric principle means that the literal recognition of trauma is not part of psychoanalytic treatment and that work with it cannot have the direct and inescapable significance that it has for interpersonal and relational analysts (see especially Boulanger, 2007).[3]

Trauma has the significance it does for interpersonal and relational analysts because real experience with other people, and not unconscious phantasy, lies at the heart of this point of view. "Real," of course, is a problematic word and concept for any psychoanalyst, since all of us, interpersonal and relational analysts included, recognize that all experience is created by acts of interpretation (I don't mean psychoanalytic interpretation here, but the continuous interpretations that constitute every experience) that, most of the time, we do not even know we are committing. Like any other psychoanalysts, interpersonal and relational analysts accept that we bring interpretive skews and proclivities to any situation in which we find ourselves.

For most psychoanalysts, these interpretive proclivities are conceptualized as unconscious phantasy, and unconscious phantasies, in turn, whatever the overarching theory in which they are embedded, generally originate in sources conceived as some form or elaboration of drive. For interpersonal and relational analysts, on the other hand, interpretive proclivities grow from experience with what we have no choice but to call "real" other people who construct between them states of relatedness. States of relatedness, in turn, are internalized, thereafter contributing to the shape of the interpersonal field as it is constantly shaped and reshaped in ongoing living. For interpersonal and relational analysts, in other words, the unconscious scaffold for experience is not biological, or even individual, but social—not unconscious phantasy but unconscious patterns of relatedness (Stern, 2014). There is every reason to imagine that these unconscious relational patterns, rooted in "real" experience, are just as thoroughly suffused with affect, and just as likely to be non-rational, as unconscious phantasy (Stern, 2014).

This orientation is the reason that, for interpersonal and relational analysts, patient and therapist are continuously involved with one another in ways that neither of them has any way of knowing. A significant part of analytic relatedness, probably the largest portion, has unconscious sources—for both patient *and* analyst. How could it be otherwise? After all, in making a relationship, both participants, from this perspective, cannot avoid depending on their own unconscious patterns of relatedness. Interpersonal and relational analysts commit themselves to practice analytic restraint and to conduct treatment in a way that is as thoroughly devoted to the patient's interests as possible. But they also assume their own continuous unconscious involvement and participation with their patients, an involvement that it is the central task of the treatment to reveal.

Clinical illustration

Let me offer a brief and simple example, one that I intend as an illustration of the way I work, and of the ideas I have just offered you. This vignette is written from a point of view I have taken for many years: interpretations, while of course they are defined by their content and symbolic meaningfulness, frequently lead to therapeutic action for another reason altogether, one that has to do with the events of the interpersonal field (Stern, 1997, 2010, 2015, 2018b). The material comes from my work with a patient about whom I have written before (Stern, 2018b; Chapter 6), a highly successful middle-aged business executive who often must, because of the continuous demands of her work, hold her sessions with me with on the telephone, often talking to me at such times from the back seat of a car, a hotel lobby, or an airport. She is devoted to her treatment, however, and never misses a scheduled appointment, however unconventional its setting may have to be. One of this woman's primary problems is her relationship with her husband, who is warm, talented, extremely narcissistically vulnerable, and brutally critical. He frequently deals with my patient in ways that lead her to feel rejected and shamed; yet, as is so often the case with those whose narcissism is easily injured, he usually feels that he is merely defending himself against his wife's unreasonable criticism. The patient has had thoughts about leaving her husband for many years but has never done so. Recently there has been a new development in her treatment: she has begun to examine her own feelings and her participation in these sadomasochistic enactments with her husband, without her usual self-criticism. Until now, her self-critical understanding of her own participation has usually seemed to result in the need to make her husband see his own sadism. She wants him to see that he is at fault, not her, in order that she can be relieved of her self-blame. Routinely, though, he refuses to acknowledge his role, and she is then left miserable and self-hating. Recently, though, she has seen that her insistence on her husband's embrace of culpability gains her very little, and she has ceased most of her insistence that he accepts responsibility, simply refusing to engage with him at such moments. As a result, the intensity and frequency of his attempts to humiliate her have declined.

One day recently, in the course of talking about one of these painful episodes, the patient said something about her belief, discussed many times between us, that she didn't seem to be able to escape replaying the destructive aspects of her relationship with her mother, also an emotionally warm, extremely self-involved person whose neglect had made it possible, tragically, when the patient was a little girl, for a doorman in the patient's building to repeatedly sexually assault her in the basement of her apartment building. On this particular occasion, after listening to the patient's account of this latest episode with her husband, and her lament about the self-destructive repetition of her relationship with her mother, I said, "Yes, and maybe you're also staying with your husband because you hope that this time, things will turn out differently."

The patient started to address another, related topic, but then she halted and said, in a thoughtful, wondering tone, that she wanted to stop and recognize this moment. She said that what I had said to her had made my point in such a succinct way that she felt she understood it for the first time, despite knowing that I had said such things many times before. "This is what you mean, isn't it," she said, "when you say that the only way I will feel ready to leave my husband is when I no longer need to." I told her yes. I had told her many times that I felt she was glued into the relationship with her husband because she could not bear to leave him until she could do it without feeling that it was her fault, and I had added on many of those earlier occasions that she could only feel that it wasn't her fault if he had begun to treat her lovingly. That is, it had been my claim that she could only leave him if she no longer had a reason to do so.

The patient then went on for a few minutes about how strange it seemed to her that it was only at this particular moment that she had been able to really hear what I was saying. Why now? I pointed out that it had probably taken both of us to manage it, even if neither of us could say how we had done it. We had created a situation (by which I meant a state of the field) in which she was ready to hear what I said *and* I was able to say it in a way that took advantage of that readiness. She responded that the process seemed quite mysterious to her. "You must have been saying this to me for years," she said. "And if I hadn't stopped myself and talked about it, I would just have gone on without paying attention to the strangeness of it. I wonder," she said, "how often that happens." I didn't say anything, but what I thought was: it happens all the time. It's the way thinking happens. *What* the analyst says or does isn't necessarily remarkable. It seems to me that my patient could have experienced what I said in this instance, for example, as downright trite. It is hardly a new idea that the repetition compulsion is partly motivated by the wish that things will work out differently this time. No, thinking is not just a matter of what is said. It is not a simple matter of semantics, at least not *primarily* a matter of semantics. Thinking is what happens when the field takes on a configuration that allows certain new thoughts and feelings, thoughts and feelings that the field had not been able to accommodate prior to that time, and that therefore could not be formulated, and when that happens, even the most commonplace observations, if they are authentic expressions by the analyst and are received that way by the patient, can create unexpectedly profound meanings.

We are all familiar with experiences like this one, and most of the time we let them pass by without really noticing that we cannot specify how they came about—as my patient was tempted to do in this instance, but did not. This unthinking acceptance of the remarkable is the most common form of joint unconscious process, the everyday presence of what I will call (in a moment) the dream sense in interpersonal life, and so, on those rare occasions when we pay explicit attention to such episodes, they feel alien or other—as unconscious process must. Elsewhere I have written that,

It is our accomplishment of freedom that makes an hour good, but often enough, as long as we are working to capacity with a deeply involved analysand, we do not really know why freedom comes to us when it does.

(Stern, 2004, p. 232)

Part 2: Emergence

It seems to me that the most compelling evidence for the significance of unconscious process in our emotional lives is the experiential phenomenon of *emergence*. I am going to take some time to tell you what I think this quality is. For now, let me just say that I mean the word phenomenologically, and I intend it to refer to experience in which we lose ourselves, experience that feels unbidden, as if it simply arrives in our minds.

Bionian field theory is particularly well suited to an account of emergence: it seems natural that the emphasis on transformation in Bionian theory—the way *beta* elements are said to metamorphose into *alpha* elements, and then into waking dream thoughts—encourages a feeling-sense or awareness of the emergent quality.

But how does interpersonal/relational theory account for that same emergent quality? I address this topic in the hope that by doing so, despite our differences, I can encourage more dialogue between the two kinds of field theory.

I have offered already, in *Relational Freedom* (2015), an account of emergence in interpersonal/relational field theory. In that account, I substantiated the point that the emergent clinical process is vital to interpersonal/relational clinical work by citing relevant clinical material from the work of prominent relational and interpersonal writers. Here I will take a different tack. I will describe the feeling of emergence as "the dream sense," hoping to show how emergence comes about in the work of analysts like me, while simultaneously arousing some of the same conviction and mystery that I find in the literature on clinical process that matters most to me, whether written by interpersonal/relational analysts or Bionians. I will end by using the implications of the dream sense to describe commonalities between the two schools. I begin the project with clinical material.

I have worked with George, a married, white artist in his 70s, for a number of years, and I have written about this work before, in the earlier discussion of emergence that appears in *Relational Freedom* (Stern, 2015). I wrote about a day when George talked about a poem by Ovid in which a nymph was raped by a river god. The nymph then turned herself into water and flowed into her attacker, becoming part of him. George felt the poem was "sexy," and it moved him. After he had talked about this for a minute or two, I told him I was reminded of his vague memories or fantasies (we could never be sure of which, although I leaned decidedly toward memory) of being repeatedly sexually abused in the cellar of his house as a little boy. George was shocked at the connection, which surprised me, but of course he understood immediately what I was talking about, and the episode turned out to be very useful to us. Here is part of what I wrote then:

> I did not *figure out* my way into the connection between the cellar and Ovid's tale, I *felt* my way into it. Even that way of putting it, though, makes what I did sound more consciously volitional than it was. What I said to George grew from living under the spell he and I, without conscious intention, had cast together around our mutual history, the story of the nymph and the river god, and ourselves in this room, in this moment. My experience was the manifestation of the interpersonal field, in other words, not just of my individual capacity to think, know, or understand. Or put it this way: we should *always* understand the analyst's capacity to think, know and understand in the clinical situation as a phenomenon of the field, not as the creation of the analyst's solitary mind. The analyst does not stand back and observe. She does her best work when living under the kind of spell George and I cast. My thought grew from what was happening between us. It would have been impossible without it.
>
> (p. 12)

George and I, in fantasy or memory, were often in that cellar together for whole sessions at a time, with George reporting whatever he could about the experience, especially how it felt. When I first presented the material that follows, my purpose was to illustrate the significance of the process of emergence in the work George and I did together, the way meanings come about as spontaneous products of the interpersonal field.

> When George and I are in the cellar, the outside world retreats. It is quiet, the office is dim, and I have noticed that colors tend to darken. There is the illusion that I am there, right there in that cellar. I know something

about how it looks, because George has told me the details, and I find that I imagine a version of those details for myself, and I inhabit them. (I am an onlooker to this process of imagining.) The ends of our sessions can be startling. It can be wrenching to return ourselves to the everyday world. That shock testifies to the depth of our involvement, our mutual absorption in the matters at hand. We are thoroughly immersed in a joint fantasy. What comes to exist between us is woven from the strands of George's inner life, from my fantasy of his fantasy life, from George's fantasy of my fantasy, and on and on. *Someone* is weaving this experience between us, but it doesn't feel to George or me that it's either one of *us*.

(p. 12)[4]

The dream sense

The emergent quality of experience tells us that we are on the right track in our work—or at least a good track. We don't know what's going to happen next, but whatever it is, we feel confident at these moments that it is where we want to go or perhaps where we need to go. Our feeling of losing ourselves in clinical process comes with an intimation of freedom, and experience tells me that greater freedom really does generally follow its intimation, even if the freedom that comes is not pleasant.

But what is this emergent quality? Where does it come from? How does it arise?

Oddly enough, to be spontaneous, and thus most yourself, is to be unaware of yourself (Stern, 1990, 2015), in just the way I felt with George. This is as true outside the consulting room as it in inside it. To be spontaneous is for experience to fall together in such a way that it all "just happens." Sometimes this is colloquially described as "being in the zone." Elsewhere I have cited a few of the thousands of creative people—artists, writers, scientists, dancers, musicians, and others—who have described artistic accomplishment or scientific insight coming into being through them, as if they were conduits (Stern, 1990; Ghiselin, 1952; Merkur, 2001). For example, Gabriel Garcia Marquez, the great novelist, wrote,

I'm very curious, as I'm writing this book, to see how the characters go on behaving. It's a true investigation. I could almost say that one writes the novel to see how it will turn out. And to be able to read it.

(Simons, 1985, p. 18)

Any number of writers have described this process as a dream state, occurring in literal dreams or in experience akin to dreaming. There is the famous story of the scientist Kekule, who went to sleep after spending fruitless hours trying to think through the elusive problem of the molecular structure of benzene. He dreamed the Ouroboros image—snakes eating their own tails—and woke up knowing that benzene was structured as a ring (Mackenzie, 1965, p. 135). Robert Louis Stevenson (1925) regularly received finished stories in his dreams from what he called "the Brownies." Coleridge's poem (1816/2019) "Kubla Khan" and Newbold's (1896) sudden comprehension of cuneiform writing came to them in the same way. The process of copper engraving was bequeathed to William Blake in a dream by his dead brother (Raine, 1971, p. 43). The list goes on and on.

In the last few years, no doubt partly as a result of becoming more familiar and fascinated with Bion and those who have been inspired by him, such as Ferro and Civitarese, I have been newly impressed with the power of dreaming. When I use the word "dreaming," however, I am using it a bit differently than Bion does. In the next part of this chapter, when I say "dreams" or "dreaming," I will be referring to the dramas we create in sleep, and to metaphors of those nighttime dramas that may inform us about day-time experiencing. I will generally not be using "dreaming" to refer to the process of thinking, as Bion does. And yet, as we shall also see in what follows, in some respects I do find myself drawn to this view. In my clinical practice, for instance, and in my understanding of creative thought in general, I have expressed (Stern, 1983) since the very beginning of my work my fascination with, and commitment to, Keats's principle of "negative capability." I did not know enough about Bion when I started to write in psychoanalysis to realize that this principle was central to him; and Ferro, too, cites negative capability just about as frequently as he cites "reverie" in his accounts of the genesis of thought. In 1817, Keats, the poet, in criticizing Coleridge and others who sought to formulate theories and categorize knowledge, wrote,

> it struck me what quality went to form a Man of Achievement, especially in Literature, and which Shakespeare possessed so enormously – I mean Negative Capability, that is, when a man is capable of being in uncertainties, mysteries, doubts, without any irritable reaching after fact and reason.
>
> (Li, 2009, p. ix)

The sense that thought originates from thoroughly non-rational processes is one of the important points that, despite our other differences, I share with Ferro and Civitarese.

The phenomenology of dreaming

Even disturbing dreams, dreams with frightening, dysphoric, or melancholic affect, rivet me. Often I am ambivalent about having them interrupted, even on those occasions when the dream is troubling or frightening enough that, when I awaken, it comes as a relief that "it was only a dream." When I wake up in the night, I find that I can go back to sleep most readily if I can find my way back to the dream that was interrupted by the awakening. At those times I often slip back into the dream with a kind of gratitude, because I know that finding my way back into it will also take me back to sleep. The dream ushers me back into that other world. This observation is not exactly what Freud (1900) had in mind in describing the dream as the guardian of sleep, but it is a gloss on that idea.

I have fallen into calling the spontaneity, depth of involvement, and loss of the awareness of myself I experienced with George as "the dream sense." For me, it partakes of all the characteristics I have just mentioned in describing creative thought: it is emotionally compelling, narratively absorbing, and happens by itself; I am a conduit for it. It seems reasonable to imagine that the dream is, in fact, the model for all creative imaginings of this kind. Joyce Carol Oates recently expressed, in describing what it is like to write fiction, exactly what I want to say about clinical psychoanalysis: "Writing is a process—like life," she said, "It is not so very different from dreaming, if one could consciously shape and reshape one's dreams" (Oppenheim, 2015, p. 65).

There is something magnetic about the proximity of unconscious thought. To exist in the dream sense, especially in dreams themselves but also in waking life, can be uncanny or repulsive; sad to the point of tragedy; frightening to the point of terror or horror. But it can also be elegant, winsome, wondrous, exquisite, majestic, hilarious, rollicking, exhilarating, or profound. The dream sense is one description of the quality of depth in experience (Foehl, 2014). Winnicott (1971) would have recognized the dream sense. His terminology was different, but I think he would have agreed that it is something like our appreciation of the dream sense that draws us to art, music, literature, and spirituality. We can say, in other words, that the dream sense is one of the primary manifestations of transitional space. Those of us who take up the practice of psychoanalysis recognize the power of the dream sense to express ourselves more than we otherwise know how to do. In fact, it has been my experience that an appreciation of the dream sense is often a portal to the very activities, such as psychoanalysis, philosophy, and artistic endeavor, that Winnicott (1971) located in the domain of the transitional. The presence of this sense, whether in dreams or waking life, is sometimes fierce and vehement, sometimes muted and subdued; it may suffuse a poem, a painting, a piece of music, or a psychoanalytic moment with power and mystery or insinuate itself into the spaces between words like a melody so faint it might not be there at all.

I would go so far as to propose that, although it doesn't often come to our explicit attention, the quality of emergence, represented by the dream sense, is the prototype of unobstructed thought—not often in the dramatic forms I have just described, of course, but in its more prosaic, everyday aspect, such as in the first vignette I presented above, the one about the woman who suddenly understood something I had said to her over and over again. I will explain in a moment what I mean when I use that word "obstruction," but I hope you have begun to see what I meant earlier when I said that, despite not being Bionian, I am drawn to broaden the reach of dreaming. I believe that the dream sense, because of its emergent quality, is a highly significant aspect of clinical psychoanalysis. Psychoanalysis, of course, is one of the activities during which people, both analysts and patients, pay the closest attention to the workings of their own minds. Analysts and patients ceaselessly hope to lose themselves in the dream sense, as I did with George, the other patient I discussed briefly, because there is an undeniable validity, even profundity, to the experience that comes to us then. The analyst grasps the patient's meanings effortlessly, and the patient feels understood. We seldom insist on interpreting what the experience that comes to us this way means, at least as long as we are in the midst of it. It is like poetry in that respect: it often cannot be reduced to anything more basic than itself. We know that the thoughts we have at such moments can be nothing else than our own creations, but they don't necessarily feel that way.

The phenomenon is not limited to reflective thought. We are also frequently involved, and without planfulness, in creating parts of the therapeutic relatedness for which there may be no words, but that we can see and feel are mutative for the patient and, often enough, even for ourselves. We have no idea these things are coming, nor do we usually have any sense of having created them after they arrive, however grateful we may be for their arrival.

But even with its dangers, this use of the unconscious—that is, consciousness as a conduit, a channel tuned to frequencies we can only try to imagine—is not your grandfather's understanding of the unconscious. For an increasing proportion of psychoanalysts, the unconscious is not merely the land of drive and instinct; it is not just a threatening ego-psychological nemesis to be conquered by psychoanalytic treatment and replaced by ego. This is not an unconscious we should tame, even if we could—which we can't. It is an unconscious we should celebrate. Because its power and mystery often threaten us, we must continuously charge ourselves with the rediscovery of our collaboration with it. We are always hoping to deepen our willingness to open ourselves to it, to link ourselves with it, to be aware of the ways we are tempted to turn away from it—all of this with the aim of being clearer about inviting its influence.[5]

Bionian field theory and interpersonal/relational theory: What do they have in common?

I am ready now to offer some thoughts about what the two types of field theory have in common, and my thoughts take off from what I have said about the dream sense.

Both varieties of field theory, interpersonal/relational and Bionian, center their accounts of therapeutic action on the freedom of the field to evolve spontaneously, and spontaneous evolution is exactly what we see in the dream sense. It is an ironic freedom, as I've said, because it cannot be consciously chosen; it must simply arrive. But it is freedom nevertheless: it is the kind of freedom in which meaning is created with little or no obstruction.

One implication here is that meaning comes about *because* of unconscious process, not (as certain ego-psychological accounts would have it) in spite of it. As Loewald (2000b), Bion (1963), and Ogden (e.g., 1992, 1994), among many others, have emphasized, it is not the defensive exclusion of unconscious influence that serves the growth of mind and meaning, but the accessibility of unconscious influence to the rest of the mind. I promised earlier in this chapter to return to the question of obstructed thought. Now I can do that: obstructed thought is the relative absence of unconscious influence. The isolation of the secondary process from the primary process, says Loewald (1978/2000a), leads to intellectualization and sterility. Ogden (1992) makes the same point about the hardening of the boundary between consciousness and the unconscious. One of my favorite expressions of the theme that full-bodied thought requires unconscious influence, a passage I have quoted before, and that also links the theme to the interpersonal field, is from Edgar Levenson (1982): patient and analyst feel, says Levenson, that

> *some* process is going on which they have not initiated or energized. There is the remarkable experience of being carried along by some-thing larger than both therapist and patient: A true sense of an interper-sonal field results. *The therapist learns to ride the process rather than to carry the patient.*
>
> (pp. 11–12, italics in original)

I myself have also written over several decades about the generative quali-ties of unconscious process. Unformulated experience, my term for uncon-scious process, like Bion's *beta* elements, is not symbolically represented. Unformulated experience is *potential* experience, embodying in primitive, global, nonideational, affective states the myriad possibilities for future consciousness. I have argued that the process of selecting which of these possibilities is eventually given conscious, explicit form depends upon the nature of the interpersonal field in which that conscious form comes to be. When the relational configuration of the field threatens to encourage expe-rience that would be intolerable if it were formulated, we turn away from the creation of these formulations and therefore cannot use them in think-ing. Instead, we enact them, by attributing to the other person—the analyst, in the case of treatment—the very parts of our own experience that we cannot bear. When analyst and patient are able to work successfully with an enactment (a crucial process that I cannot address here, but that I have often addressed elsewhere (Stern, 2010, 2015)), it loses its inhibiting effect on thought in the same moment that it dissolves, and the experience that had been dissociated becomes available to the ongoing task of constructing creative living (Stern, 2018a).

I hope I have written that last passage, and this whole chapter, in a way that makes it unsurprising for me now to suggest a significant relation between this dissociation-based account of therapeutic process and Bion's conception of projective identification. I did not intend this link at the time I began to devise my own contribution in the early 1980s, and had not even read Bion yet, but the link is there. In both Bionian theory and relational dissociation theory, meaning that has been inhibited, or prohibited, now becomes accessible via a field process: in Bion's theory, and especially in Ferro's interpersonalized version of it, this field process is the passage of *beta* elements from the patient's mind to the analyst's, where they are given symbolic form and then returned to the patient, who now is more likely to be able to use them in thinking. In relational dissociation theory, including my own, the meanings of unformulated experience that would be hard to bear if that potential experience was given symbolic representation are dissociated—by which I mean that they are maintained in their unformulated state for defensive reasons, and by the configuration the field assumes in order to serve those defensive purposes. This defensively motivated unformulated experience is free to resume evolution toward conscious formulation only when the field changes in such a way that such evolution can take place without undue anxiety or other psychic discomfort.

I believe that this picture of the relation of the two theories is accurate, as far as it goes—but it goes only halfway. There is another, more significant link between them. In both of them, we have seen, unconscious process plays a generative role in the creation of new experience. But in addition we can say, actually, that in both cases *this generative role of unconscious process is possible only when it is not interrupted by rigidities in the field.* When the field is not free to evolve spontaneously, new symbolization cannot take place. Those interruptions in the field's spontaneity are described by the Baranger and Baranger (1961–1962/2008, 2009) as "bastions" or "bulwarks"; from the interpersonal/relational perspective, they are known as enactments. Such interruptions are understood in both theories as rigidities, knots, or frozen places in the field, and in both theories, these rigidities have the effect of reducing the patient's (and the analyst's) freedom to think, feel, and be. We can say that they interrupt the dream sense. The clinical route in both models to the return of the spontaneous transformation of non-meaning into meaning—that is, the repair of mind—is not, as in traditional accounts, the reduction or redistribution of unconscious conflict inside the patient's mind, but rather the melting of the frozen places in the field. For Bion and Ferro, satisfying this aim requires the successful sojourn of projective identifications in the field and the analyst's mind; for relational dissociation theorists, it means the successful engagement of enactments, which provokes the formulation of that which had been maintained by dissociation in its unformulated state. In both cases, therapeutic action does not have to do with the understanding of psychic contents; it has to do instead with the mind's capacity to *create* psychic contents. Treatment aims to repair the mind, and sometimes to create it. In both theories, when this therapeutic ambition is successful, the field melts or relaxes in a way that allows new meaning once again to arise spontaneously.

I accept that interpersonal/relational field theory and Bionian field theory are different in some ways that may be unbridgeable. (I think here, for instance, about the attitudes of adherents of the two models toward the analyst's revelatory and expressive participation.) But in closing, I also want to emphasize their similarities. In both models, unconscious process is generative unless it is interrupted by rigidities in the field. For Bion, the unconscious is a storehouse of *alpha* elements, always ready to be used in the spontaneous construction of dream thoughts, which are the least elaborated (and most crucial) forms to qualify as thoughts, and which are used as building blocks in the spontaneous evolution of more complex, abstract thinking. In relational dissociation theory, the unconscious is potential or unformulated experience, which, if it is to be generative, must percolate without interruption until it is "ready" to become meaningful (Stern, 1983, 1997, 2018a). As in the process of transforming projective identifications, unformulated experience is generative as long as it is free to evolve. In both these conceptions, the unconscious has ceased to be the enemy (if it ever was), and is, in fact, our greatest ally. The enemy is the failure of thought, and the consequent meaninglessness, that are the results of turning away from psychic pain so disturbing that it cannot be borne.

Notes

1 Both Ferro and Civitarese are highly prolific, so it is impractical to cite exhaustively their work on the psychoanalytic field. Whenever a source has particular relevance, I cite the relevant bibliographic information in the text, but for general reference, see their most recent books (Civitarese, 2017; Ferro, 2019; Ferro & Civitarese, 2019), which contain references to their earlier contributions.

2 Jacobs (1991, 2013), a contemporary Freudian who writes about what he learns about the patient from the private resonances of his own history that are set off by the events of the treatment, is perhaps the premiere example of such a writer.

3 I use this word "literal"—and just below, the word "real"—because I think I need to do so in order to stake out my position. But I use these words ambivalently because, if what is meant by "literal" or "real" is "objectively present," as if there exists only one

meaning of experience, then in psychoanalysis there can be no such thing as "literal" or "real" experience. There can be no single meaning of anything—all meanings in psychoanalysis are multiple. And so, taking this point into account, when I use the words "literal" and "real," I mean to refer to experience in the everyday sense, with the understanding that even that kind of experience—because it, too, has unconscious sources—has more meanings than one.

4 Note that I do not spell the word "fantasy" with a "ph," a choice I make to differentiate what I mean from the Kleinian view. By "fantasy" I intend to refer to an imaginative mental and emotional construction that has significant unconscious sources, as all experience does, but fantasy itself, even if its meaning remains obscure, may be quite conscious, as this one was.

5 I have reservations about referring to "the" unconscious, and for using the pronoun "it" to refer to unconscious process. I feel that such usage often reflects reification, i.e., a misleading characterization of ceaselessly shifting process as stable, unchanging structure—the unconscious as a thing. I have allowed myself this usage in this case, though, because what I am trying to describe is the way that unconscious process so often does *feel like* (even if we know better) an "it" or a "thing," an alien presence that doesn't feel like part of our minds at all. In fact, the sense of unconsciousness as a thing, a thing-in-itself, an alien presence, is usually about as close as we can come sensing what it is.

References

Baranger, M., & Baranger, W. (2008). The analytic situation as a dynamic field. *International Journal of Psychoanalysis,* 89(4), 795–826. (Original work published 1961–1962 in Spanish. This is a translation of the 1969 revision of the original article). https://doi.org/10.1111/j.1745-8315.2008.00074.x

Baranger, M., & Baranger, W. (2009). *The work of confluence: Listening and working and interpreting in the analytic field* (L. G. Fiorini, Ed.). Karnac.

Bion, W. R. (1962). *Learning from experience.* William Heinemann.

Bion, W. R. (1963). *Elements of psycho-analysis.* William Heinemann.

Bion, W. R. (1982). *The long week-end, 1897–1919: Part of a life.* Fleetwood Press.

Blass, R. (2017). Reflections on Klein's radical notion of phantasy and its implications for analytic practice. *International Journal of Psychoanalysis,* 98(3), 841–859. https://doi.org/10.1111/1745-8315.12674

Boulanger, G. (2007). *Wounded by reality: Understanding and treating adult onset trauma.* The Analytic Press.

Civitarese, G. (2017). *Sublime subjects: Aesthetic experience and intersubjectivity in psychoanalysis.* Routledge.

Coleridge, S. T. (2019). Preface to "Kubla Khan". In Christabel & Kubla Khan: A vision in a dream. e-artnow. (Original work published 1816)

Ferro, A. (2009). Transformations in dreaming and characters in the psychoanalytic field. *International Journal of Psychoanalysis,* 90(2), 209–230. https://doi.org/10.1111/j.1745-8315.2009.00131.x

Ferro, A. (2019). *Psychoanalysis and dreams: Bion, the field, and the viscera of mind.* Routledge.

Ferro, A., & Civitarese, G. (2013). Analysts in search of an author: Voltaire or Artemisia Gentileschi? Commentary on 'Field theory in psychoanalysis, part II: Bionian field theory and contemporary interpersonal/relational psychoanalysis' by Donnel B. Stern. *Psychoanalytic Dialogues,* 23(6), 646–653. https://doi.org/10.1080/10481885.2013.851549

Ferro, A., & Civitarese, G. (2016). Psychoanalysis and the analytic field. In A. Elliot (Ed.), *The Routledge handbook of psychoanalysis in the humanities and the social sciences* (pp. 132–148). Routledge.

Ferro, A., & Civitarese, G. (2019). *The analytic field and its transformations.* Routledge.

Foehl, J. (2014). A phenomenology of depth. *Psychoanalytic Dialogues, 24*(3), 289–303. https://doi.org/10.1080/10481885.2014.911597

Freud, S. (1900). *The interpretation of dreams. Standard Edition.* Hogarth Press.

Ghent, E. (1990). Masochism, submission, surrender—Masochism as a perversion of surrender. *Contemporary Psychoanalysis* 26:108–136.

Ghiselin, B. (1952). *The creative process.* University of California Press.

Jacobs, T. (1991). *The use of the self: Countertransference and communication in the analytic situation.* International Universities Press.

Jacobs, T. (2013). *The possible profession: The analytic process of change*. Routledge.

LaFarge, L. (2014). Psychoanalytic controversy: How and why unconscious phantasy and transference are the defining features of analytic practice. *International Journal of Psychoanalysis, 95*(6), 1265–1278. https://doi.org/10.1111/1745-8315.12292

Leed, E. J. (1979). *No man's land: Combat and identity in World War I.* Cambridge University Press.

Levenson, E. A. (1982). Follow the fox: An inquiry into the vicissitudes of psychoanalytic supervision. *Contemporary Psychoanalysis, 18*(1), 1–15. https://doi.org/10.1080/00107530.1982.10745675

Li, O. (2009). *Keats and negative capability.* Continuum International Publishing Group.

Loewald, H. (2000a). Primary process, secondary process, and language. In *The essential Loewald: Collected papers and monographs* (pp. 178–204). University Publishing Group. (Original work published 1978)

Loewald, H. (2000b). *The essential Loewald: Collected papers and monographs.* University Publishing Group.

Mackenzie, N. (1965). *Dreams and dreaming.* Aldus Books.

Merkur, D. (2001). *Unconscious wisdom: A superego function in dreams, conscience, and inspiration.* SUNY Press.

Newbold, W. R. (1896). A dream detective solves Professor Hilprecht's famous dream. In R. L. Woods (Ed.), *The world of dreams* (pp. 525–530). Random House.

Ogden, T. (1994). *Subjects of analysis.* Aronson.

Ogden, T. H. (1992). The dialectically constituted/decentred subject of psychoanalysis. I. The Freudian subject. *International Journal of Psychoanalysis, 73,* 517–526.

Oppenheim, L. (2015). Interview with Joyce Carol Oates. In L. Oppenheim (Ed.), *Psychoanalysis and the artistic endeavor: Conversations with literary and visual artists* (pp. 65–82). Routledge.

Raine, K. (1971). *William Blake.* Praeger.

Simons, M. (1985). Love and age: A talk with Garcia Marquez. *The New York Times Book Review,* April 7.

Soffer-Dudek, N. (2015). Of losing oneself: Bion's traumatic war experiences as a foundation for his outlook on psychoanalysis. *Journal of the American Psychoanalytic Association, 63*(5), 959–963. https://doi.org/10.1177/ 0003065115607561

Stern, D. B. (1983). Unformulated experience: From familiar chaos to creative disorder. *Contemporary Psychoanalysis, 19*(1), 71–99. https://doi.org/10.1080/00107530.1983 .10746593

Stern, D. B. (1990). Courting surprise: Unbidden perceptions in clinical practice. *Contemporary Psychoanalysis, 26*(3), 452–478. https://doi.org/10.1080/00107530.1990.10746672

Stern, D. B. (1997). *Unformulated experience: From dissociation to imagination in psychoanalysis.* Routledge.

Stern, D. B. (2004). The eye sees itself: Dissociation, enactment, and the achievement of conflict. *Contemporary Psychoanalysis, 40*, 197–237.

Stern, D. B. (2010). *Partners in thought: Working with unformulated experience, dissociation, and enactment.* Routledge.

Stern, D. B. (2013a). Field theory in psychoanalysis, Part I: Harry Stack Sullivan and Madeleine and Willy Baranger. *Psychoanalytic Dialogues, 23*(5), 487–501. https://doi.org/10.1080/10481885.2013.832607

Stern, D. B. (2013b). Field theory in psychoanalysis, Part II: Bionian field theory and contemporary interpersonal/ relational psychoanalysis. *Psychoanalytic Dialogues, 23*(6), 630–645. https://doi.org/10.1080/10481885.2013.851548

Stern, D. B. (2014). A response to LaFarge. *International Journal of Psychoanalysis, 95*(6), 1283–1297. https://doi.org/ 10.1111/1745-8315.12291

Stern, D. B. (2015). *Relational freedom: Emergent properties of the interpersonal field.* Routledge.

Stern, D. B. (2018a). *The infinity of the unsaid: Unformulated experience, language, and the nonverbal.* Routledge.

Stern, D. B. (2018b). How does history become accessible? Reconstruction as an emergent product of the interpersonal field. *Journal of the American Psychoanalytic Association, 66*(3), 493–506. https://doi.org/10.1177/ 0003065118781493

Stevenson, R. L. (1925). A chapter on dreams. In *Memories and portraits, random memories, memories of himself.* Scribner.

Winnicott, D. W. (1971). *Playing and reality.* Tavistock.

Wolstein, B. (1959). *Countertransference.* Grune & Stratton.

Chapter 15

Otherness within psychoanalysis

On recognizing the critics of relational psychoanalysis[1]

This chapter was written for a book of essays by relational analysts charged with critiquing their own school of thought.Addressing this question offered me the opportunity to think about comparative psychoanalysis as an ideal. Consider the unification of psychoanalysis that would take place if all of us studied one another's work, granting it respect ("How exactly could a reasonable person come to this conclusion?") even if we don't agree with it.

This attitude, I think, is the psychoanalytic equivalent of being a citizen of the world, not simply an adherent of the policies of one's own country. My attitude about psychoanalytic thinking is anti-nationalist, so to speak, and anti-chauvinist. And so I often refer to being a good citizen of the psychoanalytic world. We all want to see psychoanalysis survive and prosper, free to develop and change over a much longer history than we have had to this point. I believe that mutual respect between psychoanalysts from different schools of thought is essential to the preservation of our field.

Just as the challenge to nationalism and patriotism requires facing the otherness of those who do not live where *we do, or* as *we do, so the challenge to psychoanalytic "patriotism" requires finding ways to acknowledge the otherness of psychoanalytic portrayals of human experience that differ from our own.*

Some years ago a book of mine (Stern, 2010) was reviewed by a respected colleague, a North American Freudian with Bionian and French psychoanalytic sympathies (Levine, 2010). He liked my book in many ways and I appreciated his interest and the effort he expended in reading the book and offering his thoughts about it. But he was critical on one score. He felt that it was "problematic that [Stern's] arguments are narrowly rooted in the idiom and context of contemporary interpersonal/relational discourse

DOI: 10.4324/9781032688893-18

and thinking, to the exclusion of Freud and of so much else in contemporary psychoanalytic literature" (p. 1169). He was referring to my thinking about unformulated experience, dissociation, and enactment. He went on to say that, "while being anchored somewhere in some theory is probably inevitable for all psychoanalytic authors, I suspect that readers who are not fully committed to an interpersonal/relational perspective may find this book constricted in scope" (p. 1169). My work, Levine said, risked being so narrowly cast as to avoid a deeper engagement with contemporary authors from other psychoanalytic schools and traditions (such as Bion, Ferro, Lombardi, Matte Blanco, Tabak de Bianchedi, Cassorla, Hartke, W. Baranger and M. Baranger, Green, de M'Uzan, Aisenstein, Widlocher, C. Botella and S. Botella, and Faimberg).

Even in the context of the otherwise positive emphasis of the review, that seemed to me to be an indictment. In the days following my reading of this review, though, as I digested my reaction, a thought occurred to me. I realized that in my book I actually did cite many of the very writers who my reviewer had criticized me for not considering. It is certainly true that comparisons between those views and my own were not my primary consideration in that book but I did mention them, indicating my interest in their work. The other side of this thought was that despite the fact that I had been writing about ideas relevant to that list of writers for 30 years, not even one of these same writers had ever cited me.[2]

And so I called the colleague who had written the review and pointed out that, while it was true that I hadn't compared my ideas in any detail to the ideas of the writers he enumerated, I had at least indicated that their ideas and mine bear a significant relationship to one another. But, I went on, because none of those writers had ever cited me, to criticize me for not integrating my ideas with theirs without making the same argument about the absence of their citation of me, seemed to me to reflect a kind of prejudice. My colleague did not agree. And I have not changed my mind.

Nevertheless, I felt he had a point, even with my reservations, and I resolved to do something about this. In the following years I found myself increasingly interested in the work of the Barangers, Bion, Green, Laplanche, Lombardi, and others. Eventually, I wrote about the relationship of the work of the Barangers and the Bionian field theorists, primarily Ferro, to the work of Sullivan (Stern, 2013a) and then to the thinking of contemporary interpersonal/relational writers (Stern, 2013b).[3]

Here is the twofold lesson I took from my colleague's review, my response to it, and other episodes that took place in my professional life during those years. (1) We interpersonal and relational analysts need to become more familiar with the work of European and Latin American psychoanalytic writers. We need to grasp the nature of the intellectual and clinical commitments held by those analysts, especially the commitments that lead them to their perceptions of us. If we comprehend their points of view from their perspectives—that is, not just from our own—we are in a position both to learn from them, and, when it is necessary (and it often is) to take issue with their criticisms. We have a chance to answer effectively those who criticize us, in other words, only if we understand them. The problem is really no different than one of our primary, commonsense, clinical principles: there is no sense in addressing someone about a sensitive subject unless you communicate in a way that really speaks to that person, and that generally requires that one grasp what the point in question means to them. (2) The second lesson to be taken from all of this is the converse of the first: in the same the way I have just described us learning the perspectives of others, those others should become better acquainted with ours.

What we are really talking about here is a specific instance of the general problem of otherness. In all of life's contexts, we must grasp the experience of the other if we are to diminish the emotional distance, alienation, discomfort, and dislike we can feel about the other, experience that so often breeds suspicion, contempt, and even hatred. That otherness may exist between us and actual other people, but of course, in psychoanalysis we are familiar with otherness as an internal problem, as well—that is, as the problem of the unconscious, or of alien self-states. For relational analysts, otherness has become a central clinical concern, a phenomenon that is neither altogether inner nor completely outer, but suspended between the two.

But for my present purpose I am talking about the experience of otherness that takes place between schools of psychoanalysis: in particular, between relational psychoanalysis and Kleinian and Bionian groups, and the various French schools. Of course, the problem we have within psychoanalysis is paltry when compared to the ethnic, racial, nationalistic, and gendered versions of the problem of otherness. Yet it is a problem we psychoanalysts live with on a daily basis, and it is a problem I believe we must solve if psychoanalysis is to endure.

Not all of us share the view that this is a problem that must be solved. I know that some do not see the value in trying to make common cause with those who object to our perspective. Those analysts feel we should simply chart our own path and leave those who disagree with us to chart their own. Isn't there something the matter with offering a respectful hearing to people who often don't approach us in the same way?

I feel, though, that we have so much more in common with other psychoanalysts, no matter how different their views, than we do with anyone else, that it behooves us to find a way to come together. I am convinced that respecting one another and coming together on the basis of that mutual respect is the only way to ensure a future for our field.

And so, with that aim in mind, I discuss in this chapter what interpersonal and relational analysts can do to become better citizens of the psychoanalytic world. Our recognition of analysts who think differently than we do requires greater familiarity with what they have to say, more sympathy with what is dear to them, and a clearer understanding of their perceptions of us.

I hope that analysts with clinical and theoretical commitments different than ours take up the reciprocal challenge to recognize us, and I believe they should, but that part of the problem I have no choice but to leave to them—and to the expansion of the contact between them and us that has become a welcome part of psychoanalysis today.

With Benjamin (1990, 2004, 2017), I generally think of recognition as an intersubjective process, something that occurs mutually, between people, as it does in the philosophy of Martin Buber (Benjamin, 2017)—which means that recognition cannot simply be adopted unilaterally by one of the affected parties toward the other (as Benjamin [2017] and Orange [2011] tell us Emmanuel Levinas describes our unilateral responsibility to the "suffering stranger"). But perhaps mutual recognition can *begin* unilaterally. In fact, Benjamin (2017) does suggest that there are circumstances in which we can jumpstart or awaken a reciprocal, intersubjective process by beginning with one-way recognition. It would seem that adversarial relationships, or aspects of otherwise congenial relationships that have adversarial qualities, must be one of the circumstances in which one party must begin without knowing if the other will reciprocate. Under such conditions, after all, *someone* has to begin the process of recognition. Whether or not reciprocity or intersubjectivity (in Benjamin's way of understanding this term) is the eventual outcome of unilateral recognition, though, it does seem desirable to me to understand and acknowledge how analysts from other schools see us.

In this chapter I consider those criticisms of relational psychoanalysis held by European and Latin American psychoanalysts, which means that I am not considering the philosophical critiques of relational psychoanalysis that have been mounted in recent years by North Americans (e.g., Mills, 2005, 2012). I also will not consider the literature in which North American analysts take issue with relational ideas on clinical, theoretical, and empirical grounds (e.g., Bachant, Lynch & Richards, 1995; Busch, 2001; Eagle, Wolitzky & Wakefield, 2001; Sugarman, 1995; Wilson, 1995).

I want to sound a cautionary note about the way I'm setting up the problem: there can be heuristic value in referring to "us" and "them" because it allows the problem to be conceived in the terms of otherness. But of course nothing is as simple as a dichotomy can make it appear, and not to recognize the complexity of the situation is to risk hardening group boundaries in a way that does not diminish the experience of otherness, but instead inadvertently encourages it. I want to keep in mind in what follows, in other words, that there are many psychoanalysts, with any and all of the passionate theoretical and clinical commitments that are routine in our field, who accept that serious and responsible colleagues can disagree in profound ways and nevertheless deserve one another's respect. In a recent email exchange, my friend and colleague Riccardo Lombardi, a widely known writer who finds inspiration in the work of Bion and Matte-Blanco, lamented the fact that he would not be available to meet me in Rome, where he lives and I was about to visit. In one of the emails of this exchange (Lombardi, personal communication, June 7, 2016), Lombardi spontaneously expressed exactly the sentiment I am trying to describe. After referring to my most recent book, which he described as "beautiful" despite the difference between my orientation and his own, he wrote: "We are fortunate that in our grey time of political monopole we are able to defend our spontaneous interest in the different ways of writing about clinical psychoanalysis." It is this kind of respectful recognition and acceptance of otherness, and perhaps even appreciation of it, that I admire. Lombardi reminds us that it can be done without giving up one's own commitments.

The criticisms we need to understand

So what criticisms do we need to understand? For heuristic purposes, the criticisms that interest me here fall into two broad categories: (1) scholarship and the sources of psychoanalytic concepts and practices; (2) the nature and role of the unconscious in psychoanalytic thought.[4]

All in all, those who criticize what they believe are relational positions on these matters (I put it this way because I do think that a significant part of the problem is a simplistic, and sometimes just mistaken, understanding of relational positions) are often also convinced that the way we think and practice represents a flattened and diluted version of what psychoanalysis should be. By encouraging acceptance of these views I hardly mean that we need to agree with them. I mean that to understand what these views are and why they are held, we need to start out with an acceptance of the situation we face.

I address separately the two issues I have just described. First, I discuss the issue of scholarship and the sources of psychoanalytic thought, which can also be understood as a controversy over who deserves to embrace psychoanalytic identity; then I turn to the question of the place of the unconscious in relational psychoanalysis, which I will address as the issue of who has proper psychoanalytic values.

The sources of psychoanalytic thought: Psychoanalytic identity

My early reading in the field left me with the impression that the citations of Freud that appeared in the introductions of so many psychoanalytic articles were often more a formulaic obeisance than a genuine intellectual engagement: the price of saying what you want to say, it seemed, was to subordinate it to something in Freud's corpus. I still think that is the case more often than it should be, although obligatory obeisance of that kind seems to be less frequent today in most of our journals than it was then.

There is a long history, though, of psychoanalytic writers in the United States and Canada ignoring this tradition and trying to revise psychoanalytic thought to reflect empirical observations. As a matter of fact, whole psychoanalytic schools have been constructed on the basis of such observations. Take psychoanalytic ego psychology. Not all ego psychology belongs in this category, but much of it does. Hartmann's (1958) conflict-free sphere of the ego and focus on adaptation were conceptions that brought much of academic psychology (notably perception, language, and cognition) under the umbrella of psychoanalysis, and simultaneously brought unconscious motivation into academic psychology. Good examples of bringing unconscious motivation into academic psychology are areas of empirical, quantitative research in which unconscious motivation was understood to play a new and significant role—the New Look in perception research, for example (e.g., Bruner & Postman, 1949), or the beginnings of the new cognitive psychology that in the late 1960s began to supplant learning theory as the dominant academic psychology paradigm (e.g., Neisser, 1967). As an indication that the influence was just as great in the other direction (that is, the influence of empirical research on psychoanalysis) consider the mother-infant observational studies that have been so influential in American psychoanalysis in recent decades, or the voluminous literature on attachment. Or note that the *Festschrift* for Heinz Hartmann (Loewenstein, Newman, Schur & Solnit, 1966) was entitled *Psychoanalysis: A General Psychology.* Much of the literature of ego psychology during those years in the United States concerned matters of general psychology. It is no accident that these were the same years— the 1930s through the 1970s—during which psychoanalysis had its greatest political influence in American academic psychology, psychiatry, and social work.

But ego psychology also preserved much of the psychoanalysis that academics in mental health fields of that era loved to hate. And the academics were not alone: a group of American psychoanalysts—the interpersonalists, or as they were often known, the cultural-interpersonal school—was also critical of many of the same concepts and practices of the mainstream American psychoanalysis of that day (although, of course, being psychoanalysts themselves, they were less thoroughly rejecting than many empirically minded academics). On the basis of their empirical observations of the centrality of relationships in psychological development and psychoanalytic treatment, what Harry Stack Sullivan (1940) referred to as "interpersonal relations," and what they understood to be the profound formative properties of social life and culture, the interpersonalists rejected many mainstream verities of the day: the inevitable centrality of the Oedipus conflict; the inevitability of the transference neurosis; the insistence on defining psychoanalysis as the application of a single, standard technique in which the analyst as a particular individual should make no difference, resulting in rigid definitions of psychoanalytic neutrality and anonymity; the belief that experience unfolds more or less exclusively from the intrapsychic world; the death instinct; penis envy; drive theory in general, with its internal, biological emphasis, and its deemphasis of the "real" experience with "real" people that interpersonalists stressed; and the resulting biologized understanding of psychological development, with its theories of libido and inevitable, rigidly unfolding psychosexual stages.

Of course, it is thoroughly understandable that those for whom these rejected positions lay at the heart of psychoanalysis found it difficult to accept the ideas of apostates such as the interpersonalists. But the rejection of the interpersonalists by the psychoanalytic mainstream went far beyond mere disagreement. For generations, the analysts of the American Psychoanalytic Association, largely made up of the same ego psychologists I have already described, excluded the interpersonalists in any way they could. This exclusion was often poisonous and contemptuous: the interpersonalists were characterized as shallow and too focused on the social and environmental—the kind of claim that is always code for the perception that the in-group analysts believe that the out-group analysts not only hold unacceptable views, but are not really psychoanalysts at all. Code was unnecessary, though. In those days the rejection of the psychoanalytic credentials of interpersonalists could be stated quite publicly, and often was.

Eventually, in the 1980s, relational psychoanalysis came into being. To begin with, relational analysts were subjected to the same treatment. Stephen Mitchell, for instance, was invited to speak at the New York Psychoanalytic Institute and then was disrespectfully excoriated in public by the senior members of that organization. But eventually relational thinking was easier for American ego psychologists to accept as part of their discipline than the work of the earlier interpersonalists. Why relational thinking has met with greater respect in mainstream circles is an interesting question that deserves more scholarly inquiry than has been devoted to it to date (but see Stern, 2015b). Some would no doubt point to what they believe are differences in the theoretical contents and clinical practices of interpersonal and relational psychoanalysis (e.g., Frankel, 1998). My own inclination is to attribute the difference to an increasing willingness among mainstream psychoanalysts, as time passed, to consider alternative views.

Today, it seems to me, while disagreements are still frequent between contemporary American Freudians and relational analysts, these are much more respectful disagreements than they once were, and in fact, I find contemporary American Freudians more and more willing actually to consider what relational psychoanalysis has to say. Today, for instance, in stark contrast to the treatment Mitchell received at the New York Psychoanalytic

Institute, I teach a required course on interpersonal and relational psychoanalysis at that same institute, and I have spoken to respectful audiences in the auditorium there a number of times in the last few years. I think that the physical proximity of contemporary Freudian analysts and relational analysts in New York, and the sharing of the American cultural context, has finally led to the beginning of more or less regular contact between these groups. Add to these changes the fact that the William Alanson White Institute recently accepted an invitation to join the American Psychoanalytic Association. None of this could have happened even 20 years ago.

Don't get me wrong: there is still a good deal to work out, and there are still highly conservative contemporary American Freudians who do not approve of the changes I have just described. But I believe that this battle is on its way to becoming a thing of the past. Today, reading the *Journal of the American Psychoanalytic Association* or *The Psychoanalytic Quarterly*, it is impossible not to see the influence of interpersonal and relational psychoanalysis—not in every article, and not always without ambivalence, but the influence is so clear that a colleague of mine has made the cogent observation that certain aspects of contemporary Freudian theory and practice remain "inscrutable" and "historically incoherent" if one does not relate them to the interpersonal and relational theory that preceded them (Blumberg, 2013). Today it seems to me that the relationship between relational psychoanalysis and contemporary American Freudian psychoanalysis is not really a central dilemma for either group. The identity of the North American psychoanalyst has grown to include both.

Ironically enough, as a matter of fact, a good many analysts from the rest of the psychoanalytic world, mainly analysts from Latin America, Great Britain, France, and Italy, have been, and are, critical not only of American relational analysts, but also—and for many of the same reasons—those American Freudians identified with the remnants of ego psychology. The willingness of relational analysts and ego psychologists to find the origin of some of their views in empirical observation that comes from outside psychoanalysis itself, especially when that observation concerns the so-called external world and not the inner one, has provoked criticism that their work is not rooted either in the Freudian canon or in a sufficient appreciation of the power and influence of the unconscious, reflected (so the attitude goes) in an overemphasis on adaptation to the external world. (I take up the points regarding the unconscious and the problem of adaptation in the section below.) Neither relational nor ego psychological thinking, for those who take this view, are really psychoanalytic. It seems to me that, as a result of all this, certain American Freudians, in other words, and many relational analysts, have become, in their relation to the wider psychoanalytic world, the proverbial strange bedfellows.

But what I have said so far about anchoring psychoanalysis in Freud is only one part of the story. Yes, of course it is true: some of that anchoring in Freud has been, and continues to be, little more than a rhetorical device, a marker of group membership or belonging, and the criticism of relational thought that grows from such a rhetorical position, while we need to understand it, is not a matter of substance, and therefore not something that we need to recognize (in the sense of giving it a respectful hearing). But there are many other writers whose views are more thoughtfully rooted in Freud, while simultaneously diverging from him. Three analysts who immediately come to mind are Loewald, Lacan, and Laplanche. Loewald had nothing to say about interpersonal psychoanalysis, as far as I know (relational psychoanalysis did not exist in his era), but it is rumored that he did learn from Sullivan during his years in Washington, DC. Laplanche did have critical things to say about what he usually referred to as the "intersubjective" view. According to Wainstrater (2012), Laplanche felt that relational psychoanalysis represented a "'vulgar' pragmatism." Wainstrater comments that, "We can see how clearly his thought contradicts the tenets of the intersubjective movement" (p. 298). Lacan did not specifically address relational psychoanalysis, since it came about after he wrote, but he would no doubt have been highly critical of relational thinking, since he rejected object relations, just as he rejected ego psychology, and in fact tended to think of the former as a form of the latter.

All three of these analysts were, at one and the same time, great innovators and staunch defenders of the necessity for psychoanalysis to grow directly from the work of Freud. A brief examination of how they derived their views seems to me to demonstrate that the criticisms of relational psychoanalysis by analysts outside North America do not arise simply as a result of intellectual and clinical disagreement.

I begin with Hans Loewald (2000), who created an important and innovative view of the development and functioning of mind that he always insisted was true to Freud's vision.[5] He claimed that he was merely developing implications of Freud's thought that Freud himself did not see. In the process he created very beautiful ideas about the processes of differentiation and de-differentiation that resulted in the growth of the internal structures that compose the mind. These ideas were so different from Freud's own that it can be hard sometimes to imagine that Freud was their source. In fact, I have heard what seems to me to be the churlish and cynical claim that Loewald professed fealty to Freud only so he could say what he pleased. For my part, when I read Loewald I find his commitment to Freud utterly convincing, even if I must admit to wondering whether he may have been more original, and less inspired by Freud, than he thought he was.

Lacan, while he was accused by some psychoanalysts of being a "recalcitrant, idiosyncratic charlatan" (Nobus, 2000, p. 2) with views that, for many psychoanalytic readers, did not represent Freud, nevertheless did not hesitate to denounce the Freudian ego psychology of Hartmann, Kris, and Loewenstein—the dominant psychoanalysis of Lacan's day—as anti-Freudian and to characterize his own thinking as "strictly loyal to the Freudian enterprise" (Nobus, 2000, p. 1). Lacan's rallying cry was the "return to Freud," a goal Lacan thought could be accomplished only by seeing that the unconscious was structured like a language—and for him language, and therefore the mind, was in continuous flux and conflict, and outside the ego's control. He believed that the ego was established via identifications, and that it was therefore most closely related to the imaginary, the mode in which experience is (falsely and deceptively) stable and unchanging. Therefore, to base psychoanalysis in the ego was to betray Freud. (Frankly, it is not hard for me to sympathize with this view of the mind as a realm fragmented by unconscious events that we can only accept and try to understand.)

Jean Laplanche is perhaps my favorite example of a writer who differs radically from Freud while finding his inspiration in him. What makes him such a good example is the specificity of his very critical reading *of* Freud, and therefore the specificity of his inspiration *by* Freud. Laplanche began his writing career by translating Freud into French, and then, on the basis of this very close study of Freud's body of work, by creating with Pontalis one of the essential psychoanalytic books, *The Language of Psychoanalysis* (Laplanche & Pontalis, 1973). In that work, organized as a kind of dictionary, Laplanche and Pontalis selected Freud's key conceptions and offered pithy and insightful definitions (more like brief discussions, really) of them. During these years, and continuing until his death in the early years of the new century, we see in Laplanche's brilliantly original theoretical work the fruits of these years of immersion in Freud. Every point Laplanche makes—in fact, his entire theoretical corpus—is based on what he analyzes as Freud's "goings astray" (e.g., Laplanche, 2006), which Laplanche "elevates to the rank of a methodological concept" (Fletcher, 2011, p. 83). Laplanche argues that Freud made crucial mistakes and that we must identify those "goings astray" if we are to create the "new foundations" (Laplanche, 1989) that psychoanalysis needs. Over and over again, Laplanche identifies clearly and precisely where he feels Freud diverged from what should have been the implications of his own thought, and then Laplanche fills in the ideas that he claims Freud himself would have come upon if he had been able think more uncompromisingly than he did. Laplanche's work is one long struggle with Freud, who is like a contentious sibling—or perhaps better, a parent one loves and with whom one tangles one's whole life. As in the case of Lacan, Laplanche's ideas, while meaningfully related to Freud's, are not Freud's ideas at all, but elaborations in new directions.

Given what can be accomplished in a single chapter, I cannot actually demonstrate in these pages how significantly Loewald, Lacan, and Laplanche diverge from Freud. I must ask instead that the reader simply accept my contention that they do. I cite these writers not in order to present their thinking, but to make the point that ideas very different than Freud's own—quite possibly, no less different from Freud than relational ideas— have been welcomed in the broader psychoanalytic world when they have been anchored, however imaginatively, in Freud's work. I mean "welcomed" in a particular way, since all of these writers have been controversial (especially Lacan) and so were not welcomed in the most simple sense, as if they were eagerly anticipated guests. But they were welcome in the sense that there was never any question in the mainstream literature, or (so I believe) in the minds of most mainstream analysts, about whether they deserved serious consideration—an attitude that is not always what one encounters among these same analysts in regard to relational thinking.

Examples such as Loewald, Lacan, and Laplanche show that it is not necessarily only the differences between mainstream psychoanalysis and relational psychoanalysis that makes mainstream analysts critical. Yes, of course, differences matter enormously (see the following section of this chapter) but the reason for mainstream criticism also lies in the fact that relational writers do not necessarily (and sometimes cannot, because the ideas do not allow it) ground their ideas in mainstream psychoanalytic scholarship, and Freud in particular, in a way that encourages traditionalists to grant us psychoanalytic identities.

I am not advocating that relational analysts respond to rhetorical pressures, or to calls for submission to tribal discipline. On the other hand, I do share a profound respect for scholarship with most other psychoanalysts, and therefore I do think it is desirable, when it is possible without twisting ourselves into pretzels in the process, to ground our ideas in all of the relevant ideas that have come before us. I hasten to add that I recognize the fact that many relational analysts already do anchor their work in psychoanalytic tradition.

What we should do in response to this criticism we face is not really my primary point, though. What I want most to convey is this: we need to understand that our approach grows from our pragmatic American approach to empirical observation; our (also typically American) tendency to say things straight out and thereby sacrifice a focus on the emergence of our work from what has come before; and the valorization of individualism in American culture, which I suspect also plays a role in discouraging our awareness of our dependence on our intellectual and clinical forbears. (Bloom's [1973] classic discussion of "the anxiety of influence," despite the fact that it concerns the influences of "strong poets" on poets who came after, is apposite here.) To the extent that these things are true of North American psychoanalysis, our writing can seem disrespectful and shallow to some of our mainstream colleagues. They can feel that we are violating what they most value, the intellectual substance that actually underpins what a psychoanalyst is. For our colleagues in Europe and South America, Freud is an inexhaustible resource, still the font of new thought in psychoanalysis. We need to understand that interaction with Freud is the necessary generative source for our colleagues. Freud is more a father to them than he is to most of us, and their struggle with him is therefore more crucial to them. We should understand this not only as rigidity, but as a creative impetus that we relational analysts are to some extent deprived of, because our relationship to Freud is less intimate, and therefore less precious to us. We need to understand that when they read the parts of our work that do not grow from our encounter with Freud, or in which Freud is at least not an obvious source, even some of those traditionalists who are willing to grant that we have a point will feel that we are disrespecting the history of our field, reinventing the wheel, practicing irresponsible or inadequate scholarship, and/or doing something other than psychoanalysis.

The place of the unconscious in relational psychoanalysis: Psychoanalytic values

I have tried to recognize critical views of relational *scholarship*, including my own. Now I turn to an attempt to recognize the critical views of relational *theory* held by the same analysts I have already been discussing. This is a more challenging task, because while there is often at least some truth to the claims made about the paucity of scholarly citation of Freud and other mainstream psychoanalysts in the relational literature, the same cannot necessarily be said about claims made by other analysts about relational theory. Some of those who hold the most critical views of relational theory and practice actually do not seem very familiar with the views they are criticizing. Stephen Mitchell (1995), writing about certain American Freudian views, wrote that: "The most appalling thing about these critiques of relational theories is how little effort these authors appear to have expended in trying to understand what it is they think they are arguing against" (p. 574). It doesn't seem unreasonable to take the same view of the familiarity of French, Italian, and Latin American analysts with the relational literature. The job of offering recognition to such views can therefore be quite difficult.

It is true that conceptual and clinical divergences between us and our critics lie at the heart of the views most critical of us. But I have come to believe that the reasons for the negative attitudes toward relational psychoanalysis held by many European and Latin American analysts are not only a matter of simple disagreement. The problem is more profound than disagreement over psychoanalytic questions, just as questioning the willingness of relational writers to anchor their ideas in the history of psychoanalysis is more than a question of scholarship. In the same way that the scholarship issue can be seen as a matter of psychoanalytic identity, the question of theoretical divergence can be understood as a matter of psychoanalytic values.

It is not that European and Latin American critics argue that relational analysts hold *different* psychoanalytic values; the critics claim, rather, that there exists a single set of psychoanalytic values, and that relational analysts do not hold them. Waintrater (2012), for instance, in a very useful explanation of the French response to relational psychoanalysis (for another useful comparative account, see Kemberg, 2001) writes: "Mitchell's (1988) audacity in replacing the drive theory with the relational theory is perceived as a danger, a Trojan horse that could destroy psychoanalysis from within; therefore all such attempts must be fought" (p. 300).

The French characterization of relational psychoanalysis is not a matter of simple disagreement on empirical or philosophical grounds. That kind of disagreement we could probably discuss profitably. Instead, the claim is that relational psychoanalysis is not properly psychoanalytic. This is the kind of criticism that no psychoanalyst, relational or otherwise, can accept. Yet I think—and it is the burden of this chapter to show—that we must accept that these views exist and try to understand how they came about and why they persevere.

For those of us who live in North America, the extremity of these positions about us can come as a shock. Relational and interpersonal psychoanalysts are used to thinking that the wars are over, or at least on the way to being over. We are used to the idea that there has been a significant "interpersonalization" of American Freudian psychoanalysis. And there has been, of course. But to the extent that we treat North American psychoanalysis as the psychoanalysis of the world, we are being short-sighted and narrow-minded.

If we are taken by surprise by the force of the criticism of us from the rest of the world, in other words, it is because of our arrogance and chauvinism, however unrecognized these attitudes may be. Most of us have conceptualized psychoanalysis as if it were simply what we have always thought it was. Only at this late date are we granting the same significance to the psychoanalysis of Europe and Latin America that we have always assumed for our own, homegrown varieties.

Of course, we are not alone in this: Mitchell's work, Waintrater (2012) tells us, is "virtually unknown" in France, and none of his books have been translated into French. *Psychoanalytic Dialogues* "is never mentioned in bibliographies" (p. 296). In France, says Waintrater, ego psychology (hated by Lacan, whose view on this subject remains influential) and object relations (including relational psychoanalysis) are equated, and even though it is understood that relational psychoanalysis and self psychology developed in reaction to ego psychology, all these schools tend to be tarred with the same Lacanian brush.

> French analysts react with perplexity, if not astonishment, to such ideas as the relative nature of interpretation, the primacy of the here-and-now,

and the deconstruction of authority, especially the analyst's. In the French view, such ideas reflect an ideological tendency, close to cultural relativism; they mark the end of the specificity of psychoanalysis, reduced to a branch of psychology.

(Wainstrater, 2012, p. 296)

For the French, "anything referring to cognitive processes, to notions of will and change, belongs to motivational theories and is incompatible with the very idea of the unconscious" (Wainstrater, 2012, p. 296). And:

The idea of a subject with a unified sense of self gained through understanding and experience is completely at odds with the French conception of a subject divided by the very nature of what constitutes the psyche, that is, infantile sexuality, fantasy, and repression.

(p. 296)

The French reject a central role for affect, according to Wainstrater, continuing to insist instead on the importance of verbal associations and the analyst's interpretations of them.

If the analyst's interpretations are by essence just as subjective as the patient's own experience and both are considered equivalent, then the only thing that matters is shared meaning and knowledge. Thus, according to many French analysts, the relational and intersubjective schools are tantamount to theories of communication.

(Wainstrater, 2012, p. 297)

And of course there is the question of drive: for Laplanche, for instance, "the idea of resolving conflict, and resulting anxiety, through shared understanding and elucidation [as relational writers are understood to recommend] can only be a defensive stance vis-á-vis the drive impulses and their strange and inexplicable nature" (Wainstrater, 2012, p. 298). Perhaps the most critical difference for the French is the Anglo-Saxon rejection of the death drive, which the French see as the "cornerstone of human conflict" (p. 297).

Put these and other points together and the conclusion looks like this:

A watered-down unconscious, or even no unconscious at all: this is how intersubjective theories are perceived in France. For French psychoanalysts, the indomitable force of transference and of the drives cannot be reduced to a transaction between two persons: intersubjectivity and the entire relational movement are criticized as ignoring psychic conflict and the unconscious.

(Wainstrater, 2012, pp. 295–296)

I do not have an equivalent example from South America to quote, but it is clear to me that there is no shortage there of this same kind of critique of relational psychoanalysis. Lest it appear that these criticisms come only from France, though, let me offer an example from Italy that echoes some of the same themes. In the passage that follows, Ferro and Civitarese (2013) refer to "interpersonalists" when they actually mean both interpersonal and relational psychoanalysts. Read the comment, therefore, as if it applies to both groups.

The clinical vignettes of the interpersonalists sometimes convey the impression that, first, interpersonal psychoanalysis is based on an interactionism not guided at all times by a model of the unconscious functioning of the individual and group mind as versatile that of BFT [Bionian field theory], which also takes account of the micrometry of the analytic dialogue; and that, second, [interpersonal/relational psychoanalysis] sees change as underlain principally by rational understanding and conscious agreement (which admittedly often rest on a reading of unconscious dynamics and on the joint experience of analysis).

(p. 647)

This chapter is not the place to offer detail about the views of the European and Latin American critics of relational thinking. What I intend here is just to offer enough detail to indicate the scale of the problem. The scale is huge, as even this brief sampling of views indicates.

Given this situation, what can we do if we wish to make better relationships with those who disagree with us? It is simple to begin to answer this question: we must talk to them with the assumption that their attitude toward us is not simply critical, but that, in fact, they wish to have better relationships with us, just as we wish to have better relationships with them. It's just that they, like us, are unwilling to compromise either their psychoanalytic identities or their psychoanalytic values in order to create this state of affairs.

This is all well and good, but let me make sure I am not misunderstood: I am not advocating Pollyannism, nor am I denying that forceful argumentation and rejection of the other's point of view are sometimes necessary and unavoidable.

Let me tell a story. A number of years ago, a group of about a dozen training analysts from two of New York's APsaA institutes asked me to meet with them all day on a Saturday to talk about clinical material. These analysts had read relational and interpersonal literature, but they felt that they weren't able to feel and know what doing this kind of work was really like. We met for about ten hours around a large table one day in the apartment of one of them. Sandwiches were delivered for lunch, and we kept talking. I presented clinical material and did my best to explain how I thought and felt about each clinical situation as it happened, how I intervened when I did, and why I didn't intervene when I didn't. For the first hours, I could tell from their expressions and their comments that a number of these analysts were quite leery of me. I felt defensive, but I tried to be as open as I could, feeling that the only opportunity to create a bond between all of us—and I didn't see any sense in doing this if I didn't aim for that—lay in making an authentic emotional connection through the work we shared. As the day went on, all of us relaxed, and by the end of the day the feeling among us was respectful and collegial, even excited. We felt we had shared something important. I feel confident in saying that it was a terrific day for all of us. You may remember that, earlier in this chapter, I mentioned that I now teach a required course on interpersonal and relational psychoanalysis at the New York Psychoanalytic Institute. That course grew out of this day.

I have had similar experiences with colleagues from Europe and Latin America—although none that were quite as transformative. Often there is discomfort to begin with. But the mere fact of the contact is important. I think that, like some of our colleagues in our own country, Europeans and Latin Americans often imagine relational analysts to be undisciplined and unthoughtful, and perhaps even irresponsible clinicians. They may think we shoot from the hip and do very little besides chat comfortably with our patients. When they see that we are seriously interested in the same clinical problems they are interested in themselves, and interested in the same way, things tend to relax. It is only then that theoretical differences can begin to be discussed.

We cannot have these discussions without accepting our divergences from each other. We do so with the hope that accepting these differences will result in a mutual respect for them. Imagine being an analyst who thinks that negotiation of difference in the clinical situation is simply a defensive maneuver. Imagine believing that the intention to grasp and understand unconscious processes is a superficial accommodation. Imagine thinking that the goal of comprehending the analytic relationship is ephemeral, that such "comprehension" is nothing more than an enactment, an illusion, and that the patient's mind is most usefully contacted by interacting with the patient's unconscious in ways you learn from theory. Imagine thinking that affect is not necessarily your clinical guide, and that the best way to affect the patient's mind has nothing to do with what feels like intimacy, but is instead a matter of correctly interpreting the patient's verbal associations. Imagine believing that the analyst's authority rests on the theoretically mediated grasp s/he has on the patient's unconscious process, an authority the patient needs to accept if s/he is to get better. (And imagine having patients who accept this proposition!)

And then imagine sitting with a fellow clinician who thinks in these ways, someone who sits with people in a consulting room, just as you do, someone who hopes that the time and effort they spend with patients is productive. Imagine trying to absorb these enormous differences in the way you and this other analyst think about psychoanalysis. Imagine thinking that, given the aims you share, what you do and what they do must not be as incommensurable as they seem to believe. And then talk about it.

Notes

1 I thank Phillip Blumberg, PhD, for his editorial advice and creative additions to this chapter.
2 I have gotten to know a number of the writers on this list over the last several years, and I imagine that the same is true for many other interpersonal and relational analysts. I suspect that as a consequence of this greater contact across theoretical boundaries, which used to be so much less permeable, citations of relational psychoanalytic literature by analysts of other schools will increase in the coming years.
3 Longer and more complete versions of these articles appear elsewhere (Stern, 2015a).
4 I would prefer not to use the term "the unconscious," because of the reification inherent in it. I prefer something like "unconsciousness" or "unconscious processes" but those expressions are often awkward, and so I often settle for common usage.
5 Loewald is known as an American, and he was, of course. But his cultural identification was European, which is why I include him here. He was one of Heidegger's most prized students prior to arriving in the United States (although he disavowed Heidegger after the war because of Heidegger's Naziism, and refused all attempts by others to

arrange a meeting between the two) and while he was usually classified as an ego psychologist, he was really never part of the psychoanalysis established by Hartmann, Kris, and Loewenstein.

References

Bachant, J.L., Lynch, A.A. and Richards, A.D. (1995). Relational models in psychoanalytic theory. *Psychoanalytic Psychology,* 12:71–87.

Benjamin, J. (1990). Recognition and destruction: An outline of inter-subjectivity. In: *Relational Psychoanalysis: The Emergence of a Tradition,* Ed: S.A. Mitchell and L. Aron. Hillsdale, NJ: The Analytic Press, pp. 183–200.

Benjamin, J. (2004). Beyond doer and done to: An intersubjective view of thirdness. *Psychoanalytic Quarterly*, 73:5–46.

Benjamin, J. (2017). *Beyond Doer and Done To: Recognition Theory, Intersubjectivity, and the Third.* New York and London: Routledge.

Bloom, H. (1973). *The Anxiety of Influence: A Theory of Poetry.* New York: Oxford University Press.

Blumberg, P. (2013). Personal communication.

Bruner, J.S. and Postman, L. (1949). On the perception of incongruity: A paradigm. *Journal of Personality,* 18:206–223.

Busch, F. (2001). Are we losing our mind? *Journal of the American Psycho-analytic Association,* 49:739–751.

Eagle, M.N., Wolitzky, D.L. and Wakefield, J.C. (2001). The analyst's knowledge and authority: A critique of the "new view" in psychoanalysis. *Journal of the American Psychoanalytic Association,* 49:457–488.

Ferro, A. and Civitarese, G. (2013). Analysts in search of an author: Voltaire or Artemisia Gentileschi? Commentary on 'Field Theory in Psycho-analysis, Part II: Bionian Field Theory and Contemporary Interpersonal/ Relational Psychoanalysis' by Donnel B. Stern. *Psychoanalytic Dialogues,* 23:646–653.

Fletcher, J. (2011). Editor's note. Countercurrents. In: J. *Laplanche*, Freud and the Sexual, Ed: J. Fletcher. New York: International Psychoanalytic Books, pp. 83–97.

Frankel, J.B. (1998). Are interpersonal and relational psychoanalysis the same? *Contemporary Psychoanalysis,* 34:485–500.

Hartmann, H. (1958). *Ego Psychology and the Problem of Adaptation,* trans. D. Rapaport. New York: International Universities Press.

Kernberg, O. (2001). Recent developments in the technical approaches of English-language psychoanalytic schools. *The Psychoanalytic Quarterly,* 70:519–547.

Laplanche, J. (1989). *New Foundations for Psychoanalysis.* Trans. D. Macey. Oxford: Basil Blackwell.

Laplanche, J. (2006). Exigency and going astray. *Psychoanalysis, Culture and Society,* 11:185–189.

Laplanche, J. and Pontalis, J.-B. (1973). *The Language of Psychoanalysis.* New York: Norton.

Levine, H.B. (2010). *Partners in Thought: Working with Unformulated Experience, Dissociation, and Enactment.* By Donnel B. Stern. New York/ London: Routledge. *Psychoanalytic Quarterly,* 79:1166–1177.

Loewald, H. (2000). *The Essential Loewald: Collected Papers and Monographs.* Hagerstown, MD: University Publishing Group.

Loewenstein, R.M., Newman, L.M., Schur, M. and Solnit, A.J. (Eds.) (1966). *Psychoanalysis: A General Psychology. Essays in Honor of Heinz Hartmann.* New York: International Universities Press.

Lombardi, R. (June 6, 2016). Personal communication.

Mills, J. (Ed.). (2005). *Relational and Intersubjective Perspectives in Psychoanalysis: A Critique.* Lanham, MD: Jason Aronson/Rowman and Littlefield.

Mills, J. (2012). *Conundrums: A Critique of Contemporary Psychoanalysis.* New York: Routledge.

Mitchell, S.A. (1988). *Relational Concepts in Psychoanalysis: An Integration.* Cambridge, MA: Harvard University Press.

Mitchell, S.A. (1995). Commentary on "Contemporary Structural Psychoanalysis and Relational Psychoanalysis". *Psychoanalytic Psychology,* 12:575–582.

Neisser, U. (1967). *Cognitive Psychology.* Englewood Cliffs, NJ: Prentice-Hall.

Nobus, D. (2000). *Lacan and the Freudian Practice of Psychoanalysis.* New York: Routledge.

Orange, D.M. (2011). *The Suffering Stranger: Hermeneutics for Everyday Clinical Practice.* New York and London: Routledge.

Stern, D.B. (2010). *Partners in Thought: Working with Unformulated Experience, Dissociation, and Enactment.* New York: Routledge.

Stern, D.B. (2013a). Field theory in psychoanalysis, Part 1: Harry Stack Sullivan and Madeleine and Willy Baranger. *Psychoanalytic Dialogues,* 23:487–501.

Stern, D.B. (2013b). Field theory in psychoanalysis, Part 2: Bionian field theory and contemporary interpersonal/relational psychoanalysis. *Psychoanalytic Dialogues,* 23:630–645.

Stern, D.B. (2015a). *Relational Freedom: Emergent Properties of the Interpersonal Field.* New York: Routledge.

Stern, D.B. (2015b). The interpersonal field: Its place in American psychoanalysis. *Psychoanalytic Dialogues,* 25:388–404.

Sugarman, A. (1995). Psychoanalysis: Treatment of conflict or deficit? *Psychoanalytic Psychology,* 12:55–70.

Sullivan, H.S. (1940). *Conceptions of Modern Psychiatry.* New York: Norton. First published in book form 1953.

Waintrater, R. (2012). Intersubjectivity and French psychoanalysis: A misunderstanding? *Studies in Gender and Sexuality,* 13:295–302.

Wilson, A. (1995). Mapping the mind in relational psychoanalysis. *Psychoanalytic Psychology,* 12:9–29.

Chapter 16

Can there be a psychoanalysis without unconscious phantasy? Unformulated experience and the multiple self[1]

In recent years a series, "Psychoanalytic Controversy," has appeared periodically in the International Journal of Psychoanalysis. *In each installment of the series a prominent analyst is invited to write a position paper on the particular controversy under consideration in that issue, and that paper then is discussed in commentaries written by others. In 2013, Lucy LaFarge contributed an essay to this series, "How and Why Unconscious Phantasy and Transference Are Defining Features of Psychoanalytic Practice." This chapter is my commentary on that essay. The symposium was introduced by Rachel Blass; the other discussant was Michael Feldman.*

A substantial part of my response to LaFarge was devoted to a presentation of my position on the matter of unconscious phantasy. I explained how it is that many interpersonal and relational psychoanalysts work without the idea of unconscious phantasy—a position that I knew that many readers of IJP *would find impossible to imagine. That was the reason I took the tack I did in the response, because familiarity with interpersonal and relational psychoanalysis could not be assumed among the readers of* IJP, *for many of whom my presentation may have been their first exposure to such views.*

I take the point of view that the idea of unconscious phantasy is not demanded by clinical experience. All psychoanalytic theories, of course, are anchored in unconscious process; and so all psychoanalysts, including me, agree that the idea of unconscious process and structure *(of some kind) is indeed demanded by clinical experience. It follows that we can also agree that all psychoanalytic theories must posit some means by which unconscious process is shaped into conscious, explicit experience. These two ideas—unconscious processes/structures, and some means by which they are given conscious, thinkable shape—must be part of any psychoanalytic theory.*

DOI: 10.4324/9781032688893-19

LaFarge and I come from two different North American psychoanalytic traditions. Mine, interpersonal psychoanalysis (and, starting in the 1980s, relational psychoanalysis), diverged in the 1930s from LaFarge's, which at that time would have been described as ego psychology. Today her frame of reference might be better described as contemporary Freudian psychoanalysis—although clearly LaFarge is also conversant with, and influenced by, modern Kleinian thinking.

In the beginning of their collaboration, during the 1930s, the men and women who eventually became the first generation of interpersonal psychoanalysts differed from their contemporary Freudian colleagues over the centrality of culture and interpersonal relations in the formation of mind and the practice of psychoanalysis. They shared a rejection of libido theory, Freud's dual instinct theory, and the theory of psychosexual stages; they questioned whether the Oedipus complex was inevitably central; they focused attention on the significance of language in the formulation of experience; they asserted that therapeutic action revolved around the identification of unconscious patterns in the patient's interpersonal life—in the past and the patient's current outside life, but especially in the transference and the countertransference; and they therefore argued that therapeutic action resided more in analytic work in the here-and-now than in genetic reconstruction. But perhaps the most important contribution of the early interpersonalists, in the long run, was their insistence that the analyst was continuously and personally involved, consciously and unconsciously, in the clinical situation. (For a review of interpersonal psychoanalysis, including these issues, see Lionells et al., 1995.)

The interpersonalists, in other words, were the first to introduce the idea that the analyst's subjectivity is a ceaseless and inevitable component of the analytic situation, co-determining with the transference the nature of the analytic relationship (see Hirsch, 2014). The contribution of the subjectivity of both participants in any relationship to the experience each participant has in that relationship was recognized by interpersonal writers from the beginning (e.g., Fromm, 1955; Sullivan, 1940), and some of these writers (e.g., Crowley, 1952; Fromm, 1955; Tauber, 1954; Thompson, 1961; Wolstein, 1959) saw that this point was no less true in the analytic situation than it was in any other relationship. A full and widespread appreciation of the role of the analyst's subjectivity in clinical practice, however, came about in the interpersonal literature only in the 1970s and early 1980s

(Gill, 1983), largely as a result of the work of Levenson (1972, 1983, 1991; Levenson, Hirsch and Iannuzzi, 2005; Foehl, 2008) and Wolstein (1959; Hirsch, 2000; Bonovitz, 2009).

From the 1930s to the 1990s, these ideas and others clearly differentiated interpersonal psychoanalysis and Freudian ego psychology. In the 1990s, though, the idea that unconscious mutual influence is continuous in the psychoanalytic situation, an idea that constituted the core of the concept of interpersonal field, began to appear in the work of North American Freudians (see Hirsch, 1996; Stern, in press a), but without reference to the earlier interpersonal contribution. This development in the Freudian literature took place at least partly because of the 1980s advent of relational psychoanalysis, a form of psychoanalytic thought that drew much from interpersonal psychoanalysis, but which has had more impact on North American Freudians than interpersonal theory alone had had over the previous several decades. Between the 1990s and the present day, many contemporary North American Freudian writers have come to accept a way of understanding what happens in the psychoanalytic situation that, in significant respects, bears a notable similarity to interpersonal and relational psychoanalysis.

LaFarge's conception of phantasy

Certainly we see such an acceptance in LaFarge's article. LaFarge writes with sophistication and subtlety about the conscious and unconscious influences passing back and forth between analyst and patient in the analytic situation, and her clinical vignette effectively illustrates these themes. LaFarge believes, as I do, that the analyst's subjectivity participates in shaping every clinical moment—consciously, yes, but especially unconsciously.

But I also note that nowhere in LaFarge's article is there a reference to drive, which I do not know how to interpret. Does LaFarge consider phantasy in traditional ego psychological terms? That is, does she understand it to be an amalgam of wish, defense, and superego qualities? And if she does conceptualize phantasy in this way, is wish understood to be a drive derivative? (I adopt the Kleinian convention that Lafarge also adopts: the "ph" form of the word indicates unconscious fantasy.) I do not have a way of answering these questions, but in any case, LaFarge offers us an elegant ego psychological view, one reminiscent of Arlow's (1969a, b) well-known metaphor of conscious experience as the combined or integrated image formed on a screen by projections of external reality from one side and phantasy from the other.

LaFarge believes, if I understand properly, that the *contents* of mind (even if not the *nature* of mind) begin in our experience of living (i.e., contents are not significantly predetermined) and develop along lines established by the way that contemporary experience interacts with what mind has become up to that point. Furthermore, even if LaFarge contends that thoroughly intrapsychic events play a larger role than I believe they do in the ongoing creation of mind, she does accept that many events that matter in the growth of mind are interpersonal transactions of various kinds (although I cannot tell, from this essay, exactly how present experience contributes to the ongoing construction of phantasy). And LaFarge believes, as I do, that these interpersonal transactions are deeply affected, and given their meaning, by the non-rational, unconscious involvements of their participants.

I accept all these very broad principles, and so, despite the fact that I do not use the concept LaFarge considers central to psychoanalysis (phantasy), I find a good deal of common ground here.

I recognize that a substantial number of contemporary Freudians do not accept any version of the interpersonal field, continuing to espouse a conservative and more thoroughly intrapsychic point of view that allows them to maintain their commitment to the theory of neutrality. But because of the fairly widespread acceptance in North American Freudian circles of the kind of field theory that interpersonal/relational writers have long espoused—in which the traditional theory of neutrality must at least be stretched, and for some cannot be maintained at all—it has become more complicated and difficult than it once was to contrast the two perspectives.

Nevertheless, there is a contrast to be made. I now move to the more specific consideration of phantasy.

Is the concept of phantasy demanded by the phenomena? Is it inevitable?

I turn below to the task of describing an alternative to LaFarge's view. First, though, I want to present the grounds for questioning the inevitability of the concept of unconscious phantasy.

Consider this key passage from LaFarge's paper:

A second, unconscious reality at all times shapes our experience and is evoked by it. We perceive the present through the lens of this unconscious, psychic reality; and at the same time, contemporary, conscious reality appears to bring to life elements of psychic reality, which, blended with, and represented by, contemporary events, press toward the repetition of familiar dramas (Arlow, 1969a; Isaacs, 1952). Although these elements draw upon historical events and are linked to specific developmental phases, a close examination indicates that they are not replicas of historical reality. Rather they are organizations of phantasy.

LaFarge's wording here, if taken conservatively and literally, suggests that what is established by "close examination" is only that certain "elements of psychic reality" are "not replicas of historical reality." But we hardly need to employ "close examination" to establish this point. That is, the contrast between "historical reality" (a vexed concept since all reality is constructed, and therefore heir to many influences, conscious and unconscious, never simply stamped onto the mind by historical events) and certain other elements of mind is obvious to anyone. I think, though, that the very next sentence reveals the reason for LaFarge's sentence construction. That sentence reads: "Rather they (i.e. those certain psychic elements) are organizations of phantasy." I read Lafarge to mean here that the most important thing indicated by "close examination" is the existence of phantasy.

I may be right to read LaFarge this way; I may be wrong. Either way, though, the kind of reasoning I am trying to highlight here is common to all schools of psychoanalysis, my own included. We infer an idea (in this case, unconscious phantasy) from what we can observe (in this case, the fact that certain elements of psychic life are not replicas of "historical reality"), and we then use that inferred idea to construct future understandings of clinical material. Over time, the inferential origins of the idea become wispy and eventually vanish altogether, and we are left with the sense that the idea is an inevitability, an "objective" observation rather than an interpretive construction. This is what Foucault (1995) referred to, in his account of disciplinary power, as "normalization": what begins as a particular view, or one among many actions, comes to be taken for granted, the natural order of things.

So it is with the concept of phantasy. Yes, it is true: everyone agrees that, being unconscious, phantasy cannot be directly observed, and in that sense everyone agrees that phantasies are inferred. But many psychoanalysts would claim that, even if our attribution to the patient of any *particular* phantasy is an inference, the more general idea that unconscious phantasy exists is *demanded* by what they observe in the consulting room. That is (so the idea goes), what we observe clinically cannot be explained without positing phantasy. It is this broader inference—the habit of thought that makes us imagine phantasies to explain our clinical observations—that is often treated as a "natural" feature of the world, an inevitability.

It is my contention, though, that the inferences that lead to the concept of phantasy, however useful they may be to many clinicians, are not demanded by the phenomena. One can certainly argue that unconscious phantasy is the *best* way of accounting for the phenomena we observe (and many of those who disagree with me certainly would make that argument). But that conception simply is not the only way the observations in question can be accounted for.

I hasten to add, though, that, like all psychoanalysts, I accept that rational thought, and "literal" or "historical" reality, are insufficient to explain clinical process. *Something* non-rational, and from outside consciousness, must be invoked or inferred. We all therefore agree on the necessity for *some* kind of inference about unconscious processes, but we do not necessarily have to agree on *what* is to be inferred, or exactly how such inference ought to work. I will present my own inferences in a moment.

Given the inferential status of the ideas in question, the differences that exist between our various conceptions of that-which-is-inferred cannot be answered empirically. We certainly can argue for the clinical superiority of one process of inference, and one kind of unconscious content, over others—and of course, as I have already acknowledged, we do argue in that way. Those disagreements revolve around the consequences for our patients of our theories.[2] The differences between schools of psychoanalytic thought reflect differing beliefs about what is most important in treatment and in life. Our theories of technique and therapeutic action are therefore expressions of values (Stern, 2012).

I take the hermeneutic perspective that, no matter how timeless our theories may seem to us, or how inescapably they seem to impress themselves on us, all ideas are created to serve their time and place (e.g., Gadamer, 2004). They are not eternal verities. But in the case of theories of the unconscious, because the object of study is invisible, we have an additional reason to question the utility of empirical evidence. We are in the ironic position of having to recognize that our understandings of unconscious process are not only inventions, but inventions made by consciousness—the very aspect of the psyche that we have no choice but to accept has the least to do with the phenomena in question. As Laurence Kahn (2013) recently wrote in a provocative essay on this same problem: "The surface creates the depths each time" (p. 125).

And so for all these reasons, while we can all support and defend our preferred theories of the unconscious on the grounds of their utility and clinical value, we cannot validly conclude that one such theory is true and the others false.

What is not known?

The writer who has had the most to say about the differences in the way that Freudians and interpersonalists view fantasy (and phantasy) is Edgar Levenson, who wrote in 1988 that in the case of intrapsychic theories:

> once incorporated into the patient's intrapsychic world, real events become perpetuated anachronistically on [sic] into adult life as part of a motivating fantasy system. In contrast, an interpersonal position might argue that the perpetuation of the neurosis occurs because the patient is continuing to have the kinds of relationships he or she experienced as a child, and that the interpersonal matrix is a self- perpetuating and self-equilibrating system and depends, not on the fuel of fantasies for its viability, but on repetitive interactions.
>
> (1988, p. 219)

For Levenson, the patient selects people who "collude with his or her system or can be bent into colluding," and the repetition compulsion is therefore not motivated by phantasy, "but by an adaptive way of being-in-the-world, of manipulating the interpersonal context so as to minimize anxiety in the self and in the significant other person" (p. 219).

The interpersonal or relational analyst, in other words, is liable to see fantasy (and here I mean imaginative content that is consciously appreciable) not as the motivation for interpersonal life, but as a *reflection* of it. Fantasy is shaped as much by what must not be known (because of the consequence of anxiety) as it is by the attempt to grasp it. In Levenson's (1981) frame of reference, fantasy "reflect(s) an attempt to grapple with a poorly understood reality"; it is not "an autonomous fantasy process, internally driven and motivated" (p. 97), but an ineffective attempt to understand, a kind of "semiotic incompetence" (Levenson, 1983). It is shaped as much by what must not be known (because of the anxiety that knowing would provoke) as it is by the attempt to know. For Levenson, "Psychoanalysts can be roughly divided into two categories: those who believe that the essence is the *demystication of fantasy* and those who believe that the essence is the *demystification of experience*" (Levenson, 1982, p. 127). Elsewhere, Levenson puts it this way: "the clear line of schism between interpersonalist and Freudian ... remains *the search for the truth behind appearances* versus *the search for the truth inherent in appearances*" (1985, p. 154; italics in original).

For interpersonalists, then, the most important things that the patient does not know are not internally generated (or embroidered) phantasies, but aspects of the interpersonal world. What the patient cannot experience—the nature of unconscious process—is best understood as certain aspects of experience with others, including the analyst.

For Harry Stack Sullivan (1940, 1953), whose work was an important inspiration for interpersonal theory, anxiety is created by contagion, most influentially in the parent-child relationship, but also continuing through the rest of life. When the child behaves in a way that sets off parental anxiety, anxiety is induced in the child. The whole process occurs outside consciousness for both parent and child, and in this way the behavior and experience in question, which cannot be tolerated in awareness, come to exist in dissociation, outside the bounds of the self, in what Sullivan (1953), and then Bromberg (1998, 2006, 2011) and I (Stern, 2010), have characterized as "not-me." That is, like trauma, this aspect of subjectivity is not symbolized anywhere in the mind, and appears only in anxiety-laden interactions which threaten to bring it to the fore. But of course such interactions are avoided, and the experience that would come about if they were consciously lived is therefore never formulated. In this way, anxiety (trauma, if you like) is transmitted across the generations (cf. Faimberg, 2005), perpetuated in dissociation.

Unformulated experience

From within this interpersonal/relational frame of reference, I have proposed a conception of mind (Stern, 1983, 1997, 2010) that does not depend on phantasy. I did not set out to exclude the idea of phantasy; that theoretical conclusion instead followed as an indirect, but inescapable, consequence of the conception of unconsciousness to which my thinking took me. Because of space concerns, I cannot accompany the ideas that follow by clinical illustration. I refer the interested reader to the numerous illustrative case reports that appear in other sources (Stern, 1997, 2010, in press b).

I have always been deeply impressed with the emergent quality of conscious experience, the way it arrives unbidden in the minds of my patients, and my own, in each new moment. I was also deeply impressed by Freud's powerful and respectful characterization of this emergent quality and its unconscious sources. But I found equally compelling the interpersonal or relational emphasis on conscious and unconscious interpersonal relations—the events of the interpersonal field. I wanted to be able to think of unconscious process in a way that respected all these currents.

At about the same time (the early 1980s), in the course of following my interest in constructivist epistemology, I discovered ontological hermeneutics, which was introduced by Heidegger and then developed further by Gadamer (2004) and others. These writers hold that all being comes about through understanding, and all understanding is a matter of interpretation, and they therefore conclude that all being is interpretation. While verbal language is crucial, this "interpretation" is much broader than articulation in words. Language is understood as all our systems of symbols—that is, semiotics, the sum total of culture. All interpretation requires the creative metamorphosis of the traditions into which we are born, and this metamorphosis happens in the very moment of understanding. Understanding, then, can never be fully predicted; it is always to some degree unexpected, and does not pre-exist its own creation. It comes into being in the same moment that it appears in the conscious mind.

Furthermore, in these hermeneutic terms understanding is always a dialogic event. The one who understands creates what Gadamer (2004) described as "true conversation" with the object of understanding—whether that object is a work of art, a text, a person, or an experience of another kind. Life is the continuous creation of meaning, and meaning is more or less free to develop, depending on the degree to which we can allow language (in its broad meaning) to work freely within us.

It seemed to me, as I began to read ontological hermeneutics, that there was every reason to define the degree of the mind's freedom, as it was defined by Gadamer and others, in psychodynamic terms. This is a familiar thought for psychoanalysts, of course: the degree of our freedom to think and feel is significantly compromised by certain unconscious processes, especially unconscious defensive processes, and significantly augmented by the successful analysis of these processes.

The acceptance of emergent properties of the mind and experience poses a problem for psychoanalytic theories that rest on psychic determinism. Practitioners of these theories believe that, on the basis of a sufficiently thorough knowledge of the unconscious mind, it would be at least hypothetically possible to predict every psychic event. My position, on the other hand, is that much of what is most important about psychic life is unpredictable—and by "unpredictable" I do not intend the colloquial meaning of the word: that such events are hard to imagine in advance. I mean that the processes of mind are non-linear and emergent. I am not alone in this view; many psychoanalysts today accept some version of it. Some of them come to it from a philosophical perspective, as I do (Cushman, 1996; Hoffman, 1998; Mitchell, 1993, 1997); others come to it from non-linear dynamic systems theory (Boston Change Process Study Group, 2010; Coburn, in press; Galatzer-Levy, 2004; Harris, 2008; Piers, 2000; Seligman, 2005).

I began to wonder how I could imagine whatever it is that pre-exists conscious experience in a way that respected all the sources and attitudes I have mentioned (and others: see Stern, 1983). My answer to this question was, if conscious experience is the result of an implicit interpretive process, then that which pre-exists consciousness, or unconsciousness, must be whatever precedes interpretation—that is, whatever precedes the establishment of meaning. And so one part of the answer to my question seemed to me to be that whatever precedes meaningful experience is *potential* experience, what conscious experience might become. Another part of the answer seemed to be that what precedes consciousness is *ambiguous*, since it precedes the interpretive process that will articulate it as explicitly meaningful. The unconscious from this perspective is not symbolically represented in some hidden or distorted way. It is not like a stage set behind a curtain, ready to be revealed when the curtain is raised. Because it is instead potential experience, what conscious experience might become, it has no single predetermined shape.

In this way, I concluded that the combination of sources I was attempting to respect implied that the unconscious is not fully formed, requiring only discovery or revelation to become conscious. Unconsciousness (I prefer to avoid the reification inherent in the term "the unconscious") is instead *unformulated experience*, a vaguely organized, global, non-ideational, affective state. This conception, I realized with time, is inconsistent with the existence of phantasy, among other things—if we mean by phantasy a structured unconscious phenomenon.

I wanted to be sure, though, that, like the work of the hermeneutic philosophers, the conception of unformulated experience respected that both current reality and past history are indeed "there," and that they therefore set limits on what we can think, feel, and perceive while remaining sane and truthful. For Gadamer, because reality is multiple and manifold, it leaves a certain degree of indeterminacy or ambiguity, to be resolved by the way we construct conscious experience. Both reality and history provide constraints on what experience can become, but both leave enough ambiguity to make the interpretive construction of conscious experience necessary.

I have learned that, whenever I discuss hermeneutics, I need to be absolutely clear on a point that seems to be continuously misunderstood: this is not a relativistic view, and I am not a relativist. It is perfectly reasonable that reality is simultaneously characterized by both ambiguity that requires interpretation and constraints that must be respected. For the grounds of this position, I refer the reader elsewhere (Stern, 1997, 2010). For the present purpose, I just want the point to be registered.

It follows from the account I have given that the most crucial events in the construction of experience, inside and outside the consulting room, are those that resolve the ambiguity of unformulated experience into some explicit, conscious shape. Most interpersonal and relational analysts would agree that the factors responsible for resolving that ambiguity are relational phenomena—that is, the conscious and unconscious events that comprise the interpersonal field. For these analysts, the interpersonal field is composed of the intersections and interactions of the patient's and the analyst's conscious and unconscious experience and conduct. The greater the freedom existing in the relatedness between patient and analyst, therefore, the wider the range of possibilities available for each participant's conscious experience. And conversely, the more the analytic relatedness is characterized by constriction, inhibition, distortion, and other rigidities, especially unconscious rigidities, the fewer the possibilities for conscious experience. The degree of freedom available to consciousness, in other words, is determined by the nature of the interpersonal field. The more the constrictions of the interpersonal field can be relaxed, the greater the freedom available to the minds of both analyst and patient.

Dissociation

The model for defense in theories rooted in phantasy is repression. In such theories, the stability of the mind requires the creation and preservation of a state of tolerable conflict between conscious and unconscious contents. Phantasy is one of the primary unconscious mental contents, its unconscious status maintained by the continuous application of repression.

If the mind is conceived in terms of unformulated experience, the model for defense must be reconceptualized as dissociation (see especially Stern, 1997, Chapters 5–7). By dissociation I mean the maintenance of experience in its unformulated state for unconscious defensive reasons. Unconscious content is not distorted or hidden, as it is in models emphasizing repression. Rather, the primary defense is not to create the experience in the first place.

The question that immediately arises here is how one can know which experiences to avoid creating without first creating that same experience. The answer is that it is possible, on the basis of glimmers of meaning—what William James (1890) called "signs of direction in thought" and "feelings of tendency"—to avoid, without awareness of the act, the formulation of particular meanings. See Stern, 1997, Chapters 4–6, for a detailed presentation of this argument. In that book I draw from the work of many artists and writers, and from the work on self-deception of the philosopher Herbert Fingarette (1969), who addresses the key question of how it is that we can manage to avoid the formulation of experience *without awareness* of doing so.

Dissociation is also understood from my perspective as the sequestering of states of being from one another (see below).

Field theory

Phantasy has been approached in two ways in Freudian and Kleinian theory, and these same two theoretical strategies appear in interpersonal and relational theories of the analytic field.

In Freudian and Kleinian writings, phantasy is created early in life, and these archaic forms then continue to exist in the unconscious, unchanged through life, participating in the shaping of experience. LaFarge embraces this traditional view partially. She writes:

[The most central phantasies] – those that exert the greatest influence upon conscious experience – have to do with early memories, wished for satisfactions and dreaded anxieties pertaining to the body and the self in relation to early objects.

But LaFarge also takes the perspective that each phantasy is created anew at every developmental level, and that all these versions are preserved in the mind, so that in everyday life all participate in the creation of experience. The influence of phantasy thus becomes quite complex and variable.

LaFarge's point of view can be fruitfully compared to the view of phantasy from Bionian field theory (e.g., Baranger and Baranger, 1961–62; Baranger et al., 1993; Ferro, 2008, 2009, 2011; Ferro and Basile, 2009; Civitarese, 2010, 2013), in which phantasy also does not necessarily persevere in its original shapes, but instead ceaselessly changes and develops over time as the result of continuous interchange between participants in the field. The field in this frame of reference is defined as jointly created unconscious phantasies continuously coming into being between analyst and patient. As a matter of fact, phantasy is so much a matter of change and flexibility for these writers that psychopathology is defined as frozen aspects of the analytic field, resulting in rigid and unchanging parts of the field referred to by the Barangers (1961–62) as "bastions" or "bulwarks."

We can compare interpersonal and relational writers along this same dimension. Some of these analysts (e.g., Aron, 1995, 1996; Cooper, 2000, 2010; Davies, 1994, 2001, 2006) tend to conceptualize the most significant of the formative unconscious influences as unconscious relational configurations or internal objects, archaic influences ultimately derived from aspects of relatedness with the most important early caretakers. All these writers, though, are eager to avoid the implication that meaning is preformed, and therefore they are careful not to reify internal objects. Instead, they understand the meaning contributed by internal objects to emerge dialogically in the analytic situation, in the context of the therapeutic relationship (e.g., Bass, 2001). In this particular way—i.e., in conceiving the most significant unconscious structuring influences to have been formed far in the past, and to be persevering in unconscious life to the present day—these relational analysts and LaFarge share a view of phantasy.

In another interpersonal or relational view, though, the influence of the past is not maintained so much in archaic relational configurations that have a separate existence from contemporary interpersonal life, but instead in the phenomenon of the interpersonal field (e.g., Bromberg, 1998, 2006, 2011; Ehrenberg, 1992; Levenson, 1972, 1983, 1991; Stern, 1997, 2010) as conceptualized by Harry Stack Sullivan and others, and closely related to the work of Kurt Lewin (1935). (The concept of the interpersonal field is to be differentiated from Bionian views of the analytic field—see Stern, 2013a, b.) Two early interpersonal commentators, Murphy and Cattell (1952), described the role of the past in field theory as follows:

> Strictly speaking, the past as such is not properly used in the formulation of field events; the past has, so to speak, its surrogate, its aftermath, in the present; we cannot mix past events as such in the field forces which are the determination of each individual's conduct.
>
> (pp. 175–176)

From this point of view, that is, the past cannot be considered separately from the present. Archaic phantasies and relational configurations are therefore not natural to such theories. This does not mean, of course, that the past has any less significance in these views; it has, rather, a different *kind* of significance, a significance that is represented in forms of the present. As Murphy and Cattell write: "It is only the present – rich as it is in heirlooms from the past – *only* the teeming present that counts" (p. 175).

We know how to understand the formative influence of phantasy and unconscious relational configurations: these phenomena are conceived as unconscious templates that stamp their imprint on conscious experience. Or perhaps that is too restrictive an expression. Perhaps, since phantasy does not simply produce copies of itself, we should use a less restrictive metaphor and say, more generally, that phantasies and unconscious relational configurations are *structuring* influences, leaving aside the means by which the influence is exerted.

In a similar way, we can understand the formative influence of the joint phantasies posited by Bionian field theory. These phantasies may change over time, but we are meant to understand that they influence the form of conscious experience in the same way as the more traditional, persevering (even if also changing with developmental level), archaic phantasies.

But how do we understand the articulation of unformulated experience if we cannot, in the terms of the theory, conceptualize something like an unconscious template? How do we understand the structuring influence?

Multiple self theory

Here we arrive at the theory of the multiple self (Bromberg, 1998, 2006, 2011; Stern, 2010, in press b). It is the activity of the multiple self that, by comprising the interpersonal field, opens and closes the possibilities for articulating unformulated experience and thereby, for analysts who use these ideas, plays the structuring role in creating the contents of consciousness played by phantasy in the thinking of other analysts.

I define a self-state as a configuration of identity. Each self-state is one of the ways I recognize myself to be. Self-states are defined, for me, according to the conscious experience that can be formulated or articulated from within them.

Sullivan (1953) described the self as part of the personality. We would capture Sullivan's meaning if we were to say that: (1) the personality is the sum total of subjectivity, unconscious as well as conscious; and (2) the self is that part of the personality that we know, or personify, as "me." "Good-me" is composed of those states of being that we accept and value, developed around experiences with significant others that were characterized by affects of approbation, approval, affection, appreciation, and love. "Bad-me," on the other hand, is the part of self that developed around experiences of disapprobation, disapproval, dislike, shame, humiliation, and so on. Good-me and bad-me are each composed of multiple self-states. "Not-me," on the other hand, is that part of subjectivity that, because we cannot tolerate recognizing it as part of what we are (as part of "me"), has never been symbolized. It came into being as the result of interactions with significant others so suffused with intolerable affect—shame, self-hatred, rage, humiliation, terror, loathing, and so on—that they came to exist only in dissociation, unformulated for unconscious defensive reasons.[3] The task of psychoanalytic treatment is for not-me to become me, for the self and the personality to become coterminous.

The interpersonal field is in ceaseless flux. One way to represent this flux is by recognizing that each state of the field calls out a state of self in its participants, and each self-state in one participant influences the state of self that comes to the fore for the other participant. Most of these state shifts go on imperceptibly, although a clinician who thinks this way develops a sixth sense for the signs of self-state shifts, both in herself and in her patient. As the field shifts, and in response to the self-state of the other, one is called upon to formulate experience in different ways. Each self-state, remember, is defined by the experience that can be formulated from within it—so as the field shifts, and the other's state changes, one is influenced to shift one's own state in order to be able to respond in an affectively tolerable and appropriate way to the changed circumstances.

Events in the field, while they vary in degree of comfort (it is more comfortable, of course, to be good-me than bad-me) are relatively smooth as long as the states of being called forth are tolerable—as long as they are pre-existing parts of the self, part of what I experience as "me," good or bad. But when the state of being that is called forth is dissociated—when it is *not-me*—the relational outcome is more difficult. One is called upon to occupy a part of the personality that has never come been recognized as oneself, and therefore, if one were to accept the influence, one would become someone who would not be recognizable to oneself as "me." At that juncture, what takes place is enactment, a term I reserve for what I call "the interpersonalization of dissociation" (Stern, 2004). That is, one treats the other as the dissociated part of one's own experience. (The links with projective identification will be immediately obvious to readers. For a comparison, see Stern, 2010, pp. 17–18.)

I hope I have conveyed, despite the highly condensed nature of my presentation, that therapeutic enactment—all unconsciously motivated relatedness, of course, but the interpersonalization of dissociation in particular—is crucial. Keep in mind that dissociated experience is unformulated—which means that it is unsymbolized. It therefore cannot be analyzed via interpretation. Because it has never been symbolized, it cannot even be noted, or (metaphorically) pointed at. The only way dissociated experience can enter the treatment—and thus the only route along which not-me can ever become me—is enactment. It is only via the eventual resolution of enactments (Stern, 2010, in press b) that the self expands.

Conscious experience is always a construction from this point of view, never merely a given; mind does not record experience but creates it. No more than other psychoanalysts do interpersonal and relational analysts limit their consideration to "what actually happened" and how it was registered. The constructivism of this perspective leads to the rejection of objectivism and the idea of veridicality. It is not only that we do not *know* "what actually happened"—rather, the existence of something that could be described that way is called into question.

Self-states are no more "objective" or "veridical" than any other aspect of mind, so that, despite being a very different conception than phantasy, the structuring properties of self-states bear a relation to the structuring properties of phantasy. As a matter of fact, in an effort to translate my thinking into a more traditional psychoanalytic frame of reference, one sympathetic commentator recently described my clinical interest as the interplay between personal participation and internal objects (e.g., Cooper, in press).

I have focused on the question of phantasy because, conceptually, it is the heart of the matter in the comparison I have tried to make. But LaFarge described the core of psychoanalysis as both phantasy and transference, and so let me say just a few words about transference before I end. What I want to say is closely related to what I have said already. In the scheme I am outlining, I think it may already be clear that the nature of the analytic relationship—the transference and the countertransference—is a ceaseless outcome of the ongoing interaction between the self-states of patient and analyst. That is, the ongoing conscious and unconscious sense that patient and analyst have of one another in the analytic situation is an especially significant case of the same kind of structuring influence self-states have on all ongoing experience.

I hope that this very brief description indicates how shifting self-states can provide, within the terms of the theory of unformulated experience, the kind of structuring influence on consciousness that is provided by phantasy in other theories. I have very briefly introduced an alternative psychoanalytic account of mind and treatment that does not rest on the concept of phantasy, but nevertheless remains a theory of psychodynamics with a conception of unconscious process and conscious and unconscious analytic relatedness.

Notes

1 I thank Philip Blumberg PhD for thoughtful editorial assistance.
2 I note but cannot address here the long-standing controversy over whether theory really does affect practice. Suffice it to say for the present purpose that I believe it does.
3 That which is dissociated, however, is not understood by me or by Bromberg to be the affect itself, or even the memory, but an aspect of identity. Remember that a self-state is defined according to the experience that can be formulated from within it. A dissociated state of being, then, is dissociated precisely in order to prevent the person who could formulate the experience from existing: I *cannot, must* not be the person who experiences x.

References

Arlow JA (1969a). Unconscious fantasy and disturbances of conscious experience. *Psychoanal Q* 38:1–27.
Arlow JA (1969b). Fantasy, memory, and reality testing. *Psychoanal Q* 38:28–51.
Aron L (1995). The internalized primal scene. *Psychoanal Dialog* 5:195–237.

Aron L (1996). *A meeting of minds: Mutuality in psychoanalysis.* Hillsdale, NJ: Analytic Press.

Baranger M, Baranger W. (1961-62). The analytic situation as a dynamic field. *Int J Psychoanal* 89:795–826, 2009.

Baranger M, Baranger W, Mom JM (1993). *The work of confluence: Listening and interpreting in the psychoanalytic field.* Fiorini LG, editor. London: Karnac, 2009.

Bass A (2001). It takes one to know one: Or, whose unconscious is it anyway? *Psychoanal Dialog* 11:683–703.

Bonovitz C (2009). Looking back, looking forward: A re-examination of Benjamin Wolstein's *interlock* and the emergence of intersubjectivity. *Int J Psychoanal* 90:463–85.

Boston Change Process Study Group (2010). *Change in psychotherapy: A unifying paradigm.* New York, NY: Norton.

Bromberg PM (1998). *Standing in the spaces: Essays on clinical process, trauma, and dissociation.* Hillsdale, NJ: Analytic Press.

Bromberg PM (2006). *Awakening the dreamer: Clinical journeys.* Hillsdale, NJ: Analytic Press.

Bromberg PM (2011). *The shadow of the tsunami: And the growth of the relational mind.* New York, London: Routledge.

Civitarese G (2010 [2008]). *The intimate room: Theory and technique of the analytic field,* Slotkin P, translator. London: Routledge.

Civitarese G (2013). *The violence of emotions: Bion and post-Bionian psychoanalysis.* London: Routledge.

Coburn WJ (in press). *Psychoanalytic complexity: Attitudes that matter in psychoanalysis and psychotherapy.* New York, London: Routledge.

Cooper SH (2000). *Objects of hope: Exploring possibility and limit in psychoanalysis.* New York, London: Routledge.

Cooper SH (2010). *A disturbance in the field: Essays in transference-countertransference engagement.* New York, London: Routledge.

Cooper SH (in press). The things we carry: Finding/creating the object and the analyst's self-reflective participation. *Psychoanal Dialog.*

Crowley RM (1952). Human reactions of analysts to patients. *Samiksa* 6:212–219.

Cushman P (1996). *Constructing the self, constructing America: A cultural history of psychotherapy.* Cambridge, MA: Da Capo Press.

Davies JM (1994). Love in the afternoon: A relational reconsideration of desire and dread in the countertransference. *Psychoanal Dialog* 4:153–70.

Davies JM (2001). Erotic overstimulation and the co-construction of sexual meanings in transference- countertransference experience. *Psychoanal Q* 70:757–88.

Davies JM (2006). The times we sizzle, and the times we sigh: The multiple erotics of arousal, anticipation, and release. *Psychoanal Dialog* 16:665–86.

Ehrenberg DB (1992). *The intimate edge.* New York, NY: Norton.

Faimberg H (2005). *The telescoping of generations: Listening to the narcissistic links between generations.* London: Routledge.

Ferro A (2008 [2006]). *Mind works: Technique and creativity in psychoanalysis,* Slotkin P, translator. New York, NY: Routledge.

Ferro A (2009). Transformations in dreaming and characters in the psychoanalytic field. *Int J Psychoanal* 90:209–30.

Ferro A (2011 [2007]). *Avoiding emotions, living emotions,* Harvey I, translator. Hove: Routledge.

Ferro A, Basile R, editors. (2009). *The analytic field: A clinical concept.* London: Routledge.

Fingarette H (1969). *Self-deception.* London: Routledge & Kegan Paul.

Foehl JC (2008). Follow the fox: Edgar A. Levenson's pursuit of psychoanalytic process. *Psychoanal Q* 77:1231–68.

Foucault M (1995). *Discipline and punish: The birth of the prison.* 2nd edition. New York, NY: Vintage.

Fromm E (1955). Remarks on the problem of free association. In: Stern DB, Mann CH, Kantor S, Schlesinger G, editors. *Pioneers of interpersonal psychoanalysis,* 128–34. Hillsdale, NJ: Analytic Press.

Gadamer H-G (2004). *Truth and method.* Weinsheimer J, Marshall DG, revised translation from the 2nd edition in German (first published in German, 1965). London: Continuum.

Galatzer-Levy RM (2004). Chaotic possibilities. *Int J Psychoanal* 85:419–41.

Gill MM (1983). The interpersonal paradigm and the degree of the therapist's involvement. *Contemp Psychoanal* 19:200–37.

Harris A (2008). *Gender as soft assembly.* New York and London: Routledge.

Hirsch I (1996). Observing-participation, mutual enactment, and the new classical models. *Contemp Psychoanal* 32:359–83.

Hirsch I (2000). Interview with Benjamin Wolstein. *Contemp Psychoanal* 36:187–232.

Hirsch I (2014). *The interpersonal tradition: The origins of psychoanalytic subjectivity.* Hove: Routledge.

Hoffman IZ (1998). *Ritual and spontaneity in the psychoanalytic process: A dialectical-constructivist view.* Hilldale, NJ: Analytic Press.

Isaacs S (1952). The nature and function of phantasy. In: *Developments in psycho-analysis.* London: Karnac, 1989, 67–121.

James W (1890). *Principles of psychology.* New York, NY: Henry Holt.

Kahn L (2013). If one only knew *what* exists!. In: Levine HB, Reed GS, Scarfone D, editors. *Unrepresented states and the construction of meaning,* 122–51. London: Karnac.

Levenson EA (1972). *The fallacy of understanding.* New York, NY: Basic Books.

Levenson EA (1981). Facts and fantasies: On the nature of psychoanalytic data. In: Feiner AH, editor. *The purloined self: Interpersonal perspectives in psychoanalysis,* 97–110, 1991. New York, NY: Contemporary Psychoanalysis Books.

Levenson EA (1982). Playground or playpen. In: Feiner AH, editor. *The purloined self: Interpersonal perspectives in psychoanalysis,* 127–33. New York, NY: Contemporary Psychoanalysis Books, 1991.

Levenson EA (1983). *The ambiguity of change.* New York, NY: Basic Books.

Levenson EA (1985). The interpersonal (Sullivanian) model. In: Feiner AH, editor. *The purloined self: Interpersonal perspectives in psychoanalysis,* 151–65, 1991. New York, NY: Contemporary Psychoanalysis Books.

Levenson EA (1988). Real frogs in imaginary gardens: Facts and fantasies in psychoanalysis. In: Feiner AH, editor. *The purloined self: Interpersonal perspectives in psychoanalysis,* 211–23, 1991. New York, NY: Contemporary Psychoanalysis Books.

Levenson EA (1991). *The purloined self: Interpersonal perspectives in psychoanalysis.* Feiner AH, editor. New York, NY: Contemporary Psychoanalysis Books.

Levenson E, Hirsch I, Iannuzzi V (2005). Interview with Edgar A. Levenson, 24 January 2004. *Contemp Psychoanal* 41:593–644.

Lewin K (1935). *A dynamic theory of personality: Selected papers of Kurt Lewin.* New York, NY: McGraw-Hill.

Lionells ML, Fiscalini J, Mann C, Stern DB, editors. (1995). *The handbook of interpersonal psychoanalysis.* Hillsdale, NJ: Analytic Press.

Mitchell SA (1993). *Hope and dread in psychoanalysis.* New York, NY: Basic Books.

Mitchell SA (1997). *Influence and autonomy in psychoanalysis.* Hillsdale, NJ: Analytic Press.

Murphy G, Cattell E (1952). Sullivan's field theory. In: Mullahy P, editor. *The contributions of Harry Stack Sullivan: A symposium on interpersonal theory in Psychiatry and Social Science,* 161–179. New York, NY: Hermitage House.

Piers C (2000). Character as self-organizing complexity. *Psychoanal Contemp Thought* 23:3–34.

Seligman S (2005). Dynamic systems theories as a metaframework for psychoanalysis. *Psychoanal Dialog* 15:285–319.

Stern DB (1983). Unformulated experience. *Contemp Psychoanal* 19:71–99.

Stern DB (1997). *Unformulated experience: From dissociation to imagination in psychoanalysis.* New York, London: Routledge.

Stern DB (2004). The eye sees itself: Dissociation, enactment, and the achievement of conflict. *Contemp Psychoanal* 40:197–237.

Stern DB (2010). *Partners in thought: Working with unformulated experience, dissociation, and enactment.* New York, London: Routledge.

Stern DB (2012). Implicit theories of technique and the values that inspire them. *Psychoanal Inq* 32:33–49.

Stern DB (2013a). Field theory in psychoanalysis, part 1: Harry Stack Sullivan and Madeleine and Willy Baranger. *Psychoanal Dialog* 23:487–501.

Stern DB (2013b). Field theory in psychoanalysis, part 2: Bionian field theory and contemporary interpersonal/relational theory. *Psychoanal Dialog* 23:630–45.

Stern DB (in press a). The interpersonal field: History and politics. In: *Relational freedom: Emergent processes in the interpersonal field.* Hove: Routledge.

Stern DB (in press b). *Relational freedom: Emergent processes in the interpersonal field.* Hove: Routledge.

Sullivan HS (1940). *Conceptions of modern psychiatry,* 1953. New York, NY: Norton.

Sullivan HS (1953). *The interpersonal theory of psychiatry.* New York, NY: Norton.

Tauber ES (1954). Exploring the therapeutic use of counter-transference data. *Psychiatry* 13:332–6.

Thompson CM (1961). *Interpersonal psychoanalysis: The selected papers of Clara M. Thompson.* Green M, editor. New York, NY: Basic Books.

Wolstein B (1959). *Countertransference.* New York, NY: Grune & Stratton.

Index

For Product Safety Concerns and Information please contact our EU
representative GPSR@taylorandfrancis.com
Taylor & Francis Verlag GmbH, Kaufingerstraße 24, 80331 München, Germany